EXPLORING THE WORLD
OF HUMAN PRACTICE

EXPLORING THE WORLD OF HUMAN PRACTICE:

Readings in and about the Philosophy of Aurel Kolnai

Edited by
Zoltán Balázs and Francis Dunlop

Central European University Press
Budapest   New York

© 2004 by Zoltán Balázs and Francis Dunlop

Published in 2004 by

Central European University Press

An imprint of the
Central European University Share Company
Nádor utca 11, H-1051 Budapest, Hungary
Tel: +36-1-327-3138 or 327-3000
Fax: +36-1-327-3183
E-mail: ceupress@ceu.hu
Website: www.ceupress.com

400 West 59th Street, New York NY 10019, USA
Tel: +1-212-547-6932
Fax: +1-212-548-4607
E-mail: mgreenwald@sorosny.org

ISBN 963 9241 97 0 cloth
ISBN 963 7326 01 4 paperback

Library of Congress Cataloging-in-Publication Data

Exploring the world of human practice: readings in and about the philosophy of
Aurel Kolnai / edited by Zoltán Balázs and Francis Dunlop.
   p. cm.
Includes bibliographical references and index.
 ISBN 9639241970 (hardbound) ISBN 963 7326 01 4 (paperback)
 1. Kolnai, Aurel—Congresses. 2. Philosophy, Modern—20th century. I. Kolnai,
Aurel. II. Balázs, Zoltán. III. Dunlop, Francis.

 B1646.K7774E96 2005
 192—dc22

2004   021705

Printed in Hungary by
Akaprint Nyomda

Contents

Preface

This volume took its original impetus from the first international conference to be held on the work of Aurel Kolnai, the "Aurel Kolnai Memorial Conference", which was sponsored by the Central European University, Budapest, and the Lajos Batthyány Foundation. It was held at the university on 8 and 9 December 2000, a few days after the one-hundredth anniversary of Kolnai's birth at 10 Báthory Street, Budapest. We are glad to have this opportunity of repeating our thanks to the sponsors in print.

Because the Central European University Press does not, as a matter of policy, publish conference proceedings, they agreed last year to publish an introductory volume on Kolnai's work, which would include a variety of papers both by Kolnai and about his thoughts. This collection is the first of its kind and gave us, the editors, the chance of including some little-known but important and representative papers by Kolnai, including some previously unpublished ones, together with some papers delivered at the conference and some others which would serve to fill out a little more the reader's knowledge of his oeuvre. We have added an introduction, which sets out the main events of his life, the character of his philosophy, and a brief survey of the papers which, respectively, exemplify and explore it.

We should like here to thank all those concerned for allowing us to reprint already published papers, and David Wiggins for his additional permission to publish hitherto unpublished material from the Kolnai Nachlass. Unfortunately we were unable to trace those entitled to be asked about "The Indispensability of Philosophy".

However, we are glad to end this businesslike preface by expressing our conviction that, after decades of relative neglect, the world of professional philosophy may be gradually coming round to the view that, in ethics and political philosophy, there are few more remarkable thinkers in the twentieth century than the one who is the focal point of this collection.

Zoltán Balázs
Francis Dunlop

About the Contents of This Volume

PAPERS ABOUT KOLNAI

(*"AKMC"* indicates papers invited as contributions to the *Aurel Kolnai Memorial Conference* held in Budapest at the Central European University, in December 2000.)

AMBRUS-LAKATOS, LÓRÁND, "Aims in Games and Moral Purposes", *AKMC*, first publication.

BALÁZS, ZOLTÁN, "Kolnai and Kant on (Human) Dignity", *AKMC*, first publication.

BEACH, JOHN D., "The Ethical Theories of Aurel Kolnai", first published in *The Thomist*, 45, 1, 1981, pp. 132–43.

CONGDON, LEE, "Kolnai's Mature Political Philosophy", *AKMC*, first publication.

DORSCHEL, ANDREAS, "Is Love Intertwined with Hatred?", *AKMC*, first published in the *Journal of the British Society for Phenomenology*, XXXIII, 2002, pp. 273–85.

DUNLOP, FRANCIS, "Kolnai's Dissertation *Der ethische Wert und die Wirklichkeit*: A 'Completion' of Scheler's Value-Ethics", *AKMC*, first publication.

HITTINGER, JOHN P., "The Democratic Subversion of Political Liberty and Participation". An earlier version was published in *Appraisal*, 2, 1, 1997, pp. 26–36, but the paper has been extensively rewritten and abbreviated for this volume.

MAHONEY, DANIEL J., "Liberty, Equality, Nobility: Aurel Kolnai and the Moral Foundations of Democracy", *AKMC*, first published in *Perspectives on Political Science*, vol. 30, no 4, 2001, pp. 206–12.

MANENT, PIERRE, "Aurel Kolnai: A Political Philosopher Confronts the Scourge of Our Epoch", first published as the introduction to *The Utopian Mind and Other Papers*, ed. Francis Dunlop, London: Athlone, 1995, pp. xiii–xxvi.

NORGAARD, THOMAS, "Kolnai's Idea of Emotional Presentation", *AKMC*, first publication.

RADFORD, ROBERT, "Aurel Kolnai's 'Disgust': A Source in the Art and Writing of Salvador Dalí", first published in the *Burlington Magazine*, January 1999, pp. 32–33.

STONE, M. W. F., "The Nature and Scope of Ordinary Morality: Some Reflections in the Spirit of Aurel Kolnai", *AKMC*, first publication.

WIGGINS, DAVID, "Aurel Kolnai and Utopia", *AKMC*, first publication.

Introduction

FRANCIS DUNLOP

For some time now there have been a small number of Hungarian philosophers, historians and other academics who know something of the life and work of Aurel Kolnai (1900–1973),[1] but it cannot be said that Kolnai is as yet well known in his native land, despite the efforts of Zoltán Balázs, György Litván,[2] Endre Kiss and others. There is, firstly, the fact that most of Kolnai's relatives and friends from his youth were victims, direct or indirect, of Hitler's Final Solution, since his family was Jewish. Secondly, Kolnai moved to Vienna before his twentieth birthday, only returning occasionally to visit his parents up to 1937, when he said a definitive goodbye to Central Europe. Certainly he published in Hungary during that time. *Századunk* brought out several papers of great interest by him. But the historian Ferenc Fejtő told me that he thought his own review of *The War against the West* (1938), Kolnai's ideological accounting with Nazi thought, was probably the only one to be published in Hungary.[3]

Kolnai had, in fact, severed his emotional ties with Hungary after his youthful hopes for the "Chrysanthemum revolution" had been so quickly shattered in 1918–19, and he never returned after 1937. However, he still kept in touch with Hungarians, both in Hungary and elsewhere, and with what was happening in his old homeland. A significant example of Hungarian contact was his correspondence and reunion with his former mentor Oszkár Jászi in 1941, after he reached the United States. However, he refused to get involved with any "national committee", or similar patriotic organisation, at any stage of the Second World War. Apart from this voluntary withdrawal, the strong and resolute anti-Communism of this former Galilei Circle member ensured that, after the war and the Communist take-over, there could never be anything like "official" recognition. Nevertheless, as he got older, the old emotional ties with Hungary grew stronger again, and he began to use his native tongue more frequently for personal notes and memoranda.

Kolnai never regarded himself as an "academic" in the modern sense, that is, as a person hired, probably by a university, to teach and do "research"

in some specialist area of a particular subject. As the paper "The Indis-pensability of Philosophy" reveals, Kolnai regarded philosophy as far too important to be counted merely as a "subject" taught in educational insti-tutions. As he argues in that paper, the level of thinking, and hence of debate, publication, and even conduct, in any society depends to a great extent on the quality of philosophical thinking in that society. But one does not have to be employed as a university teacher to engage in it. He himself, being passionately concerned about the reinvigoration of the best rational and spiritual traditions of the West after the First World War, but also under the necessity of earning a living, was faced with a real choice about what to do with himself after graduating *summa cum laude* from Vienna University in 1926.

He had already tried to support himself as an independent scholar and writer in 1921–22, before entering the university, but had not forgot-ten the "sobering experiences of unsuccess"[4] the attempt had brought, despite some moments of glory in the ambit of psychoanalysis.[5] On the other hand, a university career in philosophy "was both an uncertain affair in itself and certain to yield no income whatever before many years had passed". His banker father in Budapest, poorer than he once was, would hardly have been willing to support him totally for so long, even if his son had wanted him to. Kolnai was also acutely aware (long before this was generally known) of the real threat posed by the growth of Nazism in Germany, even in Austria, and of the urgency of the task of trying to fight it. For these reasons he decided to turn more actively to political journalism.

Accordingly, with the help of Karl Polányi, Kolnai won for himself a "permanent connection" with *Der Oesterreichische Volkswirt*, was for a time on the editorial staff of *Schönere Zukunft*, and contributed to various other periodicals, both in Vienna and in Berlin. Later, in the early thirties, he wrote for *Der Oesterreichische Ständestaat*, founded to combat Nazism at the instigation of Chancellor Dollfuß, and edited by Dietrich von Hilde-brand. But these articles never brought in an adequate income, even when supplemented by his earnings from more strictly philosophical writing. Although his revised dissertation *Der Ethische Wert und die Wirklichkeit*[6] had received some excellent reviews, especially in Germany, his earnings fell short of the publication expenses. However, it led to the commission-ing of his *Sexualethik*,[7] also very well received, followed by a "textbook of phenomenological ethics", but, as luck would have it, the publication of the textbook was indefinitely postponed by the publisher because of the political situation, and its text destroyed during the war. What he received for those two books, or for various substantial papers, including "Der Ekel" (one of the best-known of Kolnai's papers today)[8], "Der Inhalt der Politik"[9] and "Versuch über den Haß"[10], is not recorded. But, in any case, Kolnai felt in later life that his early decision to concentrate on politics rather than philosophy, for which he was far better equipped, had been "over hasty", and had shed a "deadening air of unreality over (his life)". "Politics interested me in their ideological aspect alone", he wrote; he was not concerned with politics in a properly "functional" way. There is, he explained, an intrinsic tension between the phenomenological attitude (the basis of his philosophy) and the active outlook of politics. Though he could employ his philosophical talent in many of his analytic articles for political journals, political thinking "requires a certain capacity for 'arbitrary' decision 'here and now', a reasonable but not properly rational response to the 'thisness' of a situation", which went against his grain. The result was that, while he failed to influence political thought in Austria and Germany, he also failed to work properly towards the production of a philosophical *magnum opus*, which would certainly have been within his reach. Nevertheless, he consoled himself, his having "borne witness" to the high values of Western civilisation during an age plunging ever faster into barbarism may not have been entirely in vain.

Having decided against a university teaching career in 1926, Kolnai found it difficult to change course in later life. Once he had left Vienna in 1937, both to see his anti-Nazi book, *The War against the West,* through the press[11], and because he knew that, unless he left Vienna, the Nazis there would, sooner or later, dispose of such a pernicious opponent, he lived the life of a refugee for about eight years. This "homelessness" (in French and Swiss hotels and boarding houses, and later in American apartments) was soon compounded by statelessness. Kolnai had become an Austrian citizen in the early twenties. When the Germans swallowed up Austria in 1938, he found himself, to his disgust, "a citizen of the Third Reich", and immediately hurried to Paris to renounce the privilege, creating in the process new difficulties for himself.

French internment as an "enemy alien" in 1939, followed by marriage to Elisabeth Gémes in 1940, to whom he probably owed his personal survival on at least one occasion, and then more internment, were major distractions. But the eventual escape of the Kolnais (both of Jewish birth, though also Catholic converts) from Vichy France, where Jews were now being rounded up for deportation to extermination camps, and their eventual arrival in the United States, might have been expected to bring with it opportunities for university teaching. Unfortunately, the supply of posts had now dried up and Kolnai had to pursue his writing career largely on a research grant and charitable handouts.[12]

But all this changed at the end of the war, when he was invited to apply for some teaching at the Catholic University of Laval, Quebec, where, to Kolnai's great satisfaction, he was soon recognised as a full-time "professeur". This was in fact the only time that Kolnai ever held such a position. Unfortunately, the religious, political and cultural climate in Quebec began to weigh so heavily on him, who saw in it another form of the totalitarianism he had so strenuously combated in the forms of Nazism and, after the war, Communism, that he felt forced to resign in 1955. He went to England, supported by a handsome Nuffield Foundation Travel Grant, to do research on utopian thought, having resolved that, come what may, he would never return to live in Quebec. When the grant ran out he secured another one, and then another after that, but he had still not finished the book, since he was beset by anxieties about how he would live when the grants ran out and was, in any case, in very poor health. By now he had realised that he could only settle in a British academic environment, yet, despite an impressive list of publications (most of them in foreign languages), no British university seemed willing to take the risk which the appointment of this highly eccentric, diffident, shabby and philosophically unorthodox foreigner seemed to present. However, eventually he secured some part-time teaching in London. Thanks to Professor Harry Acton, and to Acton's successors Bernard Williams and David Wiggins, this was gradually converted into a secure part-time "Visiting Lectureship" at Bedford College, part of London University. Kolnai, however, who had now been haunted by the fear of real poverty for at least thirty years, was in constant fear of its being withdrawn, despite his year's research fellowship at Birmingham (1961–62) and a Visiting Professorship at Marquette University, Wisconsin, in the USA, in 1968. It was in fact maintained up to the year of Kolnai's fatal heart attack.

One Hungarian whom Kolnai got to know well in Quebec was Mgr Francis Ibrányi. Ibrányi had been closely associated with Cardinal Archbishop Mindszenty, who was sentenced to life imprisonment in 1949 by the Hungarian Communist regime for "treason".[13] Kolnai and Ibrányi met frequently and had long conversations together in Quebec and elsewhere, and, when the former applied for his Nuffield grant, Ibrányi wrote a testimonial which included the following:

> Aurel Kolnai is a scholar, a thinker and a writer. It is his personality that largely supplies the key to his scientific and literary oeuvre. Kolnai lives in a state of inmost mental response to his environment—its stimulating and enlivening, its provocative and oppressive factors. On the one hand, he becomes aware, with unusual sensitivity, of every aspect, down to the smallest details, of his ambit of life. On the other hand, all experiences interest him by reference to their objective meaning and their content of value only. He applies to everything the test of ideas and ponders all things with a passionate objectivity devoid of pragmatic compromise. ...(Thanks to) his fastidious integrity of mind...no kind of "party line", whether so styled or not, has ever been able to bend Kolnai into its service.[14]

Ibrányi puts strong emphasis here on Kolnai's receptiveness and sensitivity. This was indeed a constant in Kolnai's life from a very early age, when one of his main occupations was walking the streets of Budapest and systematically recording the different "atmospheres" of its districts. It is this same receptiveness to the "feel" or "sense" of things, coupled with a desire to record these intuitions, "rectified" where necessary by further intuitions, which enables him to talk in such detail and with such assurance of moral *experience*,[15] and to pass "behind" or "beneath" the tendencies of moral language, especially in moral philosophy, towards uniformity and reductionism, to reveal a far more variegated "world" than most moral philosophers have been willing or able to acknowledge. His concept of moral "emphasis", in its various modes, ranging from strict obligation to a range of "obligation-like" tensions, is a case in point.[16] For Kolnai this was a genuinely objective phenomenon; his acute ear for what lay behind people's *claims* about moral matters encouraged him to assume that it was a phenomenon familiar in some form to all moral agents.

Contemporary moral philosophers sometimes talk as though morality were a human, "social", *invention*, devised for a purpose and thus capable of being revised. Whether we are to take this seriously or not is unclear, but what we are actually faced with in "morality" is a humanity-wide phenomenon, with surface differences but considerable underlying uniformity.[17] Kolnai points out that all human beings come into a world where morality, in some form, is simply "given"; in so far as we are talking of human persons, then morality is part of our constitution. On the other hand, whereas moral values and moral emphases are both aspects of moral experience, and therefore a human datum, moral rules for realising them *are* in some sense "devised". This raises the problem of how we talk philosophically about what is directly experienced. Kolnai started from the assumption that ordinary language was, as far as it went, a fairly reliable guide, but one that lacked conceptual subtlety and needed to be supplemented in various ways. Once he had settled in England, in the orbit of "linguistic analysis", for which he had a great respect, he was concerned to add that this method was much more fruitful when the thinker could appeal to more than one language. But he knew that the fundamental analysis of experience meant the use of metaphor (see his discussion of *fiat* in "Agency and Freedom"), and a willingness to use several alternative ways of referring to phenomena, in the attempt to get the reader to recall or imagine the salient features of what is under investigation. Hence, also, Kolnai's habit of immediately qualifying some observation he has made, in his anxiety not to mislead the reader, so that he sometimes seems like one walking a knife-edge between two contrary beliefs.[18] In all this he was much influenced in his university days by the phenomenologist Max Scheler, who talked of the philosopher's attempt to get people to "see what can only be seen", and preferred, with other early phenomenologists, to talk about pointing to things rather than defining them. As Kolnai puts it: "...Philosophy is precisely about what is *not* accessible to...rigorous logical clarification."[19]

This receptivity to the phenomena underlying language,[20] and the attempt to convey them adequately in words, goes with an exceptional *strength* of feeling, of powerful loves and hates, and strong preferences between things which many observers might hardly distinguish at all. In many ways this was a tremendous handicap, one that could only have been compensated for if his life had been lived in a more settled age and without the "urgent pressure of material cares". Kolnai, it could well be said, was, to an unusual extent, *at the mercy of* events in the outside world and of the powerful (predominantly moral) feelings and preferences that welled up from his own depths (hence his inability to continue in Quebec). Tolerance was not a virtue that could have come easily to him, though his general devotion to the moral good was such that he could be just and fair to students whose ideologies he found abhorrent, and even to the Nazi thinkers he analysed so searchingly in *The War against the West*.[21]

Kolnai's natural phenomenological method,[22] and his belief in the importance of philosophy for *human life*, went closely with a belief that it not only arises out of the everyday reflection of the "plain man" (not to be confused with the "common man"),[23] but must remain in close touch with it. "Common sense is the metaphysics of the Stone Age", said Bertrand Russell. Kolnai was as far as one could be from this belief. Without for a moment disregarding the contradictions, lack of conceptual subtlety, and other defects to which it is subject, he regarded it as a source of real knowledge, though of course it needed much clarification and correction. In thus respecting the beliefs which arise again and again in the predominantly practical life of man, he may have shown himself a truer democrat than most of the thinkers who would despise his qualified praise of, say, social privilege and hierarchy. In keeping with this, Kolnai never goes deeply into metaphysics or epistemology as usually understood. Where he did have occasion to say something about, say, free will or knowledge-claims, he might approach them from the practical point of view, or phenomenologically, as he does with the difference between evaluative and factual cognition. In the same way, though much of his writing exhibits acute psychological and sociological insights based on everyday experience,[24] he rarely touches on physics, chemistry or mathematics, branches of knowledge whose pursuit quickly removes us from the world of shared human experience altogether. Such was his unshakeably robust sense of the *reality*, or *objectivity*, of, say, ordinary material objects and living things, moral values and practical emphases, that he could never have surrendered his common-sense grasp of them. It is not that he lacked imagination to appreciate the "evidence" for, say, idealism, or various forms of scepticism. Rather, he never ceased to regard these considerations as clearly outweighed by the ordinary and manifold evidence of the "given". John Mackie's "error theory" of values would have been for Kolnai a further example of what he somewhere calls the post-Renaissance "suicide" of Western thought.

Kolnai's exceptional strength as a moral philosopher, taking "moral" in the broad sense in which it encompasses human practice in general, including politics and the general features of the human condition, lies, then, in his ability to bring to light and hence illuminate the underlying phenomena; his supporting "argument" is precisely the appeal to human experience and intuition, "necessarily" supported by the appeal to consensus. It can be no surprise that Kolnai does not produce moral or ethical "theory" in the sense of a moral calculus.[25] Recall now, in Ibrányi's striking phrase, Kolnai's "objectivity devoid of pragmatic compromise". In a review of one of Bernard Williams's works, Martha Nussbaum argues that Williams's well-known refusal to produce ethical theory is a defect because only the "illuminating simplicity and systematising power" of theory is likely to make the "radical critique of existing judgements and the experiences which are their basis" effective. She had in mind Catherine MacKinnon's feminist theory, which made people see what had previously been "avoided or suppressed".[26] The effect of all this is to suggest that moral philosophers *ought* to produce ethical theory *because of* its "practical function" (even though she implies that MacKinnon's theory ignores "the nuances of individual human lives"). In his review of *Ethics, Value and Reality*,[27] W. D. Hudson suggests that the attentive reader may be led to ask himself whether Kolnai, with his continual qualifications, re-phrasings, and so on, "is...muddying the waters, or have I been oversimplifying things in order to get them clear?" It sounds very much as though Hudson would have adopted the first alternative. But, as Kolnai frequently points out, the desire for neatness and clarity at the cost of oversimplifying is an intellectual vice.[28]

Kolnai is perfectly well aware that moral education and political and social influence are important. But he insists that there is a hard and fast distinction between the philosophical intention on the one hand and the practical one of the politician, pedagogue and reformer on the other. He saw himself as a philosopher, primarily concerned with truth,[29] not with any useful or even noble extra-philosophical end the truth might serve (though he did also think that the calling to mind of moral truth would itself activate moral impulses and moral energy). If, despite this, it should still be thought that he was actually making any waters muddier than they already are,[30] then the proper response is to ask for chapter and verse. The generalising impulse of philosophy is important, but only when the object under investigation is respected.

In fact, Kolnai, who recognised early on his own penchant for "structure analysis", is continually trying to bring order into his data by classifying them in various ways and exhibiting various relations between them. Good examples are his frequent recourse to the complicated relation between the "moral emphasis" and the "practical emphasis",[31] his distinction between "emphatic" and "implicit" morality,[32] and the apparent "paradox" of "erroneous conscience".[33] The point is that, where he can, Kolnai does "draw logical lines", as Ernst Mally said in his review of Kolnai's doctoral dissertation,[34] but he does not impose them *on* otherwise unrelated, or not clearly related, phenomena for some extrinsic practical end (even the moral improvement of institutions); he simply points to relations already *in* the phenomena. Philosophers who are used to dealing with clear-cut logical distinctions, which, in the prfessional ethics, are often of the "imposed" kind, may well talk of "muddying the waters", but that is probably because they are unused to the sustained examination of moral phenomena themselves.

The last element of Ibrányi's analysis I would like to dwell on is the inability of Kolnai to toe a "party line". Kolnai was a highly unusual person, a thinker of exceptional originality and integrity, but, as we have emphasised, of very strong loves and hates, one who saw almost everything in terms of values and universal meanings, especially moral ones. But the moral and ethical values of real things are partly conditioned by changing circumstances (this is the main theme of his doctoral dissertation). Hence the changes of political allegiance that marked his life. As he said himself in a letter to Oszkár Jászi: "I couldn't say whether I am Left or Right, or between the two, since I think too much about the question. So much is clear, that I am both Left and Right and an opportunist, and that I could not be any of them without qualification and balance…My world-view is centrist and its directing value is personalism."[35] A similar difficulty may strike anyone trying to classify Kolnai's moral philosophy. The safest course is to acknowledge not only that he is primarily a thinker who stands alone, often on territory not previously occupied, but that he actually felt driven to do so. The price of this has, of course, been that, although one meets increasingly with discussion of isolated Kolnaian themes, there is rarely any attempt to engage with his moral or political philosophical position as a whole.

But, above all, the fact has to be faced that Kolnai is difficult, especially for an age which lacks the time and patience to read his often highly demanding papers, and in the absence of any philosophical *magnum opus* which could gather everything together and reveal its order. Kolnai sometimes writes plainly enough, but he always has to be read meditatively and probably repeatedly. He may be dealing with familiar areas of philosophy, and with what look like familiar problems and questions, but the approach is likely to be eccentric, the fastidious use of language may be off-putting, the asides may well irritate the still wary reader. He has nothing of the laboratory researcher, neatly laying out his novel theory or application, or cleanly advancing a new schematic *argument*. He does not exhaustively analyse the work of others.[36] He addresses us, in a leisurely fashion, as one cultivated thinker speaking to another, but about important matters that he hopes will be *recognised* as true. For every philosopher who is deeply influenced by the (still unfashionable) content of Kolnai's philosophy, there will be many more who find his approach stimulating and thought-provoking.[37] For, even if Kolnai sometimes sounds like a lonely and isolated voice (the early phenomenological writers mentioned above are still almost unknown in the United Kingdom), he will have done what he set out to do if he contributes, ever so little, to raising the standard of thought and intellectual culture among his readers. At the very least, he will have shown us the range and extent of the moral and social data that would have to be accommodated in any philosophically adequate moral or political theory.

Finally, a brief word about the papers that follow. The Kolnai selections were chosen to exhibit the range of his characteristic concerns, with a bias towards papers little known or unknown. I have already said something about "The Indispensability of Philosophy", which, though it is a translation of a translation and hence lacks many of the marks of his style, is nevertheless a highly characteristic production of Kolnai's Quebec period as regards content. This introduction to "the abstract science of objects inserted just as they are in reality" can be compared with the better-known paper "The Sovereignty of the Object".[38] The other translated paper, "What is Politics About?", is a response in a German periodical to Carl Schmitt's (at the time) influential attempt to define politics. "The essential mark of the political sphere is not the relation between friend and foe [as Schmitt had argued] but the coexistence of opponents on the basis of a [shared] social unit of reference." Far from its being the case that "…with liberalism the state became perverted and ceased to be,…'politics' in its real essentials only begins with liberalism and its building of general discussion into the form of the state". This long paper is an important statement of Kolnai's political position when, out of concern for what was happening to democracy in Austria in the early thirties, he had joined the Marxist Socialist Party. But his acceptance of an "irrational element" in politics shows that his liberalism was always in need of some qualification, and anticipates his later fears (explored by several contributors to this volume) that unrestrained liberalism would inevitably produce a form of totalitarianism.

Of the three papers previously published in English, the least known must be "A Note on the Meaning of Right and Wrong". Here Kolnai illuminatingly compares and contrasts two theoretical descriptions of the "high-principled" or "virtuous" man: "the scrupulous duty-performer of

Kant (and) the Aristotelian virtuoso of 'prudence'". This paper has much to teach the champions of both deontology and "virtue ethics". It is also important as an early exposition of what Kolnai calls "emphatic" and "implicit" morality. "Erroneous Conscience" explores the apparent "paradox" that people are generally commended for acting according to conscience, even though their conduct may be objectively wrong. In the course of this paper, Kolnai explores many of the basic features of his commonsense view of morality. The last section is relevant to his exploration of morality under totalitarianism. The third of these republished papers is "Agency and Freedom". Kolnai here puts forward "an experiential account of free will in terms of a positive and indispensable 'decree' or 'fiat'". Although he accepts that there may be something "illusory" about free will, he argues that it "cannot, in common sense, repose on mere illusion or misinterpretation".

The earliest of the three hitherto unpublished papers is "The Concept of Practical Error". The distinction between Morality, here glossed as "submission to a specified set of demands on me, conceived in universal terms", and Practice, "the management of my concerns", together with detailed considerations about their "convergence", is a major theme of Kolnai's moral philosophy. The paper published here, for all the "unfinished" impression it gives, is the best and clearest examination of these relations from the negative point of view. The "universality" characterising the moral theme is, in Kolnai's understanding, subject to several kinds of qualification. "Are There Degrees of Ethical Universality?", which explores them, does justice to R. M. Hare's insistence on the basic universality, but criticises it for being "purely formal": "Universality is...a distinctive feature of our ethical dimension of being: not merely a logical precondition of its being possible for moral judgements, just like any other judgements, to have a truth value; (Hare's) insistence on 'universalisability' is 'a misdescription of moral experience as it really is'." The third previously unpublished paper, "Actions and Inactions", is an interesting attempt to argue that, in many contexts, it really matters whether we use positive or negative language to describe something, despite the fact that, in purely formal terms, the two sentences would mean the same. The last two sections of the paper show the importance of the question for moral philosophy.

Of the papers written *about* Kolnai's philosophy, it might help readers new to Kolnai's philosophy to know that both John Beach's "The Ethical Theories of Aurel Kolnai" and Lee Congdon's "Kolnai's Mature Political Philosophy" are clear and helpful surveys of their subject matter and can serve as introductions to the moral and political aspects of Kolnai's thinking. Congdon's paper is especially useful for relating the themes of utopia, morals and politics fruitfully together, to show the coherence of his thought.

But if we take these papers as a whole, pride of place must be given to the two devoted to the theme of the Utopian Mind, not only because of the distinction of their respective authors but also because of the intrinsic importance of the theme. David Wiggins's "Aurel Kolnai and Utopia" and Pierre Manent's "Aurel Kolnai: a Political Philosopher Confronts the Scourge of our Epoch" approach the topic in very different ways, which makes their close agreement on essentials all the more striking. Wiggins's detailed analysis of Kolnai's main anti-utopian argument is set against a useful sample and refutation of the ways in which well-known contemporary thinkers evade or even blur over this vital matter. Manent's broader and more historical treatment of the theme contains a valuable section on the significance of Kolnai's "phenomenological conservatism", comparing his approach to the social and political world with that of his contemporaries Karl Popper and Michael Oakeshott.

Kolnai's positive political thinking in his American and Canadian period is given special attention by Daniel J. Mahoney and John P. Hittinger. Both writers stress that Kolnai was not in the least averse to equality and democracy, but was concerned that the moral and social preconditions of the Western democratic tradition were being too easily forgotten. Mahoney, in "Liberty, Equality, Nobility: Aurel Kolnai and the Moral Foundations of Democracy", compares Kolnai illuminatingly with de Tocqueville, whereas Hittinger's "The Democratic Subversion of Political Liberty and Participation" puts more stress on Kolnai's argument that the rise of the "common man" (as opposed to the "plain man") spells death to freedom; he ends his paper by stressing the Catholic elements of his social thought, associating Kolnai's philosophy with that of Pope John Paul II (himself a disciple of Scheler), and with Maritain, Gilson, Newman and Edith Stein.

Kolnai's meditations on the various "logics" of human practice may have started with his theoretical interest in games (especially chess). In the course of his thinking he brought to light many instances of human institutions where the participants can only serve the personal, social and cultural ends the institutions serve by focussing on some subordinate end standing in a "paratelic" relation to the primary end. Loránd Ambrus-Lakatos's informative paper "Aims in Games and Moral Purposes" explores the relations between games and morality in this perspective. Zoltán Balázs's "Kolnai and Kant on (Human) Dignity" expounds Kolnai's well-known article "Dignity", arguing that, just as Kolnai found the specific concept of *human* dignity "deeply problematic", so Kant himself, to whom many contemporary writers on human dignity appeal, fails to show that human dignity is "a solid or thick concept, i.e. more than a weak metaphor", though he does "establish[es] the concept of *human sublimity*". Francis Dunlop's paper, which introduces Kolnai's little-known dissertation *Der ethische Wert und die Wirklichkeit*, looks at the most prominent themes of this remarkable and definitely non-naturalistic work. It concentrates on the idea of "moral emphasis", which reflects the claim that what is morally important (in various modes) for an agent here and now cannot be simply "read off" from some universal maxim or table of values but is heavily dependent on particular facts about the agent's real situation and character, in a way which invites some systematisation. The last primarily ethical work is M. W. F. Stone's "The Nature and Scope of Ordinary Morality: Some Reflections in the Spirit of Aurel Kolnai". He argues that, although both Aristotle and Kant intended their ethical works to uphold "ordinary morality", most contemporary moral philosophers assume that morality can only serve the modern world if it is systematised in a reforming spirit. With the help of a careful analysis of Sartre's famous example of the would-be resistance-fighter's dilemma, Stone argues that the modern assumption is not justified, since it ignores the problem-solving resources already available within ordinary morality.

Thomas Norgaard's paper is primarily epistemological. As he writes himself, it expresses an aspect of "a broader interest in cognitivist axiology and ethics" and is inspired by the hope that it "may be of help to those of us interested in affectivity's role in evaluation and motivation". Such painstaking analytic work has an important part to play in showing how unjustified is the disdain still often shown to ethical thinkers who rely to a great extent on intuition. Andreas Dorschel introduces Kolnai's paper "Versuch über den Haß" (An Essay on Hatred). Although Dorschel's primary interest is in the substantive question of whether love and hate are "intertwined", a good deal can be learnt about Kolnai's method and style in the course of this systematic analysis. Lastly, Robert Radford discusses the surrealist painter Salvador Dalí's interest in the phenomenological method of Kolnai's paper "Disgust". Although Kolnai would himself have been disgusted, had he learnt of Dalí's interest in this essay[39]—better known, probably, than any other of his works—we may be thankful that Radford, who is not himself a philosopher, has brought this most interesting relation to our attention.

NOTES

1 The most complete account of Kolnai's life and work is Francis Dunlop, *The Life and Thought of Aurel Kolnai*, Aldershot: Ashgate, 2002.
2 Litván, one of the very few relatives of Kolnai's still living, and Endre Kiss, entitled their joint introduction to the issue of *Világosság* devoted to Kolnai and his work (Vol. 38, 5-6, 1997) "Az itthon ismeretlen Kolnai" (Kolnai, unknown in his own country).
3 "Háború a Nyugat ellen", *Korunk*, IV, pp. 362–65, 1939.
4 Quotations in this and the following paragraph come from the unedited text of Kolnai's memoirs.

5 Notably, the publication of *Psychoanalyse und Soziologie: zur Psychologie von Masse und Gesellschaft*, Vienna–Leipzig: Psychoanalytischer Verlag, 1920, translated into English by Eden and Cedar Paul as *Psychoanalysis and Sociology*, London and New York: Allen & Unwin, 1921.

6 Freiburg im Br.: Herder & Co., 1927.

7 Paderborn: Schöningh, 1930.

8 Now translated as "On Disgust" by Barry Smith and Carolyn Korsmeyer, Chicago: Open Court, 2004. See also Robert Radford's contribution to this volume.

9 Translated for this volume as "What is Politics About?"

10 *See* Andreas Dorschel's paper in this volume.

11 It was published by Gollancz of London and finally appeared in 1938.

12 The grant was for a projected book *Liberty and the Heart of Europe*, which examined the principles which Kolnai hoped would inspire the Western powers in influencing the political arrangements in Germany and the Central European countries they had occupied, now that an allied victory seemed probable. But once the likely victors, including, of course, the Soviet Union, had agreed on their respective "spheres of influence" he abandoned the half-completed book as "overtaken by events".

13 Ibrányi left Hungary in that year. He had been Professor of Moral Theology of Esztergom and for ten years Prefect of the Seminary there.

14 *See* the Kolnai Nachlass, awaiting transfer to a university library.

15 *See* especially "A Note on the Meaning of Right and Wrong" and "Are There Degrees of Ethical Universality?", both in this volume, where the appeal to experience is very prominent.

16 *See* §3 of my paper on Kolnai's dissertation in this volume. It is vital to grasp that Kolnai's appeal to differences of moral experience is not supposed to be of merely "psychological" relevance. *See* "Are There Degrees of Ethical Universality?" towards the end of §3.

17 *See* "Moral Consensus", in *Ethics, Value and Reality*, ed. Francis Dunlop and Brian Klug, London: Athlone, 1977.

18 As in his many attempts to distinguish between "morality" and (the rest of) "practice".

19 "Moral Consensus", p. 166.

20 Explored from the epistemological point of view in Thomas Norgaard's paper in this volume.

21 *The War against the West*, p. 19.

22 This is poles apart from Husserl's obsession with "constitution", and from anything to do with existentialism, but close to the method of Pfänder, Reinach, Hildebrand and the early Scheler.

23 *See* the papers by Daniel J. Mahoney and John P. Hittinger in this volume.

24 *See* especially "Agency and Freedom" in this volume.

25 *See* the last section of the addendum to "Erroneous Conscience" (in this volume) for Kolnai's view of the uncertainty of moral cognition in particular situations.

26 See *Ethics*, vol. 107, pp. 526–29.

27 *Times Higher Educational Supplement*, 10/2/78 (page unknown).

28 On the concern to "reform" "ordinary morality", see M. W. F. Stone's paper in this volume.

29 Or rather with "submission to the sovereignty of the object".

30 If there is a grain of truth in Hudson's insinuation, it is more likely the result of Kolnai's literary style.

31 Discussed in "The Concept of Practical Error", in this volume.
32 *See* §2 of "A Note on the Meaning of Right and Wrong", reprinted in this volume.
33 *See* the paper of that name in this volume.
34 Translated, almost in full, in Francis Dunlop, *Early Ethical Writings of Aurel Kolnai*, Aldershot: Ashgate, 2004, pp. xii–xiii.
35 Letter from Kolnai to Oszkár Jászi, 15 Sept. 1942, Columbia University Library, New York. Printed in *op. cit.*, note 2. *See* p. 80.
36 His discussions of Carl Schmitt's *Der Begriff des Politischen* and of R. M. Hare's early theory are not typical.
37 Karl Popper was among their number. *See op. cit.*, note 1, p. 236.
38 *See* Ethics, Value and Reality, pp. 23–43, ref. in note 16.
39 *See* "Moral Consensus", p. 145.

I. PAPERS BY KOLNAI

What Is Politics About?

AUREL KOLNAI
1933

(Translated from the German by Francis Dunlop)[1]

I

1. There was a time when "politics" simply meant the way a country is governed, or, as an object of study, the theory of the state. Today the discriminating usage of the intelligentsia receives full confirmation from the systematic disciplines, and there is a general concern for a *sociology of politics*. This is definitely not supposed to be about constitutional law, the art of government or reasons of state, but about the mysteries of politics in the most confined sense. Carl Schmitt, whose work[2] has become a model for the most recent studies of this kind, has even tried to interpret the state as "*the purest example of political existence*".[3] However, "political existence" is still given a very specific, and questionable, meaning here. In view of the enormous influence that this unusually profound and spirited work of Schmitt's has had, and of its obvious connection with a very definite and tendentious interpretation of both state and politics, the champion of a different view must work out especially carefully where he stands in relation to it.

Speaking very generally, one may place Schmitt among those thinkers very widely represented among German-speaking intellectuals today, who can be briefly described as "*irrationalists of life and power*". The members of this group appeal to thinkers like Nietzsche, Klages, Scheler (?),[4] Bergson (?),[5] Sorel, Pareto, Spengler, Heidegger and so on, in this or that respect and with more or less justice from case to case. In terms of the history of ideas one might link them *inter alia* with Vitalism, the Youth Movement, Bolshevism and Fascism. Naturally this is not the place to produce a philosophical critique of this complex movement of thought. We can only indicate in the barest outline and with special reference to political theory the fundamental ideas of this way of thinking: "life" and "existence" do not serve any rational purpose, or any values, ethical or logical, which could be understood as normative; they exist simply for their own sake. It is in principle impossible to rationalise life completely, that is, to give it a pervasive structure of rational considerations and normative responsibilities; the attempt to do so falsifies and weakens life, leads to hypocrisy, half-measures and atrophy. Rational justifications of this "life-centred attitude" are mere pretences, ideological will o' the wisps. Nothing that takes place in the human world, or even the spiritual world, is really the attainment of purposes, but the unfolding of the life-drive. In the social sphere life takes the form of power. Moral legitimations of power are futile and superfluous. Since power justifies itself, conflicts between powers whose spheres of action intersect are natural and unavoidable—indeed the true test and highest intensification of vigorous life. Power can be concealed by means of laws and humanitarian ideologies—perhaps cleverly disguised or made really impotent—but there is no substitute for it as a fundamental category of social existence. Liberalism and democracy, public discussion and a plurality of parties are, on the one hand, the cover for capitalist power seizures, on the other, passing phases of weakness in the lives of states.

It would be a mistake to think that all attention to irrational motives, all criticism of customary rationalistic constructions, all sociological interpretation and relativisation of points of view and systems of ideas, must be irrational in this sense. Indeed, as we shall see, this cannot be said of all Schmitt's points. His distinction between that aspect of the life of states which can be given the quite general name of "administration", and that consisting of "politics" in the narrower sense[6], is of inestimable benefit to political science (as an example of the narrowly political we may take the basic political orientation of the regime, on the basis of which the rules of administration are worked out; this is in a *certain* sense irrational, since it cannot be unequivocally derived from normative considerations). So is his demonstration that the contemporary rationalisation of life is a historical process of a specific kind, which gives rise to distinct kinds of claim and provokes irrationalist reactions. We should also add his critique of all "rational" social theories, with their naïve pseudo objectivity and their uncouth pretensions to truth.[7] But this is quite different from putting the main emphasis on what is purely vital, irrational, and "a-spiritual", or—let us be frank—"barbaric", when writing about social existence.

2. Schmitt *bases politics, and hence the state, on the idea of enmity.* What leads him to this singular outlook, this quasi "Copernican Revolution"?

The argument goes like this: the state is the product of community-forming political groupings. (From this point of view, "in the beginning" really was "action"—not "being"!) A political grouping exists when human groups confront one another "concretely and existentially", that is, they do not represent rationally explicable points of view or value preferences, but ultimate forms of being. To help them establish themselves their members are prepared to give their own lives and to annihilate their enemies. Forms of being as such do not necessarily create community in this sense, just as not every group is a state. Politics begins where there is a readiness to die and kill, where collectives confront one another as enemies. The enmity in question is, of course, not a private, anarchic one, but a matter of groups. Jesus's commandment in the Sermon on the Mount, "Love your enemies", has no bearing on this.[8] Clearly therefore politics presupposes comradeship, kinship, community, but only when there is war and antagonistic grouping does a social collective really become a political one, that is, a state. Just as a man becomes Christian through baptism, so social existence becomes political through enmity. It is clear that the more fundamental idea here is not friendship but enmity, since the latter phenomenon is regarded as constitutive for friendship itself in the strongest sense, for the political unity of human beings.[9] It is not peaceful, economic and cultural coexistence that founds the state and brings "friendship" into being as a political phenomenon, but standing together in the face of the enemy—in other words, war.

Corresponding to the basic value polarities "good and evil" in the ethical sphere, "beautiful and ugly" in the aesthetic, and "beneficial and harmful" in the utilitarian, Schmitt *makes the distinction between "friend and foe" central to the political sphere* (pp. 14ff). Is his argument circular, when he confines the political application of this idea to "public" friendship and enmity, and at the same time reintroduces his definition of politics as a public affair? It is not, to the extent that he presupposes the fundamental phenomenon of the "Public", and emphasises the unity of conflict as the defining feature of public existence in its political form. His treatment of the contrasting ideas of friend and foe, good and evil, and so on, as analogous pairings, seems more open to question. For the contrasting pairs of good and evil, etc., quite apart from the height of the values concerned, take an ultimate objectivity of value for granted which is completely absent from the category of friend and foe. Certainly the beneficial and the harmful, and even more so the pleasant and the unpleasant, are relative to the individual person, the accidents of his body and soul and even his momentary condition; but they represent value-qualities of a general and arguable kind, so that one may justifiably speak of useful books and pleasant forest air, even though the books referred to are of no use to many, and person after person takes no pleasure in forest air. By contrast "friend and foe"— not to be confused with "friendliness" and "malevolence" as qualities of character—do not refer to value-qualities, but merely to relationships and groupings. The individual's standpoint (or that of a particular group) is in this case not only the presupposition of and criterion for his feelings and judgement, as in the case of values, but its own proper *content*. It means something to say that an upright man is in favour of good and against evil; it is less important, but still means something, to say that the hedonist is in favour of what he finds pleasant in the given case and in general, and against what is unpleasant; but does it mean anything at all to say that political man supports what he is for, and opposes what he is against? *Can a grouping that is in itself purely accidental determine the creation of a realm of meaning?*[10]

Schmitt leaves us in no doubt about this; friend-foe relations, or political antagonisms, are "neither purely normative nor purely 'spiritual' antagonisms" (pp. 14ff).[11] The friend, or better one's own group-existence, does not represent what ought in some way to be, or what is right or in order; nor does the foe in any way represent what ought not to be, what is wrong or destructive of order. The opposition is not normative, and hence not discussible; it cannot be settled through explanation or understanding; it is existential, resting, so to speak, on the collision between self-asserting forms of existence, and can only be resolved through the destruction of what exists, through the removal of one of the parties by physical conflict. Schmitt does not say that every political antagonism that arises necessarily leads to real war, but it is part of its nature that it can lead to it, and it does tend to lead to it,[12] and it can really only be properly resolved in this way. It is not so much perpetual war with all its possible foes that makes a state a real state, as a continuous readiness for war—not, of course, preeminently in the technical and organisational sense, but in a sociological, psychological and legal one.

We shall return to this sociological assessment of war. But first we must investigate the nature of political, *"existential"*, antagonisms more closely.

3. Schmitt's concept of "the existential negation of another existent" is equivocal. Is the incompatibility of the two "existents" supposed to be based on their radically *different qualities*, or on their *rival claims to possess*, say, territory or raw materials? In the latter case the antagonism would be entirely or predominantly an economic one, which Schmitt expressly excludes from the category of existential antagonism. But in the first case it is pertinent to ask why the two forms of existence "collide spatially", and why they do not go on simply existing alongside one another. I only need to risk my life in standing up for my own form of existence when its presence, that is, the existence of my community, is threatened in its given form. Certainly it can come to this; a difference in form of existence can coincide with competition for the physical space needed for effective existence. Clearly this is the case Schmitt has in mind. But as soon as one makes this clear, one at once sees that it is not simply a matter of the mystical enmity of antagonistic forms of existence, of different tribal deities, perhaps, but necessarily of situations that on one side border on interests, economics and property—on what is quantitative. War is normally also a struggle *for something*. But an analysis of the antagonism of the forms of existence seems even more important. Schmitt asserts that wars conducted for religious, moral or economic reasons are unthinkable.[13] But it is not obvious why two peoples should not fight for the possession of a piece of fertile land from the very first day they find themselves existing as separate entities. But again, if their "existential" opposi-

tion cannot be a religious or moral one either, one must seriously ask whether the two foes are really likely to confine their mutual reproaches to the scandalous charge of "otherness". A glance at the facts of history teaches us that even in wars where territory disputes play a minor part and where none of the participants is really defending its threatened political autonomy, the fighting is about *something specific*, such as religion, honour, the organisation of society. In those cases where no objective and impartial judgement can easily or, in my view, possibly be pronounced in favour of one, and against the other party, the reason is not the absence of arguments, that is, of objectively valid principles, on either side, but their actual presence. Let no one suppose that these considerations are idle. They are indispensable, should anyone wish to obtain a more accurate picture of the content of political life.

Schmitt, of course, is not unaware of the well-known motives for waging war that history provides. He concedes that "religious, moral and other antagonisms are *used* for political ends, in order to *bring about* the hostile alignment that really counts. Once this grouping for war has really taken place, however, the decisive antagonism is no longer religious, moral or economic, but political." Considerable agreement is possible with the second proposition; sociologically speaking, it is highly informative. It points to the existence of a *special political sphere* in the social world, and to the fact that its *concerns* are *derived* from value spheres more directly accessible to the senses. But in the first proposition the anthropomorphic terms "used" and "bring about" (our italics) are symptomatic. They recall the hoary old story of cunning clerics using men's fear of the dark, or of thunder and lightning, to secure for themselves fat benefices, as intimates of the deity. But such tactical and demagogic "use" of religious and other antagonisms is a secondary procedure, and it is highly questionable whether groupings for war can be deliberately "brought about" at all. Schmitt sounds more plausible when he says (pp. 25ff): "Every religious, etc. antagonism changes into a political antagonism when it is powerful enough to divide men effectively into friends and foes." This sociological insight is further refined, when he adds that "at the very moment when this realignment is effected (that is, realignment into friend and foe), the nonpolitical antagonism, with its hitherto accepted criteria, fades into the background and the parties concerned become subject to the completely new, specific and...often very illogical and 'irrational' conditions and consequences of what has now become a political situation."

If this is true—and one may go a long way towards accepting it—one may nevertheless refuse to accept unqualified the arrogant assertion that "there are no normative and no 'spiritual' conflicts". We can rather talk of "normative and 'spiritual' conflicts" now being represented by concrete powers of a particular kind, and which, correspondingly distorted and reaccented, make themselves felt in a play of concrete power mechanisms of a particular, "political" kind. The political antagonisms are now, however, not completely irrational, not impervious to meanings and objective value-qualities; their expression is no mere trial of the other's strength, no mere carnage between opponents who can only be characterised as "this one here" and "that one there". This, again, is worlds apart from Schmitt's assumption that the change from a pre-political, let us say a "material", antagonism to a political one is *brought about* simply by one party's "becoming strong enough"; and that the politicisation of the antagonism really *consists in* its new power "to divide men effectively into friends and foes".

The transformation of a material antagonism into a political motive, its attainment of political actuality, depends not only on its inherent strength, but also on a number of further conditions—how far such an antagonism can link up with current political concerns, how far leading political groups feel it and, once aware of it, actually consider it "exploitable", or how far several material antagonisms converge in one political focus, or admit of polarisation round one political axis. The political is by no means *simply* equivalent to what is most intensive, serious or weighty, although at the bottom of every great political struggle (there is also routine skirmishing of a diplomatic kind and within political groupings) there lies a selection of definite antagonisms, experienced as intensive and weighty, involving both spiritual matters and interests.

Schmitt is mistaken in his claim that the politicisation of an antagonism signifies the friend and foe groupings based on it. If friend and foe are to be taken simply as "opposed" social groups (like different churches and schools of philosophy, competing economic units, or artistic movements) his definition is too wide. But if, as he apparently will have it, they are to signify no less than totalities ready for war, death and destruction, his definition is too narrow. Can it really be maintained (to anticipate a later point) that party antagonism in the modern state is really only political when armed "party militia" stand behind each side, or their formation is somehow imminent? On the other hand it can be objected that this over-narrow criterion of the Political is quite insufficient! Do not a well-organised band of criminals and the police, or two great criminal concerns in a state of feud, equally deserve to be called "warring totalities", and does this really make their antagonism a genuinely political one? The spiritual antagonism of the supporters and opponents of prohibition in the USA today seems to us to be an antagonism that has "become political", since it is frequently at the centre of national politics, although it is hardly likely ever to lead to civil war; whereas the perpetual physical struggle between the officials of prohibition and the extensively organised bands of smugglers can scarcely be described as a political one.

It seems to us, then, that Schmitt essentially exaggerates the relationship between *politics* and *war*. This is clearly related to the striking fact that in his work *politics is treated almost entirely as a matter of external relations*;

internal relations completely vanish from sight. His sole mention of the class struggle relates to its power to push national antagonisms into the background and bring about a state of civil or international class war.[14] This neglect of internal relations on the part of one so outstandingly well informed about the problems of internal politics, as Schmitt is, obviously has a deeper meaning and cannot be the result of inattention or insensitivity.[15] Indeed, we may venture to suggest that this averting of the gaze from internal politics has without doubt an *internal political meaning*. This almost exclusive concern with external politics, this rigid holding fast to the primacy of foreign affairs, nicely corresponds to a *definite* view of internal politics, to the structure of power *within the state*!

War, then, is the cornerstone of the life of the state; and this derivation of the state from external relations, together with this, as Schmitt himself says, pluralist picture of the world as an essential multiplicity of sovereign states, and the sharp polemic we also find in this work directed against *discussion*, an essential category of internal relations, as a basic category of civic life—these things are logically very closely related and show the way in which the primacy of external relations and, as it were, the repression of internal, are both in fact directed towards the solution of questions of internal politics.

4. The *defining feature* of the state is, for Schmitt, the *jus belli* (pp. 33ff). It is from this point of view that he attacks Cole's and Laski's theories, according to which the state is one form of grouping among others. He denies that the state is any kind of grouping, "society", or, so to speak, contingent assemblage of comfortable sovereign individuals (to render Schmitt's indignant scorn in yet more drastic terms); in Tönnies's language, it is not an "association", but an absolutely real entity, a "community". This seems to us correct, in so far as we also regard the state as a special kind of community which conditions the forms of association and possesses considerable metaphysical dignity.[16] But the "state" in its developed form (such as the monarchical empire, the ancient *polis* and the modern constitutional state) is surely a poor example of Tönnies's idea of "community", an outstanding feature of which is an element of natural growth, of the familial and tribal. But a more important question is whether the state and the political sphere are really constituted by the *jus belli*. A secret society with clearly defined goals, which orders its members to kill its "enemies" and subjects them to its internal courts of justice, is not necessarily a political body in any important sense, and certainly not a state. An international movement, which makes similar claims on its adherents, though with only partial success, is certainly a political force of the first rank, but again not a state.

Nevertheless, the claim that every community at war has something political about it, and even forms a kind of "state", or perhaps only a "state within a state", when its power is really considerable and its exclusiveness well marked, is more plausible than the corresponding claims that politics only makes sense *when it embraces the possibility of asserting its own and annihilating another's existence through warfare*, and that *the state is necessarily a sovereign warrior community* confronting other such communities. But this is what Schmitt actually says. A people which devotes itself to peace and wants to have no enemies is not doing anything political but doing away with itself as a political subject (p. 41). An "idyllic" world where mankind was united and free of the possibility of war, whether or not it could ever come to pass, would nevertheless be a world containing "neither politics nor state" (p. 42). Not only would the peoples subject to a League of Nations with powers of decision not form states; the world-state itself would not be a state, "it would be neither state nor empire, but would completely lose its political character". For in respect of its earthly environment it could have no more enemies. It could not be organised for the struggle against a foe. The "friendship" of those individuals and peoples united within it could not constitute a political community, since the correlate of "antagonism" would be missing.[17]

It is hard to be polemical in the face of such exaggerated constructions, since the risk of sounding a banal note is all too great. Nevertheless, the thinker must always be mindful of his subject and take no heed of the glorious or lamentable nature of his own task. But are we really expected to nod agreement when told that in the world-empire there would be no more distribution of power, no more hierarchy, rivalry or resolution of public antagonisms? No more ups and downs in the cultural, economic and even the straightforward power relations of the federated nations and their appointed personnel? Would there be no more disagreement about how certain central decisions (of a religious kind, for example, or concerned with the planning of the world economy) were to be resolved, or how the individual nations and districts were to be governed? Would there be no more state taxes, no legislation for state education, no state courts and police? It seems to us much more likely that politics would simply acquire a new dimension, that of the organised super-state, although it would, in exchange, lose important, though not unreservedly "pleasant", elements. There would certainly be no more armaments debates or diplomatic alliances, as we know them.

One might object (as we ourselves do): Even a world-state cannot completely do away forever with the possibility of enemies, revolutions and armed collective action. Indeed, no! Schmitt adds the bitter comment that, in the future, man will not speak of wars but of "means of compulsion" and of "executions" (pp. 64f).[18] But he never completely denies the possibility of a world-embracing organisation at perpetual peace, his concern being the thesis that such a condition would signify the end of the state and of politics. But it is by pressing our first objection that we come to the really important point. It may be generally acknowledged that every state-like formation, and every political power, must be prepared to consider rising up in arms (not necessarily only "defensively") should the need arise, or be capable of considering it in an emergency. An absolute rejection of this possibility seems in fact tantamount to the dissolution of all civil society. For a single man who is "of another mind" could then overturn the whole defenceless world-state. Even the existence of party groupings of any kind, in even the best-balanced and most freedom-loving democracy, would probably make no sense unless it were at the same time "thinkable" that if the impossible happened and an attempt to suppress them completely were made, it could be met with forceful resistance. *But this is not the essence or heart of the matter.* Schmitt's ghastly vision of a united world-empire helps us to see this clearly. Here too "war" would still be part of the picture, but its possibility would be so small and remote that it would be quite obvious that war and the concern for war, that is, the "friend-foe" relation in Schmitt's sense, have very little to do with the basic determination of politics and the state. (In the same way it would be manifestly false to speak of a civilisation dying out or fading away simply because crimes were so rarely committed that only a feeble remnant of its police and law-courts still continued to function.)

Let us now leave consideration of the "world-state" and go on to consider the relation between municipality and state and, in particular, the federal state. The supreme authorities for taxation and police, for example, in the large municipalities resemble and stand in for the state itself, but in no way are they organised for possible wars against other regions of the same state. Apparent exceptions turn out to prove our point. Paris in Jacobin days, "Red" Vienna in contemporary Austria, in their pointed struggles for power with the rest of the country do not simply represent themselves as demographic or residential units, but as the political Left at state level, a party division intended to embrace the state as a whole. The important regional power struggles in the German Empire furnish an almost vanishing prospect of military engagement between the states concerned—for example, Bavaria and Prussia—and one that bears no relation to the political weight of the antagonisms. One might perhaps put forward the American Civil War, the largest post-Napoleonic military operation of the nineteenth century, as evidence that even regional antagonisms in a federal state lead on to the "real thing" (so Schmitt), that is, to war, once they achieve real political significance. But in fact the Civil War was by no means an abstract collision between Northern "existence" and Southern "existence" as such, but resulted from the combined effects of various antagonisms, those, namely, between the different cultures of North and South, between a factory and a plantation economy, and between the moral and the utilitarian, racial and aristocratic attitudes to slavery (thus providing a superb example of how political oppositions develop).

And in any case nobody would ever claim that the complicated and eventful internal political history of the United States from the Declaration of Independence to our own day merely amounted to a kind of "background" to the Civil War, or a step on the way to an inevitable civil war of the future.

The American example—that strange combination of revolutionary and territorial warfare—may well show that "the beast merely sleeps", that in certain circumstances internal politics develop into foreign affairs, "discussion" into war. But it also shows the reverse. The war was ended by the reunification of the realm and survived by the Democratic Party, which, largely under the banner of Free Trade, brought together the "aristocratic" white population of the South and the second-class citizens and lower-class dissenters of the East (Catholics, Jews, and so on) into combined opposition (radically opposed to civil war) on internal affairs. And who would see today, in the dispute between church and radicals in France, a "possible" revolt of the Vendée, or in England's class and party struggle a (potential) war with Scotland? The Irish question has received an "internal" and federative solution, which may well prove lasting. Can all this be called "the death of politics", an "extinction of the state"?

In no way is war *the culmination or essence of politics*; it is simply a *means*, notwithstanding the fact that once it has come about it brings its own far-reaching problems and is, to a great extent, subject to its own laws, like any situation of comparable urgency and decisiveness. We shall later have more to say about the actual *material* goals of the state and, especially, of politics, and about the grain of truth one-sidedly exaggerated by the "friend and foe" theory. Here we must simply concede that the controversy over the sociological assessment of war is certainly supported by a total view of things not wholly lacking in value. Schmitt's way of thinking sees war as the life of a community raised to its most intense and solemn pitch. This is the view we utterly reject. We certainly do not think that war or conflict between organised and armed powers is, under all circumstances, reprehensible and barbarous. In our view the ability of men to assert themselves by going to war, especially when their cause is just, is intimately bound up with the value and dignity of persons and communities. Life is not the highest good, nor is death the greatest evil. But we are no less clearly convinced that the essential meaning of life can never be found in death or the prospect of death, but in life itself—and then not in "life" as such, or in "life" as the luxuriancy of experience, as crass naturalists or scintillating vitalist philosophers hold, but in the ranges of meaning life offers, and in the shaping of its goals. A positive value can be attributed to the warlike attitude, in as much as it represents a positive and manly stance towards evil; it has absolutely no worth as a fundamental good of existence itself. But, to take a sociological point of view once more, the "friend-foe situation" is an *essentially possible borderline case* of the political process, which doubtless possesses its own dialectic and its own requirements, and which, thanks to its own special urgency, puts all current political or technical concerns into a new perspective for as long as it lasts; but for all that it is not the real fulfilment or culmination of the political process, nor does it transform every single one of its technical goals into an unimportant and contingent technical accessory to military contest!

5. Liberalism, according to Schmitt (p. 58), perverts all the categories of public life, replacing war and peace, which "clearly distinguishes between the status of the two parties", with the "dynamic of endless competition and endless discussion" (in accordance with the separation of the economic and mercantile sphere from that of ideology and the "spiritual", each the object of contempt for those inclined towards "heroism"). A strange opposition, ingenious yet absurd! In the first place war and peace are primarily concepts of external relations, whereas discussion belongs to internal politics, competition to the social and economic realm. Secondly, why should there not be something like "endless" competition and discussion and at the same time peace, for the most part, alternating with the occasional war? Analogously, one cannot play off the more rhythmically alternating activities in the life of an individual, such as work and rest, eating and not eating, against, say, the "lasting states" of breathing or thinking, on the grounds that they "clearly distinguish between the status of the two parties". We see in this forced contrast yet another expression of Schmitt's fundamental concern to ensure the primacy of external relations and to discredit internal politics, at least as the major theme of public affairs. This is merely a new-style sociological version of the age-old principle: "*It is power, not justice, that counts.*" Power, the stalwart endurance of war against the foe, that is what matters. Discussion, intended to solve questions of justice and correctness, is superfluous tomfoolery. The question is how the state is to deal with the enemy, not how the people are to be governed and life lived within the state. That is, government and life should be so ordered within it that it could bring to bear against the foe the greatest possible amount of force. To put anything else in the forefront of attention is a philosophy of "weakness". This would of necessity be exploited by "others" who are free of it, by the "enemy".

The correctness of our interpretation of Schmitt is confirmed by his denial that there can be any significant struggle of a spiritual kind (p. 59); in the concrete reality of political existence, he says, "there can be no rule of abstract orders or sets of norms; all there can be is control of specific human individuals or groups by other specific human individuals or groups". Rightly understood, this is a sociological truism which can always be used against certain formalists and rule-fanatics. But if we take it further, this sociological realism becomes a pseudo-sociological fantasy of power worship. The "discovery" that even in the case of liberal institutions neither the "constitution" nor the "people" itself "rules", but that there are always specific wielders of power, specifically privileged strata and kinds of men, injustice of a specific kind, etc., is supposed to be sufficient to "legitimate" as sociologically natural a form of institution which is primarily and, so to speak, "openly" directed towards the development of power and dominion. This ignores the fact that the second member of Schmitt's opposition (concrete power-wielding individuals and groups) is *in itself* as impossible, or in need of completion, as the first (the rule of abstract orders and sets of norms). All dominion, and even the constitution of any kind of leading group, has its own particular material principle (e.g. theocratic), all exercise of power by "concrete individuals and groups" is limited by "order" or "sets of norms" on whose basis that level of control is still possible; above all, "control" varies in kind and degree according to the type of objective rule with which it is institutionally linked. The "dominion" of morality, law, the economy or of "rule", says Schmitt (p. 59), has only "a concrete political meaning". This is correct only in the sense that that "dominion" of morality, and so on, is only possible in a particular and concrete political form. It would be totally absurd to claim that the difference between the ancient Persian monarchy and a parliamentary democracy consists "simply" in the fact that in the one case a single man "ruled" at the head of a standing army and the viceroys appointed by him, whereas in the other we have "rule" by a "clique of professional politicians".[19] The difference between a prison and a holiday camp is not just a matter of the difference in character between the persons in charge. Rather, the life of the community has in either case a different rationale; certainly we can talk of an "order" in the second case as much as in the first, but talk of "the authorities" is not so appropriate, of "rule" and "compulsion" even less so.

Thus the question of the detailed structure of the "order" in the state, the question of how it is ruled and ought to be ruled, how far, for example, there should be mastery and inequality, with what material qualifications or kinds of value power should be especially bound up, how far it should be concentrated or divided: *this is the proper object of politics.*[20] The working out of this does not mean armed struggle, but the *contrast and comparison of the ideas of order, that is,* primarily, *social discussion.*

II

1. Carl Schmitt's vision of politics is characterised by the primacy of *foreign policy,* by *war* as the supreme manifestation of community and by the *expansion of power* as the be-all and end-all of communal human life. As against this, I offer a conception of political life which gives the primacy

to *domestic politics*, to the teleological *function of the state*, and to *debate* as the rational prelude to *decisions about where the state should be heading*.

Does this mean I am just proposing a different "party" policy, or arguing about the meanings of words? A closer look at the phenomenon of "politics" should go some way towards allaying both these suspicions.

No theoretical understanding of politics, not even Schmitt's, is uninfluenced by the thinker's own position.[21] If I make the "friend or foe situation" the centre of politics and put the warlike power-seeking of foreign relations at its metaphysical heart, I thereby commend unlimited armed conflict as the normal and approved form of settling political issues; I commend aggressive and unyielding power relations, the unquestioned submission of citizens to their rulers, and a domestic social structure most suited for waging war. If I deny political debate, with its competing views, I thereby reject the idea of social adjustment and of supervision and inspection from below, and at the same time support the traditional, or perhaps newly emerging, arbitrary distribution of power. Schmitt's position is in fact counter-revolutionary in an anti-proletarian sense: the reference to the enemy without is supposed to distract attention from the experience of "class struggle" and its rational and ethical content; the canonisation of the irrational element of power and the trivialisation of "liberal" discussion are supposed to provide a relative "justification" for the antiproletarian class struggle conducted from above, a kind of "rationalisation" by courtesy of realistic sociology. The citizen with a bad conscience, still stricken with liberal illusions, offering under their spell only fainthearted and resigned resistance to the proletarian onslaught, can be filled with new zeal by Schmitt and made ready to fight. However, the proletarian desire does not have to be interpreted as an abstract will to power, since it is formed around a new and rational idea of social order. But there is one respect in which the ultra-revolutionary—or Bolshevist—will to class struggle might be thought to support Schmitt's conception: it offers the prospect of a complete uprooting of the enemy class—though this war-aim of absolute revolution from the Left is hardly an option for any kind of counter-revolution.

These facts could certainly be given a different kind of political interpretation. But they do not presuppose the liberal dogmas of a merely "fictitious" will of the state as the resultant of the "autonomous" wills of all citizens, of the "equal validity of every opinion" or of an "endless rationalisability of power relations", any more than they do the demand to abolish war or any kind of force whatever.

But one definite fact emerging from this discussion does support our own interpretation: the question *Who is to prevail over whom?* is necessarily *subordinate* to the question *How is the communal life of mankind to be structured?*. The *kind of existence* is a *more decisive category* than the *conflict of existences.* As opposed to "structure", "conquest" has a merely secondary importance in an objective and essential sense. If "Hinz vs. Kunz" is not primarily a question about alternative ways of structuring a given slice of social life but is actually supposed to *mean no more than* "Hinz vs. Kunz", then the issue is no longer one requiring rational treatment; it is *not "politics"* but something of no more significance than the struggle between competing football teams (a possibility almost realised with the circus factions of the Blues and the Greens in the Byzantine Empire). Lichtenberg expressed it with exemplary firmness when he said that the question is not whether the sun does or does not set on a particular empire but what it manages to see in it. This implies not, certainly, the unimportance, but the altogether secondary importance of foreign relations. Whether I "prevail" over this or that man is certainly important but is in itself a trifling matter compared with how I live. A state may or may not be at war with this or that other state, but the question about the nature of its regime, the political atmosphere in which its citizens go about their business, is always unavoidable, can never lose its topicality and can never be, as it were, accidentally on the agenda. State A and state B do not have to come into contact with each other, and they can cease to be in contact, but the relations between social groups within A and within B are the most central constituents of the "existence" of these states. Certainly foreign relations are far from being the chance "encounters" of nomadic tribes who have perhaps hitherto known nothing of one another. But we have only to think of dispositions of foreign relations such as "the balance of power in Europe", "mastery of the Mediterranean", "the Far Eastern question", "disparities in armaments", etc., to see at once that they do not concern simple antagonisms or "friend and foe" situations, but *questions of order concerning some single focus of reference.*[22] The actual powers and power aspirations of the individual nations and states represent different points of view, religious, cultural, internal political or social. Certainly in these cases the simple power interests of the individual "powers" do seem to predominate—though to different degrees. In domestic politics, however, especially in the internal relations of "states" in the self-contained, modern, sense (as in absolutism or democracy), the leaders, leading groups, parties, classes and so on absolutely never represent mere "loosely" connected and formally identical units of power, but are intelligibly bound together as the *exponents* of competing forms of life, of "positions" vis-à-vis pressing issues that concern everyone, of "answers" to current organisational questions. By the primacy of domestic politics we are then to understand that these constitute the really decisive issues for the formation of social life, though they are certainly not without "irrational" aspects which are only intelligible in the light of "historical" power struggles. In foreign relations these last dominate the picture, although in a less integral and essential fashion they carry along with them historically compelling elements of decisions relating to social organisation. That these must play some part, however small, results from the fact that *all conceivable human groups are contained in the ideally all-embracing community of the "human race"*. We can hardly conceive of a collision between "foes", however hostile and primitive, where both parties have not in some way claimed to "be in the right" and to be superior to their opponents according to some recognised objective "value".

However, as long as foreign relations remain foreign and are not, for example, the internal relations of federal partners, their material will always be contingent, fluctuating, evadable; its implications certainly cannot be extended arbitrarily far, but nor does it constitute a *clearly defined and unavoidable presence*. The case is different with internal politics, which turn on *the form of the state*. The relationship between the two is rather like that between aesthetics and ethics. Art plays an enormous spiritual role in human life, although the extent to which individual persons concern themselves with this or that art, or with any, is a contingent matter, even a matter of chance. However, there is no conceivable escape from the ethical questions of life. For the state is not a vehicle or a medley of strivings for power which equally well might not have existed, but *has two functions indispensable for social life*, that of guaranteeing the protection of the law and that of centrally regulating relationships. The proper *content of politics* is the actual structure of this central social apparatus and the way it responds to the life and power aspirations of the groups subservient to it; political *debate* is the argument between groups and points of view, not about existence and non-existence, I-live-and-you-die, but *about fashioning the destinies of all alike*. It is therefore not a bloodless substitute for war, not a degenerate shadow of fighting, but a social function with elements of both struggle and co-operation, which could not be replaced by any kind of war, even civil war. Political discussion was not invented by liberalism but has existed in every state. Just as there has to be a council of war in wartime, so in times of peace, when the state is carrying on its proper business, there must be an endless network of advisings, considerings and thoughtful assessment of powers, without which no ruling or mutual contact between rulers and their subjects (every regime in the world must take their "mood" into account) would be possible at all. Liberalism and democracy simply give political discussion a rationalised legal form and offer a stimulus and a pledge of minimal participation to all citizens and ethnic groups. In this sense it could be said that *"politics" in its real essentials only begins* with liberalism and its building of general discussion into the form of the state—in direct opposition to Schmitt's view that with liberalism the state became perverted and ceased to be.

2. For all that, there is absolutely no denying the *peculiarly "irrational" aspect of politics*, which can easily lead one to interpret all affairs of state in

irrational terms if too much emphasis is placed on it. When Schmitt attempts to understand the state in terms of politics, and to interpret politics in terms of the extreme borderline case of a sublime and pointless existential trial of strength, he turns everything on its head. It is like a proposal to define the psychophysical concept of a "man" as "smallest natural fighting unit". He simply ignores the perfectly obvious, proper and commonplace meaning of the state and makes its more "exciting" emergency function, which naturally takes this meaning for granted, into the substance of the case. Nevertheless, he is right to claim that politics has something to do with the irrational element in the life of the state.

What, then, is this irrationality, and how does it differ from the generally irrational aspects of human life? Taken in themselves, both the "common good" of politics and the individual good of any particular person can only be materially defined within limits—the trite saying "Man's heaven is his will" is true for both. It is also true that, from both the individual and the collective points of view, a cholera epidemic is indisputably bad and a well-managed currency indisputably good. One might at first think that the specific irrationality of the life of the state consisted in the fact that here, as in the individual case, no taste, lifestyle or value preference, which are all in themselves irrational, can be taken as given, since in public life man confronts man, will confronts will, value code confronts value code. There is no rational way of settling these differences, just as it is also impossible to argue an individual into accepting a way of life that differs from the one he is used to. There is, in addition, the awkward fact that even private interests, perfectly rational and intelligible in themselves, such as pure "welfare" interests, cannot be rationally weighed against one another but only pitted against each other in somewhat combative fashion. But is this correct? Are there not forms of social life, just as there are (more or less perfect) ways of regulating interests, in which, at all events, some sort of standard of adjudication is applied and a certain adjustment secured?

There is a great difference between the "irrationality" of politics on the one hand, and, on the other, the "irrationality" of the struggles between men and animals, or between nomadic tribes who encounter one another on their wanderings, contest a grazing- or watering-place, or think they are serving their gods with blood sacrifices. In these latter cases the contest between two firmly established systems of goals or effective powers is cleanly resolved through physical means, unclouded not only by convictions or appeals but also by vague influences of a "psychological" and "demagogic" kind. In the first case we have discussion at various levels, warnings and promises, persuasion, conversion, propagandising and theoretical debate; rules of procedure which can be broken, but not at all times and in all ways; corporate moods and swings; a predominant tendency to change, whose relation to the particular decisions and outlooks of those involved is always something of a mystery.

It is this last point that puts us onto the track of *specifically political* irrationality. It is not just a matter of the *multiplicity of subjects* involved, as though it were confined within a closed social circle. When a new people settles among a host people in such a way that it is clearly separated as a whole, despite there being certain economic exchange relations and perhaps even certain spiritual relations between individuals of either people, this irrationality does not yet appear in its typical form in the two groups taken as a whole. Nor is it found between the castes of a caste-ordered society, where the castes by and large, apart from certain hierarchical religious relationships and fixed economic obligations, can be thought of as living separate autonomous lives; in a stable oligarchic state, supported by a sub-class of spiritually unawakened serfs or peasants, without rights or claims, the latter are essentially untouched by the "refined", "lively" and not precisely characterisable irrationality of politics. How strange! It is precisely the allegedly so rationalistic and mechanistic modern party democracy and the age of genuine "class struggles" that have suggested the thesis of the irrationality of politics—though we do not mean to imply by this that the phenomenon first genuinely came into being in our age. But this peculiar irrationality (and today's democracy is certainly not the first case of it) is found where *the representatives of different points of view are grouped around a common centre.*[23] The single point of reference characteristic of "the state" as such, the quasi personality of the state embodied in, say, a "prince" or a "cabinet" on the one hand,[24] and on the other the manifold and opposed social groups of the leaders, thinkers, and so on, interested in the course of its activity, constitute the conditions for the existence of the "political" in the narrowest and truest sense. Political irrationality is not pure instinctive life as opposed to the supposedly "impotent" life of the spirit, but is a genuine spiritual irrationality—certainly partly conditioned by instincts—which presupposes the rational focus of all spiritual activity.

We spoke just now of *manifoldness* and *opposition.* Do we not also find this in a somewhat watered-down form in Schmitt's category of friend and foe? The state administration, which embraces the social unit, with its uniform system of goals (Schmitt would perhaps prefer to speak of large municipalities or spheres of authority rather than the state) is in itself still "non-political"; only with the appearance of friend and foe, as at least possible categories or potential relations, do we hear the note of politics. But any honest observer, whether he shared our own or Schmitt's predilections, would grant that the contrast between his and our view goes very deep. We cannot see anything political in the struggle of primitive peoples against savage beasts; we can only see very little that is political in the war of extermination between two warrior tribes, rather more in the wars of expansion of a great king; and the quintessence of political life in, say, the contest of two parliamentary parties or the competition between two tendencies in determining the policy of one and the same party. But this ascending series of "political" levels does not go with increasing scope for the friend-foe relation; on the contrary, it is gradually inhibited, relativised, given a place in an indissoluble unit of shared life. Certainly "politics" does bear in itself a specific relation to struggle, but *within* this relation it exhibits precisely an *alternative* to physical annihilation or even social elimination or the "disposal" of one's opponent. The well-known secondary sense of the word "politics" as meaning "tactics" or "shrewd diplomacy" also points to this. Naturally we have here no simple replacement of violent by crafty means in the service of the same goal of annihilation, but a fundamentally different conception of the coexistence of a plurality of policies and attitudes to power. In other words, the essential mark of the political sphere is not the relation between friend and foe but *the coexistence of opponents on the basis of a social unit of reference.* In the sphere of foreign relations this unit of reference is more or less indeterminate, a matter of culture and so on, and lacks a quasi-personal focus of conduct, while the "opponents" are primarily determined as individual products of a particular territory; in the domestic sphere the unit of reference is the relation to the state's "direction", to the policies and personnel of a central apparatus for decision making and guidance, and the "opponents" are primarily, in accordance with their social function, determinate groups and representatives of "standpoints" with direct intentional reference to the central guidance and the life of this social unit. Our concern here is, above all, the second variant—internal politics.

3. The specific irrationality of political *discussion* is *not that it lacks objectivity* or that there is something *illusory* about it, but that it inevitably has *two meanings*. It is quite true that its aim is not to adjudicate about a purely objective truth and falsity, as in science, or even about what is advantageous and disadvantageous, given some quite definite choice of goals. But that does not in the least mean that it is just a substitute, prelude or mask for the settlement of group enmities, which would as little admit of resolution by discussion as, say, an attack of hungry wolves or the destructive waves of a spring tide. The fact is that the oppositions first arise and take some definite form because of the unit of reference, through the fact of mutual dependence and concern with the "common good". Think, for a small-scale example, of the case of a father who criticises the manner of life of his son and tries to dissuade him from what he considers to be its mistaken course. He may well also have his own advantage in mind, in that he wants to ensure that he does not lose his own fortune or his social standing through his son's extravagance. In all this he is very likely to start by taking for granted some other way of life from that of his son, some relatively different set of value priorities, which he perhaps unjustly interprets as an index of the son's stupidity, depravity or imprudence. But

it by no means follows that he is not also concerned to guard his son from serious harm of a kind that even the son would clearly recognise to be seriously injurious to himself. Within limits, which change from case to case, he can get his son to see this, or else be brought by him to see that his fears have no material foundation. In their discussion a great deal may be brought to light concerning ideals of living; the son may come to see that he has shown disrespect for certain values which the family or its social circle have stood for and which he himself still finds important; the father may learn that what he is up against is a well-thought-out point of view with which he must reach some quite definite compromise.

So, too, political discussion is neither superfluous nor mere delusion. But it does also, to some extent, inevitably express the real contest of various "forces" for a share of power and goods.[25] It is in fact impossible to make a rigorous separation between this contest and the purely objective discussion of the common good, of what is "right" for the state; this is because the power interests only *reach the stage of alliances and manifestos* in their interpretations of the common good and their reference back to the given central "state power",[26] and because the "competition between styles of life in society", which comes between the struggle of interests and the objective problems of the state, can only come alive with the attempt *to solve the question about how the given state should conduct itself*. Individual tastes and interests only acquire their title to be acknowledged when they can be inserted into an objective conception of the state, one that the "general public" can accept. In a secondary sense, of course, we also find a clear demarcation between spheres of validity for forms of life (as in religious questions) and the pure conflict of interests (as in the determination of formulae for the allocation of taxes and subsidies). Political discussion also overlaps with the purely academic sphere of jurisprudence, political economy and the theory of the state. But the very heart of politics—the rise and fall of policies and parties, the trust and mistrust of the "masses" towards a regime, good and bad "conscience" in a party before "public opinion", the calculation of what may be politically possible or impossible, the practical alternatives open to the state—all this contains an inseparable tangle of ideals and interests, statesmanlike thought and the private will for recognition. An attempt to free discussion from its entanglements is as meaningless as its abolition, although there are bound to be relative solutions for particular questions[27] and although a partial, perhaps dictatorial, restraint and confinement of discussion must always be possible, though it is precisely this that betokens a degree of depoliticisation in the life of the society.[28] For the aim of discussion is not the discovery of a definite "truth" about the state, to which all its parts have then to conform irrespective of their interests and predilections; nor does it arise from the confrontation of various spiritually unrelated and impermeable wills, one of which has simply to "conquer" the others or even to "exterminate" them, or among which power has to be divided on a proportionate basis by way of compromise.[29] These "standpoints" and "factors" are by their nature not rigidly separate and individuated things like professional groups or official parties; they are always "produced" with reference to the question of the day and the policy being followed by the central government, and they change their meaning in response to changes in the relations of authority and trust between the regime and all its people, between leaders, their subordinates and subjects in general. (The role of the "non-political", of the "unpredictable crowd", of the unforeseen, the condition of the economy, swings, surprises!) The specific, one might say the paradoxical, feature of politics lies precisely in the fact that it concerns the course which *power*, the central governmental direction of society, is to take, with its manifold relations of alliance and opposition, with the various, from its point of view, *"subjective"* groups and party conceptions which already somehow presuppose the existence of society's central direction and justify their claims to it. The fact that power is more the *theme* of relationships in the political than in any other sphere has often produced the mistaken idea that the only thing that counts is the success and increase of the "one" power at the expense of "others". But we do not find either a mutual impingement of the rational plans of independent and self-seeking subjects, as in the pure market economy (where, for all that, some social substrate has always to be presupposed outside the scope of the plan), or simply a central plan as in a planned economy or a completely organised state (where at least "nature" and the wills of all concerned have still to be taken account of). What we do find is the interplay between plans conceived from different points of view and underlain by different interests and a *shared* set of goals.

Forget, then, the idea of feeble rational appearance concealing powerful irrational reality! We have, rather, the *variously coloured modifications of a generally rational concern*, always compromised and weighted but also nourished by particular interests, which are in themselves not subject to the generally rational concern, a fact which gives the impression of something especially irrational, incalculable and conflict-ridden in politics. We do not find the dull and deadly confrontation of friend and foe, but an overarching "friendship" shot through with particular friendships and corresponding enmities, alike endangered and supported by them. The undeniable irrationality is not to be found in the futility of rationality but in the manifoldness and elusiveness of its nevertheless interlocking particles. *Political activity* does not mean fighting without any consideration, or even with merely external and secondary consideration, for a total order, but means, precisely, fighting *about the total order*. Such is the internal politics of a state; the foreign relations of states will only be truly "political" when they become the worldwide internal relations of mankind actually united, even if they include wars or "executions".

4. The real content of political life, the *object world of politics*, consists, then, not of wild coalitions of "friend and foe" but of everything of importance for a society, especially relationships, above all power relationships, in so far as they relate to the bearers and ways of proceeding of the central power—the state power, but also municipal or other public power. Various material factors dictate whether, how far and when social affairs become *politicised* and become the subject matter of political discussion and pressure-group formation. Some important power relations, which thoroughly determine the entire life of the society, such as stable class relations, may be confined to a marginal place in political reality, as long as they are quietly accepted and not, or only partially, supported by the manipulations of state power; on the other hand, some in themselves minor questions concerning the occupancy of some post or rates of tax can assume a highly political character when they are symbolic of far-reaching choices or social conflicts. Indeed it often happens that seemingly tiny details are bitterly fought out and become the occasion of momentous political crises, as for example the matter of the tax on tea in the American Revolution, the dismissal of Necker or the storming of the Bastille in the French Revolution, the affair of the armoured cruiser or the nugatory differences in social policy in the recent collapse of the great coalition in Germany, or the appointment of a general manager of the railways in Austria; as for foreign relations, one may recall the causes of the Franco-German War and the Great War. The special importance of clearly isolable particular questions like these and of unforeseen events in politics is partly due to the presence of opposed group formations whose antagonisms can flare up at certain selected points of conflict and can be thus relieved. But this need for clear, limited and intelligible "catalysts" itself also points to that unit of reference within which the antagonisms are confined, and which therefore are not normally carried to extremes or brought to the highest level of current tension. Incidents can be smoothed over (Fashoda, Agadir) and government crises survived (the dying down of the Negro question to a lower level of tension after the Civil War). But this phenomenon of political details having symbolic power has other causes. Politics is, firstly, not a private business and secondly is not "social" in the aggregative statistical sense or even in the sense of a merely spiritual and material life-sphere, like culture or economics; nor is it merely a public functional device, a self-enclosed subject of activity like the administration, justice, or the armed forces. It is a "public matter" in the pointed sense of *collectives consciously acting* alongside, against and with one another. Here there is a special need for easily grasped and remembered cases for decision, which of course stand for deeper life-questions and group interests, through which the watchful interests of the masses are inserted into the ambit of rational action. This also accounts for the role of symbolic (often not, or not primarily, "leading") personalities, slogans and formulae, his-

toric events such as battles, collisions, elections and parliamentary decisions, and flags and insignia. From the point of view of the leading circles
(the government, party leaders, etc.), but also of the masses, in so far as
they are organised and capable of taking a wide view, isolated conflicts
and critical situations often function as *tests* of the scope of a political
power, the ability of the group leaders to count on their supporters, the
degree to which there is a common mind—on certain matters—within the
people, and so on.

The composition of the political object-world in a particular group of
people at a particular time is therefore dependent on all social facts relating to the group concerned (including its milieu), with special reference
to the dynamic brought about by displacements, as changes become important, generally known and in need of settlement; for the most part the
social forces themselves are already formed by the state or with political
reference to the state—perhaps through the parties; the state apparatus is
by no means merely a "mirror" of the social world, and the parties and
other politically determined groups by no means act as mere representatives of tendencies of thought and class interests, but also comprise a system of goals of their own[30] with their own traditions, even in part their
own ways of life.

Political topics differ not merely in their subject matter—derived from
their religious, economic, directly political, etc. origins—but also formally, in various ways. They may concern an entire population or, despite
their relevance to the state, merely a small group within it—for example,
the leadership problems of a single party.[31] They can vary in urgency and
topicality (think of the power position of a prominent statesman), and be
in varying degree centrally political (compare government powers and
rights to freedom). Political matters can also be more or less "deep"; questions which, especially in a relatively peaceful time, do not essentially and
directly touch current government policy (as, for example, the development and the demands of a not yet "respectable" party on the Left in a
country by no means ripe for revolution but involved, say, in industriali-
sation) may yet much more deeply affect the foundations of the system of
government itself and the relationship between state power and the classes and other social circles, than highly topical political questions which
may at any time bring about the collapse of the regime.

5. Let me, in conclusion, look once more at the *value sphere of politics*, especially in the light of the contrast between the friend and foe theory and
what we may briefly call the theory of political order. Against the idea of
essentially irrational enmity let it be at once asserted that politics is above
all concerned with the application of *non-political values*—those of religion,
welfare, justice, humanity, technological control, comfort, etc. But of course
we may also speak of peculiarly "political values". They include success,

significance, forcefulness, ingenuity, creativity, and the timing of political conduct—values, which are in general independent of any political tendency and can characterise conservative just as much as revolutionary politics.[32] So, for example, at a particular moment of crisis, both a quite definitely rightist solution and a quite definitely leftist one would make sense and would be compatible both with the preservation of the unity of the state and with national traditions. So the question of whether one is, speaking crudely, primarily of the Right or of the Left, is not an object of genuine "political evaluation" but is determined by already professed principles of ethical value preference, religious and metaphysical prejudices, personal and class allegiances. But it is a matter of political insight, political instinct and political inventiveness to discover what actual solutions are possible here on both "leftist" and "rightist" presuppositions; what still acceptable moral and mass-psychological cost is entailed by the rightist solution; what still acceptable risk to the existence of the state is entailed by the leftist one. However, the friend and foe theory of politics champions an untenable absolutism and relativism of political values. According to it, every already existing system of political goals, every already existing "battle camp" counts as absolute for its adherents, or rather its members, and as incommensurable with all other points of view; there are no political values in the space between such camps, and relativism is the only possible position for an outsider. Every political victory is both absolutely valuable, absolutely valueless (for the "enemy") and, at the same time, absolutely irrelevant. The theory of political order, however, will recognise, between the pure category of subjective success in battle and extra-political value foundations, an intermediate sphere of those genuinely political values which will correspond not simply to the victory of the better over the worse, and not simply to the victory of the one over the others, but *to the right and lasting harmonisation of the elements of a social unit of reference*, albeit certainly *from the preferred standpoint of one of these elements*. An example from domestic politics is provided by the great statesman, who, from the point of view of his party, class, confession or region, engages in "state politics" even to the extent of completely disregarding these prepossessions. At the level of inter-state relations think of a foreign policy of such a kind that it is able to create a secure and possibly also leading position for the home state (even by warlike means in the extreme case) but always acknowledges the system of goals of the given circle of states as such and co-ordinates the power position of the home state with an objective function within the wider system of goals. The formula suggested above in italics contains the suspect word "right"; by this I wish to indicate, firstly, that political values can have no validity without reference to other, more fundamental values, that is, a policy good in itself must operate with as large as possible a stock of sound and obvious values (justice, welfare, culture, etc.),[33] though it is necessarily also directed against other values of these kinds. Secondly, a good policy strives for a genuine "harmony", that is, a leading role for one's own standpoint (one's own "camp"), which, thanks to the objective function it performs, is recognised, supported and tolerated by the representatives of other standpoints, whereas the radical defeat, elimination or annihilation of an opposed power is reduced to the unavoidable minimum.

NOTES

1 Aurel Kolnai, "Der Inhalt der Politik", *Zeitschrift für die gesamte Staatswissenschaft*, Tübingen, XCIV, 1, 1933, pp. 1–38.
2 *Der Begriff des Politischen*, Munich–Leipzig, 1932, an expanded edition of the essay of that name in the *Archiv für Sozialwissenschaft*, 1927. Simple bracketed page numbers in text or notes refer to Schmitt's book.
3 "The concept of the state presupposes the concept of politics" (p. 7). "The state as the standard political unit" (p. 33). "The pluralism of the world of states follows from the conceptual criteria of politics" (p. 41). Once mankind is so organised that there is no longer any possibility of war, there will be "neither politics nor states" (p. 42). The "state" has no properties as such, since it really embraces the entire life of society; one must investigate the specifically political categories (pp. 11–12).
4 This bracketed question mark is in the printed text [eds.].
5 *See* previous note.
6 Cf. Schäffle's distinction between the routine work of the state apparatus on the basis of rules and regulations, and "politics" proper, which is a region of "novelty" (cited by Karl Mannheim, *Ideologie und Utopie*, Bonn, 1929, pp. 71–2.) Political action proper enters in "where unregulated situations demand a ruling". This sphere is irremovable: as E. K. Winter somewhat extravagantly puts it ("The True State in the Sociology of Law", *Zeitschrift der öffentlichen Recht*, 1931): "In the last analysis states can only be governed by men, never by laws in themselves". The bureaucratic conservative conception of the state is, however, mistaken in holding that this sphere is dispensable, as is the liberal conception in thinking that it can subsequently be rationalised to an unlimited extent by supra-statal Natural Law (Mannheim, *op. cit.*, pp. 71ff). Roughly, the view of the ethics of sentiment, which certainly feels the irrationality of the world, especially in its power relations, but cannot endure it (Max Weber, *Politik als Beruf*, Munich, 1921, p. 443). The recent emphatic revelation of the irrational (R. Behrendt, *Politischer Aktivismus*, Leipzig, 1932, p. 59) is supposed to be a reaction to the liberal capitalist rationalisation of the whole of modern life, at the same time a counter-consequence of that politicisation of socialised man (p. 57), which is an aspect of the liberal rationalisation already directed at the irrational. Cf. elsewhere in Behrendt the extension, or résumé and analysis, of the political conflict-irrationalism championed by C. Schmitt.
7 *See* Mannheim, *op. cit.*, I: Stages of the sociology of thought: psychological functionalisation, which detects the dependence of values on interests and affects in the social standing of their bearers, and noological functionalisation, which finds it in the commitment to formal structures of thought, to the system of categories

itself. However, this does not make the values objectively irrelevant. Relationism does not mean illusionism. The "genesis of possible truth as bound up with the social process" remains an open question. Perhaps "absolutes" are "to be found" in the course of the development of social ideas. The rootedness of thoughts in the social being of their originators does not have to be a source of error. An immanent evaluation of political preferences can be combined with sociological research, in that their objective realisability is tested within the environmental conditions actually obtaining.

8 Schmitt actually asserts this (pp. 16–17) by distinguishing the public concept of *hostis* from the private one of *inimicus*. One does not have to hate the political enemy personally, but neither does one have to love him, certainly not to support him against one's own interest. The Sermon on the Mount certainly does not command this; but then does it really command a "support" of the private enemy in a personal conflict? Certainly a genuine personal enmity may have a characteristically poisonous trait as against the more "institutional", "objective" enmity of war. But surely Christian morality excludes an ultimate and whole-hearted surrender to the latter just the same. Either it strictly forbids all personal animosity and injury, hence war also; or it tries to relativise any animosity and arch it over with love, justice, respect for the other, and in any case with ethical scrutiny, humanisation and limitation of war. Christ does not go with Treitschke, Kjellén or Bernhardi.

9 Leo Strauß says the same: "Notes on Carl Schmitt's *The Concept of Politics*", *Archiv für Sozialwissenschaft*, vol. 67, pp. 736ff. Combat is the "real thing", according to Schmitt, enmity the primary and "grouping" factor. Hobbes's "state of nature" view of society, which takes an individualist form, assumes an "original situation", in which everyone is everyone's "enemy". We find it obvious (Strauß's points take roughly this line) that Hobbes's radically naturalist fiction is far better suited to serve as theoretical subsoil for social morality than the apparently much milder theory of Schmitt, which also takes for granted an original community. If the supposed animosity of all against all comes to be restrained by treaty and judicial order, it can be completely replaced by a community of common purpose and a collaboration of all mankind. Schmitt, by contrast, regards it as the eternal or normal destiny of men to struggle against the alien community in combination with the companions of one's own community.

10 Here too we agree with Strauß's interpretation of Schmitt, *op. cit.*, pp. 734ff. Schmitt does not really have in mind any kind of close connection between politics and other spheres of culture, or the "autonomy" of politics. The thought is, rather, that politics is something fundamental and uniquely "real", not one among many "objective domains". It is "above" the other spheres of culture. "The understanding of politics implies a fundamental critique at least of the prevailing concept of culture."

11 This is put more extremely and unambiguously in the 1927 version: "neither normative nor 'spiritual' antagonisms".

12 War is not the end or goal of the state, but "the reality of an ever-present possibility", the "real thing".

13 "The rationale of war is not to be found in any defence of ideals or laws but in its being waged against a real enemy" (p. 38). But who is the "real enemy"? Even the answer that it is the economic competitor is rejected by Schmitt as "liberalistic", and, for the most part, rightly (though we would be far from saddling only "liberalism" with the one-sided perspective of "economism"). But cannot "ideals and laws", or adherence to them, make an essential contribution to some-

one's becoming a "real enemy" of mine? Is it not somehow artificial to break off an analysis and content oneself with the claim that one community somehow becomes the "real enemy" of the other in the course of history?

14 Whenever the class struggle is really "serious", Schmitt opines (p. 25), we already have a particular proletarian "state" making war on the bourgeois state. This amounts to an untenable conversion of the—certainly meaningful—metaphor "state within a state" into the basis of the concept of the state. Domestic politics cannot possibly amount to inter-"state" politics. (Cf. the text, below.)

15 Here too it is worth noting the divergence of the expanded new edition from the 1927 essay. Whereas in the latter Schmitt simply pays no attention to domestic politics and understands politics exclusively as foreign relations—except for civil war, where the parties have already become like hostile "states"—the new edition contains a discussion of internal politics, which the author of course considers as, by comparison, greatly lacking in dignity (pp. 17ff.). According to this, there are *within* the state "numerous *secondary* meanings of 'political'. Hence educational, municipal, social politics, etc. However, "opposition and antagonism within the state" remains "constitutive for the concept of politics". Are these partial "oppositions" also supposed to be simply elements of "antagonisms" in abeyance or cold storage? At all events Schmitt sees in the carrying on of "weakened" oppositions a "parasitic", "caricature-like" politics, which operates with "tricks and dodges", is identical with "party politics" and has no acquaintance with "the real thing". This is true, to the extent that the question how the citizens of a state ought to live is "unserious" as such, and the seriousness of life only begins when the living man is faced with the shadow of death. But we only need to formulate the proposition clearly to refute it. Certainly one may speak of a primacy of internal politics (p. 20) when there is a real possibility of war in this sphere, that is, when civil war impends. Elsewhere in the book edition (p. 34) Schmitt discovers that it is an achievement of the "normal" state to guarantee peace, safety and order within its territory, and speaks of the "necessity of satisfaction within the state". But what does he mean by this? That the state can itself designate the disturber of its functions as an "internal enemy", declare him a "*hostis*"! In our view those functions and the way they are met are themselves much more important than the proscription of those who disturb them. And it is surely not the meanest task of the genuine statesman to get by if possible *without* "internal enemies".

16 D. von Hildebrand, *Metaphysik der Gemeinschaft*, Augsburg: Haas & Grabherr, 1930, pp. 310–11: "*Res publicae*" as the proper sphere of the state, centred on the "protection and realisation of the law"; public safety a fundamental presupposition, an elemental good for the individual. Schäffle: "Rule-governed central apparatus for the coordination of all parts of the total life of society and organ of positive intervention in the interest of the preservation of the whole", cited by Adolf Menzel: "Die energetische Staatslehre", *Archiv für Sozialwissenschaft*, 1931, p. 165. According to Hermann Heller (*Die Souveränität*, Berlin–Leipzig, 1927, p. 81) the state is "the homogeneous collaboration exclusively of particular human acts, in this respect like any other human association, but completely distinct from them in that the acts which give it reality are the guarantee of all collaboration in this area." (Of course every society contains something "statal", but not always in the sharply characterised or constitutional form of the modern state.)

17 There would be no more politics in a pacifist world (p. 23), "despite interesting oppositions", etc., since "there would understandably be no opposition on the ground of which a man could be required to lay down his life"—and just as little reason "for killing other men". So is the presence of politics bound up with uni-

versal conscription? If not, does it only affect the personnel of the standing army? Is the question of who is to govern "interesting", but "not political"? Schmitt's special terminological position really conceals *value judgements* (see Strauß, our note 21).

18 Wars waged in a pacifist spirit, perhaps as "war to end all war", are (p. 24) "especially intense and inhuman", since the enemy is even morally disenfranchised. It may be remarked here that, e.g., those wars of certain times and peoples in which, in the case of victory the whole enemy population was exterminated or sold into slavery, were quite certainly waged without pacifist slogans and not as "wars to end all wars". Furthermore, people seek to put their opponents morally in the wrong and to justify themselves in *all* genuine antagonisms, whether between individuals or peoples and their leaders. The affirmation of abstract hostility as such is much more a matter of ideologues than of statesmen and warriors.

19 The distinction made by R. M. McIver (*The Modern State*, Oxford, 1926, pp. 306–307) between the "ruling class" of capitalism and that in the feudal sense is very true: "The capitalists did not become a governing class in the sense in which the landowners had been. They exerted of course a strong influence on government, but they were not, as by a kind of natural right, the rulers of the state. Their property power was not naturally translated into political power."

20 A recent notable critique of Schmitt by Georg Schmitt in the Catholic *Rhein-Mainische Volkszeitung*, July 1932, sees the kernel of Schmitt's position in the fact that he will not acknowledge that politics is the problem of defining an *order* for the life of the state. He is also right in his interpretation of Schmitt's concept of politics *itself* as a *polemical* one, in that it is spiritually directed against liberalism, though materially against the proletariat; however, he does not work this out at any length. Cf. what follows in the text.

21 Strauß shows this clearly in Schmitt's case, *op. cit.*, pp. 745–47. Schmitt's thought is not value-free, rather he affirms politics in his sense, and not because he regards "non-political" (i.e. pacifist) existence as utopian—he thinks its realisation is a real possibility—but because he "detests" it, feels "disgust" at it, as he shows, for example, in his mocking use of the word "entertainment" (in the description of the rich content of a "non-political" condition). For he sees "the seriousness of human life threatened" by this possibility. In emphasising the independence of the political, its distinction from "the moral", etc., Schmitt contradicts himself: it is not just as a scholar that he affirms his own sense of politics, but as an expression of his own ethos, which is certainly very different from a humanitarian ethos. "Politics *cannot* be evaluated, or judged against an ideal, at all" (Strauß, p. 739), because Schmitt has already posited it as the highest of life's values.

22 This topic is rejected by Schmitt. Strauß puts it concisely (*op. cit.*, p. 747): "The affirmation of the 'Political' is the affirmation of the state of nature." Hobbes, however, who argues from a much more extreme conception of the "state of nature", places its *overcoming* at the heart of his theory of society.

23 Mannheim writes about an objective platform for "*real discussion*" (*op. cit.*, pp. 157–58).

24 Such a sharp differentiation between the state and society in general and the other social groups within it is only found in our own culture: Alfred Weber, *Die Krise des modernen Staatsgedankens*, Stuttgart, 1925, pp. 18–19. This of course says nothing against the general sociological lawlike tendencies of the "statal" sphere at the basis of every society. Even so, the phenomenon of law can be studied only in certain societies of superior culture, and the phenomena of "caste" and "Dharma" predominantly in the culture of India.

25 Party struggles are always *also* struggles for the patronage of office, as Max Weber (*op. cit.*, p. 406) makes clear.

26 Alfred Weber convincingly argues (*op. cit.*, p. 84) that every party, even a class party, has to put itself forward as an instrument of a universal state policy.

27 The falling off of discussion in the working of today's parliament, which Schmitt emphasises in his *Verfassungslehre* (Munich–Leipzig, 1928, p. 318) and elsewhere, is certainly very significant and is connected with the increasing rationalisation of the machinery of the state and the change of function of parliament from being an organ of mere supervision to the bearer of state power; but this certainly does not bring with it a dying away of political discussion in the democratically governed society itself, but rather a more intense politicisation of society-dwelling man in general (see later in this note). Schmitt discusses the liberalistic "endlessness" of discussion in his work *Die geistesgeschichtliche Lage des Parlamentarismus* (Munich–Leipzig, 1923, p. 24): In place of the claim to absolute truth we find a "competition of opinions". But that sort of competition is not possible at all except where there is an intention to find the truth, and the discussion leads again and again to relatively valid and relatively final solutions.

28 The sphere of internal politics does not stand and fall with the presence of liberal state institutions. It is also incorporated (Max Weber, *op. cit.*, pp. 410–11) in the separation of the political civil service from specialist officialdom. The "political civil service" in the narrow sense depends both logically and historically on the existence or production (actual or at least assumed to be possible) of an "opposition", of a plurality of state-related standpoints: it represents, as against the technical executive apparatus, the predominant will of the state in its development and conception, in its opposition to real or possible alternative conceptions.

29 Majority decisions would be pointless as automatic arithmetical operations; they presuppose arguable questions for universal decision: Alfred Weber, *op. cit.*, pp. 44–45.

30 Cf. in Max Weber, *op. cit.*, p. 420, the distinguishing of political leadership, as full-time occupation, from the strata of notables in more recent democracy, especially and earliest in the United States.

31 To some extent, especially in the American system of large programmeless parties, necessarily "unofficial" (because fluctuating and requiring a continuous reformation and regrouping of standpoints) mass psychological operations of politics are all but completely transferred to the intra-party sphere. A constitutional fixation or legalising of parties would be pointless, as Hermens (*Democracy and Capitalism*, Munich–Leipzig, 1931, pp. 53–54) rightly remarks: new extralegal tendencies, new "parties" in the spirit of their original function, would immediately form.

32 Cf. note 29.

33 Roman Boos (*Wirkichkeit und Schein im modernen Staatsbegriff*, Berlin–Grunewald, 1931, p. 49) puts it very well: The fundamental requirement is "that the state should be given a form, which allows it again and again to re-submit itself to the standards of human justification".

A Note on the Meaning of Right and Wrong[1]

AUREL KOLNAI
1955

1. A CLASSIC PROBLEM IN ETHICS

Do we prefer, morally, the "high-principled" or the "virtuous" man: the scrupulous duty-performer of Kant or the Aristotelian virtuoso of "prudence" for whom doing the good has become "second nature"—who, in other words, is habitually pursuing "his" good in the perfect way that renders it identical with "the" good?

No unequivocal solution is possible to this puzzle. Absolutely speaking, the second type of "good man" may appear preferable. For, obviously, he who does the good with ease, with all or most of his "inclinations"[2] harmoniously assenting to his course of action and participating in the tracing of his conduct, must be more intrinsically permeated with "goodness"—nearer to the "saint", indeed—than he who, again and again, laboriously, loudly and sweatingly, as it were, asserts his "respect for the law" and achieves its "triumph" over his unruly, or at any rate "unsympathetic", desires. Yet, on the other hand, this latter kind of moral man lives in keener awareness of moral duty as such; if we find him less loveable we are apt to credit him with greater merit; and, as students of ethics if not purely and simply as men, we may well accord our preference to the Kantian conception on the strength of its casting into higher relief the very essence of morality as distinct from human perfections taken in a broad sense. It might be argued that the "intrinsically good" type of man was only of more agreeable converse, not worthier of being approved—which is by no means the same thing. Again, we are perhaps faced with two irreducible and equally legitimate varieties of moral behaviour: A may be a good man in the duty-conscious fashion, without being able to develop into a good man in the properly virtuous style, while B may act righteously with spontaneous ease, without being able to take much interest in the clear thematic formulation of duties; if these two contrasting temperaments, without ceasing to be such, have both attained a high level of

1 Originally published in *Scientiis Artibusque*, an anthology of essays published by Herder & Co., Rome, July 1958, for the Hungarian Catholic Academy of Science and Art in exile.
2 *Neigungen*, a term of contempt for Kant.

objective morality, it is so much the better that both should exist. It would be a poor sort of world in which it were possible to be good in one manner only. To be sure, the *objective content* of *A*'s mode of behaviour will, in analogous situations, sometimes differ from *B*'s: *A* will, on occasion, decide on a course of action that to *B* (and perhaps to us) may appear "petty"; and *B*'s conduct will, on occasion, evoke *A*'s criticism (which we shall perhaps endorse) on the count of being a trifle "lax". But, then, are we always able to ascertain, with scientific rigour, as it were, which choice or what conduct is the best in a given case? Far from it. That a loan should be paid back by the borrower is unequivocally certain; that the creditor would do well to remit a debt is obvious in some circumstances and highly improbable in others; but in still another set of circumstances it may pose a most delicate and debatable problem, which must be entrusted to the ultimately inscrutable decision of the agent's conscience. Even at the peaks of proven morality, characterological differences will retain a legitimate range of influence.

But in concrete moral discourse we are not so much interested in contrasting shades of perfection as in the likelihood of actual good conduct. In their respective one-sided coinages, both type *A* and type *B* will, on different grounds, evoke a certain distrust on the observer's (or on their neighbours') part. *A* is apt to impress us as a person of predominantly evil inclinations, inhibited, to be sure, and held in check by an enlightened and law-abiding will, devoted to right and averse to wrong—which, by the way, could hardly exist but for one set of at least actual virtuous habits—but not attacked and modified, not ennobled or rectified, in their substance. Such a man appears to do the right thing grudgingly, with an effort betraying that it really goes against his grain; the very sternness of his insistence on duty and the very emphasis of his readiness to override his interest or to spurn pleasure warn us that the whole man is far from being behind the impeccable or meritorious conduct. We do not know for certain that he will, in the long run, prove able to keep up his self-control; we do not know at what moment the checks may snap and the restraints give way—and if they do, something pretty surprising, if not fairly monstrous, may happen. Within such limits, and with such a proviso, however, we feel rather safe with our man. Until further notice, at least, we may presume him to be responsible—that is to say, ready to give account of his actions (in the proper circumstances, and to such as may reasonably demand it) under accepted or acceptable standards, in intelligible and arguable terms. It will be the other way about with the second man, *B*. Short of a miracle of evil, as it were, or, to put it differently, in the very long view, we may always count on his fundamental goodness—fairness, kindness, delicacy, sympathetic understanding, height of quality, and so on. His good behaviour gives us the comfortable feeling of proceeding from, and pledging, if I may use a metaphor, not his inner "government" alone

but well-nigh the whole "people" of his thoughts, yearnings and dispositions. But in hardly any single situation—involving any objective occasion
for doubt—can we trust him implicitly. That his inclinations are good is
all to the good and by no means "morally irrelevant"; but we do not
know that he *would* act, if need be, *against* his inclinations. So far, he
"happens" to lean spontaneously always towards the right and to shun
wrong much as we naturally shun pain; but may we not infer from this
apparent *identity* between the spontaneous movement of his will and that
which he objectively ought to do a danger of inversion: in other words,
the likelihood of his confusing the primary impulse of his "heart" with
objective duty as such, as though his likes and dislikes were a standard of
right and wrong? Should we ever come to disapprove of his conduct can
we remonstrate with him and argue the case, appealing to set rules, which
we both recognise as valid? Has not his very habit of doing the good quasi
"automatically" dishabituated him from weighing his actions carefully in
the light of principles detached from his self, the basis for discussion and
responsibility? Is he likely to possess a conscience set at a distance from
his nature? May we not fear lest he should neglect to confront his primary impulses with that conscience, mistaking them for the voice of conscience itself?

In brief, then, we seem to be on the horns of a dilemma. The morality
of type *A* is defective in as much as it fails really to *pervade* the personality;
that of type *B* appears defective for the opposite reason of not *transcending*
it. The "good will" obsessed with pedantic formalism, moralistic rigour
and puritanical mistrust of life and spontaneity suggests a fascination
with evil and a renunciation of actually being a "good man", virtuous in his
substance. And the "angelicism" of accomplished virtue suggests a naturalistic evasion of the moral theme, a state of mind subject to presumptu-
ous illusions, and the pernicious trap of the negation of evil.

It need hardly be said that, in following out the logic of our two contrasting types, we have been moving on a plane of barren abstraction and
remorseless simplification. Obviously, these types are constructed, rather
than observed, realities; obviously again, they embody characteristic tendencies or possibilities rather than anything like a compelling alternative.
In moral psychology, many other divisions into contrasting types are possible; our own types *A* and *B* are by no means invariable, rigid unities,
but are capable of further subdivision: thus, the properly Kantian duty-
moralist and believer in the formalist, monist and subjectivist concept of
"good will" is different from the Puritan proper, whose code of rules is
derived from outward objective imposition by God, or perhaps the state
or tradition; again, the morality of virtue, harmony and spontaneity may
bear a properly religious or a properly naturalistic tinge. Nor shall we, in
reason, decide for either of the two types as a general ideal, but visualise
as an "optimum" character one that unites a prevalently good quality of

primary inclinations and habitual desires and repulsions with a keen consciousness, an explicit awareness of principle and an occasionally demonstrated or transparent readiness to control appetites even should it require
a major effort. Still, few will deny that the types A and B express classic
aspects of reality and are relevant to fundamental problems of ethics. In
fact, I hold that their analysis may, to some extent, help us to approach
the most essential of those problems—the meaning of Right and Wrong.

(I should perhaps note that, in this paper, I am using the terms Right
and Wrong as suitable abbreviations, respectively, of *Moral* Good—that
which, in conduct and character, deserves approbation—and *Moral* Evil—
that which deserves reproof—that is to say, without implying any restriction to the sphere of justice and veracity as distinct from the spheres of
purity, neighbour-love, constancy and so forth; or even any restriction to
conformity to, or infraction of, a recognised code of hard-and-fast rules.)

2. THEMATIC AND IMPLICIT MORALITY

By supposition, A and B are equally "good men" or "moral persons"; but in
the conduct of A, or rather, more particularly and more conspicuously in
its motivation, reference to Right and Wrong plays a more central and
emphatic part. For example, let us imagine that either of them renders a
certain service to a third party, C, which involves a fairly tiresome kind of
labour and which C has been more or less vaguely "promised", or at any
rate allowed to count upon. A will say, "I hate to do it, but I've as good as
promised it; I cannot default on my duty." B, however, will mutter, "I
can't let good old C down", though perhaps C is not so very "good" after
all nor a close friend of B's; and B will perform the service, in spite of the
inevitable discomfort it entails, with some amount of pleasure—referred,
not to the abstract sense of "doing one's duty" or "being right with the law",
but to the resultant good of C himself, vicariously "shared", as it were, by
B. I propose to call A's conduct *thematically moral* to a very much greater
extent than B's; yet B's conduct is *not* for that reason *less moral* than A's; it
is even more so—more "virtuous", we might say—in that B's mind partic-
ipates more thoroughly, with a much greater volume of inner resonance,
in the good action he is performing. Thematic morality does not necessarily mean a more perfect morality, nor a less perfect: for instance, B is
likelier than A to fail to redeem his promise, at least a not very clear
promise, if he happens to dislike C personally (which would be less likely
to affect A's behaviour); or again it may be that A will refrain from a dis-
reputable act for the right reason, with a keen sense of indignation, while
B will do so with a rather indifferent state of consciousness, because it
would somehow offend his "taste"—in which case, though the conduct of
both would of course appear perfectly satisfactory, that of A would impress
us as imbued with a higher sense of morality. Put over against A's, and

evoking either a slightly higher or a slightly lower degree of approval as the case may be, *B*'s conduct will on the whole be not so much thematically as *implicitly moral*.

Prescinding from other possible shades of distinction, the word "moral" is used in three main senses. First, in a sense referring to the sphere of moral values and disvalues, to accents of approval and disapproval and their objects as such: thus, we speak of a "moral life" or "moral conduct" (i.e., conduct as judged from a moral point of view), "moral defects", "moral problems", "moral difficulties". In the second sense, "moral" means what is morally commendable and opposed to "immoral": a moral action in this sense is the same thing as a "good action", a moral man the same thing as a "good man", or again, a "moral play" a play morally innocent or even pointing a wholesome "moral". The third sense is that of thematic morality. It means, in short, not moral goodness but emphatic attention to moral themes. Moral goodness is actually impossible without some measure of thematic morality: a person deficient in conscience—lacking awareness of Right and Wrong—may not behave immorally in every possible respect but cannot behave morally at all; in the language of moral theology, "habitual" or even "virtual" good intention cannot subsist without a core of "actual" good intention, a basic determination to fulfil the moral law. But neither is moral goodness *proportional* to the degree of thematic morality. The predominantly duty-conscious is not necessarily better than the spontaneously virtuous or noble character; the professional ethicist, moralist or educator may be, but need not always be, morally superior to those whose interests and preoccupations are centred in other subjects; a certain type of sinner and backslider, living with a strong awareness of sin and tormented by his conscience, is surely not the worst of men but may well be worse, not better, than the "happily conditioned" kind of man who, on the whole, lives a decent life but devotes little thought to problems of morality. Nor is "integrity", akin to thematic morality, a sure index of moral goodness: one may live strictly according to one's conscience but have a misinformed, distorted and falsified conscience and thus be, actually, rather more evil than the average humdrum person liable to succumb to passion without even minding it much; whose conscience then is obtuse and undeveloped but not perverted. Again thematic morality is less conspicuous—its presence more discreet—in the man of saintly life, with whom morality is implicit in his love of God, than in the man honestly anxious for moral correction who has but few and vague religious beliefs or for whom, even though he be a Christian believer, religious life is merely peripheral. On the other hand, an atrophy—let alone, a negation—of thematic morality is necessarily prejudicial to the moral quality of conduct and character. One who would *despise* doing the right thing except spontaneously—even though he habitually *does* the right thing spontaneously—is open to criticism, and so is the pietist who shuns sin and pursues good ends *merely* out of "obedience to God", without any insight into the nature of Right and Wrong, or slighting the intrinsic distinction of Right and Wrong: for one thing, he can attach no meaning to the tenet that God is "good" or "righteous", and misconceives of the holiness of God.

Implicit morality, which means not the absence or exclusion of, but only the restricted, or "background", role of thematic morality, should not be confused with a mere resultant "goodness"—that is, usefulness, either in a self-regarding or in a social perspective—of conduct. The mere accidental, or even statistically probable, effects of conduct, as detached from the underlying intention, have nothing whatever to do with its morality. The difference between thematic and implicit morality is not that the former presupposes a good intention while the latter is independent thereof, but that the good intention, essential to both, is emphatically and prevalently the intention to "do the *right thing*" as such in the case of thematic morality, whereas in the case of implicit morality it is the intention to do *a certain thing* in which the agent is interested *apart from* the theme of Right and Wrong, but which he *knows* to be *a right thing* not a wrong thing. In the vocabulary of moral theology it is *secundum legem* rather than *propter legem*; but it need not for that reason be merely "licit", it may be properly "meritorious". Nay, according to its subject matter and the particular quality of the motives, it may even be a great deal more meritorious than many a thematically moral action: thus an act of gratuitous, self-denying, and at the same time well-advised and fruitful, generosity in favour of someone we personally cherish and hold in esteem, as compared with the obligatory act—informed by thematic morality—of resisting an immoral temptation.

Thematic morality might as well be labelled "pure morality", and implicit morality, morality "alloyed" or "mixed" with extra-moral concerns. This does not, to put it bluntly once more, mean that thematic morality as such is superior and preferable and implicit morality a mere second-best substitute for it. For man is ordained, *not* to confine his interest to morality but to *live morally*, which is an entirely different thing. Indeed, "by" morality alone, in the exclusive mode of thematic morality, that is to say, he could not live at all; the all-round entelechy of his life—in other words, the value of the "good life"—consists in implicit rather than in thematic morality. The stuff of life, material and physical, is not primarily moral but ought to be realised and worked out in a morally good fashion, in view of the distinction of Right and Wrong, in fulfilment of moral laws. Thus, commutative justice and the wrongness of cheating are eminently moral considerations, but the purchase of an object for which one pays the full price in due time is not a thematically moral act; Christian marriage as opposed to promiscuity is an eminently moral theme, but Jack wants to marry Jill here and now because he feels the need to live with a woman and is in love with Jill, not primarily in order "to posit a moral act"; intellectual integrity is a strict moral duty, but the scientist who sets out his findings with scrupulous reserve and honesty is still primarily interested not in intellectual integrity but in the object of his research; we may keep an onerous promise by thematic obedience to the moral law—under the prompting of our conscience, that is—but we do not generally make promises in order to set in motion the machinery of the moral law that commands us to keep them. Implicit morality is not, then, merely "instrumental", "unconscious" or "inferior" morality, but actual morality *entwined* in the non-moral primary concerns of life, necessary for the existence of any kind of human morality, seeing that thematic morality itself cannot subsist except in the framework of life.

However, if implicit morality cannot be replaced by thematic morality, neither can it render thematic morality superfluous. But for an actual or virtual recourse to "pure" morality—to the explicit standard of Right and Wrong—it is doomed to lose its bearings, seen from the agent's side, and indeed to lose its meaning, considered from a general perspective, for moral life *as a whole* would be impossible without express moral judgements—acts of approval and disapproval—which have their locus in the medium not of implicit but of thematic morality. In particular, thematic morality comes into its own whenever the necessity of *abstention from wrong* arises. Thematic and implicit morality can by no means be *per se* identified, respectively, with negative and positive morality: on the one hand, thematic morality may lie at the back of our positive duty fulfilments (when, for instance, we feel it to be our duty to warn X of a danger which is threatening him) or of our generous initiatives; on the other hand, we may recoil from many a temptation by implicit morality: an unanalysed feeling of shyness or modesty, a movement of habitual tact or taste, and the like. Yet there is a marked asymmetry between thematic and implicit morality, as to their respective preponderance in the emphasis of Wrongness and Rightness. In its full weight and majesty, the theme of Right and Wrong emerges, primarily, from the conflict of vital impulses—passions, interests and self-assertion tending to sovereignty over our will—and moral prohibitions. "Taboos" and "Don'ts", the accusing or monitory voice of Conscience in the proper sense of that term, and critical discussion of the behaviour of others, are basic to moral experience and are the most powerful stimulants of ethical reflection. It is the "Thou shalt not" that stands out, from the outset, in sharp relief against the non-moral primary texture of life. Inversely, on the positive side our awareness of morality tends to recede into the status of a discreet overtone. Our conscience is more concerned with our wrongdoings than with our moral merits—and in confession we do not narrate our good deeds. Again, though in a broader view, the Law as a whole is a highly moral institution, the criminal courts are much more concerned with thematic morality than the civil tribunals. Moreover, negative moral precepts have, over positive ones, a priority of *urgency* which goes to strengthen their thematic emphasis: it is more important (though, in the favourable supposition, not more but less meritorious) to abstain from murder than to succour the needy, and to tell the truth—meaning not to tell lies—than to disseminate knowledge, and so forth.

Absolutely speaking, no doubt, morality is destined to ensure "the good life" rather than the mere absence of evil; the perfection of being rather than the non-existence of stains, which could most securely be provided for, as some oriental currents of thought would indeed commend it, by the extinction of being altogether. But, apart from some exceptional cases of ethical attention, the pursuit and the appraisal of approvable positive achievements in life carries a less sharply and distinctively moral accent than our resistance to, or reprobation of, moral evil. Life, meaning "the good life", is never all morality in the sense in which the struggle against Wrong is all morality. Valuable achievements, performances and creations, whether ordinary or extraordinary, whether private or public in scope and significance, connote properly moral accents, intentions and emphases to varying degrees, yet as a rule in combination, or rather intimate interblending, with *not* properly moral—although natural, legitimate and approvable, and perhaps noble and sublime—biological, practical, intellectual, esthetical and religious preoccupations. In our appreciation of the achievements of prudence, fortitude and wisdom, of statecraft or high literary art, we do not as a rule separate the moral aspect from the aspects of natural yearning, skill, knowledge and intensity so neatly as we separate moral guilt from unsuccess or incapacity: the passage between moral virtue and virtue in general is smoother and more imperceptible than that between sin and other kinds of deficiency. Positive moral values, though of course distinguishable in their concept, are inextricably fused into the texture of life and, accordingly, much more carefully toned than the acts of virtuous abstention. The motives of action are not and cannot be, in general, primarily moral: in the achievements of life, positive moral values come to be connoted, implied, more or less indirectly intended and exhibited *ex post*—the avoidance and combating of Wrong representing, predominantly, the "pure", "central", originally experienced and sharply characterised moral theme whose emergence punctuates life at its various turning-points.

Implicit morality postulates, then, the background of thematic morality: to deny this is to fall into some kind of naturalist, vitalist or perfectionist fallacy. No type of human nature, however propitiously "bred", "educated", "conditioned" or "enlightened", will produce implicit morality by following its bent in a spontaneous and automatic fashion, without painful checks and restraints, without awareness of evil and the pressure of conscience. Morality as a whole is bound to be defective, spurious and, as it were, evanescent, unless it is sustained by the agent's habitual readiness to act against his nature and curb his self-assertion (his concupiscence, pride, impulsiveness and self-centredness) for the sake of morality. But so also does thematic morality, on its side, postulate implicit morality. An exclusive fastening on thematic morality—in its puritanical, Manichaeist and formalist shades—not only conjures up distasteful excesses and threatens to stifle the manifoldness of human values in its obsessive fear of sin and of imperfection uncritically equated to sin, it also tends to be self-defeating and indeed proves, on closer scrutiny, to be logically untenable. For, in their contents, all moral themes, even though negative in emphasis, involve the background of the business of life and presuppose the world of non-moral concerns. The moral evil is not in strictness "deducible" from the value of earthly life but supposes the pre-moral value (the "physical good") of life and without this foundation would lose its meaning. Disrespect for alien property could not be wicked unless ownership itself connoted an implicit moral value. The moral taboo on profligacy is certainly not "deducible" from the natural purpose of generation or the positive morality of orderly marriage, but it is largely grounded on the irreverence, implied in debauchery, towards a vital sphere susceptible of the realisation of high moral values closely allied to "happiness" and the good of the race. More generally, by virtue of their content all moral laws, including those purely prohibitive, carry in them an obscure and potential reference to non-moral concerns accepted as legitimate, and thus an innuendo of implicit morality; yet if we rescind contents and place all emphasis on the sheer formal concept of "the moral law" we shall find that we have reduced the moral law itself to an empty verbalism stripped of all meaning: Kant's "imperative", taken entirely seriously, would be like a person in authority who is constantly proclaiming the absolute validity of his authority but, that being his sole theme, *cannot actually command anything*. This objection cannot be levelled with the same force against G. E. Moore's one-time "intuitionism", which held that "the good" was an irreducible ultimate quality, inexpressible except in terms of its own immediate perception: but this view, which stretches the truth that moral values cannot be *deduced* from natural concerns into the fallacy that they cannot be *interpreted* in the context of life and its non-moral primary concerns, at any rate greatly impoverishes the meaning of the moral good and deprives it of *weight*.

It remains to be noted that implicit morality, as such neither inferior nor superior to thematic morality, has a far wider *range* extending both "downward" and "upward". In practical morality, whether we think of the small child or the uncouth or primitive man (so far as he exists), moral life begins with mere drill, discipline and training which carries an inchoate and confused moral connotation inseparable and hardly distinguished, as yet, from concrete arbitrary imposition by the habitual and somehow beloved authority of a superior human will (that of parents or rulers, or crystallised in custom) and the sanctions of pleasure and pain attaching thereto. Again, the "fully virtuous" man may live by implicit morality to a higher degree than the ordinary well-intentioned person, who needs the proddings of his conscience to refrain from a good many mean or naughty things he may be tempted to do. And the blessed in heaven cannot attend to thematic morality in any practical sense, seeing that they live in a world without Wrong and therefore without the tension of Right and Wrong: perhaps, to change the terminology, in a world where Good alone is present and thus Right proper can have no place.

Although, in their typical forms, the overrating of thematic and that of implicit morality entail the opposite dangers of tense and narrow puritanism and of lax and complacent naturalism, their high-pitched varieties may converge into much the same effect of ethical perversion—the mystical identification of the agent's own will as such with "the good", in contempt of codified laws, concrete rules of judgement and responsibility in the court of moral argument and discussion. This may be couched alike in the Kantian phraseology of a "purely moral" will which is "its own lawgiver" as opposed to the historical contingence of particular and determinate laws, and in the Aristotelian phraseology of the "rectified will" being the measure of right conduct rather than inversely, and of "prudence" judging a particular situation with impenetrable sovereignty, over and above the need for casuistic self-justification. Neither thematic purity and the mirage of an "exclusively moral" motivation, impatient of non-moral admixtures and particularised objective values, nor acquired personal virtue pretending to be the *test* of conduct, of which it is in fact merely the basis in the order of causation, can raise man above the ineluctable duality of a thematic and an implicit relation to Right, both equally necessary. One-sided affirmation of either may easily result in a disguised refusal to submit to the moral law as such.

3. RIGHT AND WRONG IN THE CONTEXT OF THE BUSINESS OF LIFE

The above reflections do not enable us to attempt a definition of the unitary meaning of Right and Wrong, but may contribute some relevant hints. These I propose to outline in the form of four remarks.

(a) The experience of thematic morality, with its stronger negative emphasis and its sharply *sui generis* character, shows that Right and Wrong have a meaning that cannot be drawn simply from the securing, protecting and coherence of the practical concerns of man—the business of life in the widest sense of the term—or the un-evident commands of a superior authority (more perfect than man) *as such*. The uncontrolled self-assertion of our nature, sensuous as well as egoistic and formally self-centred (appetites, interests and pride), is itself *part* of the meaning of Wrong, again and again experienced in particular moral "taboos"; and our general readiness to self-restraint, self-detachment, self-criticism and self-abnegation is, accordingly, part of the meaning of Right. The stark experience of morality is primarily that of a barrier to vital unfolding, a brake upon self-assertion, a split between conscience and the "given", non-moral complex of the emotive and volitive self; this negative emphasis *implies* and *presupposes* the positive framework of our being and our endeavours, our needs, our reason and our beliefs, but is not a mere abridged *expression* of their affirmation nor a mere *condition* of their proper order. The self-restraint meant in thematic morality—in the concentrated emphasis of Right and Wrong—is not of the merely technical, functional, instrumental or transitory kind but has an *essential* edge: it embodies not a mere reference to the enhancement, refinement, discipline and "reasonableness" of life but an act of self-transcendence imposed on the practice of life. Morality, in other words, does not stand for the immanently "best" practice of life, though still less, of course, for a negation thereof; the relation between morality and practice as such is a "dialogic" one, involving tension and points of negation set in a vaster perspective of consonance.

(b) The "immanent" realisation and perfection of the concerns of life is not, however, a merely "neutral" affair, subject to the avoidance of Wrong and compliance with "strict moral duties"; it constitutes a *moral* performance, primarily not in the sense of "thematically moral" but in the sense of "morally valuable" and enclosing a multitude of morally sanctioned tasks, interwoven with morally thematic accents. Implicit morality is not a mere intentional remnant, a residual memory or a remote reflection of thematic morality, but an essential mode of the moral life. The "good" practice of life, taking its departure from primarily non-moral ends, enters in its turn into the very meaning of Right, which cannot be grasped fully except in its particularised *contents* and therefore in its correlation with the manifoldness of positive values. Although, for example, social institutions cannot as a rule be defined in terms of thematic morality, they essentially connote moral themes (more general or more specific), and even the pure ethical analysis of Right and Wrong, as distinct from the establishment of concrete moral codes or the descriptive pursuits of moral sociology, will have to include, with a view to its completion, an aspect of institutional references. In much the same way as the abstract definition "An embodied rational being" does not really tell us what is meant by "human nature" without a complementary knowledge of man in his empirical (including historical) manifestation, the "meaning of Right and Wrong" cannot be fixed definitively so as to be "applied" to concrete problems of ethics or "illustrated" by the same afterwards: rather, its discussion will imply a provisional raising of the question, different to be sure but not strictly separable, as to "*what* is right and *what* is wrong".

(c) It is important to note, though the subject can be no more than touched upon here, that if Right and Wrong cannot be defined primarily in terms of the immanent success or harmony of practical concerns—which would mean skirting round the practical core of moral experience—nor can they be defined, as some forms of "axiological" ethics would have it, in terms of intrinsically "higher" and "lower" *qualities* of value and the "maxim of preference" for the higher over the lower value in emergent situations of choice. This is one cardinal aspect of the business of life and of morality but not the touchstone, let alone the meaning, of Right and Wrong. In particular, such an ethical theory would be out of keeping with the substantive thematic weight of Wrong and with the characteristic pressure of *urgency* which aligns moral demands with the basic "lower" values—such as the preservation of life—rather than with the values of high culture and refinement of life. Rational control as opposed to the unchecked assertion of animal appetites is doubtless fundamental to morality, and the spiritual height of life obviously has a positive moral significance, but neither the practical management of practical concerns nor the tone of spirituality as such define the meaning of Right and Wrong.

(d) In correlation with the manifoldness of primary non-moral values which make up the medium of the "business of life", morality itself is essentially and in a *sui generis* manner, *polythematic*. The unitary meaning of the precepts of the Decalogue—or, to put it differently, of the themes of justice, veracity, purity, self-control and others—is not, in our view, a mere figment of verbal usage but constitutes an "open" or "incomplete" unity of convergence rather than a massively unitary principle, of which the particular moral themes would be mere mechanical applications to different *materiae* of life. We experience Right and Wrong *as* Right and Wrong (not as essentially unconnected types of pleasing and unpleasing human conduct, which we subsume by a technically convenient verbal habit under the category of morality), but at the same time we experience Right and Wrong *in* their classic modifications which specify our experience more deeply than would a mere variable manifold of "circumstances" as confronted with one "identical" principle. Not only is morality an "obligatory" theme of life: its special accents inherent in the various dimensions and junctures of the business of life are likewise inescapable. This means that we cannot bring Right and Wrong, by analysis of concept, deductive argument and observation of cause and effect, to the full evidence of one formal axiom of "rational endeavour as such", "submission to a higher will as such", or "the equilibrium of all purposes of life". Moral experience itself points to the necessity of a concrete "code of law", not of our own making nor an object of our clear and unproblematic primary perception as is sense-evidence or the evidence of formal logic. It invites, *specifico modo*, our *intrinsic submission* to Divine Authority: "submission" in as much as the moral commands carry in them a residuum of the non-evident and irreducible, as well as an appeal to conform our own wills, over and above our "good pleasure", however rationally pruned and canalised, to the Will of God; and "intrinsic" in as much as they acquaint us with Right and Wrong in their knowable objective Rightness and Wrongness as *indicated* by Divine direction, not as a matter of mere opaque and arbitrary precept to which blind obedience without intrinsic cognition were an adequate response.

Erroneous Conscience

AUREL KOLNAI
1958

1. THE PROBLEM: SUMMARY OF ITS ASPECTS

(a) On the common-sense suppositions that moral judgements are true or false and that, therefore, conscience can be correct or erroneous, whereas on the other hand it is morally right to follow and wrong to disobey one's conscience, we seem to be faced with a paradox in ethics. That some kinds of conduct are morally right while some are wrongful and blameworthy is presupposed in moral discourse and in conscience itself ("I am ashamed of having broken my promise"; "My patriotic duty commands me to..."); yet if the agent is doing what he, in entire "good faith", thinks to be right, his conduct cannot very well be immoral, while if he is doing what he thinks to be evil his conduct *eo ipso* is immoral. The traditional solution to the puzzle is that one ought to follow one's conscience, whether correct or erroneous—the agent, anyhow, cannot possibly know that his conscience is erroneous, so long as it is his conscience—but that to hold an erroneous conscience denotes, so far as it is not reducible to mere "invincible" ignorance of *fact*, a moral defect which implies some degree of guilt. From this we may conclude a general duty for men, but especially for such as hold a *dissentient* conscience and again for such as find themselves confronted with moral dissent not obviously preposterous, to allow for the possibility that their conscience may be erroneous and to examine loyally the arguments against their moral opinion.

In actual practice, at least in our capacity as appraisers and advisers if less perhaps as agents, we nearly always take this dualist view, commending a person's moral insight as well as a person's conscientious "integrity", and blaming moral misjudgement or lack of percipience as well as the various types of unconscientious behaviour. We expect a man to behave rightly rather than either merely appraise rightly or merely behave according to his appraisal, and thus we consider "sinning against the light" essentially guilty but also attach a moral disvalue to a person's following his errant lights. And a conflict between these two apparently disparate points of view would strike us as more shocking, more paradoxical, more in need of a special elucidation, than the tension we continually experience between different moral criteria, all on the same level of intrinsic moral appraisal. We find it natural enough that a man's morality should be not worthless, indeed, but imperfect, in that he, say, displays a strong sense of justice but little human sympathy, or yields to his generous impulses at the expense of justice; but if a man sticks to his conscience we feel tempted to regard his morality not merely as better than nothing but as *perfect*, and yet if at the same time he thinks right what we and the like of us think wrong, we again feel tempted to regard his morality as *invalid* rather than merely imperfect.

(b) Theorists fond of neat system and sturdy simplification may, of course, try to get round the dilemma by applying "Occam's razor" to either of its terms. I propose to call "formalism" the view that the agent's acting or not in conformity with his conscience is the only test of his behaving rightly or wrongfully, though apart from that his conduct may be prudent or unwise, and socially useful or harmful. The converse view I propose to call "intellectualism". On this view, subjective "good faith", regardless of *what* the agent believes to be right or wrong, has no tangible meaning; right conduct depends on true moral knowledge (and, perhaps, on a normal capacity for action) alone, and all wrongful conduct expresses a moral error (or perhaps weakness of will, but never a wilful disregard of what the agent thinks right). I shall argue in section 2 against formalism, and in section 3, more briefly, against intellectualism—endeavouring to show that both Erroneous Conscience and Ineffectual Conscience exist and that, while distinct from each other, they reveal a certain interdependence.

   The point I am chiefly concerned to bring out is that the moral status we feel inclined to concede to Erroneous Conscience is attributable to it not by virtue of conscience representing an inscrutable and unjudgeable supreme principle of "formal" morality regardless of its "material" contents, but in as much as genuine conscience, however erroneous we may reasonably deem it by reference to a specified province of morality, expresses and presupposes the agent's general response, assent and submission to the valid intrinsic principles of morality as we know them. Accordingly, in sections 4 and 5 I shall try to establish a distinction between genuine Erroneous Conscience and the type of comprehensive principles of conduct to which this description no longer applies. Such principles, seeing the eminently "conscientious" attitude (in a technical sense) they may command in those who profess them, seem to pose the problem of Erroneous Conscience in a particularly baffling and paradoxical form, claiming as they do the respect due to consistent devotion of self while at the same time arousing moral revolt. I shall distinguish, then, Erroneous Conscience proper from what I propose to call Overlain Conscience, informed by the agent's surrender to a "non-moral absolute". I cannot, in the limits of this paper, deal with Dissentient Conscience as such—its argumentative and social aspects, its relation to the moral consensus and traditions of mankind, its possible reformatory and exemplary functions—nor with the interesting topic of supererogatory moral aspirations and of moral obligations experienced with a non-universal, personal or vocational, emphasis.

(c) It is well to bear in mind that—owing to the problematical *sui generis* status of moral truth and the impossibility of grasping it adequately, and especially of applying it to the actual moral governance of conduct except through personal insight, reflection, emphasis and judgement—every conscience is virtually dissentient and we constantly live in the presence of at least mild and marginal forms of what impresses us as Erroneous Conscience, including, often enough, our own states of conscience reflected upon at some distance. But it is only in certain conditions that Erroneous Conscience confronts us with the necessity for a practical decision between conflicting moral claims—tolerance or responsibility, respect for conscience or prevention of a public danger, and similar dilemmas—thus making us more keenly aware of the underlying philosophical problem. Apart from such obvious distinctions as that between a conscientious position with a purely private range of reference and one essentially implying public pretensions, between an explicit or rigid and a doubtful or undecided state of conscience, and between various modes of *pro* and *con* attitudes on the spectator's or the public's part (e.g. tolerance and admiring respect, or essential contempt for some kind of dissent and the conviction that it calls for coercive measures), it may roughly be said that the classic conflict only arises between *contrary* positions of conscience: that is, when neither dissentient conscience nor consensual opinion about the controversial point is merely permissive but both are imperative, one being prescriptive and the other prohibitive, or inversely. Even for the philosopher, however, a greater interest may attach to antithetical positions like "Fairness to our adversaries is the mark of high morality.—No, it is a detestable weakness, a sign of degeneracy" than to anything in the way of mere disagreement about degrees or limits.

(d) On the context of Erroneous Conscience, we use the word conscience chiefly in the sense of sustained moral opinion, that is, of moral rules which the agent professes as obligatory or moral standards he recognises as valid. In so far as the agent feels committed "in conscience" to principles not properly or purely moral (for example, religious, political or expressive of whatever particular loyalty or appreciation of value), or again, to some particular standard of conduct he would not conceive of as universally binding (cf. *Noblesse oblige, Aliis licet, tibi non licet*, or the various forms of vocational "ethos" and of gentlemanly ideals), these are still, more or less, in the nature of specified contractual or professional duties, derived from universal moral rules or at any rate referable to universally meaningful moral standards, seen in conjunction with the particular circumstances and previous acts of the agent. However, conscience primarily and properly means not moral convictions but moral awareness and self-criticism—remorse, warning, acquittal or approbation—in reference to one's own conduct, past, present or tentatively planned. Conscience means, further, moral judgement in the shaping of one's conduct. It is the office of my conscience not only to enforce my concrete obligations under a permanent and universal body of moral laws it apprehends as binding upon me, but to apply, to specify and to supplement them so as to fit the moral aspect of any actual situation I find myself in; in other words, not only to represent my general knowledge of right and wrong on the one hand and to prod me to do right and to shun wrong on the other, but to tell me what is right or wrong here and now, and thus to inform the morality of my actual conduct.

No doubt, it is easier to discuss Correct and Erroneous Conscience in terms of the agent's express moral beliefs, which are a more solid, knowable, communicable and arguable thing than is the succession of his single moral decisions or of his single states of moral self-awareness; but in speaking of conscience we should not lose sight of the original and full meaning of the word. Morally relevant beliefs are not all morally centred beliefs, and a man's quasi-moral beliefs, both express and operative, are not all conscience, nor all his conscience. If one who has carried out, in strict obedience, the monstrously unjust and cruel decrees issued by an authority to which he is subject by a kind of ideal conviction, maintains that he has been acting "according to his conscience", this may be a very inaccurate description of the real state of affairs. Again, Dissentient Conscience, in the full force of the term, amounts to more than a mere unusual moral belief: it may connote a significant moral experience, unknown or repressed in the dominant social ambit of the agent, and open up a valid but hitherto undiscovered or evaded new dimension of moral sensitivity.

2. The Existence of Erroneous Conscience

(a) On the formalist view, Erroneous Conscience—except in the trivial sense of conscience as moral decision *hic et nunc*, misinformed as to facts—is logically impossible, seeing that conscience is the ultimate test of morality, with no standard above it by which it could be verified or falsified. There is one apparently formidable argument in support of this view: the intuitive evidence of the reflection that nothing can be more obviously moral than to intend to do the right thing, and nothing more obviously immoral than to intend, from some non-moral motive, to do a wrongful thing. The argument does prove something, but decisively less than what it purports to prove. It is indeed never morally indifferent but always highly important whether the agent believes himself to be acting rightly or wrongfully. But the assumption that the most *obviously* good or bad feature in the agent's conduct exhaustively defines its goodness or bad-ness is nothing but a plausible fallacy. It is somewhat like believing that, say, any even number must have more factors than any odd number. In fact, the moral rightness of an action I perform with a wholly satisfied conscience may be greatly impaired by the defects of my conscience—for example, my failure to understand that even a scoundrel must never be judged unfairly; and the badness of an action I perform with an uneasy or guilty conscience may be slighter than it would otherwise appear if I have a morbidly scrupulous conscience or if my illicit action is inspired by a morally good motive—for example, compassion or righteous indignation.

In a recent novel about intelligence-service intrigues, I read the sen-tence: "It was obviously Dr Thompson's duty, as a patriotic British citi-zen, to announce his discovery to Major Macpherson." This sounds so peculiarly silly, not because it is slightly redundant, but because, though in fact it is only a piece of careless writing, as it stands it seems to invite a formalist interpretation: there are two classes of British citizens, patriotic and non-patriotic; for one of the latter, it would not be a duty to inform Major Macpherson; but the hero, unfortunately for him, happens to belong to the patriotic set, thus in his case that duty, with its attendant discom-forts, did arise. This strikes us as preposterous because to "be patriotic" is not a distinctive natural characteristic or a matter of taste, entailing moral obligations when it is present, but is itself a moral obligation on men by reference to their respective countries. It is true, none the less, that if Thompson had had a non-patriotic or unpatriotic, a defective or erro-neous, conscience, his omission to inform the Major would in one sense have been less wrongful, in that he would then have acted "in good faith" as contrasted with prevarication. As it was, this act of disloyalty to his conscience might have marked the beginning in him of a process of moral backsliding; whereas, if he had not been a patriot anyhow, he would have suffered no such moral "fall". And yet, do we, as patriots or even on gen-eral moral principles, prefer the "integrity" of a non-patriotic, to the guilty lapse of a patriotic, Thompson? Hardly—at least certainly not *a priori* and regardless of the possible qualifying circumstances. Our con-science tells us that we ought to be loyal citizens not because we have that kind of conscience but because men, including Thompson and ourselves, ought to be loyal citizens; it tells us that we, including him, ought to obey our consciences, but also that we ought to have the right kind of con-science, which, among other things, implies a patriotic conscience.

(b) As I have just admitted, conscience is *also* reflexive and self-emphasis-ing. I may have the remorseful feeling that in a certain complex and morally charged situation I did not listen to the voice of my conscience, or warn myself, in view of an impending practical decision, in terms like "Well, this course seems to offer great advantages, and something might be said for it on moral grounds; still, in some essential way it would go against my conscience." But all such modes of conscience are secondary; they presuppose a primary reference to moral categories outside conscience— in a similar way as my promise to pay £100 to Jones does indeed create my obligation to pay £100 to Jones but does not create my obligation to keep the promises I make. My conscience of yesterday, which I am now sorry to have silenced or cheated, or the present one that I am now telling myself to obey, was not or is not a conscience about conscience but a conscience about duties of honesty, loyalty, neighbourly love and the like, and about offences opposed to such duties or virtues. The moral qualities and rules thus referred to are not a function of my conscience but prior to it and constitutive of it, even though my conception of them has been shaped and amplified in a way involving the workings of my conscience. Just as a general whose orders did nothing but enjoin upon his subordinates the duty of obeying his orders would not actually command anything, a conscience demanding only to be always obeyed would in no wise direct the agent's conduct and would not in fact be conscience at all, but merely a phantom of misguided philosophical lucubration.

Any attempt to save formalism by propounding a weaker variant of it, which would no longer entail an infinite regress, is doomed to failure; for it must either surreptitiously bring in objective moral standards over and above conscience, or lapse into arbitrary naturalism and immoralism, superseding conscience by the agent's or somebody else's good pleasure. Thus, if we construe the sovereignty of conscience in the sense that a man behaves rightly in conforming unhesitatingly, from moment to moment, to the random hits and improvised glimpses of his conscience, we no longer imply that right conduct *means* conduct in conformity to conscience. We have switched to the gratuitous assertion—wholly out of accord with experience and common sense—that conscience *finds* what is right and what is wrong here and now by a succession of unreflective intuitions and unarguable decrees; or else, abandoning this mystical and unanalysable object of inerrant intuition, we simply mean that what a man ought to do is what he wants to do, and that conscience is nothing but the dominant impulse, craving, fancy or whim of the moment.

Again, if we suggest that the agent should adopt as a rule and incarnation of his conscience some extraneous interest, system or authority, serving henceforth that objectified Principle with punctual fidelity and unflinching zeal, we are no longer holding on to a morality of conscience. For if the agent chooses to lean on a specified authority for intrinsic moral reasons, his conscience is no longer the definition but merely, as in the common-sense view, the guide and director of his morality, dependent on objective standards of right and wrong which it is meant to represent and to divine, not to supplant or freely to invent; whereas if the agent decides to subordinate his conscience to some outside concern or entity from any vital or historical, morally irrelevant and contingent motives, he will be adjusting his conduct not to his conscience but to something else. A conscience thus put out to lease is not conscience but the evasion of it, except for that specious semblance of conscience which may be discerned in one's blind obedience to the authority that happens to be in command.

Conscience that cannot hope to be correct, and accordingly cannot fear to be erroneous, is not conscience in the established and dignified sense of moral self-criticism, judgement and belief—which essentially aspires to truth and tries to escape from error, and in fact expresses the agent's endeavour to ponder and argue his decisions in universally valid terms and to make his conduct *justifiable* in the open court of objective morality. Mere "conscientiousness" as a habit of discipline, a descriptive psychological feature opposed to impulsiveness and whimsicality, is indeed one moral requirement and is independent of true or false moral beliefs; but it is only a subordinate aspect of Moral Conscience and anything but a supreme directive principle of conduct. A "conscientious", that is, painstaking, methodical and devoted, secretary or accountant of a burglars' association is hardly a better man than a generous and high-principled but somewhat self-willed and unpredictable servant of an estimable philanthropic cause.

(c) Another argument for the existence of Erroneous Conscience lies in the fact that we sometimes feel remorse over such past actions of ours as we performed not against our conscience but with a definitely assenting conscience. True, in regard to some moral mistakes in our past history we may feel shame and annoyance rather than remorse proper; this points to Erroneous Conscience not through any fault of the agent's but operating guiltlessly in perfect good faith—"invincible ignorance", as traditional language has it. But whether I say "What a fool I was to believe that! Alas, I couldn't help it!" or "Damned fool that I was! I ought to have known better", my present conscience criticises not only my past conduct but my past conscience. More, when in the grip of a present or recent moral problem of some complexity, I am likely to say in a tone of bemused hesitation, "My conscience tells me I'd better do this, and mustn't do that"—revealing a tinge of reserve and doubt, an admission that my conscience might be mistaken. Indeed, when we feel very certain in a moral matter we rarely invoke our conscience: "My conscience tells me I mustn't forge bank-notes" is less natural language than, say, "My conscience tells me I ought to inform Smith that Brown is plotting against him." We recognise, then, that we are responsible not only *before* our conscience but also, within limits, *for* our conscience; that we are obliged to "apply reasonable care" in shaping our conscience (*se faire une conscience*) so as to keep it sensitive, enlightened and well informed, and to safeguard it from error.

(d) Finally, Erroneous Conscience exists in virtue of the intimate linkage between our moral judgements and sensibilities on the one hand, and our knowledge and interpretation of facts on the other. Of course, owing to a gross error of fact a person may commit grievous "material" wrong without any trace of guilt or Erroneous Conscience on his part. But sometimes the position is altogether different. Erroneous Conscience may lean on intellectual delusion or misconception as a kind of collateral support, or indeed be occasioned by it. In such cases, theoretical error not only causes the agent's conscience to be misapplied in fact but colours its intrinsic content and distorts its emphasis. Thus, the moral error that it is not wrong to maltreat animals is often fused with, and perhaps conditioned by, the factual error that animals are scarcely more than unconscious automata and incapable of feeling pain in any sense comparable to human suffering. The Erroneous Conscience of pacifists is mostly linked with false opinions about the nature and causes of war; that of nationalists and racialists with certain historical delusions; that of Marxists with their sham-scientific theory of social institutions. In general, our vision of things as they are is largely dependent on our emotive and valuational attitudes; and conversely, our valuations, including our moral views, are largely contingent upon our perception and construction of reality and our appraisal of the factual importance of various things and forces in its order.

Perhaps it might be said that misinterpretation of facts, as distinct from isolated errors of fact, will, in a morally relevant matter, contextually imply Erroneous Conscience, for the connection of our more specific and psychologically more vulnerable moral intuitions with the more general and more incontrovertibly evident ones implies our knowledge of facts and their connections. Therefore theoretical error may not only alter our actual conduct, inducing us to misapply our valid moral insights, but may interfere with some of our more specific moral intuitions, depriving them of their central support—their resonance in our more general moral experience as it were—and thus cause them to wither or force them out of our dominant consciousness. Thus, for example, my spiritual infatuation with a man of brilliant qualities (including, perhaps, some moral accomplishments) may mislead me into overlooking the fact that he is mainly an impostor. By virtue of this neat error of fact I may further be goaded into the moral error of believing, not indeed that imposture is right, but that there is nothing morally wrong with the habitual use of specious persuasive rhetoric in furthering some magnificent-sounding design, failing as I do to realise the categorical nexus of this looseness of discursive practice with the cruder and more blatant forms of dishonesty with which it is frequently and significantly, though not necessarily, associated.

3. ERRONEOUS CONSCIENCE AND INEFFECTUAL CONSCIENCE

(a) I shall take for granted, rather than argue at length, the thesis, opposed to intellectualism, that conduct can be at variance with the agent's conscience and that, accordingly, a correct conscience may not ensure right conduct: *Video meliora proboque, deteriora sequor.* Whoever is unable to confirm this from his own experience is entitled to our boundless admiration either as a born saint or as a prodigy of Erroneous Conscience. The intellectualist view originates, I think, from three main sources: (i) the pedagogical postulate that right conduct should be "teachable"; (ii) the failure of moralists—a Greek heritage still far from wholly discarded—to distinguish in a sustained manner between morality and practice; and (iii) the false assumption that the agent's conscience must be a simple thing all of a piece—for it seems logically odd that one should, even for a moment only, "choose evil" unequivocally and wholeheartedly. I will forgo (i) altogether; but (ii) and (iii) are more relevant to the subject of Erroneous Conscience.

(b) How can one possibly choose what one believes to be wrong and reject what one believes to be right? Ineffectual Conscience might appear to be an unreal, a merely conventional, pretended conscience; and all wrongful conduct based on Erroneous Conscience (including complete lack of moral awareness in certain respects). But the fact is that we constantly choose on some grounds what we would reject on some other grounds, or conversely. This is precisely what choice means: our numerous, and in part changing, concerns clash mutually in various ways, and we cannot pursue them except by restricting and postponing them, by choosing to favour one and renounce another temporarily or perhaps definitively. The mutual attunement, scaling and ordering of our concerns, with "ends and means" as one of its aspects, is called Practice. The course of action we thus choose as practically best, or better than the nearest possible alternative, would appear analytically to constitute our actual conduct. If I have decided that *this* is the best thing for me to do here and now, how could I go and do something else?—unless, betwixt the cup and the lip, some change in circumstances supervenes or some factor which I forgot when taking my decision now makes itself felt. Suppose I decide to undergo an operation, or to approach a person in authority, but panic and fear then prevent me from carrying out my resolution, whether I formally revoke it or just leave the matter in abeyance; in this sense even practical decisions may turn out to be ineffectual.

Moral approval, however, is not practical choice. My moral concerns are only one among my classes of concerns, although it is true that the practical ordering of my concerns as a whole is itself to some extent a moral requirement, and that, on the other hand, moral obligations as expressed in my conscience essentially connote an overriding claim to absolute validity—analogous, in this, to the concern of self-preservation. Yet an imperious claim, demand or command is not (and is strictly inconsistent with) an irresistible motion. However perfectly my will may conform to my conscience, my conscience is not my will. It is bad, but quite possible, that my sense of moral obligation should be outweighed by non-moral concerns (and awareness of this possibility lies at the root of conscience). There is such a thing as a hypocritically pretended or a weak and vague conscience; but Ineffectual Conscience in itself is no more unreal than, say, my craving for this or that pleasure is unreal because, for reasons of morality, health or economy, I refrain from satisfying it.

However, the habit of living with a defeated conscience may wear down the vigour of conscience and thus indirectly lead to a displacement of moral emphasis, sophistic self-justification and a form of Erroneous Conscience: Aristotle's "incontinent" deteriorating into an "intemperate" man. Again, Erroneous Conscience may come to involve Ineffectual Conscience in that it may dislocate, without altogether uprooting, the agent's stock of sounder moral sensibilities: a fanatic who believes it to be his duty to kill heretics or to kill kings and presidents may yet be keenly aware of the general evil of murder, and in perpetrating or planning his misdeeds may act in some fashion against his conscience, albeit prompted by his prevailing Erroneous Conscience. In fact, though it is certain that he is not acting unconscientiously, like a teetotaller who in cheerful company yields to the temptation to drink, it is open to question how far his conduct is governed by Erroneous Conscience proper and how far by a *sui generis* type of non-moral concerns loaded with a high spiritual tension, that is, emotive dedication of self to a set of abstract concepts and varnished with a tint of moral overtones. For non-moral concerns, whether morally rightful or objectionable, are by no means all of a self-seeking, sensual or material order. To this I shall presently return. Let it suffice now that if the force of non-moral concerns obviously accounts for Ineffectual Conscience, their intertwinement with moral accents and aspirations accounts, in part, for Erroneous Conscience; and that Ineffectual and Erroneous Conscience, though plainly distinct, may coexist and, as it were, conspire mutually.

(c) Conscience is a composite thing, so much so that we precisely speak of conscience in a more exquisite sense of the word when referring to the agent's moral decision or judgement in the face of conflicting obligations than when referring to conduct in obvious accordance with an unequivocal moral belief. The more, in a given context of behaviour, the agent's conscience is called upon to *decide*, not merely to register and to emphasise, what he ought to do, the more likely it is that he will be expressly obeying the dictate of *his conscience* (as distinct from a straightforward moral imperative) *and* doing so with a slightly uneasy conscience, seeing that he has to silence or to argue into consent some protesting voice within his conscience. No doubt a really conscientious decision (warped or not by moral error) may be reached and may forthwith determine the agent's practical decision; but moral conflict provides a special point of application for the pull of non-moral concerns, and this makes it even easier to understand the possibility of Ineffectual Conscience and of its interblending with Erroneous Conscience.

Immoral conduct, particularly of a more consistent kind, is usually underlain by a guiltily falsified conscience, implying both moral errors and a more or less robust disregard for the muffled protests of such elements of conscience as have been relegated to the margin of consciousness: a state of affairs that might be called Specious Conscience. The point I am trying to make here is that Erroneous Conscience does not necessarily imply "good faith" but may, without thereby being a mere conventional pretence alien to genuine conscience, connote an aspect of Ineffectual Conscience and thus embody a state of *mauvaise foi*, in the sense of self-deceit as contrasted with mere "labouring under a deception". Neither is conscience *a priori* endowed with inerrancy, as formalism would have it; nor is Erroneous Conscience *a priori* exempt from blame and merely in need of material rectification, as it would appear on the intellectualist view.

4. SOME FORMS OF ERRONEOUS CONSCIENCE

(a) What we call an eccentric, cranky or idiosyncratic conscience may be described as an arbitrary over-emphasis or extension, a supersensitive and obsessive application, or a disproportionate observance, of some recognised moral rule or standard; in some cases, indeed, as a fictitious moral emphasis attached to what is normally considered a moral adiaphoron. Thus beliefs such as that (moderate) drinking, or smoking, or meat-eating, or dancing, are sinful; that all violence and all participation in war are sinful; that one always ought to be not only honest but completely sincere; or, again, that one ought never to enjoy anything that all or most people on earth are not yet in a position to enjoy. These and similar errors—so far as they are errors—mark a deviation by excess, though of course they may impel the believer to offend against some more plainly valid moral rule which he comes to disregard, or at any rate to undervalue. Such consciences, though often a social irritant and sometimes perhaps a social danger with grave moral implications, are not *in themselves* opposed, that is, *contrary*, to current standards: we do not think that peace or gentle behaviour are evil, or that smoking is a moral duty.

Erroneous Conscience of the foregoing kind does not essentially interfere with the agent's general conception of morality; his moral consciousness as a whole may be much like the normal, though it is vitiated by obsession or irrelevancy and by some displacement of accent. But let us not forget that no two of us, either, are likely—or obliged—to maintain exactly the same proportion between our respective moral emphases. My own conscience is anything but sure about the moral legitimacy of meat-eating; some of you may disagree with my moral disapproval of hunting or fishing for pleasure, or even of bull-fighting; whereas my conviction that it *may* be necessary to deal sternly with the wicked might expose me to censure under certain Christian, Buddhist or humanitarian standards. Very often, anyhow, a supersensitive conscience will compel our moral respect, even if it appears to us to be tainted with error and to be a practical nuisance; and it may always be worth pausing to reflect whether, perhaps, it heralds a new moral truth—in however overstated a shape—or, rather, a moral truth badly neglected, underestimated or flouted in the agent's social environment.

(b) Primitive, undeveloped or crude conscience, or again a conscience shrunken and obliterated in some respects, may be said to err by defect. Thus some people tend to believe that whatever is not illegal is morally licit; that they are morally at liberty to do anything they please so long as it does not actually harm others; that if they only comply with their strict duties their morality can leave nothing to be desired; that, say, mercy, or intellectual probity, or courtesy and good manners, have no moral significance at all; and so forth. This defective type of Erroneous Conscience is closely related to rank unconscientiousness or to Ineffectual Conscience; precisely for that reason it is less of a problem theoretically and more open either to intrinsic mending by instruction or at least to correction by social pressure. Deficient morality, as far as its range *does* extend, is still much like ordinary morality, with elements of genuine, unfalsified moral consciousness in control of the agent's behaviour. For example, a person who disbelieves that there is anything wrong with sexual licence may nevertheless as scrupulously refrain from lying and cheating as any of us, and from the same motives. It may also happen that an apparently defective, like a supersensitive, conscience is not actually erroneous but, rather, justly critical of some set or other of conventional moral attitudes; for there may prevail, in a given social medium, rigoristic attitudes, one-sided in emphasis and largely sustained by non-moral concerns of doubtful legitimacy.

(c) I would define as Immoralistic Conscience a type of Erroneous Conscience informed by a *doctrinal* negation, explicit and operative, of the intuitive and consensual standards, traditions and rules of ordinary morality. Immoralistic Conscience can, so far as I am able to see, only exist in an incomplete sense, seeing that moral appreciations, with a feeling of obligation, inalienably belong to the constitution of man (as does, also, at least a virtual reluctance to comply with the moral demand). An integral and consistent "Evil be thou my Good" attitude—or, say, a "morality" of the Ten Commandments professed with an opposite sign—is, I think, quasi-logically inconceivable, in that consistency as such has a positive moral aspect akin to honesty, and the self-transcendence implied in "..be thou my Good" could not but work out in a way involving some elements of true conscientious morality. In fact, immoralistic moods are often directed, concretely, against the servitude of moral *conventions* (valid and legitimate as these may be) and fasten on positive and recognised moral motifs like honesty and sincerity as opposed to hypocrisy, or responsible personal decision as opposed to routine devoid of moral experience.

Again, an immoralistic conscience informed by the philosophical doctrine of hedonism—as distinct from the Christian-gentleman conscience of a John Stuart Mill, spuriously interpreted in utilitarian terms—will, at any rate, compound with various standards of ordinary morality, accepting them as ingrained canons of taste or respecting them as social facts one can only ignore at one's peril. In the most typical case, perhaps, Immoralistic Conscience is a proud ego's way of putting up with Ineffectual Conscience: suppose the things, decried as immoral, which I practise or want to practise, are not really immoral but the mark of a higher morality, or of a higher perfection of man which soars above morality, beyond good and evil; petty philistine minds may call me immoral and confuse me with a common rogue, but this is only the ransom of being actually a superman. This type of character will usually develop a compensatory overemphasis on some moral standards against which he is not tempted or not able to offend: utterly depraved rakes may nurse a deep moral contempt for homosexuals, and corrupt people take great moral pride in not being like the Pharisees.

Apart from its express revolt against some classic contents and some formal aspects of morality (e.g. traditions and conventions, the concept of obligations, or the distinction between "my good" and "the good"), Immoralistic Conscience implies the general subordination of conscience to some non-moral concern installed in the position of a supreme maxim of conduct. This mental state of affairs is what I call Overlain Conscience, and I am going to devote the remaining section to its most characteristic and important "totalitarian" form.

5. Overlain Conscience

(a) By this I mean that the agent subjects and adapts his conscience to some non-moral "absolute", which thus comes to usurp the office of an ultimate and comprehensive moral authority—taking the place of the recognised universal rules of morality as interpreted, modulated and particularised by personal conscience. What is best fitted to play the part of such a non-moral absolute is a concrete human entity, individual or collective, more or less institutionalised, with an impressive display of values or "perfections"—seen in terms of vitality and energy, power and success, aesthetic and even moral qualities—and, in the most complete and typical cases, connoting a high "ideological" pretension: an inherent claim to intellectual and practical direction, to power and influence, and to educative action by inspiration and example. The agent's conscience will, accordingly, be disconnected from its proper background of overt and discursive moral appraisal and mediatised or overlain, as it were, by a kind of "possession", that is, infatuation with a concrete human object; possibly by ideological and institutional loyalty erected into an ultimate criterion of value and a supreme rule of behaviour.

Such a state of conscience is obviously different from mere laxity of conscience and the *de facto* predominance of non-moral concerns over the sense of moral obligation; and it is plainly compatible with a keen response to some moral demands, with moral effort and performance, and, in particular, with conscientiousness in the technical sense of discipline and subordination of self. The personal or social entity to which the agent clings in idolatrous attachment will be experienced by him as embodying, also, certain objective moral values: the religious or political authority to which he fanatically adheres in unreserved surrender will necessarily exhibit genuine moral features and lend itself to some interpretation in terms of morality.

Again, the salient characteristic of Overlain Conscience is not erroneous judgement or the displacement of emphasis concerning such and such intrinsic moral points, though this is inevitably implied, but the wholesale supersession of Moral Conscience proper by an overriding principle of, shall we say, *supra-moral* devotion to a concrete being. This principle, whatever spiritual or other values it may represent and whatever moral references it may enclose, *ex suppositis* cannot stand for Morality as such: just as Jones's will, character or temperament, be Jones ever so enlightened, conscientious, virtuous and saintly, cannot be *the* definition, standard and principle of morality. The agent's conscience, of the type here considered, will be erroneous by excess, defect and disproportion in various ways (by conscientious overemphasis on devotion, "orthodoxy", discipline and zeal, and a corresponding disdain for "abstract" moral standards like honesty, fairness, kindness or propriety). It will also be ineffectual in that the agent has to suspend, dispossess and repress many a residual or rudimentary, but not wholly absent, element of his ordinary moral conscience: for it is connatural to man to act morally and immorally, in awareness of the fact; to think and to appraise in moral categories. Totalitarian language itself, though kept carefully distinct from current usage so as to impress on men's minds the superior validity of the special mode of being it is meant to convey and to subserve, abounds in ordinary moral references whose meaning is independent of the ideology in question; these ostensible moral appeals are systematically and unscrupulously misapplied in a tactical design but are by no means necessarily and invariably fallacious or irrelevant to the subject they bear upon.

However, unlike Erroneous or Ineffectual Conscience proper, Overlain Conscience means an abdication of conscience as moral judgement—as a representative and interpreter of universal moral demands. In developing an Overlain Conscience, the agent alienates the sovereignty of his conscience, transferring it to a concrete Being, Force or Will to whose dictates he chooses to submit or with which he emotionally identifies himself. At the price of his morality being a radically falsified and degraded one, a sham morality thrown out of focus, as it were, he may have secured some psychological advantages: a feeling of greater and more tangible certitude as to the rightness and meaningfulness of his single actions; a feeling of splitless unity between his conscience and his deepest emotive self; and the feeling of acting on behalf of, and of being pervaded by, a superior Force which embodies the Good or Perfection in an objectified and fully real sense of the word.

(b) I need hardly insist that there is a close correspondence between a moral attitude of this kind and the philosophical position that is termed the Naturalistic Fallacy. There is, on the practical plane, something attractive in the idea of leading a life more infallibly insured against error, more at one with itself, and more "sublime" by virtue of its communion with a thing metaphysically superior, at the cost of a mediatised conscience: in a word, of evading conscience with a satisfied conscience. This moral temptation is matched to, and partly, I think, identical with, the philosophical temptation of construing morality in terms of more manageable sets of concepts, assimilable to the order of facts and of logical evidence (thus concepts biological, prudential, legal or psychological, etc.) with the slight inconvenience only of explaining something else in place of morality while implying morality, at the opportune moment, in a surreptitious, casual and question-begging fashion. Whereas Erroneous Conscience proper is not necessarily linked to any particular philosophical position, Overlain Conscience entails a doctrinal error *about* morality.

(c) It seems to me that Overlain Conscience cannot, in general, like Erroneous Conscience proper, claim intrinsic respect on the strength of its expressing a fundamental allegiance to Right as such and opposition to Wrong as such. For, precisely, the agent's supreme allegiance is not, here, owed to right but to a particular interest he has espoused, *a priori* other than right as such; and his distinctive, "conscientious" hostility is not levelled at wrong as such but at that which is in the way of the interest he is upholding. Somebody's supreme *pro* and supreme *con* attitudes, even though associated with some moral biases and with the use of various moral words, do not define right and wrong. Right and wrong may not hinge upon this or that specified precept or taboo of the Decalogue or of some similarly apposite code of genuine morality, but they lack all meaning in severance from such codes of rules—or tables of moral intuitions—in general. Formal morality (the sense of obligation) and material morality (the sense of kinds of conduct intrinsically right or wrong) can be distinguished but cannot be separated as if there existed a deontic blank, to be filled indifferently by any contents fancied at random or pleasing on whatever grounds, or, inversely, as if right and wrongful kinds of things could be described without reference to their deontic force.

I respect what I believe to be Erroneous Conscience in virtue of its being genuine conscience, that is to say, of its interlacing with the rest of the agent's conscience, which for the most part I know or presume to be correct conscience. The moral error to which he is a prey nevertheless reflects his stock of authentic morality. Thus a total abstainer or a non-violence pacifist may agree with me on most of the other main points of morality. Furthermore, although I am definitely opposed to both these attitudes, I appreciate the abstainer's "erroneous" conscience also in virtue of my own moral aversion to drunkenness and abhorrence of enslaving passions, and the pacifist's also in virtue of my own moral aversion from violence and abhorrence of wilful killing. But Overlain Conscience is a conscience in inverted commas only; it is erroneous in its basis and ensemble and correct by accident—though, as the case may be, correct perhaps on many important points.

I do not expect a religious person of the fanatical, obscurantist and sectarian type, a totalitarian partisan or a nationalist or racialist idolater—or, indeed, the infatuated disciples of "great men" erected into spiritual idols—to display a sound and valid conscience in all kinds of indeterminate respects. Rather, I should be prepared to find the obsessive concern emerging at any moment: invading, mutilating, falsifying and throwing out of proportion whatever fragments of true moral insight and sense of obligation may be present, and possibly discarding or blurring today what was overemphasised yesterday in a different pragmatic context. That Erroneous Conscience proper may, in its turn, connote an obsessive feature and exercise a distorting effect in its area of emphasis, and that Overlain Conscience may itself have sprung originally from excessive attention to one genuine moral theme, is beside the point. What matters is the differentia of Overlain Conscience, namely, its transfer of sovereignty from moral awareness, insight and judgement to a concrete object of loyalty and infatuation; even though, in the agent's formal belief, this may still be underlain by a kind of syllogism with an impeccably moral major premise. The mechanism of Overlain Conscience, with its naturalistic bent, is superbly, if somewhat indirectly, depicted by Coleridge in a passage of *Aids to Reflection*: "He who begins by loving Christianity better than Truth, will proceed by loving his own Sect or Church better than Christianity, and end in loving himself better than all." "Himself," that is, the particular attachment of self to the idolised object as a natural fact, in contraposition to the self-transcendence implied in the agent's relation with truths, values and imperatives not defined in terms of the vital and historical context, situation and incorporation of his self.

Again, Overlain Conscience essentially tends to afford an enlarged scope to *derived* obligations at the expense of the intuitive evidence and discursive appraisal of intrinsic right and wrong. I feel I ought to act in such and such a way, not because it is the honest, humane, decent or earnest, or even the high-minded, the prudent or the courageous, way of behaving in a given situation (though it may be all that), but because it is in keeping with the decree of a particular authority, suits a particular "higher" interest, or distinctively expresses the style of behaviour proper to a particular human type or community to which I belong. In as much as the idol in question is supposed to represent an intuitively evident moral ultimate—for example, the due response of man to divine perfection, or social justice, or lawful authority, or the imitation of high examples of moral virtue as known to the agent—the special duties thus recognised by him may be described as derived moral obligations. They are derived from a moral ultimate through the intermediary of his attachment to a concrete entity. Normally, however, they (or the most important among them) would have their place among the direct intuitive data of conscience; and their possible connection with moral principles of a higher order, even though implying various kinds of factual knowledge, would be of a quite different, a far more intrinsic, nature.

One of the most prominent instances of Overlain Conscience, seen from this aspect, is the Communist "party line" rule of thought and conduct; another, always somehow mitigated of course by the Christian affirmation of intrinsic and universal moral standards, is the totalitarian form of the Roman Catholic attitude and conscience, often called *intégrisme*. It is well defined by Lord Acton's distinction between asking "What is true?" and asking "What shall I believe?" In the words of Jean Domenach, a contemporary French Catholic writer, "*L'intégrisme consiste en toujours majorer l'orthodoxie.*"

(d) The test of genuine conscience lies not in the agent's profession of a universal moral principle, nor in his rejection of concrete, particular and embodied moral guides, authorities, exemplars and ideals, but in his recognition as a moral basis and standard of the open consensus of mankind. That consensus is not accurately or exhaustively represented by any specified system, creed, person or collective. It is laid down in the universe of moral intuitions, traditions and codes, which are necessarily incomplete and fraught with ambiguities and inadequacies, and are therefore in need

of being interpreted, supplemented, restated and re-emphasised by conscience. Without this primary assent to consensus—to "what men think to
be right and wrong"; the classic standards of intrinsically right and intrinsically wrongful kinds of conduct—the agent's morality is out of focus. To
apply the term "morality" or "conscience" to a private set of maxims and
loyalties, not thus grounded and accredited, is a misdescription. Again,
this primary acceptance of consensus entails a secondary acceptance of a
critical and active participation in it—in other words, the selective and cod-
ificatory task of conscience. Far from excluding, it also entails a manifold
of positive references to concrete authorities, models, depositaries of value
and means of orientation in the agent's spiritual and social environment.

The religious, doctrinal, institutional, personal, and various other inspi-
rations and allegiances of the agent are not irrelevant to his morality; rather,
they are a condition of his keeping in touch with the moral consensus of
mankind and of his building up a conscience of his own. The Naturalistic
Fallacy is not *all* fallacious; morality, for all its distinctive emphasis and
claim to sovereignty, is confined within the context of Practice, and, however irreducible to other concerns or to the all-round management of
concerns, it overlaps in all kinds of ways with non-moral concerns, needs
and endeavours.

What constitutes Overlain Conscience is not the fact of this interdependence, or the agent's awareness of it, but the arbitrary marking-out of
one determinate allegiance as a supreme rule of life, over and above intrinsic—intuitive and consensual—morality. It is not, for instance, the attitude of a Jewish or Christian believer whose moral consciousness is centred in the Ten Commandments, but the attitude of one who believed
that the moral prohibitions against perjury, murder and so forth would be
meaningless or trivial *if considered outside their nexus* with particular historical circumstances, metaphysical beliefs, salvational superstructures and
devotional practices.

In a purely formal fashion, arbitrary monism and infatuation can easily be dressed in the deceptive cloak of a universal moral rule "containing
no reference to a proper name": thus, "Act always in conformity with the
instructions, and so as to further the interest, of a specified and identifiable social Force, highly representative of human perfection and effective
for human improvement" is, so far, strictly universal. The agent's choice
may then fall (or have fallen) on such or such other Entity, according to
his "inscrutable" taste or the contingencies of his history—and, of course,
to the different aptness of different social entities to claim and to command
a totalitarian kind of loyalty. Such an attitude, though connected with some
moral ideas and achievements, is one of spurious morality, not because
the prefacing rule is not universal but because the preface is not the substance of the book; because the detour implied in a supreme principle

thus fashioned is out of accord with the basic moral intuitions of mankind and entails an alienation of conscience.

(e) The objection might be raised that "different moralities" were possible, "each as justified as the other": in particular, totalitarian surrender to a specific "absolute" as well as the morality of intrinsic intuitions and consensual tests. But this is a misuse of language and an attempt to muddle and confound our vision of things as they are. Men, when using moral language—moral and immoral conduct, right and wrong, good and bad character, honesty, knavery, and so on—mean not an esoteric appraisal by reference to any of their respective and divergent "absolutes", but an appraisal they suppose to be virtually universal and arguable in the open forum of mankind, of certain types of conduct and their decisive relevancy for judging a person's worth. And they keep on using moral language thus, even if they profess some totalitarian loyalty, though they will then inconsistently mix it with distorted totalitarian idiom. Moreover, the philosophical relativism of "several moralities equally justified" is incompatible with actual adherence to one of *these* alleged moralities.

The relativist philosopher may take an aesthetic delight in the devotion of all manner of sectarians to their respective "absolutes", but he cannot himself be, say, a Communist, a Nazi, an *intégriste*, and an Anthroposophist at the same time. Indeed, should he choose actually to make any one of these causes his own he must cease to be a relativist philosopher, for the rival absolutes exclude not only the ordinary outlook but one another as well, as also the broad-minded relativism which commends them on an equal footing. The real sectarian will naturally withhold his appreciation from the abstract admirer of the "concreteness" of his self-commitment. Certainly my morality and my moral philosophy are not the same thing; but a doctrine that precludes its professor from really adopting the morality it is meant to supply with philosophical credentials can hardly escape the charge of logical oddness. (It should be noted that the mutual exclusion of rival "absolutes" is quite unlike the clash of conflicting obligations in ordinary moral conscience, or the points of divergence between the genuine consciences of different persons. It belongs to the essence of infatuations and idolatries to assert the unique validity of their respective objects and to evade *bona fide* argument under consensual standards.)

(f) On the philosophical plane, the relativist doctrine of "different moralities, equally legitimate" issues from the plausible overextension of the concept of morality: the inveterate confusion between morality and the higher forms of emotive attitudes and practical maxims as such. We all cherish more or less strongly particularised—personal and collective—

convictions, loyalties and aspirations, of high import and linked in manifold ways to our moral beliefs; but these are not so many "moralities". It is part of their meaning to support, to safeguard and to bring out more effectively our moral positions according to our various temperaments, histories and circumstances; if they take the place of morality it is by way of moral aberration.

Thus the social entities to which we naturally belong or which we join by free choice embody, among other things, certain distinctive moral features, performances and accents. Again, our loyalty towards them conforms to a general moral demand, and in its turn begets certain derived moral obligations: from our familial, national, religious, political, etc., affiliations will arise for each of us a set of moral bylaws, as it were. But our loyalties, though in themselves morally valuable and to some extent morally obligatory attitudes, are at the same time, materially speaking, non-moral facts of natural inclination and personal taste, perhaps passion.

For example, the moral obligation of patriotism is different in logical structure from the moral obligation of honesty. The latter does not in any way raise the various indeterminate Joneses, Browns and Robinsons (to whom I tell the truth and hand genuine cheques, or whom I judge fairly) to the status of a permanent moral term of reference or a quasi-absolute or epitome of value. To the normal patriot, on the other hand, his country will be not just an incidental point of application for the moral rule "Be loyal to your country", but a permanent object of devotion, a framework of life and centre of a sphere of duties. Patriotic loyalty may thus come to hold a disproportionate place in the agent's conscience. "My country, right or wrong", at least as a consistently applied maxim, marks a typical and frequent case of Erroneous Conscience; beyond that, it may degenerate into an actual rejection of the moral concept of patriotic duty, in that the agent fails to recognise its validity in regard to other countries and denies respect to patriotism in foreign nationals. This attitude means an inchoate form of infatuated Overlain Conscience; the totalitarian stage is reached by the kind of nationalism whose devotees look upon the interests or the peculiar genius of their nation, or both, as the supreme standard and test of morality. Here we have a species of Overlain Conscience, never perhaps so comprehensive and so fundamentally distorted as that which goes with sect or party totalitarianism, but philosophically important for being more generally intelligible and observable. National affiliation is a more universally and inevitably given aspect of life than are ideological positions, and few of us who recognise patriotic loyalty as a moral obligation may be free from all traces of the state of conscience warped by nationalist moods and habits of thought.

It is thus, by contrasting Overlain Conscience as vestigially present in ourselves, with our normal and valid conscience in regard to the same matter, that we can best gain an insight into its nature. Overlain Conscience is not conscience standing for "another morality". It is falsified conscience under the spell of a non-moral "absolute" and grafted onto that irrecusable interpenetration between moral demands and natural or preferential loyalties which may, in certain conditions, give rise to a submersion of morality by non-moral concerns that usurp its imperative accents and its *sui generis* dignity, and that we all know from our own experience.

ADDENDUM TO "ERRONEOUS CONSCIENCE"

Editors' note: Aurel Kolnai did not usually keep his preparatory notes for papers, once published. Exceptionally, he did this in the case of "Erroneous Conscience". Whatever the reason, the following may be found useful to readers of the paper.

Provisional Summary
I

1. Brief exposition of the classic problem: whether or how far we owe respect to such conscientious positions of others as we consider materially false. Again, whether it is necessarily immoral to try to persuade a person to act against his conscience. This conflict falls under the heading of Conflict of Obligations but with a particular status of its own. *Prima facie*, a problem for the appraiser and adviser (those who represent the agent's social environment) only, not for the agent himself.

2. The stricter meaning of Conscience, referred to the actual or intended conduct in a concrete situation, and its broader meaning as an equivalent of "moral maxim" or "moral principle believed in and professed by the agent". In the present context, Conscience in the broader sense is chiefly meant; but Conscience (1) and Conscience (2) are interdependent, and it is important not to lose sight of the more proper meaning (1) of the term.

3. That Erroneous Conscience exists in fact. Inferred from the objective validity of moral rules and criteria of judgement, implied in the fact of Conscience itself which is *primarily* the agent's moral awareness by reference to a code not of his own making. Inferred, further, from the essential defectiveness of moral "experience", "evidence" or "intuition": but for which, Conscience as such would lack function. *Error facti* and *error juris*, in the moral field, not unequivocally separable. Moral argument proper, impossible unless Erroneous Conscience is possible. False consciousness sometimes directly experienced in remorse. Conscience necessarily "private" and "personal": therefore virtually dissentient, and therefore correct or erroneous.

4. That Conscience can be disobeyed (Aristotle's "incontinent" type); though this is more obviously true of Conscience (2), in the broader sense of "principle", than of Conscience (1), which is more closely linked with actual decision or "will". Just as there are more "conscientious" and more "virtuous" styles of morality, the aspect of "conscience disobeyed" or that of a "vitiated conscience" may prevail in transgression. But the two aspects interlock in as much as Conscience is *not of a piece* but encloses a plurality of points of view and a discursive phase. Except perhaps for marginal cases, some element of error present in all wilful wrongdoing, and some element of guilty blurring of Conscience in all false conscience. The moral obligation of "forming a correct conscience". The moral demand bears mainly on "the right conduct" rather than on either "correct convictions" or "living according to one's convictions". Deceptive appeal of intellectualism on the one hand, formalism on the other, arises from craving for simplification.

II

1. Conscience a necessary but not an infallible arbiter of Conflicting Obligations. The latter ("collision") a moral undesirable, to be reduced to a minimum. Standard forms of "collision" require subsidiary moral rules; a starting-point for ethical reflection and theory building. General (and trivial) principles relative to "circumstances" and "proportions". Emphasis on the "sovereign and ineffable concrete decision", a pretext for moral nihilism, and from a philosophical point of view, an *aveu d'impuissance*.

2. Differences in the position of Dissentient Conscience according to its prescriptive or prohibitive character, and the prescriptive-prohibitive or permissive character of the received code with which it is at variance. The types of "stricter", "broader", and "contrary", conscience. Some fairly obvious hints for their respective appraisal.

3. Distinction between moral maxims or principles—Conscience (2)— and (chiefly or centrally) *non-moral practical principles* with their morally indifferent, morally positive and morally negative aspects. Such principles are indispensable; may be morally legitimate or not; may be simple, straight-forward "maxims" or tend to form comprehensive, doctrinal and emotionally charged rules of life. Various types and standard examples. Attempt to distinguish between attachments and ideologies pretending to the place of a substitute for morality on the one hand, and inadequacies and malformations of the morally proper (e.g. the undeveloped, the narrow, the "cranky" or eccentric conscience) on the other hand. How far "substitutes for morality" (e.g. sectarian and totalitarian) nevertheless connote an aspect of genuine morality; how far integrity of conduct under such principles may be considered worthy of respect. Consistency and devotion to

a cause necessarily connotes an element of moral performance. Again, "respect" may connote an element of non-moral appreciation.

4. "Conscience" meaningless except on the basis and in the context of a traditional moral code or conjunction of such codes. "Formal" not strictly separable from "material" or intrinsic morality. Dissentient Conscience expressed in terms of traditional morality. The arbitrary phraseologies used by totalitarian or otherwise immoralist systems: a device for dodging Conscience. This does not preclude the use of subordinate moral appeals. Emphasis on "supra-moral" values and powers, and infatuation with concrete (individual, collective, historical) entities not subject to the test of universal moral standards: stigmata of the "perfectionist" attitude, one classic expression of the Naturalistic Fallacy. Erroneous Conscience proper, on the contrary, centres in its arbitrary overemphasis on some recognised moral point of view (or at any rate, some moral point of view closely related to recognised standards) without subordinating it to a non-moral "absolute".

5. The argumentative, social and dialogic nature of conscience. Conscience (1) as actual and Conscience (2) as virtual (and permanent) self-criticism of the agent; it is ineluctably "my" (i.e. the agent's own) conscience, yet as necessarily represents appraisal from outside. Conscience never *identical* with the agent's "will" or "character" as such, however "virtuous" or responsive to moral appeal. Conscience means not a self-justifying decision indifferent to objective standards but the endeavour to achieve justification by such standards; not moral solipsism but responsibility; not moral self-sufficiency but a striving to be able to give account of one's conduct. Moral enquiry and the act of "forming one's conscience" tend not to preserve and cultivate but to reduce the "impenetrable residuum" of personal decision outside the reach of clearly valid obligations.

6. Conscience, and with it the possibility of Dissentient (and, therefore, of Erroneous and of "creative" or reformatory) Conscience, is, on the one hand, rooted in the fact that all explicit moral rules are inadequate to the exigencies of concrete situations; all moral codes incomplete; and, in particular, all moral traditions somehow imperfect, biased and lopsided, alloyed with various non-moral accents or interests; and all social units, communities, bodies and authorities open to moral criticism and falling short of embodying anything like the achieved, valid and comprehensive moral consciousness of mankind. Dissentient Conscience stands not for "the individual" versus "society", nor necessarily for a vaster as against a narrower unit of group consciousness, but for a different social perspective as against the automatic pressure of the immediate social environment. In virtue of its pretension to correct the ambient moral tradition by its

reflective confrontation with other moral traditions and extraneous data of human experience, it may assert morality proper in the face of current misuses of moral language and sentiments for purposes more or less alien to morality, and may act as a stimulus of moral awareness and a vehicle of moral reform. On the other hand, it is also liable to set in a position out of focus, relinquishing contact with important and perennial elements of morality and embodying, as Erroneous Conscience, an impoverished, narrower and more biased form of moral consciousness as compared to the standards prevailing in its social environment. Dissentient conscience, even though possibly erroneous, is entitled to a *prima facie* respect but is also justly received with a *prima facie* distrust. Erroneous Conscience, not necessarily better morally but only less *obviously* guilty than acting against one's conscience.

Are There Degrees
of Ethical Universality?

AUREL KOLNAI

1967–1968

1. The Axiom of Universality

Moral discourse presupposes, and moral experience connotes, a constitutive reference to universal concepts as standards of morally right or wrong conduct, of duty and breach of duty, of morally good or bad conduct, intention, motive and character. This is inseparably bound up with the descriptive contentual or material element of moral appraisal (Hare)[1], as distinct from its prescriptive or formal element of pro or con appraisal, that is, the act of approval or disapproval, of commendation or condemnation. In other words, moral judgement cannot but imply a reference to universal concepts in virtue of its being judgement: that is, of asserting (predicating) something of its object rather than merely expressing the appraiser's smiling or frowning mood. Moral evaluation is a cognitive act, which must needs be cast in the mould of universal categories. Jones has done right in that, for example, he has kept his promise; Brown has done wrong in that, for example, he has pulled a fellow-passenger's wallet. The bystander who forms and utters these judgements is logically committed to judge identically when, on another occasion, Jones and Brown respectively do the same things, and also to judge identically if next time, instead of Jones or Brown, it is, say, Robinson who does either of these two things. Keeping one's promise is an obligation; theft is a transgression. True, here-and-now appraisal of the single action may sometimes legitimately vary in spite of the act typifying the same category. But such an exception, in other words such a latitude of appraisal, is only apparent. Were it to issue from subjective factors—for example, that the next honest Jones happens to be the appraiser's competitor in local politics or that the next light-fingered Brown happens to be a close friend of his—his change of valuation would be illegitimate: it would be inconsistent, invalid, making nonsense of his status as a moral appraiser, and itself an immoral act. A modified or indeed contrary judgement may, however, be appropriate in view of a change in the relevant circumstances of the actions in question. An act of promise-keeping may be morally questionable or even downright condemnable if the agent is aware that by performing it he is inflicting grave and undeserved harm on a third party, or if what he has promised is in itself a gravely immoral thing. An act of theft will appear in a more favourable light if it turns out to have been committed with a view to saving a sick child from starvation or to discharging a peculiarly pressing debt of honour. But such an exceptional configuration of "relevant circumstances" again implies recourse to universal ethical categories, which are part of the description of the action from a moral point of view. One and the same action may, at the same time, typify a standard kind of right action and a standard kind of wrong action. This fact frightens Hare into distrusting highly general moral standards as such and into looking for invulnerable universality in the ideal of laboriously particularised "foolproof" rules.

I dissent from him on this point. A universal standard does not mean a rule invariably obligatory and always directly fitted to be "action guiding"; it means a moral point of view invariably and intrinsically valid, a moral demand always and unconditionally entitled to earnest consideration. It can, in the given case, be opposed and even nullified by another, countervailing moral claim (or several such claims) equally applicable to the circumstances. Descriptiveness and universality stand unshaken; but description may have to record a factual togetherness of contrary features without any contradiction creeping in, and universals are multiple without in the least becoming irrelevant or expendable. In fact, I do not think that Hare quite does justice to the specific ethical status of universal standards, which in a stricter sense do imply a higher degree of generality, in interpreting them in terms of descriptive content alone. The point is that life as we know it is so constituted as to offer an area of application to highly general moral standards; and it is inherent in the peculiar nature of moral judgement to depend on justification—more so than do other kinds of valuation, for example aesthetical—in terms of such standards. Again, I think that the nexus between ethical universality as a logical postulate and the substantive moral demands of consistency and impartiality is closer than Hare would have it.

We come here to what Mayo,[2] devoting greater attention to this aspect than does Hare, calls "the third level of universality" (the first two relating to universal categories being applicable to "essentially similar" actions carried out on different occasions and by different agents). By the third level of universality, men's consensual awareness of the self-same universal standards is meant, but for which moral discourse, communication, argument and indeed consciousness would be impossible: for moral experience and its conceptual framework are embedded in the individual's awareness of a "mankind-wide", an indefinitely extended and virtually universal unison of intuitive evidence and evaluative understanding. And here universality does involve generality, seeing that beyond the mere reference to universal categories it has come to mean a field of actual universal consciousness, belief and response which cannot be centred in a directly and infallibly utilisable "action-guiding" code of endlessly specified rules and instructions. It can only be centred in a perspicuous body of highly general axioms—although differentiated according to content—carrying widely consonant evidence and claiming the evaluative assent of "men" *qua* spiritual persons capable of communication and identical insight into objective validities, regardless of their membership of groups or camps and their particular conditioning circumstances. Universality is, then, a distinctive feature of our ethical dimension of being, not merely a logical precondition of its being possible for moral judgements, just like any other judgements, to have a truth value.

2. Pseudo and Vacuous Universality

However deeply imbued, personally, with the experience of ethical universality, Hare gets stuck (as Mayo does not) in this purely formal and pretty trivial conception of it: that also underlies his preference for the term "universalisability". In his view, my moral judgements are primarily "prescriptive" and "decisional" acts; but, so as to vindicate the objective validity of the descriptive content which inevitably attaches to them once they are judgements rather than mere smiles or frowns or, again, here-and-now commands (these *have* a descriptive content but one shorn of all claim to objective validity and truth value), I must be ready, at a second remove, to "universalise" them—a misdescription of moral experience as it really is. Now Hare does not seem to notice that the principle of universality thus formally and vacuously conceived, and dislodged from its habitat in the consensual stock of moral intuitions, can quite easily be circumvented and stultified by a simple logical trick, and so rendered ineffective for sustaining the kind of ethical reference that Hare, with his sound instinctive bias in favour of that mode of reference, would expect it to sustain. In virtue of its descriptive connotation and claim to objectivity, a moral rule must be couched in universal concepts; it must not be based on any reference to singled-out, ostensively defined individual entities, to pronominal indicators, proper names or other verbal agents of brute singularity such as "hers" or "now". Well and good. What if various kinds of immoralists resort to the stratagem of defining their non-moral fetish, the extra-moral sovereign bearer of a thisness they elevate above Right and Reason, the object of their amoral infatuation, in some foolproof, tidy, impeccable and respectable verbal terms which fully satisfy the requirement of logical universality? Examples abound, or can be constructed as you please. Here are some supreme moral principles. Be thyself. May thy action always be authentic. Thou art nothing; thy People or Race is everything. Give thyself over to the strongest force of nature; become a part of the wave of the future; surrender thyself to, and serve with boundless devotion, the most progressive historic force of thine epoch.[3] These are hardly the kind of universals that for Hare (or myself) would fit the bill; they are anything rather than universal moral standards, genuinely descriptive categories, or ubiquitously occurring (or missing and missed) qualities of conduct or character. But as a logical class exercise they can be trimmed to the disciplinary requirement of concept universality. Or would you object that they opaquely or obliquely refer to ostensively picked-out singulars, for example, "Be thyself" to the ego of the hearer? But so does "Thou shalt not swear falsely". And what about the moral prohibition against cheating? I can only cheat people, and these will be nameable concrete individuals with actual proper names. In the critical situation, when the effectiveness of the prohibition is put to the test, my conscience will tell me that I must not cheat Harry Miller or Billy Burton or the members of an identifiable commercial firm.

I have thus, I hope, succeeded in complicating to some extent the thesis of Ethical Universality (in which I firmly believe) and have thrown some amount of obscurity upon it. I dare not call it "creative" obscurity, but I do feel that a certain problem may, if properly encouraged, emerge from the havoc I have wrought. To be sure, no existent, no historically or ostensively identifiable entity (impersonal, unipersonal or collective) embodies a self-contained epitome of Goodness as an independent standard of Right or Wrong or a moral ultimate; any belief to the contrary is tantamount to ethical obscurantism and idolatry. The moral significance of any existent can only be spelled out, and examined and assessed, in the system of co-ordinates provided by universal types, by conceptually intuitable qualities of what constitutes moral goodness or badness, with their characteristic innuendo of obligatoriness and forbiddenness. To vary the metaphor: the basic idiom of ethics is adjectival; it accords to nouns a no more than derivative and exemplary status. (And this first principle of Ethical Universality, let it be noted, also debars from criterial position the universe itself, a logical singular; cosmic teleology, whether susceptible of any meaning or not, cannot decide about right and wrong.)

3. Crypto-Universality

Granted this, it might nevertheless still be the case that non-universal objects, non-categorised presentations of value and singular-directed sentiments have some legitimate place in moral experience and orientation. It might be that one or the other, perhaps most, of the fake-moral principles or appeals just listed acquire some genuine axiological meaning, not altogether irrelevant to morality, if diverted from the claim to supply a principle *of* morality and demoted to a subordinate status, to an ancillary function, or to the office of a collateral, as it were, in the ethical establishment. Thus the "ego-emphasis" which the obscure demand of "authenticity" really means is plainly unfit for the role of a first principle or a conceptual matrix of moral valuation as such, but it might furnish a supplement, not devoid of moral significance, to our really "authentic" moral experience of truthfulness or our experience of the spiritual stature and self-assertion of the person. Again, the imitation of, and allegiance to, existent models of virtue, holiness or spiritual grandeur would grievously usurp the place of an overriding duty and, worse, of a basic moral principle; but they do constitute both a modality of moral endeavour and, given the proper checks and restraints, a vehicle of moral insight and a stimulus to ethical thought. Again, the naturalistic and historicist enthusiasms for idols of power, trend, progress, fruitfulness etc. might at least sharpen our interest in the practical theme, with its definite moral connotation, of meaningful and worthwhile, as contrasted with futile and unrealistic, activity. But if that is so, the question arises as to whether, notwithstanding the full basic validity of the universality principle, we should not allow for possible differences of kind and degree in the mode of reference to that principle as displayed by moral experience. No doubt the principle is fully manifest and directly and focally experienced in such classic standards of moral conduct as, say, self-control, "universal" benevolence and, the most important example perhaps, the rules of fairness, honesty, veracity or contractual justice. Although in the given case it is Harry Miller I must not cheat, all the emphasis lies on not cheating and none on Harry Miller's person; it will next be a Billy Burton, next another fellow again, and always, in the perspective of "Thou shalt not cheat", an indifferent somebody—an indefinite and exchangeable dummy. Similarly, ethical individualism, that is, respect for the individual's rights and dignity, implies a strict indifference to the individual traits or specification of any individual. But, I submit, not all modes of moral experience, not even all classic, familiar and ever-recurrent modes of it, may *exactly* conform to this structural schema. Herein lies my "question". Nor would I defer to the objection that I am here tackling a merely psychological topic, to whit the varieties of moral experience, which is not a properly ethical theme and is out of bounds for the philosopher. Not so: for what I mean by the question has nothing to do either with a differential psychology of men's moral experiences as dependent on their subjective dispositions, or with a causal enquiry into the varying factors that condition the growth and the typological varieties of moral experience. Rather, what the question bears upon is the possible presence of significant differences of structure between modes of moral experience corresponding to, and determined by, their purely ethical objective content. In other words, what interests us here is the possibly unequal experience of ethical universality seen as a quasi-logical function of the different aspects or dimensions of morality itself. In the perspective, for example, of honesty, the "partner"—the existent object of our attitude, or the target of our impact—is comparable to a featureless dummy (Justice is "blind"). But in some other subdivisions of the moral perspective this may not be entirely so; and if not, the difference exists in virtue of a sort of logical necessity.

4. Toned-down Universality: First Group

It seems to me that the realm of what I would call Toned-down Universality divides into three fields, no doubt subject to overlaps and possible further subdivisions, yet plainly distinguishable. The first of these, and the one that sets up the least incisive challenge to the Universality Principle, is the field of supererogatory moral endeavour or self-demand, which in its more elaborate and sustained form takes on the character of moral ideals, voluntarily chosen and personally embraced (or perhaps personally constructed). Such commitments are by definition not—normally and legitimately—felt to represent a straightforward and therefore universal obligation. Yet the person who possesses them does credit them with particular, perhaps with the utmost, moral significance; and his pursuit of them, like every assenting response to a moral value or theme or task that has confronted the mind, is distinct with a note of obligatoriness. This mode of experience underlies such aspirational principles as *Noblesse oblige* or *Aliis licet, tibi non licet* (the heraldic motto of the Sonnino baronial family in Italy), or the heroic or saintly pursuits of excellence or perfection (recently noticed and acutely analysed by Urmson),[4] or again, in a different way, certain morally significant ambitions or projects adopted in answer to a particular call of which the agent believes himself to be the recipient, and again, in a somewhat different fashion, such trains of thought as "I must commit myself to this noble and arduous task because I happen to be specially qualified to carry it out (though I may fail)". Now the joint presence of the aspect of obligation and the aspect of non-universality in these and similar forms of conscientious awareness cannot but evoke in us a sense of paradox. This finds a plastic expression in Admiral Sir Richard Grenville's dying words in Tennyson's ballad *The Revenge*—logically odd words meant to wave aside yet also tending to agree with the tribute of praise and admiration addressed to him by his Spanish captors:

> I have served my Queen and country as a valiant man and true:
> I have only done my duty as a man is bound to do.

To be "a valiant man and true" is not exactly "a man's" duty, and each of us is hardly bound, with one warship only under his command, to defy a fleet of 53 enemy ships, some of them bigger than his sole one and superior in firepower.

Ah, but *if* one is an admiral, not a farmhand or a city merchant or a humble scribe etc., and has for one's job to fight enemies as dangerous and as odious as those Popish fiends, "those dogs of Seville", then merely by refusing, in a situation like that of the battle of the Azores, to accept the role of a quixotic hero, that man would prove a coward, a moral *minus habens*. And that, indeed, *no* man ought to be. And so we are led back to the safe moorings of moral standards, in which every "particular duty" fitting a particular situation must be grounded; without this back-reference or matrix or sounding-board it could not be argued as a duty or possess any demonstrable moral meaning at all. A saintly ascetic may similarly hold that it is somehow his bounden duty to be what he is and act as he does, yet it is not everyone's duty; still, the linkage between his exceptional state of obligation and the stock of ordinary moral obligations binding on everybody is easily discernible: he exhibits a surplus of ordinary righteousness as contrasted with wickedness and all kinds of moral defects, "only more so", making the contrast more trenchant and glaring and emphatic; he incarnates, to borrow a phrase of Professor Findlay's,[5] a "prolongation of pattern" superimposed on the warp and woof of ordinary morality—a refinement upon it. So we may rest assured. We need not worry about the defence of Universality. But perhaps the whole story is not told therewith, and some vestige of the paradox lingers on. Discard the basic scaffolding of ordinary and universal deontic morality, and all supererogations, extra-subtle sensitivities, generously embraced particular ideals and commitments lose their meaning and weight and value index; they are disembodied ghosts wandering in a vacuum, exiled from their place in the consensual system of moral co-ordinates on which their meaning ineluctably depends. To be sure; but the point is that the world is so made that, *given* the established validity of universal moral standards, supererogatory aspirations and morally inspired ideals *do* come by a meaning and appear to be something *called for*: as if, in some more hidden way, ordinary morality in its turn depended on *them*. Perhaps the moment may come for me when, unless I assert myself as a hero, I shall stand convicted as a coward; perhaps mere elementary and correct duty fulfilment *needs* the complementary luxury of what is more than it, on pain of decaying beneath its level into moral laxity and indifference; perhaps, in the ultimate and global perspective, whoever stubbornly dodges the call to glory is doomed to perdition.

5. TONED-DOWN UNIVERSALITY: SECOND GROUP

The second standard type of (apparently) de-universalised moral position presents a sharper break with the purely universal-directed one than does the first, in that it marks not a pattern of prolongation (i.e. the voluntary choice by the agent of a more exacting code of norms for his own governance) but a kind of transfer of allegiance, within limits, from conceptual and intrinsic standards to morally accredited existents. These are models (exemplars) to be followed in the sense of imitated, or authorities to be followed in the sense of being obeyed (believed, as regards the validity, wisdom and relevance of their injunctions). Model and authority may, but need not, coincide—though the status of a model tends to imply a connotation of authority, the converse is not true: if, say, a zealous Catholic venerates a saint, he will necessarily tend also to believe, or at least to ponder very earnestly, that holy person's opinions and assertions as well as to mind his exhortations, whereas he has no reason to install, say, his bishop or the reigning pope as a model of virtue and holiness except possibly on the merits of the case. Models are persons or groups of persons (e.g. perhaps the early Christians, or social types such as the *homme honnête*, the gentleman, the Prussian officer, the perfect trade-union man, etc.); authorities in their turn are persons (whether "in authority" or not) or institutions (governmental, sectarian, academic or anything else), but implying a status to some extent formalised.

Normally and legitimately, the status of a morally relevant model or authority is of necessity anchored in the soil of straightforward and universal standards. A further and decisive condition, however, is their particular affinity or proximity to the agent in question—I mean the disciple or follower or subject who accords them his reverence, belief or allegiance. (Either his essential preferences and free choice or his existential or circumstantial, "given", involvement or location may lie at the origin of the relation and remain in the focus of its working-out.) The immense part played in moral orientation and education by exemplars and authorities needs no stressing. But the inherent danger of abuse and perversion, or obscurantism and blind infatuation, of an adulteration of conscience and distortion of the sense of values, is equally obvious and familiar. It lies in the temptation, perhaps seldom wholly absent from the follower's mind, to elevate the object of his allegiance *supra legem*, to see in it no longer a representative and vicarious transmitter, a servant and a vehicle of universal moral standards, but a self-contained source and creator, a fountainhead or an epitome of intrinsic "adjectival" standards; in a word, there is a temptation to substitute the standard-bearer for the standard itself. A non-moral value experience, to formulate it in the most lenient and cautious way, thus comes to take the place of moral value experience; something else comes to be substituted for morality and to usurp its appeal and simulate its voice. A sham has been delusively invested with the trappings of morality—its unique dignity, intuitive evidence and deontic force.

Yet *abusus non tollit usum*. In itself, so long as a direct and pervasive reference to the firmament of universal moral standards is maintained over and above any allegiance to value-embodying entities with their magic of attraction and power, his awareness of exemplars and authorities will tend to sharpen and enrich rather than to distort the subject's moral percipiency or sensitivity. Our contact with what we experience as "moral realities" is logically secondary but may be highly conducive to our insight into the evidence and the mutual connection of ethical universals. Here, once more, it would be misleading to say that the entry of what I have called toned-down universality means the supersession of moral experience by something else, that is, by a non-moral emotive attachment virtually destructive of the moral sense; this is merely a danger, not the essence of the thing. Attention and reverence accorded to morally significant entities is not as such an alternative to morality proper but is itself part of moral experience.

6. TONED-DOWN UNIVERSALITY: THIRD GROUP

Lastly, I must mention the most conspicuous and, if I may so put it, most universally present, mode of non-universal reference: a type of non-universal reference inherent, precisely, in one of the straightforward universal standards of deontic morality.

This is the group of what we may best call, by a common label, duties of loyalty—the commandment "Honour thy father and thy mother", patriotic loyalty and the like; in general, the allegiance and diversified obligations a person owes to the concrete (social) entities to which he belongs in view of his antecedents and history. (There is an obvious nexus between duties of loyalty and, bearing on the relations among individuals, the obligation of gratitude; and, so far as the person's affiliations partly rest on his own free choices made in the past, between duties of loyalty and what is sometimes called "fidelity", that is, being faithful to one's word, observing a contract faithfully, and in general the sphere of justice—in modern terminology, honesty and reliability.)

The objects of loyalty are singulars, and, notwithstanding certain more normal or more exceptional changes in life (marriage and progeny; change of nationality; friendships forming and dissolving, etc.), as a rule highly *constant* singulars. Patriotism is a full-fledged universal moral principle and is identically, or almost so, meaningful for everybody; yet for, say, a Swede, the "country" or "fatherland" is not an indeterminate and variable dummy like the Harry Millers and Billy Burtons we are forbidden to overreach in business, but the unique and ever-identical Sweden. At the same time, the objects of loyalty are *not*, except accidentally, ethical paragons (or thought to be so) nor privileged depositaries of moral wisdom. The duty of allegiance owed to them is underlain by no such premise: that would be contrary to its very meaning. For supposing there was a country "by far the best" and that country was Switzerland, then the value-response that all men including, for example, Swedes, virtually owed to Switzerland would be something totally different from Swiss patriotism, that is, from the universal duty of patriotism as applying to Swiss people and to them alone. Consequently, we are faced here with a universal moral principle prescribing a differential attachment to a singular, not justified in terms of the distinctive and superior values embodied by that singular but determined simply by the factual, historical situation—the "belonging to"—of the individual. Moreover, if, on the one hand, duties of loyalty enjoin a primary (and, in general, the most potently operative) break with crude egoism, on the other hand they converge with, and sanction, a natural bent of man which has aptly been described as extended egoism. Hence the manifold well-known abuses, perversions and illusions, masquerading as virtue, which go by the names of family obsession, uxoriousness, tribalism, chauvinism, jingoism, (partly) nationalism and racialism, etc. Hence also the logical oddness of our moral position in cases of conflict: the problem which was hotly and brilliantly, but somewhat helplessly, debated between Gellner and Hare in their memorable Aristotelian Society papers (1954–55),[6] and which is rooted in the fact that duties of loyalty are essentially divisive and agonistic (while at the same time, of course, essentially unitive *qua* intra-familial or civic duties). In war, and more generally in situations of international conflict, we as patriots must be interested in the opposing power's citizens being as *un*patriotic as possible (most distastefully to Hare!): thus, we are morally obliged to wish that a large group of our fellow-men should be refractory to the *same* moral demand and behave immorally under the *same* category of obligation. Naturally, as Hare emphasised, the position is essentially modified if we are aware of a definite note of Good versus Evil attaching to the conflict in question. Being seriously and sincerely convinced that "our" side represents Evil, we may, or perhaps even ought, to question the validity of our patriotic obligation; and in the inverse case we need have no moral scruple in trying to suborn enemy citizens and to undermine their sense of patriotic obligation. If no such note can obviously be assigned to the conflict, I think that the obligation of loyalty maintains its validity but is subject to various reservations—supposing we are not *just* patriots but morally conscious and conscientious persons and therefore *also* patriotic but a good deal else besides.

To conclude. If the loyalty type of Toned-down Ethical Universality is peculiarly vulnerable to abuse, no more should the counterpart of this evil be overlooked. The attitude of "seeing through" the moral inferiority and intellectual delusions of vulgar patriotism, which is especially common among intellectuals, easily lends itself to a perversion equally pernicious, if not more so—that of ideological nationalism, a thing vastly different from patriotic loyalty but apt to interfuse with its excessive and immoral forms (the "religion of patriotism"). In other circumstances their rebound from "unthinking loyalty" and "primitive", "herd-like" patriotism encourages them to imagine that by actually taking sides against the cause of their own country or type of civilisation they have given conclusive proof of their spiritual height and moral purity. What they have in truth demonstrated is their being victims of a philosophical fallacy: the simplifying misconception of Ethical Universality. And, linked to that, a moral defect to which the ordinary man, whose simplicity harbours a sense of complex reality rather than the passion for conceptual reduction and simplification, is less prone—a prideful contempt for the limitations of perspective inherent in the human condition: limitations, the acceptance of which is not only a practical necessity in the face of cheap and uncontrolled moral afflatus but indeed an integral constituent of morality itself.

NOTES

1 Kolnai is here referring to R. M. Hare, *The Language of Morals*, London: Oxford University Press, 1952. [Editor's note.]
2 The reference is to Bernard Mayo, *Ethics and the Moral Life*, London: Macmillan, 1958. [Editor's note.]
3 The last three principles mean typical *sham* universality in that they are meant to point to singular entities. There is no true opacity of reference present, only a persuasive phrasing in terms of universals.
4 The reference is to J. O. Urmson, "Saints and Heroes", in A. I. Melden, *Essays in Moral Philosophy*, Seattle: University of Washington Press, 1958, pp. 198–216. [Editor's note.]
5 The Reference is to J. N. Findlay, *Values and Intentions*, London: Allen & Unwin, 1961 (see index). [Editor's note.]
6 E. A. Gellner, "Ethics and Logic", PAS 1954–55, pp 157–178; R. M. Hare, "Universalisability", *ibid.*, pp 295–312. [Editor's note.]

The Concept of Practical Error

AUREL KOLNAI

1959

I

The concept of Practical Error (PE) is, on the face of it, nonsensical. Nevertheless, there are two reasons why it may be worth while investigating what it might possibly mean. First, the central position it occupies in Aristotelian ethics, which is bound up with the naturalistic confusion between a person's good (i.e. what is good for him) and a person's moral goodness: that confusion has something irrepressible about it, and, in however oblique and distorted a fashion, the Aristotelian doctrine may at least hint at a real problem and suggest one way towards its solution.[1] The second reason, unconnected with the use of the technical term PE, lies in the amplitude of meaning proper to such ordinary-language expressions as "a foolish action", "a mistaken action", "he committed a great error", or "foolish" as opposed to "wise" but at the same time possibly distinct from "stupid", "erroneous" or "ignorant", from "mad" or "crazy", from "rash" or "reckless", and, of course, from "wicked" or "wrongful". So far as we could single out some principal and characteristic meaning of "foolishness" or "folly", neither simply dependent on error proper, misinformation or fallacious reasoning, nor simply identical with rashness and lack of deliberation or unskilful technique, we should have succeeded in giving body to a concept very close to that of PE.

II

Common sense clearly distinguishes between a foolish and an immoral action (their philosophers' speculations should not inveigle us into doubting that this was also the case with the Greeks) but at the same time, rightly or wrongly, tends to assume a more or less obscure correlation between practical and moral defect. Talleyrand's comment on the murder, by Napoleon's order, of the Duc d'Enghien, *"C'était plus qu'un crime, c'était une faute"*, provides an illustrative example. Obviously it implies that a *crime* is one thing and a *faute* another; but, allowing for the possibility of evil deeds not practically unwise and of foolish actions not evil at all, it appears also to imply that the fact of this action being both wicked and unwise is not wholly accidental. The underlying assumption is that a man who has achieved great success by ruthless and crafty methods and has so far brilliantly got away with his tricks will be tempted to believe that he is infallible in this practical sense and to overreach himself with possibly fatal results. If I am deficient in moral sense I may easily commit the miscalculation of underrating its strength in other people and may take it for granted that by acting astutely and without moral restraints I am *necessarily* furthering my own interests. Being himself a cynical politician and an outspoken wit delighting in cynicism, Talleyrand emphasised that the element of practical un-wisdom weighed more heavily in the scales than the element of immorality, but this also expresses the immanent perspective of political action as such; others would have said more drably and perhaps more hypocritically: "This piece of knavery was, moreover, an act of folly from his own point of view."

Our moral consciousness is pleased to imagine that right conduct must in some ultimate and supreme sense work out to the agent's own advantage, and on the other hand is pleased to imagine that a truly good action cannot have any self-regarding motive. "Pleasure" will "accompany" the results of virtuous conduct, and man should know this in general but forget it every time he is actually shaping his own conduct. It is easy to get rid of the antinomy by tempering both propositions appropriately (my acting morally must benefit me in an important sense, no matter how much it may also harm me; moral action necessarily implies non-self-regarding, but need not and indeed cannot exclude self-regarding, motives); but the problem of adjusting practice to morality and fitting morality into practice remains a complex one. Perhaps so much might be suggested, that moral transgression connotes the idea of practical blunder if only in virtue of the loss it inflicts on the agent's self-respect and claim to the respect of others, and that, on the other hand, practical misperformance bears in it an innuendo of moral failure at least in as much as a reasonable management of one's concerns may itself be recognised as a second-order moral demand.

I will now turn to the subject of PE as (possibly) distinct from theoretical error and technical mistake in a practical context. An action may be called "foolish" or "unwise" in a looser, I might also say trivial, sense from four different points of view (III–VI), which nevertheless may help us to grope towards a definition of PE.

III

Sometimes a man is said to have acted foolishly if he has failed in his objective, which he would have, or might have, attained if he had acted differently. But success or failure also depend on outward factors independent of the agent's operation and wholly, or largely, or to some extent unforeseeable. If a roulette player stakes on red and the ball alights on black, we do not for that reason say that his choice has been false or foolish—although reckless gambling, and in some people's opinion all gambling, may be foolish. Perhaps our man did miscalculate in that he fallaciously believed that after a long series of reds the probability of the next turn giving red was greater than 1/2; even then staking on red would have been no whit wiser than staking on black. However, failure may at least indicate a certain, or probable, or at any rate conceivable defect of practice. Though we cannot isolate this as *the* cause of the German defeat in the Battle of the Marne in 1914, it was foolish of the Germans to put the Schlieffen Plan into execution and yet mass superfluous troops in Lorraine and at a crucial moment transfer two army corps to the East in order to halt the Russian advance on Königsberg. Most likely their mistake was due not to plain technical, military miscalculation alone but also to the morbid fear on the part of a power-mad and swashbuckling yet insecure state leadership of facing the calamity of invasion in the East while achieving the decisive victory in the West. Perhaps such a mismanagement of conflicting concerns—the inability, as it were, of putting first things first precisely when all is staked on one card—may convey a hint at the meaning, if there is any, of PE: for it is not ascertained simply by the test of success or failure, nor defined in the terms of either theoretical error or of moral transgression.

Another way in which failure, or an unsatisfactory result, may conjure up the idea of PE is presented by the kind of successful performance that disappoints the agent's expectations, not because the aim he has attained proves to be an inefficacious "means" to some other, higher "end" but because, having been desired for its own sake, it fails to yield the intrinsic satisfaction the agent imagined would attach to it, evoking a sense of hollowness, surfeit, or "too-lateness" instead. Its realisation reveals to the agent that he has misconceived of his own good.

IV

Error proper, that is, theoretical error—plain ignorance of relevant factors, error of fact, fallacious reasoning, or miscalculation arising from inadvertence or lack of time for reflection—error, then, fully definable in itself and neatly separable from its practical context, often underlies false practice; for all practice is based on theoretical ("speculative") suppositions. There appears to be no place here for PE, seeing that just as felicitous practice is not truth (is not cognition or true belief), false practice is not error, whereas the error it involves is not practical but theoretical. If, owing to misinformation or misremembering, I believe that the Piccadilly line leads to Waterloo and take it in order to reach that station, my failure to arrive there cannot be called an error, and the proposition that the Piccadilly line leads to Waterloo is false independently of whether anybody is bound for Waterloo on any given occasion. And *so far as* it is true that virtue (temperance, justice and the like) is indispensable for happiness, a man who sought for happiness consistently outside virtue would be the victim of a theoretical error (ThE) and his practice would miscarry for that reason. Yet we sometimes do loosely call "foolish" an action vitiated by ThE. This we tend to do, of course, if that ThE consists in an emotively conditioned illusion or piece of ignorance rather than in straightforward, so-called "invincible" ignorance or in miscalculation concerning a technically complex matter. Censures like "fool" or "foolish", "ass", and so on, do not (in paradigm cases) simply or necessarily express a diagnosis of substandard intelligence even with reference to its actual or foreseeable unfortunate consequences; they connote blame and therefore an element of moral reproof. They are uttered with a tone of moral vexation—though their prominent emphasis is not moral. I would sum up tentatively: PE emerges in a practical context and is embodied in a practical act or attitude, while it displays an implicit ThE—which the agent may even express in so many words, though perhaps as an *obiter dictum* on the spur of the moment only, in the given practical context—and also appears to bear a tinge or semblance of moral inadequacy.

V

"Foolish" conduct not subjectively translatable into ThE, that is to say, not involving a ThE which the agent would maintain in the face of warnings or criticisms, is that which reposes on rashness, lack of circumspection, neglect of relevant circumstances, "omission of reasonable care", or decision without sufficient deliberation. This is what may most properly be labelled "imprudence", taking "prudence" in its closer technical sense.[2] By contrast with the agent's being deluded into a false belief through emotive allurements, and again with his lapsing into miscalculation as to the efficacy and workability of a scheme of means destined to secure a determinate end, the man who acts imprudently turns a blind eye to a set of relevant circumstances just because one aim in the forefront of his attention has taken a disproportionate hold of his will, or out of habitual impatience ("precipitancy"), or under the pressure of urgency which prevents sufficient reflection. In the last case, practical "misperformance" may be no more than apparent, and in fact no more than a manifestation of the "exigencies of practice", that is, the necessity of making a practical decision in the face of the incertitude of theoretical judgement and the impossibility of taking all factors into consideration. Habitual precipitancy may involve the *general* ThE *about* practice that complete, short-range solutions to isolable practical problems ("taking one thing at a time") are usually possible and tend to add up to a satisfactory whole.

Obsessive concentration on one aim, or rather on one type of concerns or some selection of concerns, to the detriment of others is of greater interest. It must be emphasised, however, that no "error" is implied here unless the disregarded or neglected concerns really are the agent's concerns. Only on that supposition can the bold assertion be risked that the agent is mistaken about what he actually wants, takes an erroneous view of his own subjective good, and is acting against his own interests—not unwittingly, for that would be simply ignorance of facts or miscalculation, but with a kind of obfuscated consciousness. Poverty or triviality of concerns as such, oddness or perversion of character as such, will impair the goodness of the agent and diminish his cultural, civic, moral or personal value, but they do not imply—*as such*, I repeat—any erroneous belief about his own concerns and therefore do not express PE. A man may just as truthfully hold that he prefers Coca-Cola to burgundy, strip-tease to Ibsen, and material advantages to obeying a sensitive conscience, as that he prefers peaches to apricots or inversely. A preference can be wrong, deplorable or reprehensible in many ways, but it cannot be false, seeing that it involves no propositions contrary to fact. To act in conformity with it or to indulge it may, however, be false in the somewhat fragile and circuitous sense that it clashes with other preferences of the same agent which are of greater keenness and weight though less intensely present to him in a given situation, or that it is at variance with his enduring and ordered stock of concerns.

The problem of potential or virtual, evolutionary and interpretative concerns arises, of course, at this point. The concerns of man are the only logically conceivable principles of his practice, but they are not sacrosanct, unalterable and definitive. Children in some respects grow into adults and are often aware very early that they cannot help doing so and had better assent to that destiny, with the discomforts it entails; tastes often come to be enriched and rectified, and responses evoked to new and objectively higher values; a blunted, dormant and seemingly inexistent conscience is sometimes dramatically aroused or gradually nurtured into life by diverse kinds of experiences. In view of his new scale of preferences, the agent will then deem it "false" to continue in some of his former habits, and in the light of his present state he may be said to recognise some of his earlier attitudes as "erroneous" in that they precluded him from the appreciation of a "greater good" which he by now has actually proved to be able to appreciate and would be reluctant to sacrifice. But, while pragmatic idealists, moral pedagogues and social utopians would find in this consideration the ultimate truth about the matter, for the disinterested common-sense philosopher it represents, as I called it a minute ago, a *problem*.[3]

Suffice it here to observe that the changes in the state of our concerns may be objectively for the worse as well as for the better (although the memory of the "greater goods" for which we have lost taste is still likely to be more real than a purely supposititious future concern); that many such changes are axiologically and morally indifferent, or important but at the same time highly debatable as regards their goodness or badness, a clear delimitation between these and the obvious improvements being impossible; and that many of a person's valuations, concerns and pursuits hardly change at all in his lifetime. To say nothing of the fact that a society composed of equally and maximally wise, noble and high-minded individuals could not survive materially at all, or if it could would promptly die of boredom. The identification of practice with the pursuit of *the* objective good as such is not only an arbitrary falsification of the data of experience but self-stultifying into the bargain. The problem of a virtual convergence or consonance between them, however, remains. Moreover, there remains, I suggest, the insight that awareness of a possible amplification, refinement and moral revision of the agent's dominant concerns and preferences is itself in the agent's interest—that is, part of the immanently correct management of his concerns as a whole, although no complete and conclusive tests for the appraisal of a correct or less correct practice are so much as conceivable—whereas a hidebound disregard for one's virtual concerns or probable future cares may be said to constitute one form of PE.

VI

Criticising a person's conduct from the perspective of practice, that is, of the co-ordinated pursuit of his own concerns, sometimes involves a use of qualificatives like "foolish", "stupid", "preposterous", or "crazy", so extended and un-self-critical as to be obviously illegitimate. But however sloppy, careless and misleading ordinary usage may be, it can always be made to convey some valid point of common sense. Thus, in a given social medium or even within the area of a certain community of tastes, a man may be called foolish for following, in his behaviour, a different order of preferences. "Strangeness", "oddness" or "eccentricity" are all the more liable to be accounted for in such terms if they conflict with widespread and fairly constant human habits of preference, even though the agent may not be ignoring or overlooking the fact but consciously resisting the persuasion of the "normal" in spite of examples, explanations and remonstrances. Yet clearly no error need be implied in a man's not loving "wine, women and song", in his not putting either life or honour above everything else, in his being very particular about his accommodation but utterly indifferent about food or dress, and so forth. Nevertheless, eccentricity may, as the word itself happens to suggest, express a vision out of focus, a sort of partial blindness or lack of conspectus relative to the agent's realm of concerns, and may point to obsession and perhaps to an unhinged mind. Some would say that strangeness (by reference to common standards and even habits) at least raises, or renders meaningful, the problem of "justification". There is indeed nothing foolish—nothing indicative of error—in marked individual tastes or comparatively unusual preferences as such; but in a *prima facie* sense they logically place in doubt the agent's capacity for taking properly into account what *are* his concerns.

Somewhat similar considerations, which cannot all be followed out here, apply to such peculiarities of character as rigidity, on the one hand, and inconstancy on the other; to indecision and practical cocksureness (the erroneous common presupposition of these two being that action requires certitude about its correctness); and again, to *a priori* disregard for so-called practical maxims, or, inversely, dogmatic reliance on or conscientious conformity to a set of practical maxims, as if they were scientific truths or basic moral imperatives. In fact, they are reminders and plausible points of view destined to aid the shaping of practice, and some of them can actually be arranged in pairs of contraries. Disregard for a current practical maxim can underlie practical misperformance but also the exercise of practical genius;[4] many a battle has been won, and not necessarily thanks to a fortunate accident, in violation of established strategic principles. Rigidity, with the artificial narrowing and overweighting of the agent's operative concerns that it implies, is likely to indicate an element of error in his conception of them; and inconstancy may harbour, on the intellectual plane, something like the false belief that one's concerns can effectively be taken care of without their sustained mutual confrontation and co-ordinated management. Such defects of practice as a one-sided attachment to short-range satisfactions only (e.g., the spendthrift) or long-range projects only (e.g., the miser) may involve characteristic errors about one's concerns and about the constitutive aspects of practice: for example, that vital concerns endure into the future and that, on the other hand, possession is primarily a means to enjoyment; and, being wholly embedded in the texture of practice, such errors are apt to evoke the idea of PE.

VII

A more rigorous determination of the meaning of PE, if it has any, might be attempted by enquiring into how PE could be *tested*. Now, practical failure provoked by technical slips and inadequacy and limited to the region of a well-defined and circumscribed pursuit is perfectly testable ("I got into great trouble because I missed my train under the mistaken impression that the Piccadilly line would take me to Waterloo"); because obligations can conflict, and can also be disputed and nugatory, practical failure is more easily testable than moral transgression. But the correctness or falseness of practice in a more intrinsic sense, and indeed of practice in any comprehensive sense, is extremely hard to test, very much more so than conduct as an object of moral appraisal.[5]

For Aristotle, the test of the practically wise or foolish action resides in the prudence—or lack of it—of the agent himself, which is almost like saying: "The right solution to a problem in algebra is the one found by the best mathematician, whoever that may be." To make bad worse, the prudent agent is at the same time identified with the right-acting, that is, virtuous agent: thus, moral testability comes to be engulfed in the unjudgeableness of practice, the test of which is displaced into the empty postulate of a causal relation. Yet Aristotle's notion of the agent being the proper judge of his own practice, and of a close interdependence between his practical thought and his actual practice, is not wholly unhelpful.

Setting aside morality and other objective standards by which conduct and character may be judged, it is only by reference to the agent's concerns, of which he alone (whether prudent or not) can attain a true and living conspectus—inseparable from his actual shaping of preferences and poising for decisions—that the state of his concerns as served or disserved by his actions can be estimated. Such an estimate is not a matter of self-knowledge in a purely psychological sense, that is, of unmixed theoretical knowledge.[6] It embraces not only a registration and scaling of the agent's wants but also an emerging experience of what he is ready to do and to endure, of the concern or concerns into which he is able to fuse his will and which he is able to set up, confirm and maintain as a centre of gravity, with other relevant aims and preoccupations attuned to it. Decision based on the conspectus of given concerns is *also* an active modification of the agent's concerns, perhaps the creation of a new concern; it involves inchoate action, action already in exercise as it were. Part of its rightness (its practical correctness, that is) lies in the true production, the efficiency and the intrinsic satisfactoriness of the action it calls forth—in addition to the correct theoretical presuppositions about the given concerns and capacities of the agent, the relevant circumstances and the prospects of success, and considered *prima facie* irrespective of the moral rightness or wrongness of the action. Thus, there attaches to practice an aspect of *predictive truth*, theoretical in as much as truth cannot but be theoretical, but at the same time inherently practical in as much as the agent himself works out, though he does not simply decree but also fore-estimates, the fulfilment of his implicit prediction. The apparently nonsensical Aristotelian phrase about practical "truth", which consists in a correspondence of reasoning with the "right" movement of the will (which in its turn is defined in terms of a so-called "right reason"), suggests, I think, this insight—that correct practical thought is able to map out, set in motion and guide the agent's *real* willing, his effectual self-dedication to the course set, and thus to forecast "truthfully" the unfolding of the pursuit in hand and its place in the landscape of his concerns. So far as morality *is* somehow everybody's actual and unevadable concern, practical truth also connotes a correspondence with "right" (i.e. righteous or virtuous) willing. But furthermore, it would seem that correct practical deliberation, in the sense here adumbrated, depends to some extent on the moral equipment of the agent in as much as it supposes courage and self-mastery—in other words, the pre-moral capacities which Laird has called "qualities requisite for morality".[7]

Practice can be immanently better or worse, more or less wise and less or more inept, rather than analysable into truths and falsehoods like a theory composed of statements; but single, salient practical decisions may perhaps bear on them the stamp of intrinsic "truth" or "falsehood" accord-ing as the agent is eminently ready or tangibly unprepared to "verify" them by, shall I say, wholehearted and inwardly efficient action, or sustained attention to the concerns they represent as dominant. We should then have to distinguish PE in this proper and intrinsic but admittedly abstruse sense from the far more easily testable PE in the improper and extraneous sense of practical misperformance underlain by ThE or technical blun-der: ignorance, fallacy, oversight, precipitancy and narrowness of vision. But there are manifold intertwinements and intermediary levels. Thus it might be argued that all PE "proper" could be interpreted in terms of an insufficient knowledge of one's own concerns. Again, PE "proper" is apt to breed quite palpable and detachable theoretical errors about extraneous objects and relations: to manifest itself, for example, in illusions, chimeras, and groundless apprehensions. It may thus become more testable for the agent himself and particularly for outside observers of his conduct.

VIII

Practice is inalienably the agent's own and responsible only in the forum of his own concerns (though this is not to deny the possibility and necessity of a presumptive, interpretative and persuasive or educative approach to the concerns of others, under proper reservations; nor the biological, tra-ditional and environmental background of concerns). Hence, practice cannot be tested by objective standards, structurally on a par with techni-cal achievement, health, morality, erudition, etc. PE can be properly ascer-tained, if at all, only by the agent himself—though it can be surmised or conjectured by others—and by the agent, again, only in the perspective of his state of concerns at the time of his behaviour in question. No doubt this proviso must be taken with a certain qualification: I may judge a PE I committed some ten years ago, though I cannot be exactly the same man nor put my present self experimentally back into the same configuration of interests, perceptions, emphases, desires and anxieties. The changes I have since undergone, the insights I have since gained, and the mental losses I have suffered cannot but colour somehow my conception and expe-rience even of those among my former concerns which I feel have endured immutably and form the permanent scaffolding of my concrete self. Yet I have to set aside everything that represents a perceptible discontinuity or dislocation in my state of concerns between then and now: the fact that, in a closely analogous situation, I would act (or estimate) differently today than I did in the past does not justify me in thinking that I was foolish then and am wise today. The question is whether, on reflection, I find that "I was another man then", "My taste has changed since", "I did not suspect at the time that..." and the like, or, on the contrary, "I recklessly left it out of account that...", "I ought to have known", "How could I have failed to foresee that...", "I did it against my better judgement", "It's the kind of mistake I *would* commit (even now), but I am more keenly aware now of why it *is* a mistake", and similar expressions of strangeness. Thus, for example, it is pointless for a mature or elderly man to recall it as a "folly" that he once was a young man, but he may quite meaningfully recollect PEs committed in the past which are more connatural to young men yet by no means inherent in the fact of being young (e.g. failure to *realise* that one is not to remain young for ever, though a young man jolly well *knows* this): such meditations in an elderly man are part of wisdom, especially if at the same time he keeps mindful of the truth, extending to a wider area than that of senile amorous infatuations, that "There is no fool like an old fool."

The nearest test of PE, then, seems to lie in the sense of frustration and perplexity, of being baffled and proved silly, of quasi-guilt and quasi-repentance (not in face of the law but in the context of his own aims and cares) evoked, or at any rate evocable in principle, in the agent as identical with the "erring" agent in regard to his concerns though not in regard to his state of mind. Others who are in touch with him may vicariously anticipate or guess or suppose such a quasi-repentance on his part, or indeed evoke it on some occasion by putting matters before him and piercing the cloak of his purblindness. But even this test is apt to be a precarious one. Self-criticism is occasionally more foolish than the act it condemns. Moreover, the critique of practice is faced with the formidable problem of the plurality of perspectives in time, or, to put it differently, the indefiniteness of long-range views: a decision taken under the pressure of urgency or prompted by the dubious intuition of the moment may next be proved faulty in a wider conspectus of concerns but again vindicated and made to look "wise" from an even longer view.[8] Rather than forcibly referring every human act to that fictitious "ultimate end" of Aristotle's—the *ignis fatuus* of moral philosophy, as Carritt has justly called it—which is said to be pursued by everybody by "natural necessity" and yet to be actually dodged by the imprudent and non-virtuous majority of men, I would suggest that practical wisdom and folly, while indisputably real and at times judgeable by unequivocal tests, are seldom present in a pure state and are by no means such invariable characteristics of human conduct as our pragmatic eagerness, along with our moral zeal and intellectual hubris, would have it. I have no space to complicate the matter further by raising the problem of "practice on behalf of others", that is, of public, and especially political, pursuits, and historical appraisal.

Just as an instrument can be found less efficient and useful than one would have wished or expected it to be, but cannot be falsified or disproved like a theory, it is natural to speak of more or less wise, well-ordered or felicitous practice rather than of correct (let alone true) or false (let alone erroneous) practice. Error is most neatly and tangibly present in the context of practice when it is a theoretical error or a piece of faulty calculation, that is, only "practical" in an extrinsic sense; and to this corresponds, on the side of the periphery of practice, failure within the terms of a delimited, objectified concern, that is, failure to achieve a determined end: missing instead of hitting a target. The innermost core of practice, the management of concerns taken in their ensemble with an eye to their mutual linkage, tension and equilibrium—the "happiness" which Aristotle distorts into an "ultimate end" and arbitrarily centres in "virtue"—is on the whole unjudgeable except in a very crude, tentative and approximate fashion, if only because even the agent himself can form but a foreshortened conspectus of his concerns and in fact is likely to modify his concerns in the very process of judging. Important and salient partial aspects of practice may, however, be meaningfully considered, at least accidentally, in isolation. And in such limited perspectives the concept of a testable PE proper, problematic as it always remains, may be assigned a place: some practical decisions will stand out as ill adjusted to the agent's relevant concerns and unfit to be followed out by his actual endeavour in the way he has thought they would be, and will thus come to be "stultified" or "refuted" in their predictive content, much as a theory is falsified by facts.

IX

Without wanting to labour the point, I recall that PE necessarily connotes moral inadequacy (though this may not amount to sin or transgression[9]); the sense of practical quasi-guilt can come close to that of moral guilt; and that sin also involves PE at least in the sense that moral integrity is *also*, not indeed "the" good of man, but *one* peculiarly precious *possession* of man. It is all the more important to guard against the emotive and intellectual temptation to confuse practical wisdom or prudence with morality, and PE with moral deviation. The formal theme of practice (the management of my concerns) and the formal theme of morality (submission to a specified set of demands on me, conceived in universal terms) are clearly quite different; and the belief in their miraculous coincidence as regards their respective contents is, I am convinced, quite false. I will only list, with the utmost brevity, three arguments in support of my view.

(a) Some classic types of situation are charged with an eminently practical, others with an eminently moral, emphasis. Into such momentous practical problems as, for example, the choice of a profession or the choice of a mate, moral points of view only enter in a circumscribing sense, and, within the limits of the morally permissible, in a vague, accidental and variable fashion. The converse is true of situations determined, say, by the presence of a special obligation, or of one of the standard conflicts between desire and a grave sexual taboo.

(b) In any kind of situation the practically wisest and the most emphatically moral, or even the most irreproachably moral, choices are not necessarily identical. It has been said of three prominent statesmen of the same epoch that, faced with any difficult problem, "S would always seek the most directly expedient, C the most prudent (practically wise), M the most equitable and just solution". It may be a gross PE on a man's part to embark on an exacting and ambitious enterprise inspired by a lofty moral ideal, but it cannot be a downrightly evil thing to do, even if it be morally objectionable in an indirect, subtle and debatable manner. Again, around 1945 our supine policy towards Communist power was even more foolish than it was contemptible; in our present inferior position and under the threat of total annihilation, it may be slightly less contemptible but a great deal less foolish.

(c) Consider Aristotle's distinctions between the "self-indulgent" man (of good basic intentions, perhaps high-principled, but frail, deficient in virtue, vulnerable to temptation) and the "vicious", corrupt, morally indifferent or even perverted type of person. The same kind of sinful action will be less wicked in the morally weak than in the consistently wicked man; but it will plainly involve a much more blatant and grave PE in the weak man's case, seeing that it flies in the face of his own paramount, or at any rate permanent, concerns, disturbs his conscience, and stirs up remorse painfully gnawing at his entrails.[10]

NOTES

1 Anscombe in *Intention*, Oxford: Basil Blackwell, 1957, p. 74, grudgingly admits that it is perfectly possible to say "At this moment I lose all interest in doing what befits a man" and that "*if* [my ital.] Aristotle thought otherwise, he was surely wrong". See, in my sense, also P. Glasson's paper, "A fallacy in Aristotle's argument about the good", *Philosophical Quarterly*, Oct. 1957. For the difference between moral and prudential judgements, see Hare's examples in *The Language of Morals*, Oxford: University Press, 1952, p. 144.
2 Even so, "prudence" does not imply conduct governed by motives of "expediency" alone.

3 For the logical priority of *my concerns* over *this or that specified concern of mine*, e.g., moral obligations, see Nowell-Smith's argument in *Ethics*, Harmondsworth: Penguin Books, 1954, p. 224, about deontic presupposing teleological words but not inversely.

4 That great practical genius King Leopold II sent this instruction to one of his agents, about to discuss Congo affairs with a French emissary: "Be very prudent, without, so far as possible, betraying your mistrust...*I don't think it is in our interest to sound him out much: he might reveal to us plans which, once they have been revealed to us, we could not very well combat.*"

5 Pio Baroja, shortly before his death at over eighty: "On the whole, I seem to have had little luck". Interviewer: "But you're not certain of it?" Baroja: "Well, no." Taylor on Hitler and Mussolini: "Probably each was happiest in the last phase, securely divorced from reality, M. rattling the bones of the Fascist Republic and dreaming of St Helena H. reading Carlyle and preparing a stupendous *Götterdämmerung*."

6 The true and, I dare say, authentic (non-Platonic) meaning of Socrates's "Know thyself" is nothing like a "theory of the soul" but "*Know* what you know—about the things you are concerned with and the way in which you are concerned with them."

7 Cf. also A. R. White in "Good at", *Proceedings of the Aristotelian Society, Supplementary Volume*, 1958, pp. 195–206; "Some of our moral appraisals embody the notion of 'good at' whereas others do not." White very rightly rejects C. K. Grant's absurd thesis (*op. cit.*, pp. 173–94), "The exercise of any skill or capacity is itself subject to moral judgement", and rightly remarks that "Being good at" may elicit moral *blame* (*scil.* skill in the exercise of an evil activity). [Eds.: The ref. to Laird is unknown to us.]

8 Cf. also so-called "cleverness" or "false prudence": practical wisdom *exceeding* the moral point of view.

9 Cf., concerning the moral inadequacy that may attach to indecision, White (*op. cit.*, note 7): "A man such as Hamlet or myself"—I beg to be accepted as *in eurem Bunde der Dritte*—"who is very bad at making up his mind, is not immoral but has perhaps a defect of character which others may blame or despise."

10 This argument can be found in Price. [Eds.: Ref. unknown.]

Actions and Inactions

AUREL KOLNAI
1970–71

1. THE CONCEPT OF ACTING AND NOT ACTING

Although my interest in this theme is primarily ethical, the theme itself is
not. Rather, it has its place in the orbit of the "Philosophy of Mind", or
the "Description of Actions", or again the "Logic of Practice".

By Action I mean what is usually meant by it. In recent philosophy
much attention has been paid, and rightly so, to the ambiguities latent in
the concept of action and, closely linked therewith, the element of arbitrariness inherent in our description of actions. As early as about the beginning
of this century, the Hungarian humorist (later playwright) Ferenc Molnár
makes a Mr Csepi, a very rich man, who also has the reputation of being a
very wicked man, complain to a lady of being thus unjustly blamed: "Some
time ago, when my brother died, people were making indignant remarks
about my not shedding a single tear on the occasion. The absurdity of it!
As if the kindness of my heart depended on drops of salt water pouring
from my eyes! They also censure me for not having offered any money to
his destitute widow. Judge for yourself: isn't it ridiculous to hold that I am
a good or a bad man according as I do or do not put some coloured slips
of paper into a woman's hand?" The lady, however, is not convinced. She
breaks off the conversation with the emphatic final remark: "It seems to
me, dear Csepi, as though you really *are* a pretty wicked fellow." The
story goes to show that one or the same item of behaviour or action *can*
be described in different ways, but also that the essential aptness of the
description may not be a matter of wholly arbitrary choice. Here is another
example, from a German pocket encyclopaedia of 1935, where the outbreak of the Great War is described like this: "...Germany, allied to Austria,
had thus to fight Russia and France at the same time; presently England
and Belgium also joined the ranks of Germany's enemies." And it is true
that when the German columns crossed the frontier at Gemmenich, it was
the Belgian frontier guards who fired the first shots, thereby arousing
righteous indignation in the invaders' breasts. As Julius Kövesi insists, we
do tend to import evaluation into our description of facts.

It is, again, not without some difficulty and arbitrariness that we analyse people's behaviour, conduct or policy into single, as it were isolable
and self-contained, "actions". The articulation of Practice in quasi-indi-

viduated actions can be described in an indefinite number of ways; nevertheless, such an articulation objectively exists. Going from my flat in West Hampstead to Bedford College, Regent's Park, I may be said to perform an action; but, on the other hand, this is part of a larger context of policies and goals (taking my class, fulfilling my duties, enriching young people's minds and ennobling their hearts...), and, on the other hand, my "action" can be analysed into a sequence of sub-actions or basic actions (walking to West Hampstead tube station, choosing the most attractive-looking carriage of the train, rehashing in my mind the points to be developed in that day's class, etc.). Actions of this kind may be regarded as merely marginal actions in that they follow a routine pattern, but actions they nevertheless are, as contrasted with involuntary twitches and tremors, catching a cold and running a temperature. We shall later raise the subject of "significant" actions.

By Inaction I mean not, of course, what we mean when using the word as a term of blame for a passive attitude where energetic measures ought to be taken (e.g. the government's "inaction", i.e. failure to take action, when faced with the danger of uncontrolled inflation), but more generally the absence of an action or a system of actions which emerges as a possible theme in the agent's practice and which he *might* be expected or predicted to accomplish, or again exhorted to do or discouraged from doing. I mean, then, cases in which we would speak, perhaps in a spirit of blame or perhaps not, of an *omission*, or a failure to do or to try to do something, or again, perhaps approvingly but not necessarily so, of an act of *abstention* or of refraining from doing something. Like actions, inactions may be more or less significant and more or less voluntary, more or less properly deliberate; but while every "doing something", unless it be purely involuntary behaviour, is an action, every "not doing something" is by no means an inaction—not even if it might reasonably be presumed that *if* the agent thought of a possible course of action, or *if* it were suggested to him, he *would* deliberately reject it. The most typical forms of inaction are: (a) omitting to comply with a positive duty; (b) successfully resisting a positive temptation; (c) rejecting an offer, whether this offer is such that the agent's rejection of it is (in the circumstances) immoral, or the offer is immoral and its rejection a moral duty, or the offer is of a permissible kind and its rejection morally neutral.

My omission to do what I rigorously cannot do, for example levitating, is *not*, then, an inaction; it is only a non-action. Nor is it an inaction proper if I omit to do something which, rigorously speaking, I *could* do but which I neither in any way desire nor in any way am obliged or have any special reason to do. Thus my never having visited Leeds or Manchester has not been an inaction; whereas if I had refused, in 1961, a one-year research scholarship at the University of Birmingham, that would have been an inaction.

2. FULLY-FLEDGED PHYSICAL ACTIONS. "SIGNIFICANT ACTIONS"

According to Eric D'Arcy[1], *A*'s not doing *X* is "an omission only if *X* was in some way expected of *A*"; thus, if *A* for some reason omits to go and see Wilde's play *The Ideal Husband*, although he is specially fond of that lovely comedy, that certainly can be called an inaction, even though he may be a very solitary person and no-one around him may be at all aware of his being an enthusiast of it. I support D'Arcy's rejection[2] of Bentham's criterion for distinguishing action from omission: to wit, the performance or non-performance of such physical movements as may constitute an action. D'Arcy holds that, for example, relaxing in an armchair or sitting for a portrait or hunger-striking are actions rather than omissions, though they imply the agent's being physically at rest rather than in motion. I agree. In D'Arcy's opinion, a motionless state of the body or abstention from certain bodily movements is a necessary but not a sufficient condition of inaction. Similarly, *A*'s taking some (important and definitive) decision, which might well intend the accomplishment of certain physical actions but only days or even months later, is a purely mental act but does in itself constitute an action—though not the action or policy decided upon—and certainly not an inaction. Suppose that in the context of my work, say writing this paper, I meditate for some time on a question in point reclining in my desk armchair, but after a minute or two get impatient, jump up, run out of the house and potter about in the garden, dismissing the problem from my mind, until the end of the day: my rushing and pottering may be described as an "action", but in a much more significant sense I shall feel guilty of an omission. Nevertheless, the paradigm case of "an action" *is* rather a fully-fledged physical action than a merely mental performance, however strenuous and productive. After all, deliberation and decision are ordained to physical actions to be undertaken in the near or at least the more remote future; and even thought as such is normally *directed* to subsequent expression and communication, which consists in physical acts such as talking, writing, or submitting a manuscript for publication.

The more mental activity leads on to physical intervention in the course of events, and again the more intentional and deliberate, the more thought-out and calculated a physical action is, the more definitely we may speak of "an action"; and, *a fortiori*, of a *significant* action. A successful effort to check, say, the involuntary movements of my limbs when I am overtaken by fear, means of course action rather than inaction. On the other hand, my decision not to go on with the writing of a book I have begun is a more definite and significant case of inaction than my mere *drifting* and quasi-automatic gliding into passivity in relation to a project once formed.

Finally, another criterion of "significance" resides in the presence of a deliberate *change* of activity as opposed to *routine* or continuing in an established and self-perpetuating "rut" of procedures. To introduce a reform or enact new rules and measures is an exemplary case of "taking action", though it is likely to involve the abolition of some activities or types of action which have hitherto prevailed. If I "break" a habit I consider morally objectionable or imprudent, that is a more significant action than my continuing to indulge the habit, though its direct theme and goal is the cessation and non-existence of an activity.

Actions and inactions are, then, intertwined and interrelated. Is their mutual correspondence a straightforward and rigid one? Is their distinction and contrast, by any chance, merely a matter of language or our arbitrary choice of expression? Is every action expressible as an inaction, and every inaction as an action? I hope presently to show that the relations here implied are fairly complex and manifold, variable according to types of case.

3. The Problem of Mutual Translatability

There exists, of course, a minimum formal translatability, substitutability or equivalence between a positive and a negative judgement expressing an identical state of affairs. Thus, for "This book cover (BC) is not red", we may substitute "BC is non-red" or "BC is of a colour other than red"; we have here transformed the negative into an affirmative judgement. There is, however, something clearly artificial and tortured about such equivalences, which may be a matter of indifference to the practitioner of formal logic but will puzzle the linguist or the philosopher. We must have some reason for preferring, in ordinary language, "not red" to "non-red", for inclining to insist on the distinction between positive and negative *Sachverhalte* or *Objektive* (states of affairs). Furthermore, the negative is apparently parasitic on the positive judgement (and state of affairs). We express non-being by reference to the corresponding being, which, as it were, we annul or negate; whereas we express being, as it were, by a direct pointing to it. Sometimes, if the situation is such that it allows or invites us to be more informative and more succinct, we abandon equivalence in answering a yes or no question, and replace the negation by a precise affirmation which contradicts the one meant in the question: Is the cover of that book red? No, it is blue.

In virtue of their greater complexity and of their narrower range, and therefore the greater wealth of their concrete presuppositions, statements about actions and inactions may in some sense have a logic of their own; but here too we may expect different degrees and types of translatability, and also a numerical prevalence not perhaps of inactions proper but of non-actions over actions,[3] and something like a thematic or descriptive primacy of actions over inactions. Or should I say ontological primacy? Indeed, we only—or at least mostly—speak of "inaction" (omission, abstention), as distinct from not-doing pure and simple, if something like action, namely an inhibitory action, is present; true, this may not apply to the *drifting* type of inaction, but even in such a volitional state there is involved a compound of inchoate or unserious, unachieved or unsuccessful action or actions on the one hand, and shamefaced, inarticulate, fleeting and semiconscious but not totally involuntary "refusals", that is, inhibitory acts, on the other. I maintain a thesis of asymmetry: the converse, I submit, is not true. To be sure, every action objectively precludes an indefinite number of conceivable alternative actions; every action implies choice and therefore negation. But not only can the paradigm case of wholehearted action be pretty fully *described* without any reference to inaction, it is also possible that the agent performs it without any hesitancy or vacillation; whereas it is only in the poorest marginal cases of inaction, bordering on mere non-action, that inaction ensues without any act of inhibition or resistance intervening. Some inactions may take the form of elaborate physical actions, for example writing a letter in which an offer is firmly but courteously declined and the refusal circumstantially motivated; no doubt a highly active policy may in its turn involve periods of apparent passive expectancy, that is, inaction, but these are still incandescent with the flame of resolution to act. I do not deny, but definitely affirm, that action too is parasitic on inaction; I merely say that inaction is parasitic on action primarily and to a larger extent.

4. Limits of Translatability

Language shows an almost boundless flexibility in respect of affirmation and negation, which might lead us into denying any but a grammatical and stylistic distinction between action and inaction. To break a promise is the same thing as not to keep a promise. Not to obey a command or not to conform to a rule is the same thing as to disobey it, or to go against it. To act at random means to act without having reflected or deliberated. "He told a lie" means "He didn't tell the truth." Not to help others in need is a near-synonym of "being indifferent to the suffering of others", and so on. But a closer analysis of these and similar examples would obviously show the limits of translatability. In most cases, we might hesitate to use the affirmative expression for the negative meaning, or inversely. The counsel of our sense of style would itself point to the inexactitude of the possible translation, that is, the incompleteness of the equivalence in question. Thus "Jones did not respect the sanctity of human life in respect of Brown" is a barbarous circumlocution for "Jones killed Brown"—or else, perhaps, a (still clumsy and inaccurate) mistranslation for "Jones didn't mind if Brown was going to be killed." "I don't advise you to do this" is a more polite and toned-down form for "I advise you not to do this." "I don't expect victory" is a euphemism for "I think we shall be defeated", perhaps leaving open, or pretending to leave open, the possibility of a "draw". Again, inaction may similarly be clad in affirmative linguistic garments, with or without some modification or distortion of meaning: "Something must have prevented him from coming" instead of "He hasn't come"; "He attaches little importance to the outward manifestations of loving-kindness" instead of "He never helps a man in trouble"; and so on. Sometimes, of course, equivalence *is* rigorously exact and both modes of expression equally correct and normal: I am staying at home = I am not going out.

Three observations are in order here:

(a) The relation between judgements describing actions and judgements describing inactions is complicated, as already hinted, by the fact that negative predications are very often cast into a seemingly opposite form, that is, transposed from syntactic into semantic expression. Thus "He doesn't drink" becomes "He never drinks", or "He drinks very little", and so on. The use of such words as "disrespect", "valueless", "untrue", "involuntary", "inequality", "scarcely", etc. is very widespread and indeed helpful and ineliminable. But it may also give rise to misunderstandings (cf. a word like "invaluable") and obscure the distinction between actions and inactions by engendering the illusion that affirmative and negative *sentences* are always mutually translatable without remainder and thus suggesting that every doing is a kind of not-doing and every not-doing a kind of doing. My point here is just the validity of the fundamental distinction, no matter what reservations must be made and what problems may be seen clustering about it.

(b) I would further suggest that to effect an important change or turn in a situation, or, say, in the pattern of the agent's policy, as opposed to going on with an established "routine", constitutes what may be called a *significant action*, whereas to consider such a change and finally to reject that change, or to let the opportunity pass, may deserve the label of a *significant inaction*. Had the Good Samaritan of Christ's parable dismissed the call emanating from his meeting the man in trouble, he would in one sense still have been acting, not only because an inhibitory decision is also an act but in as much as walking intentionally towards a destination is doubtless an action, whereas he is praised for interrupting and postponing *that* action; yet the *significant* conduct of the Levite, who continued his journey, consisted in an *inaction*.[4] I need hardly emphasise that a significant action as well as a significant inaction may be morally good, morally bad, or morally neutral, or again hard to assess. We are sometimes faced with highly significant practical decisions loaded with very little moral charge, decisions carrying but a very slight, shadowy and possibly ambiguous moral emphasis.

(c) Actions are describable in a sense in which inactions are not. They have a describable *content* involving a wealth of details, whereas we cannot describe inactions or analyse them into parts. Robinson did *not* kill or try to kill or assault Brown: it is idle to ask whether he "not-did" it with a dagger, or poison. But, it will be objected, if I wish not to take advantage of an offer, it is meaningful to ask: "Shall I refuse it orally or by letter, or just by tacitly ignoring it?" However, the last is just the inaction itself, while the first two are *actions* meant to *convey* my refusal. Certainly my original impulse to do a thing, my toying with the idea, may be vetoed precisely by my considering the necessary means to carry it out and finding them all too distasteful, onerous or expensive. But this belongs to the manner in which I arrive at my negative decision; it is not part of my inaction, which as such is empty of content.

5. The Reality of Inactions

This emptiness, although I would not say vacuity, of inaction might mislead us into believing that inactions do not really exist or occur: that what we call an inaction is in fact action *other than* some action that has at first been considered by the agent; or that apparent inaction is in fact the action of rejecting a possible course of action; or again, that when we point out an apparent inaction, what we are really doing is describing another action "in place" of the action *not* done, but describing it *incompletely*. After all, men are always doing *something*, unless they are asleep or comatose.

I maintain, however, that this is a distorted vision of how things stand. I have already admitted that inaction is eminently parasitic on action—deciding expressly not to do something *is* a kind of mental action—but also emphasised that decision is not itself *the* action the agent decides to do: hence the decision *not* to do something is not the inaction itself; moreover, the "poor" type of inaction, bordering on mere non-action but not identical with it, is not even based on a decision not to act. Again, it is not true that when we "describe" an inaction we in fact describe an action, though only in an inchoate, or as it were "open-textured", form. When we say of an object that it is not unicoloured and not indigo we mean that it is not indigo; we do not mean that it is blood-red, pale pink, ultramarine, orange, etc., although we do not know which. Similarly, when I declare "I will not go to see this play" I make a negative utterance solidly standing on its own feet and by no means necessarily an incomplete description of what I *will* do or where I *shall* go at some future time. And that is so even if my negative statement is more narrowly specified, for example "I will not go to see this play next Friday evening." Inaction, then, exists as such; it does not *consist* in a possible alternative action, though it may certainly be set in contrast to such an action and *is* necessarily set in a context of various past, present or future, intended or contemplated, actions. A position similar to that which I have been proffering here is expounded in Jack W. Meiland's remarkable work *The Nature of Intention*.[5]

6. TRANSLATABILITY AS INHERENT IN A CLOSED ALTERNATIVE

If I enter a restaurant in Brussels one evening to have supper and am deliberating whether I should order *truite au bleu* or *paillard*, my final choice in favour of one of these will, as it were, "mean", or rather "unequivocally imply", rejection of the other. In this context-dependent sense my action translates equivalently into my inaction and *vice versa*. But suppose I am also considering a third and perhaps a fourth possibility, say rump steak and *waterzooi* (a Flemish chicken speciality). Then either one of these dishes tempts me so much at the moment that I immediately decide for it; or else I proceed by elimination. Having successfully chosen two or three inactions, one action will at last "of necessity", quasi-automatically, result. In such cases, action quasi-rigorously entails several inactions, or else inaction entails the narrowing down of the choice until a dual alternative is brought about, which again represents an exact and reciprocal correspondence between one action and one inaction. However, a relative independence or a merely loose independence reigns in "open-textured" situations: thus, in a state of quasi-inactivity I feel the urge to do something more or less significant and embark on an action, so to speak, in the mode of "invention"; or again, having nothing precise and urgent to do, I "let myself go" and indulge in daydreaming, or possibly, in a phase of "drifting inaction", I execute more or less at random some sporadic short-term projects. In these cases the schema of doing a thing *in place* of another and *not* doing a thing *as implicit* in another recedes into a pallid and as it were occult background; there appears to be no rigorous relationship between doing *this* thing and intentionally omitting *that* thing. Where, on the contrary, the pattern of a clear-cut choice prevails (ordering *what* dish for supper; travelling from A to B by *what* means of locomotion?) action can be *inferred* from inaction and inaction from action. This exact correspondence, however, is context-dependent and is tied to fore-given stipulations and principles as well as to an irremovable framework of factual possibilities. The action and the corresponding inaction do not, properly speaking, *mean* each other; their logical nexus is practical rather than strictly semantic; more like the contextually possible quasi-*contrary* opposition between, say, red and yellow than the properly *contradictory* opposition between, say, red and non-red. The frequent occurrence and high importance of situations of stark choice, with the appearance of strict translatability they suggest, does not, then, support a thesis of general and perfect translatability.

7. RIGHT AND WRONG ACTIONS AND INACTIONS

Whereas it might be held that every duty fulfilment is translatable into the negative term of "impeccability", that is, abstention from any transgression of duty, and every transgression into the negative language of moral omission (non-fulfilment of a duty), and accordingly right inaction described in the terminology of right action and wrong inaction interpreted as wrong action, this schema of linguistic equivalence is not in fact adequate to the data of moral experience and fails to account for certain obvious aspects of it.

First, it is not applicable at all to the field of supererogatory, that is, non-obligatory, right actions which we would more naturally describe as eminently *good* actions, such as acts of generosity, charity, heroism and self-sacrifice. Since they do not constitute a moral obligation, their omission would not amount to moral transgression; they are admirable and their omission would only mean the absence of an admirable example of conduct. What is not admirable is not therefore reprehensible. Significant action is not, then, reducible here to significant inaction (i.e. non-transgression).

Secondly, however, we feel impelled to extend this specifically, as it were one-sidedly, positive mark to all actions meant, or obviously likely, to be beneficent, to all benevolent actions as such, including those which we *would* regard as obligatory and the omission of which we *would* explicitly blame: in the language of moral theology, "duties of Charity". Every moral emphasis is by its very nature *somehow* a *deontic* emphasis; it is the *continuity* of gratuitously noble actions with obligatory benevolent actions (and the existence of a twilight zone of beneficence where it would be difficult to decide whether or not to recognise an actual obligation) that confers upon highly generous acts of unselfish devotion the mark of *moral* admirability. There exist obligatory actions that we not only approve of, as we do of all duty fulfilments, but praise (as "meritorious") with a warm and distinctive response, and whose omission we would condemn but to some extent excuse—in other words, deplore morally rather than actually condemn. Acts of painstaking and meticulous, as it were coruscating and "exquisite", honesty, or again of delicate tactfulness, would, I think, also fall into this category.

Thirdly, we tend to apply a somewhat, though not wholly, analogous distinction on the side of wrongful kinds of action as well. It seems as if the gravity of the matter, *per se* a mere question of degree, can be found to underlie qualitatively different modes of condemnatory response. It has been pointed out by a recent writer that it sounds odd to hear murder described as an "act of injustice", although it certainly does offend against justice. I should find it hardly less comical if it were said of somebody that he had committed a severe breach of duty, meaning that he had committed rape—which certainly does offend against two distinct classes of obligation: that of justice (in the sense of respect for another's right to non-interference) and that of chastity. In such and similar cases, the translation of action into terms of inaction seems to be out of proportion with the weight of the actions described. Starkly and blatantly *evil* actions are undoubtedly wrong actions, incompatible with duty, but they are much worse than that; our indignant and horrified reaction to them displays a transfer of emphasis from the formal aspect of what is right and conformant to duty and what is wrong and contrary to duty, to the specific malice of the *content*. Yet this response of reprobation, in spite of its probable aesthetic, and again its properly utilitarian and self- or other-protective overtones, eminently belongs to the domain of moral experience, nay to that of the most intense moral experiences.

Looking now at the problem from another point of view—that of action and inaction as such rather than their moral qualification—we shall perhaps gain a clearer insight into the limitations of translatability. At one end of the scale, beneficent or benevolent or altruistic acts are generally and typically true actions rather than true inactions. Helping others, including the most important, most urgent and most frequently obligatory form of such conduct—that of saving others from some danger and striving to relieve them from suffering, pain and discomfort—consists in actions, not inactions. If my neighbour complains of a headache, I help him by offering him a painkiller and fetching a glass of water for him. It is true that altruistic inactions also occur, such as taking care not to disturb an ill or highly strung person in my proximity by certain (e.g. noisy) actions which I have a right to perform or *per se* even had better perform; or again, tactful abstention from revealing certain truths which it is not exactly my duty to reveal and which would badly hurt someone's sensibilities; and *in certain cases* (for such abstentions are not always good but may be gravely immoral or dangerous) waiving some right, forgiving an offence, overlooking someone else's misconduct or omitting to denounce him, etc. But such abstentions lack, I suggest, the full-blooded nature of active lovingkindness and charitable devotion. Again, at the other end of the scale we find plainly that the virtues of self-control, temperance, chastity, dignified reserve, etc. are exercised in the form of inactions rather than of actions. Dull behaviour, for example, may be a disvalue but it does not offend, as does riotous behaviour, against the rules of decency. Though lust manifests itself only in actions of some kind, never in abstentions, chastity consists in the avoidance of various forms of sexual conduct.

There are, furthermore, two classes of moral, or at any rate marginally moral, activities in regard to which the primacy of right action over right inaction and wrong inaction over wrong action appears to me to be evident. First, what is sometimes called self-improvement, or striving for "perfection" in a general as well as a selective sense, relating chiefly to values of the agent's personality, and whose moral aspect is unemphatic, such as cultural and intellectual pursuits, the refinement of aesthetic sensibilities, the richness and fruitfulness of life, etc. Such strivings and accomplishments bear a positive moral sign; contentment with an inert and humdrum, tensionless and drab sort of life, and the lack of endeavour to achieve excellence in any direction, bear a (less conspicuous) moral sign, though perhaps we would only speak of moral "wrongness" here when laziness and inertia attain a duty-infringing degree, and especially when we note a tendency to wallow in triviality and vulgar amusements, in which case, however morally objectionable, inaction bends over into morally despicable action. But surely excellence, sustained or even desultory effort, eagerness for accomplishment and the enhancement of consciousness are more noticeably good than comfortable immurement in mediocrity is noticeably bad. Secondly, what we may call a thematic concentration on moral problems or on an interest in ethics as such. To take cognisance of moral demands and submit to them with intrinsic willingness is not only "right" but a basic presupposition of all deontic morality itself; and moral indifference is even more conspicuously a base moral evil. But any thematic specialisation on moral points of view, including ethical studies, though it undoubtedly bears a morally positive sign, should not be confused with a person's moral goodness.

8. The Ambiguous Status of "Contractual" Morality

By "contractual" morality I mean what we, in the orbit of the modern Western commercial, puritanical and post-puritanical, especially Anglo-American, ethos at any rate, are accustomed to regard as the very core and backbone of morals, and the focal point of juncture between formal (or conscientious) and material (or contentual) righteousness: in Aristotelian-Scholastic language justice, and in present usage the realm of justice, honesty, truthfulness, and so-called "special obligations", that is, promise-keeping and the observance of explicit contracts. Consistency, integrity and trustworthiness or "reliability" are also relevant concepts. Nowadays, when we, especially so far as we are anti-naturalists, have fortunately come to distinguish clearly between morality on the one hand and prudent or (better) practically wise conduct on the other, there have been signs of a tendency to limit the concept of morality as such almost entirely to this domain; I am in sympathy but not in agreement with this tendency.

Are we faced here with right actions and wrong omissions, or with right inactions and wrong commissions? Both of the two opposite theses can be plausibly argued. It seems to me, however, that the second thesis—right inaction as antithetic to wrong action—renders the truth of the matter more essentially, though it needs some qualifications.

For it is obvious that lying, deceiving, cheating, dissembling, stealing, robbing and defrauding are, in this context, the saliently thematic *actions*; *not* "truth-telling", sincere communications, or respect for alien rights and property. So far as I pull your purse from your pocket I *am* dishonest; so far as I *do not* pull it, I am honest. My solicitude about preventing your purse being pulled by a third party, or your brief-case getting lost, is an act not of honesty but of benevolence, kindness or friendship. But is my making true (i.e. subjectively true, *bone fide*) statements not an action? Surely it is not straightforward inaction like simply keeping silent, or making no statement at all about the matter in question. No doubt; but asserting as such is not a matter of honesty any more than of dishonesty: in the perspective of honesty, it is only a "routine" or "presuppositive" action, which *ipso facto* implies the self-evident claim to be accepted as true (i.e. sincere). The falsification and distortion of the state of affairs (the object of the statement), which makes it a *lie*, is the supervenient and *significant* action which determines the essential character of my action and the conduct it represents. So far as *"telling* a truth", communicating some news or imparting information are significant actions, they are seen under a description that opposes them not to lying and deceit but to withholding, hiding, passing over in silence, and so on. These acts, or the behaviour expressing these attitudes, may be morally neutral or again praiseworthy or blameworthy, but certainly not akin to deceit, except in cases where the intention is not so much to leave the recipient in ignorance as to create in his mind a *distorted* picture.

It cannot be denied, however, that the contrary impression arises in the types of contractual relation in which the fulfilment of one party's obligation falls due at a time remote from the point of time when he contracted the obligation—thus, in cases where he ought to keep a promise, redeem a pledge, pay a debt or live up to a trust placed in him with his consent. Paying a debt within the stipulated time limit, doing what I promised to do and the like are (right) actions; failing to do them is a (wrong) omission; nor can these be translated, respectively, into alternative (right or unobjectionable) *in*actions or (condemnable) *actions*. The point of paying my debt is not that I am not spending or am otherwise investing "the sum in question" instead; the point in keeping my promise to assist you in a difficult negotiation is not that, when I ought to be doing so, I am reading the fragments of Heraclitus instead. It is true, though, that an inaction (my not-doing something) may also be the object of my promise or the theme of the trust somebody has put in me; to follow out the implications of this variant would I think introduce a needless complication. Rather would I translate, for example, someone's promise to keep a secret, which is physical inaction (abstention) not action, into a promise to conquer any temptation he may feel to divulge that secret, and I would interpret this resistance or conquest as an "action" of self-control. I do not think I can offer a wholly satisfactory "solution" to the "paradox" we are faced with here: that lying, deceiving, cheating, should definitely appear to be actions, whereas promise breaking, failing to execute a contract, or disappointing a trust should appear at least more characteristically to be inactions. But the key to the solution cannot but reside, I suggest, in the fact itself that in the second type of dishonesty (incorrectness) two interrelated acts, say the making of a promise, so far a licit action, and the breaking of it, an illicit inaction (rather than action), constitute as it were a single unit of conduct drawn out in time. The final, objectionable act, more typically an inaction (not paying, say, £5 to Smith) would not be objectionable at all, except perhaps accidentally on other grounds, if the initial and so far irreproachable action had not been done and thus no obligation (here and now) had been engendered. In this view, which, I repeat, does not wholly satisfy me—for there seems to be something artificial in this conflation of two "individuated" behaviours into one—the moral offence committed by the promise breaker should be described not so much in the terms "He broke a promise" as in the terms "He made a promise and then went back on it". And this "organic whole" of conduct, to use Moore's phrase, would obviously constitute an action not an inaction, no matter whether the *object* of the promise were to do something or to abstain from something. Again, on this view the offence only "comes off" with, as it were culminates in, the breaking of the promise; it quasi begins with, and is virtually present in, the making of the promise—which of course we presume to have been a *bona fide* promise. This aspect is most glaringly illustrated by the case of a man who makes two promises, each to a different person, which are, if not rigorously and plainly inconsistent (in which case at least one of the promises would have to be deceitful in itself), at any rate probably and pretty manifestly incompatible with each other in a factual sense. As a corollary, we might add that the germ of the broken promise is harboured by the *careless*, the insufficiently pondered or impulsively accorded, promise. Hence the British, being obsessed with the horror of promise-breaking, as also of lying and distorting, are in general extremely reluctant to make promises, as also peculiarly incommunicative. This fine virtue, like other great virtues, naturally has its drawbacks too.

NOTES

1 *Human Acts*, Oxford 1963, pp. 41ff.
2 *Op. cit.*, pp. 40–41.
3 "Here too": we expect more non-red than red objects to exist.
4 Cf. the distinction in the syntactic use of the verb "to stop": the Good Samaritan stopped travelling and stopped to help the man in trouble.
5 London: Methuen, 1970. *See* p. 92, "Intending to do X and intending not to do X."

Agency and Freedom

AUREL KOLNAI
1966–1967

1. Freedom of Action by Choice and Free Choice

Moore, in *Ethics* (1912), chapter VII, writes—if I understand him right—that our basic experience of free-will resides in our certain feeling, in regard to our past actions, that we could have acted differently if we had so chosen; more exactly, that we should have acted differently if we had so chosen, which precisely means that we could have acted differently. He adds the qualifying adverb "sometimes"; I think we may well say "always", keeping in mind, of course, (i) that we are only concerned here with "actions" proper, as contrasted with involuntary movements, twitchings, starts, fits, etc., and also with wholly habitual, routine-like movements or manipulations performed without any attention and without the slightest deliberation, and (ii) that only such actions are meant here as are within our range of physical or psycho-physical power, which is anyhow implicit in the concept of choice: there is no sense in my saying that I might here and now "choose" to carry this building on my back to Paris, to dismiss the present government or to continue writing in impeccable Japanese. However, Moore is aware of the clearly meaningful objection that "acting as we choose" (within these obvious limits) would not establish the fact of free-will unless it were also the case that our choice itself is (often) free, in other words, that we not only choose to act so instead of acting differently but also choose to choose so instead of choosing differently. He argues that this, too, is indeed (often) the case, emphasising in this context our experience of the unpredictability, even by ourselves, of our future choices (or of many or most of them). He concludes, though, on a note of doubt which shows that he is not quite sure in his own mind that he has definitively disposed of the objection.

It is here that I propose to take up the thread again, suggesting a re-examination of Moore's proper starting point—the experience of "doing what we choose"—rather than going on to ask whether we really "choose to choose what we choose" and challenging the determinist to predict our (or again, his own) future choices. My tentative contention is that the concept of "choosing to choose, etc." is apt to lead us into a maze of infinite regress, and that a discussion of predictability[1], though certainly not devoid of interest, may well prove (as Moore himself seems to have found) to be inconclusive, whereas the incontestable fact that we act by choice may itself furnish the key to our focal experience of free-will—an experience that perhaps has something illusory about it but cannot, in common sense, repose on mere illusion or misinterpretation.

Suppose I am confronted with a classic situation of practical choice, for example two mutually exclusive offers, each of them involving obvious advantages but also some drawbacks, while to turn down both offers would land me in dire difficulties without any substantial advantage to balance them, and suppose that after weighing the respective pros and cons ("deliberation") I decide in favour of one of these offers as against the other: that is, I choose A, discarding B; I choose to accept A and, correspondingly, to reject B. I then proceed to act according to my choice, on the lines of the policy implied by my acceptance of A and rejection of B. Now, on being asked the question why I do (and omit to do) the various things I do (and omit to do) in following up my choice, I may meaningfully answer by pointing out the main advantages and disadvantages in question and by explaining how, in my estimate, "on balance" A has emerged as the more advantageous of the two alternative courses. This is indeed what my interlocutor, or perhaps I myself in surveying *après coup* the reasonableness of my decision, probably wished to know (or to test once more). But the purport of the question, and accordingly the relevance of my answer—no matter how far it, that is to say my choice itself, may be materially correct—is not unambiguous. So far as the "Why" of the question is a causal "Why" and refers, not to the justification of my choice but to the explanation of my doing such and such things rather than other things, in the sequel, the proper answer is not that I do them on the grounds listed nor because they satisfy this or that urge, inclination, interest or aspiration of mine, but that I do them because I have chosen to do them. In all exquisite choice situations, a case might be made out just as plausibly for not doing these things but on the contrary for embarking on the alternative course of action; this is implicit in the fact that I was carefully weighing the respective pros and cons before taking my decision. And my acting is my carrying out that decision, that is, my execution or "making valid" of that choice—not, as it were, the unfolding or the continuing operation of what has commended or commanded or perhaps "determined" my choice. In order that I may act in the sense so desired or urged or suggested or postulated, I must choose or decide to act thus.[2] (Between "choice" and "decision" I can see no distinction other than that of contrast emphasis: my "choice" of A as against B is at the same time my "decision" which puts an end to my previous state of hesitation or "indecision".)

I am aware of the two standard objections to this description of the phenomenon of agency, and shall presently deal with them; but let me first state more explicitly what the point of the description is. It purports, as it were, a positive rather than a negative interpretation of free-will. It emphasises a special—and very definite—mode of determination rather than a lack of determination. It suggests an experiential account of free-will in terms of a positive and indispensable "decree" or "fiat"[3] as distinct from the argument that the causal machinery of the determination of our actions has only been insisted upon as a scientific requirement but never actually demonstrated. But, admittedly, freedom is a primarily negative concept; and the view I am here proffering of agency has its essential negative aspects. If choice is the unique and sovereign author of action (or policy) which must intervene between its (let us say) determinant motives and the actual execution of action, then those motives or springs are not properly the determinants of the action—in much the same way, if a crude simile be permitted, in which we call John's father his "maker" (*l'auteur de ses jours*, *sein Erzeuger*) but do not so call his paternal grandfather, that is, his maker's maker, nor of course his more remote male ascendants on his father's side. What strikes us as a salient trait in full-fledged action is precisely this feature of "saliency": the sharp break in the agent's behaviour, the discontinuity between the action itself or the launching of the action and the multiplex of the desires, concerns, regards, etc. which—really and truly, or apparently—motivate it. That point of discontinuity is the locus of "free choice", "decision", "decree", "making one's mind up", "resolve" or whatever we may preferably call it in the context; and it is here that we touch on the nerve of "free-will", the differentia of agency proper as contrasted with mere "behaviour". In other words, action is not a "resultant" of psychic urges, pressures, yearnings, cravings, attractions and repulsions, forces or bents, not an emergent product of motives relevant to its content; rather, it is the execution of a decree[4] issued by something like a unitary "self" or "ego" or "sovereign ruler" who consults those motives and is influenced ("inclined", "pressured", "urged", "instigated" or "coaxed") by them but who, in turn, is in control of motility and directs its workings.

Kant, in this respect closely echoed by N. Hartmann, emphasises the nature of will thus understood in saying that, while physical events are universally subject to a pattern of mechanistic determinism governed by causal laws, the so-called "intelligible ego" has the power of initiating new chains of causation and thus intervenes in the mechanism of world events without upsetting or invalidating it. To whatever other objections this schematic picture may be open, Kant bungles it hopelessly by arbitrarily placing on it a peculiarly moral construction:[5] in his view, the "intelligible ego" enacts its autonomous new departures by obeying the dictates of "practical reason", that is, of a "moral law" unrelated to the natural law of causal mechanism; from which it would ensue both that morally right action was free action and morally wrong action unfree action, and that morally neutral, in particular random, choice did not exist but was in reality either evil or in some way yet determined by reverence for the moral law—that is, a farrago of absurdities. None the less, Kant rightly saw the essence of free action in its being performed at the "dictate" of the will over and above the interplay, the confluence and antagonism, of fluctuating "inclinations" and even of rationally fixed and formulated "interests".

In a sense, indeed, free agency is more conspicuously brought out by random choice, *liberum arbitrium indifferentiae*, than by the example of moral self-control, for the latter might be described by determinists as an instance of the stronger desire subduing the weaker—seeing that our desire to "be moral" may sometimes happen to be "more intense" than the sensuous desire with which it is incompatible. When we freely delegate our choice to an alien will (e.g. agree to accompany our friend to the cinema and ask him to choose the picture at his pleasure) or entrust it to sheer randomness (e.g. by tossing a coin or submitting to the blind "decision" of a roulette ball), we shall be doing something mediately "determined" by ourselves, but totally cut off from the flux and mechanism of our psychical forces or our physical constitution and condition. We have, as R. C. Skinner[6] puts it, chosen to choose in this way, but the issue (the content) of our choice is absolutely independent of any "determinants" within our soul (or body). This, however, only constitutes the extreme limiting case of free choice and agency as such. Even in the more normal case of deliberative and reasoned choice, my decision is an act in its own right—an act of "sanctioning" a policy as against others, of "setting a stamp" (of validation) on one alternative possibility, of "self-commitment" to one selection of aims and desirabilities—quite different to the calculable resultant from a parallelogram of forces or the calculated result of a problem of commensuration with its implied additions and subtractions. I may, but need not, try to work out a "wise" choice, and I may even deliberately choose what appears to me to be the less "wise" (e.g. an utterly risky) course; more important perhaps, in the case of the so-called wise choice itself I may tentatively come to scale *ad hoc* my relevant preferences or re-assess and alter my established grading of them, and the inchoate choice thus formed may in its turn intervene as an autonomous factor in the shaping of my definitive decision. Practical choice proper is unlike the "choosing", that is, picking up, of the heaviest or the lightest out of a given set of weights, or the writing of the correct sum under a column of addenda; for in the business of life we are not in general pursuing one determinate and insulated "end" but have to keep our eye on an indefinite manifoldness of mutually conspiring and competing concerns.[7] Except for limiting cases of preferring the obviously better to the obviously worse with no balancing counter-aspects whatsoever (and even the unequivocal simplicity of such types of situation may be deceptive), an element of randomness and sheer arbitrary self-causality will slip into the play of our deliberation so as to enable us to lay down our volitive position, to trace our line of conduct and to maintain ourselves at the level of agency. Reason, that is the organ of cognition and vehicle of "compulsive evidence", never "commands" the will as Aristotle, in his Greek or Platonic intellectual snobbery, and his pious commentator, Aquinas, would have it; against them, Duns Scotus—in this respect a nobler precursor of Hume—justly insists on the full practical sovereignty of the will which reason merely enlightens and informs as to the possibilities and the limits of its action, placing before it the facts which as such are independent of it and which may fall within or without its range of efficacy.

I will now turn to the two standard objections hinted at above, and in the sequel will try to confront some more objections to which I may have laid myself open in my further elaboration of the original thesis.

2 (A) THE PROBLEM OF AGENTIAL CAUSALITY

The position I have been trying to set out might be paraphrased thus: Free-will means, primarily, not so much free choice as free action (not only externally uncompelled, that is, but intrinsically free); and free action means not uncaused action but action caused, in any direct sense of the word, by the agent's choice or decision alone, not by a machinery of psychic "determinants"—regardless of how far the "motives" conducing to that decision may operate in the mode of necessary determination. To such a view the objection may first of all be made that, as has sometimes been suggested, the underlying decision is not properly a "cause" of the action at all[8] but, rather, its beginning or first phase, its initial aspect or the agent's accompanying experience of his entering upon it. A decision not followed by any corresponding action, not carried at all into execution, is indeed not a true decision but merely something like a velleity, a wish or a temptation, an unserious and illusory mood such as that of a man muttering desperately "Unless this ends within five minutes I shall instantly kill myself" or "If that happens I shall kill X and Y and Z", yet in fact far removed from being resolved on suicide or multiple murder if the abhorred condition should come true. The decision, then, seems to be an inseparable part rather than the cause of the action; to imply or entail and at best introduce the action rather than engender it as a consequence— similarly as wars are caused by developing clashes of interests or national aspirations, by threats to national security, etc., and not by declarations of war or by suddenly provoked frontier incidents and so on.

The objection cannot be lightly dismissed, but I propose a twofold reply to it. First, it is not clear to me that to call a man's decision the "cause" of his ensuing action is incorrect language just because some decision-like acts are sham decisions or because some conspicuous junctures or points of articulation in our behaviour are in the nature of formalities rather than of effective decisions. I may well—as an instance intended to serve as an argument—now conceive and proclaim my intention to take a sip of water three minutes hence, go on doing nothing of the kind and make no preparations for it during that interval, and then do it at the end of three minutes sharp; or likewise, I may decide now to ring or visit my friend X tomorrow at 3 o'clock and execute my decision tomorrow, having done nothing connected with it (not even reflected on the matter) until the said hour, though not having done, meanwhile, anything incompatible with it either, for example, not having made another engagement for the said time: in all similar—quite common—cases, it would appear unnatural to me to deny that the decision has been the cause of the action. A cause of a somewhat peculiar kind, to be sure, in as much as the decision does not, of infallible necessity, compel or conjure up the action. The water now available may no longer be available in three minutes' time, and by 3 p.m. tomorrow my friend or I may be dead, for one thing; for another, I may reconsider and revoke the decision I have taken. So that the causality in question may operate, a certain relevant substratum of factual circumstances must endure; and so must my resolution: in other words, my decision has to be maintained, or to vary the expression once more, my "will" has to remain fixed in its established position, directed towards the chosen objective. But if this is the case, it is correct to say that I do the action because I have so decided. Secondly, even though it may equally well be said that the motives that have elicited my decision—induced me to take that decision—are also the springs of my corresponding action (for, should anything happen or any consideration occur to me in the meantime which is apt materially to alter my scheme of motivation, I may revoke my decision and omit the action contemplated), it still remains true that deliberate action is never simply "caused" by its "motives" and their prevalence over contrary motives, but necessarily starts from the germinal act of decision and is performed as if it were the execution of a decree which endures in the shape of a "sustained will". A feeling of "I could have chosen otherwise" characteristically attaches to it—"I am doing this for such and such reasons and from such and such motives, but I could have accorded greater (decisive) weight to countervailing or inhibitory reasons and actualised a different set of motives"—and often, though by no means always, there is also present an express consciousness of my doing this, as opposed to something else, "just" because I have so decided rather than because I am solidly convinced that this is plainly the more expedient, the wiser or the better or "the" right thing to do. In the solution to every practical, as contrasted with theoretical, problem, the arbitrary gesture of Alexander's "cutting the Gordian knot" intervenes at least virtually, sometimes conspicuously and perhaps dramatically, as the characteristic act of volition touching off, discharging and "commanding" action—somehow comparably to the god committed to the Federal and anti-slavery cause who "hath loosed the fateful lightning of his terrible swift sword" and "is trampling out the vintage where the grapes of wrath are stored".[9] The "sword" of decision has to be "loosed" as the final determination of the indeterminate state of things which inexorably demands a settlement by the agent; the "stored grapes of wrath" may be translated into the language of tensions accumulated between competing desires, concerns and claims; and action is "marching on".

Free-will, I would argue, is not so much a gift or quality or power with which man might or might not be "endowed", as a logical postulate of Practice with its inherent incertitude and opaqueness on the one hand and its unevadable factual pressure on the other, which connotes a logical necessity of its own. The "compulsive evidence" of cognition is matched here by a compulsion to choice, implacably non-compulsive (i.e. with-holding compulsive evidence) as to the question which choice: whether to choose this or that or the other action in the given context, including pos-sibly the choice of "inaction" as an alternative to some positive action "proper" in the descriptive physical sense of the word. A theoretical prob-lem will indefinitely tolerate a "modal" answer, a reservation in the form of "conceivably", "probably", "to the best of my knowledge" or "so far it would appear that", etc., any more complete and definitive answer being disingenuous so long as sufficient "compulsive evidence" for it is lacking. Not so with practical problems. These, while sometimes susceptible to a delayed or again to a compromise solution, are in principle intolerant of any enduring answer couched in terms of probability or the like: I cannot "probably" choose this drink or that if I am here and now offered a choice of drinks but only actually take one of them (or none); I cannot "probably" go to a specified lecture next Monday night, once next Monday night has arrived, but only actually go or not go. The decisive factor has to be my decision, which can be manifoldly influenced, guided, grounded or goaded, yet for which no other factor can be substituted. (Whenever we use the verb "decide" in its improper, theoretical sense, e.g. "the doc-tor decided it was a case of perforated appendix", we mean "I find that this assumption, though not indubitably true, is more probable than oth-ers I can think of and so decide to act upon it.") The point is that action in the marked sense of the term cannot but be set off by decision, and that the agent alone can make the decision—either, which is the normal primary form, deciding directly and intrinsically, or else, which is a derivative form but conspicuously throws free-will into even bolder relief, deciding mediately and non-contentually, in that he decides to entrust or delegate or "farm out" the practical problem on hand to the decision of somebody else or even to blind chance.

2 (B) FREE-WILL AND AGENTIAL POWER

Yet, once more, a critic of the Moorian starting point might object that the crucial part which the act of choice plays in action performed or policy carried out, however significant, fails to argue for the freedom of the act of choice itself. The action, dependent on choice, may indeed be of formidable amplitude and consequence; but the amount, or indeed the range, of power exercised is irrelevant to the freedom underlying its exercise. A 1000-horsepower engine acts no more freely than a 100-horsepower engine; a man ten times as powerful as I am in the sense of muscular strength, of financial means, of intellectual capabilities or of social prestige, has not for that reason a will ten times freer than I have, and a paralysis of my limbs does not deprive me of free choice within the limits in which I can make it effective or at least express or indicate it, nor do I regain it by recovering the use of my limbs.

The last example, however, sounds a little less convincing than the previous ones. Evidently free-will does not mean power and, so far as it may admit of degrees (which is doubtless not plainly and straightforward-ly the case, as it is with physical and mental power in their various forms, or again with so-called "inner freedom", a distinctive moral quality),[10] it is not proportionate to the powers possessed by a person. Yet would it make sense to attribute free-will to a person completely inert, that is, deprived of all power of action? (Including such purely intra-mental actions as turning our attention to one object of thinking as against another, or deliberating and deciding in regard to the taking of a position that, for the time being, we cannot in any way make effective.) Reduce agential power to zero, and free-will appears to have vanished: if I cannot act at all I can-not act freely and, a slightly less tautological further step, cannot "choose". What a person "does" in a state of drunkenness or under the empire of "overwhelming passion"—that is, when the normal control and ordinance of motility by a focal and unified "self", set at a distance from desires and impulses, has well-nigh disappeared or is considerably upset and inter-fered with—will be "attributed" or "imputed" to him in a problematic and diminished sense only; it is in such contexts that we speak, without fear of paradox, of a diminished freedom and responsibility, of an impaired freedom, of (relatively) non-responsible conduct. In contrast with sleep-walking, and perhaps things done in a total state of trance or under hyp-notic compulsion, we, for various reasons, still describe what the person is doing as "actions", but in view of the "irresistible" invasion of motility by immediately effective spontaneous impulse or urge we hesitate to call them "free actions" and assume the presence of a state which, in the lan-guage of moral theology, *minuit* or even *tollit voluntarium*. Thus the con-cept of free-will appears to be linked, if not to the extraneous efficacy of the agent's choices (for he may plainly decide, in the full sense of the word, to do something that he subsequently proves altogether unable to achieve in fact), and much less to the volume and scope of that efficacy, at any rate to an intrinsic effectiveness of choice. For whatever "reasons", and regardless of the determinist assumption of a mechanism of "causes"—reflected or not in those reasons—which, in the mode of an occult background activity, "compel" my decision, I "coolly", in full possession of "reason", or rather of "my wits", but certainly not as a logical "conclusion" of my reasons, decide to displace this object from the right to the left side of the table and forthwith do so displace it: here is the basic model of free-will and of conduct informed by it. The very fact that my decision is not only the starter but itself already part of my action contributes to my experience of freedom, in that my sense of continuity between choice and action (virtually contained in it) heightens my sense of discontinuity between choice and its psychical antecedents and physical preconditions.

While, on the one hand, "sustained will", that is, the carrying out of a policy pre-decided in a possibly distant past, expresses emphatically the continuity and self-governance of the person, on the other hand it is choice directly effective, decree manifestly and in a "lightning-like" fashion transposed into terms of reality, which lays bare the very core of free-will and exhibits the indestructible nucleus of freedom as the centre of a human life inalterably embedded in a network of fore-given facts, conditions, causal machineries and constricting limitations. In a sense, all our long-term decisions, with their delayed-action efficacy drawn out in time and subject to all sorts of reservations, reverses and unforeseen reactions, are only hypothetical decisions and continue to be exposed to the pressure of our psychic "determinants" and waxing and waning rival motivations; and any action decided long in advance requires, for its actual performance, a set of renewed and revised, confirming and modifying, acts of choice, as well as of sub-decisions, so to speak, for its "application" to the emergent circumstances of the concrete situation in which it is to take place.[11] It is, on the contrary, in choice directly issuing into action—in action decided *sur le champ*—that freedom bursts forth in its raw reality, over and above the mutual push and pull of intra-psychic "forces", and presenting man as a reduced and dwarfish "godling" and his world-shaping "decree" as a caricature, and yet somehow a likeness, of divine omnipotence. Thus it comes about that man—clinging to his decisional power yet aware of its frailty and vulnerability—when he is faced with significant choices whose execution, obviated by formidable difficulties, might demand a painful "effort of will", will often fret with impatience to inscribe his choice immediately into the massive tissue of accomplished facts, translating it presently into some kind of outward action; that he will take vows or give pledges and undertake commitments, look for objective safeguards and artificially circumscribe the range of his freedom in order to buttress its validity and ensure its efficacy. It is said of Generalissimo Joffre that when, on the eve of the Battle of the Marne, 3 September 1914, he had decided to relieve General Lanrezac of the command of the Fifth Army, he hastened to appoint General Franchet d'Esperay to that crucial post of command unofficially before visiting Lanrezac at his headquarters to inform him about his decision, lest the possible indignation and remonstrances of that great and respected, but in Joffre's judgement worn-out, discordant and inopportune, military leader should make him waver and perhaps go back on his decision—he "could not" very well do so after having, as it were, "embodied" that decision in Franchet d'Esperay's fierce and stocky person. Thus there is a modicum of truth in Sartre's extravagant doctrine that men seek to find reasons *ex post* for their choices already taken, or, in Miss Anscombe's infelicitously argued contention, that men can "choose their motives".[12]

3. "DECREE" AND COMMITMENT

A further and capital objection I have now to anticipate bears on the doubtful legitimacy and merely metaphorical character of such words, used in the context of willing, as "decree", "command", the *actus imperatus* of the Scholastics (meaning a fully voluntary, deliberate and intentional mental act, preparatory or not to bodily action), or indeed "commitment" of the will. For, on closer inspection, we fail to distinguish the author and the recipient of the "decree" or to discern who "commands" whom in the act of a man's deciding something and carrying out his decision. We experience something like a focal "self", an indeterminate formal "ego" which determines a choice between contending impulses or competing aims and thereby the movements to be performed, the utterances to be pronounced, etc., by the agent; but we cannot as it were identify, as in a social situation where these words are properly used, a person who commands and another who obeys, an authority that issues a decree and its subjects or subordinates who conform (or in part are just supposed to conform) to it. My decision to, say, raise my right arm here and now does somehow look like "decreeing" that my arm shall be raised or "commanding"[13] myself to raise it, or again "commanding" my right arm to rise—a command addressed to my body—and such a model of action gains in plausibility whenever an effort is needed to make the decision effective, for example when I am tired, and yet the action ensues in effect: it appears as if I had compelled myself to do the thing ordained, or forced my body to execute the required movement. But on a more critical examination the analogy threatens to break down. I decree, mentally or aloud: "My arm shall be raised", but no serviceable occult forces will rush swiftly to raise it, and my arm remains still in its resting position. I command myself to raise my arm, but I cannot find any second self in me to do it, indeed such a self, being still "myself", would again have to transmit my command to a third "self" and so on; meanwhile, my arm stays where it is. And if I try to move my body by addressing a command to it or saying "Right arm, rise!", once more nothing happens: my body or my arm will prove entirely disobedient and unresponsive, staying inert and heeding my command as little as the most headstrong of true-bred dachshunds would. If I really am intent on raising my right arm, I must needs raise it myself—with or without effort. What, then, has become of "decree" or "fiat", of command and obedience within myself, or indeed of my being in control of my body (so far as its voluntary muscles and agential movements are concerned)?[14]

But we can seldom prescind from the use of metaphors when venturing on an account of mental phenomena; what is required is only our being aware of the metaphoric character of the expressions in question—lest, by taking them literally, we should be misled into facile allegorising and arbitrary constructions—and our making sure that the metaphors actually point to significant aspects of the phenomena we are concerned with and shed some light on what we experience as palpable reality. And this, in my submission, is true of the language of "decree", "self-command", etc., notwithstanding the pertinent criticism levelled against it. Decision is decree-like in virtue of its effectively ushering in, its enacting, as it were, action—whether immediately, flagrantly and with a strong note of "infallibility", or in a mode of action delayed, suspended and conditional as the case may be; the second type lacks the note of flagrancy and conveys a weaker suggestion of infallible efficacy, but once the effect is produced it places the power of decision over the shaping of reality in an all the more glaring light. The fact that the decree is not automatically "obeyed" by the universe but carried out by the agent himself detracts nothing from the experiential phenomenon thus described; it only shows the indissoluble unity of action, the compenetration of decision and purposeful "commanded" movement or system of movements. On the contrary, the reflection in the physical action of the underlying "motives" is merely contingent, it may or may not show forth; the action subserves some desires and interests (while it is likely at the same time to express a veto or restraint placed on others, no less real and propulsive), but the decree, not the motives favoured or concerns privileged on the occasion, is that to which it conforms and from which it proceeds with logical univocality. Further, although it is not literally possible that the agent should "command himself"—he does not harbour several "selves", for example a higher and a lower self; the promptings of moral conscience are not "commands" but demands, as are the stirrings of a turbulent passion, and may or may not prevail—still there is an aspect of decision in the agent "commanding himself", in as much as he undertakes to do a thing as opposed to another thing and then goes and does it, thwarting the tendencies in himself to do the opposite thing and silencing the apparatus of arguments he has tentatively built up in himself for the service and advocacy of those tendencies. He may, in the given case, choose the moral thing as against the pleasant, or inversely, even though the second choice may stand out in less clear outline, a veil of sham moral arguments being drawn over it to make it more palatable; again, he may choose to enjoy a magnificent sight at the cost of climbing up a steep hill, or inversely choose to rest at the cost of renouncing enjoyment of the sight, and so forth. But even if he chooses to do what, on some examination, he finds to be altogether right and very pleasant and economical and good for his health, etc., at the same time he is likely to miss some advantage or accept some hardship in so choosing; and even should he "will" to do a thing he finds to be advantageous from every point of view he can think of, in virtue of the categorial schema of choice and action at least a shadowy sense of contradictoriness still attaches to his experience—he might, after all, have decided otherwise, perhaps wilfully invoking a countervailing motive; he could have chosen an alternative course (but why do so? why should he need to "demonstrate" his free-will by an act of gratuitous folly?).[15] Again, an aspect of self-command and self-obedience is inherent in the agent's manifest ability to use his limbs (and to concentrate or deflect his attention). Certainly my arm does not rise by my summoning it to rise; but neither does it rise on its own, independently of my will, as the various glands in my body secrete their products: it obeys my command in the sense that I can raise it, and do raise it if I so choose, be it once or twice or ten times over again; and I can also feel a sort of muscular desire to raise it, yet (for reasons of manners, say) choose to leave it still, in which case it will not rise. Because my body is not just an object at my disposal but organically fused with myself, in some sense is also "myself", this "being in control of motility" peculiar to the "ego", the bearer of choice and will and issuer of "decrees", also means a kind of command-and-obedience relation within the agent, and it is through the instrumentality of this control that he can bring his will to bear on extraneous objects including other selves. Thus it comes about that some events in the world happen in conformity to our free decrees.

Another facet of free-will, however, is presented by what I have just called "undertaking" or "pledging oneself": the phenomenon of (self-) commitment. Freedom necessarily means servitude of a kind (how far Luther may vaguely have had this, too, in mind when he spoke of *servum arbitrium* I cannot say); by making a decision I am exercising and thereby of necessity consuming my freedom; in following out my decision I am operating, as it were, under a dictate. That "dictate" emanates from myself and remains subject to my control until the action be accomplished or the policy carried out; yet it appears embodied, we might say "reified", in what is no longer myself but an "order" or "rule" or "law" somehow detached from myself, projected out of myself, and a solidified "power" above me to which I owe obedience although it only exists by my grace. Commitment is obviously very like a promise and yet sharply different to it: it is not a social act, not a pledge given to another self, and does not entail a highly imperative, paradigmatic moral obligation; the subtle distinction between the self "*qua* commanding" and the self "*qua* obeying" is only remotely analogous to the massive distinction between two distinct selves (the promiser and the promisee). But though I can commit myself without making any promise (cf. the "declaration of intent"), I cannot promise at all without committing myself; and, seeing the constitutively social character of man, the assumption would seem justifiable that the concept of commitment ("engagement", *Sich-Festlegen*, "decision", "resolution", etc.) implies at any rate an oblique reference to that of promise. Similarly, "responsibility" or "answerability" or "accountability" is a concept with a social connotation, indicating that I—my "focal self", of course, not the "forces in my soul" nor the parts of my body—owe an "answer" or "account", pledging my whole person so far as I am its "master", concerning such actions of mine as have (in certain ways and degrees at least) exercised or are apt to exercise an impact upon the interests of others. Here, once more, freedom is inseparable from subjection to law. Sticking to one's commitments, or in other words sustained resolve or a consistent policy, is not *per se* tantamount to the fulfilment of moral, much less of jural or legal, obligation, yet in a germinal sense bears within it the pattern of moral obligation and points to the basically and thematically moral character of man—not to his morally good original nature, to be sure; it is, as Aranguren puts it, a matter of *moral como estructura*, not of *moral como contenido*.[16] Man as an agent is neither morally good nor morally bad—and, I hold with Duns Scotus, any single action of his need not be either right or wrong—but man as an agent is ineluctably subject to the polarity of good and evil (involving many of his choices that must be right or wrong); and agentiality itself carries in it an adumbration of goodness while the attempt to escape from it is branded with a sign of immorality. It may be morally inconsequential, and in certain circumstances obviously even a moral duty, to go back on a decision; yet, other things being equal, abiding by one's choice or maintaining one's decision and acting upon it, that is, "obedience" or "fidelity" to one's own decree, is endowed with a *prima facie* moral privilege: constancy or perseverance are rightly looked upon as praiseworthy, flightiness and "weakness of will" as blameworthy—if not always as guilty conduct, at any rate as a moral deficiency.[17]

It is by virtue of the constitutive division and distance within the person, between its multeity of concerns and between these and the central volitive or agential Self, that commitment exists and is closely comparable to promise; but though it underlies morality, it is a pre-moral rather than a properly moral concept. We make promises, as we freely commit ourselves, decide, perform acts of will, etc., *qua* "constitutively moral" beings; we keep promises *qua* "actually" moral or morally "good" or "virtuous" beings. But we only choose freely what to promise; we do not at all freely choose promise-keeping as a standard or criterion of morality. Again we are free to keep or to break our promises; yet our moral worth resides not in that freedom but in our keeping our promises, whereas our breaking them stamps us as immoral. To talk of "autonomous" morality or a "morality of freedom" is thus ambiguous and misleading, and lends itself to easy misuse by votaries of various forms of immoralism. If morality presupposes freedom, so does immorality. The locus of moral evil is not the "lower self" as prevailing over the "rational self" or the "will", but the will itself—in its perversion, to be sure. Nevertheless, freedom does not stand in relation to good and evil in complete symmetry or blank neutrality; it is attracted towards the moral good as towards one pre-eminent "good", towards evil (primarily, at least) in virtue of some non-moral "good" attaching to it. Hence our fairly universal tendency to blur our awareness of doing wrong when, or so far as, we do wrong, or again to build up in our minds the spurious sense of acting, when we transgress, not in freedom but under a sort of irresistible compulsion. Whether "vicious habits" tend to diminish our freedom of choice more than "virtuous" ones is a complex question, which cannot be argued here.

On the pre-moral, practical level of commitment, submission to objective "given" standards of rationality (not without properly moral implications) still fills an essential place, but the central postulate here is the self-limitation of freedom as a condition of its efficacy. If commitment were deprived of its force of compulsive obligation, agency and volition would vanish and the concept of freedom would sink into inane vacuity.

4. THE TWILIGHT ZONES OF FREE-WILL

It must be admitted, and has often in recent times been discussed, that the commonsensical experience of free-will is not altogether proof against philosophic criticism and indeed constitutes no wholly solid and of-a-piece datum in itself. There is some truth in the determinist contention that, whatever its basis in reality, our familiar sense of doing what we choose, and thus *eo ipso* "choosing what we choose", that is, "choosing freely", involves a kind of illusion. Even though Hampshire may be entirely correct in asserting that we cannot with certainty foretell how we shall act in a certain future situation without having hypothetically decided or deciding that we shall so act, it may well be the case that we can foretell it with a high degree of probability without being decided to act thus and perhaps without approving of our self-predicted behaviour; and this points to the probability that our sense of "not being determined to act in a certain manner" springs, in part, simply from our incomplete knowledge of our motivation in the heat and pressure of having to decide ourselves here and now. Again, looking back on some of our past choices, we may feel that they may not have been so arbitrary and uncaused, so "free" in a word, as they appeared to be at the moment of our making them, but were obviously prompted by some potent and plausible "motive" of which, at that moment, we were unaware or but dimly and marginally, inexplicitly aware: a motive "subconscious" or "subliminal" or "semi-conscious" at the time but unearthed and brought into the light of full consciousness since. True, such hindsight self-interpretations are themselves far from infallible. I would only say briefly that we are, anyhow, always conscious of having motives whenever we are acting deliberately, and that the fact of our never being fully conscious of all of them cannot affect our certainty of there being present "spots of indeterminacy" waiting for our "own" decree to fill them, and thus of an indestructible "nucleus" of freedom.[18] Moreover, our partial ignorance of what is going on in our own soul is an argument that cuts both ways. The area of our free choice may be more circumscribed in some ways but also wider in other ways than we might believe. It occasionally happens that in the end we do carry out a brave and selfless action we have in advance decided upon *pro forma*, as it were, yet in a well-founded state of apprehension lest we should prove unable to give effect to our decision when it comes to the point. If there are illusions of freedom, there are also illusions of unfreedom; and I still think that the ultimate decisiveness for our action lies with the one "motive" of our having taken this, and no other, decision.

The objection concerning the oscillations and variations intrinsic to our experience of freedom as a whole appears to me more interesting and fruitful. Given the technical possibility, I feel that I could choose—freely and effectively to "will"—to, say, kill myself, or to give away or destroy all my possessions, or to commit some heinous crime, or gratuitously to insult X for whom in fact I have the highest regard and appreciation, though I could not desire, or by any effort of will bring myself to desire, any of these things. But there is some curious inanity and abstractness about this sense of "I could choose"; only some very forced and artificial imaginary schema of circumstances might, in a dubious and tenuous way, "give body" to such an experience of "real possibility". And, if some configuration of events or pressure of adverse forces really did "compel" or "oblige" or "induce" me to do one of these hideous things, that is, to "will" to do it (for otherwise it would not be an action: if a brawny ruffian takes hold of my arm and slaps X's face with my hand, I am performing no action and thus am not insulting X), I still should not desire or want or wish to do the thing in question: hence in ordinary language we should not call that action "voluntary"—though, on pain of not being an action, it would be "intentional"—and some people would say that I did the action yet did it "against my will", did "not will it" or did not will it, choose it or do it "freely". Here the point in question is whether I can "will" a thing (or "choose" it) which I do not desire or want or wish to happen; or, rather, since that description would perhaps apply to purely random (and innocuous) decisions as well, a thing that goes against all my desires, wishes and

wanting. It might be countered, however, that my "will" to do that thing—
most unwillingly, to be sure—would at any rate be in accord with my
desire or wish to preserve my life or to avoid some other, even more monstrous, dishonour or disaster. In another type of case, on the contrary, it
might be claimed that I do "against my will" something which I loathe
morally or emphatically reject on principle but which I happen to desire
or want intensely: the case of the will faltering under the impact of passion, as when St Paul misleadingly but picturesquely speaks of "his members" doing the opposite of what he "willeth", or St Augustine speaks of
the "members of the body rebelling against the soul" in concupiscence
(as a punishment of man for original sin), though of course if my limbs
really performed any movements against my will I should be doing no
action and would not be responsible for the "sin-like" event that happened, and though the soul not the body is the seat of evil inclinations
and no action, sinful or not, is possible without the consent—the "seal"
or "sanction"—of the focal self. There are more incongruities, or at any
rate odd features, somewhat different in various linguistic media, about
the language of "will" and "voluntariness", to which I have no space left
to advert.[19]

It seems certain to me that the domain of man's will is not purely and
simply the area of *liberum arbitrium indifferentiae*, that he may in some sense
not only be compelled to suffer alien power and influence which cannot
be dislodged by his action, as well as to endure originary inner realities
(e.g. cravings and mental limitations) over which his will has only an indirect and dubious power, but he may even be constrained to adjust his
willing to imperious quasi-necessities of the situation and to decide and
act in a line that goes integrally against his grain (e.g. to yield to black-
mail or to do something of which he is thoroughly ashamed). And this
aspect of the human condition, no less than the phenomenon of free-will,
is very familiar to common-sense consciousness and is laid down in such
idioms as "acting against one's will", "I don't want to do it but I have to"
(where "I want to" is almost a synonym of the technical-language "I will
to", *je veux, ich will*, etc.); "I would but cannot" (where the "cannot" is not
rigorously but only "quasi" or "practically" true); or again "he did not of
course do it voluntarily, though neither did he do it involuntarily" (his
action having been a real action though most unwillingly done, not an
involuntary movement made inadvertently, below the level of volition and
action proper). Similarly, on the positive side, with an emphasis on spontaneity, enthusiasm and eager "willingness": "he volunteered for the army
immediately on the outbreak of war"; "volunteering an information"; "he
voluntarily offered double the amount of the obligatory subscription";
and most markedly linking the "will" to wanting and desiring, the adverb
"willingly" (the French *volontiers)* and the locution "with all my heart" (in
German *von Herzen gern)*. The focal, central, or "decreeing" and "sanc-

tioning" self is not exactly, not in all rigour of the word, an "indifferent" self; rather, it is an "undetermined" self, set at a distance from the impulses and concerns of the personal soul and a critical arbiter placed above them yet from the outset biased in favour of them as a whole and representing them in a sovereign attitude of conspectus rather than judging them as an alien and, as it were, blindfolded court of justice.[20] Thus it comes about that the legal formula *placet* stands for strictly volitive, agential decree, that the pleading lawyer at court introduces a proposal with the hedonistic tail-waving words "May it please your Lordship", and that some offenders are sentenced to detainment "at Her Majesty's pleasure". Will is free-will but it is not only free; its element of unpredetermined random "decree" can be compared to the impure randomness of loaded dice. While Austin Farrer has rightly said that "free-will" is a pleonastic term since there is no such thing as a non-free will[21], the freedom of the will is not that of an unweighted entity sauntering about aimlessly in a vacuum; and thus the expression "free-will" is not quite so starkly tautological as, say, "a female cow" and had, I think, better be retained by libertarians as a useful and significant reminder that ultimately and principally the will is free but that this fact is not so self-evidently and unproblematically established as to be in no need whatever of continued assertion and argument.

NOTES

1 That freedom, "an intrinsic characteristic of the agent", should not be based on "unpredictability" (which is "extrinsic to the agent") is forcefully argued by A. R. Lacey, "Free Will and Responsibility", *Proceedings of the Aristotelian Society*, October 1957, p. 32.

2 See the discussion, about whether actions must be preceded by decisions (acts of will), between D. F. Pears, J. F. Thomson and M. Warnock in *Freedom and the Will*, ed. Pears, London, 1963, esp. pp. 19–26. Professor Ryle's "infinite regress" argument against the necessity of decision—acts of will being themselves actions, every act of will would have to be preceded by another act of will, this again by another, and so on—is countered by M. W. with the suggestion that not every act may have to be thus preceded and that acts of will may constitute a particular class exempt from this necessity; J. F. T. rejects this distinction as subversive of the model of "action based on decision" as a whole; D. P. seems to argue (more in keeping with M. W.) that between initial thinking and planning on the one hand, and overt action on the other, an express act of decision and "effort of the will" may or may not intervene. Cf. A. C. Ewing, "May Can-Statements Be Analysed Deterministically?", *P.A.S.*, 1964, p. 172: Some voluntary acts are preceded by specific acts of volition. My own contention is that decisions ("acts of will") are not in themselves actions at all (as are "overt" or physical but also purely internal actions such as deliberately fixing one's attention on some object or contemplating the virtues of a person one dislikes) and are not of course preceded by "decisions" to make this decision, though they invariably have their intellectual and emotive-volitive prehistory, including all sorts of decisions (our choices

being partly determined by previous events: Ewing, *op. cit.*, p. 170); with Pears's account I would agree so far as that acts of choice or decision can indeed be casual, unemphatic and toned down to the point of being difficult to locate and all but imperceptible, but I would make the reservation that his vague concept of "(practical) thinking and planning" obviously already includes preliminary choices and identifiable decision-like acts.

3 The expressive term *fiat*, in this context, "let it be done!", originates, to my knowledge, from William James.

4 The scholastic concept of *actus imperatus a voluntate* is endorsed as "the right metaphor" by A. Kenny, *Action, Emotion and Will*, London, 1963, p. 238.

5 Lacey, *op. cit.*, p. 27, justly writes: "I am surely as free in non-moral situations as in moral ones" and "...it would be odd if conscientious action were alone in being unaffected by the agent's background".

6 R. C. Skinner, "Freedom of Choice", *Mind*, October 1963, p. 476. There are, I think, few attempts to defend the libertarian doctrine as admirable as Skinner's.

7 Cf. my paper "Deliberation Is of Ends" in *P.A.S.*, March 1962, esp. p. 272.

8 The case against decisional or volitive causality in action has probably been argued most subtly and insistently by A. I. Melden in his book *Free Action*, London, 1961and 1964, esp. Ch. V ("By Willing, One Does..."), pp. 43–55. The gist of his argument appears to be that volition cannot be the cause of action since it cannot be neatly separated from the action it is supposed to cause, i.e. individuated as an event distinct and independent of the event constituted by the action to which it necessarily refers. My objection to this, as set out in my text, is that decision, though not logically independent of the action decided upon, is de facto sufficiently distinct from it to form another event preceding it and—in what manner is indeed an obscure question—bringing it about. I suggest that if Melden's argument were sound, the odd implication would hold that whereas a stroke of lightning setting a house on fire could be called the cause of the house's being on fire, an incendiary's act of arson could not be so called, for "setting fire to a house" and "that house being on fire" are somehow contained in each other or fused together. Cf. Ewing, op. cit., p. 171: "I cannot see any good reason for saying that choice as part of a mental state may not be a cause of a physical action". I do not, however, deny the tendency of volition to "fuse into" action, significantly revealed by the English idiom "I will...", which Fowler describes as the "first-person-coloured future". This meaning of "I will..." (I intend or am resolved to..., and shall do it) is also, less often, similarly expressed in German (Ich will..., and particularly Wir wollen..., in the sense of "It is fit, or best, for us to..., and so that is what we are going to do forthwith").

9 Julia Ward Howe, *Battle-Hymn of the Republic*.

10 Professor B. A. O. Williams, in his postscript to *Freedom and the Will*, ed. Pears (quoted above), p. 124, emphasises the degrees and limitations of freedom of choice, particularly as dependent on the agent's true and false beliefs concerning the courses of action open to him. Light is thrown thereby on the relations, not to say transitions, between the concept of free-will as a status or constitutive attribute of man, and that of "inner freedom" as a distinctive quality or "virtue" which quite plainly admits of an infinitude of degrees. Nevertheless, the distinction is conspicuous and ineliminable. In ordinary life we simply assume freedom of the will, with responsibility as its corollary, in everybody not in a condition of insanity, intoxication and the like, though we may also recognise its being perhaps abnormally circumscribed by an amount of ignorance "extraordinary in the circumstances". We do not praise (or in any way single out) a man for his "unusually free will" or "highly developed freedom of choice". But this is pre-

cisely what we do in reference to "inner freedom". When we say that a man is "responsible for what he does", and when we call a person "highly responsible", we mean two completely different things: in the first case, that his doings are imputable to him; in the second, that he is laudably mindful of his responsibilities. "Responsible" in the first sense, is opposed to "non-responsible"; in the second sense, to "irresponsible".

11 That is why Intention, which, on the one hand, tends to outrun actual performance (since this may partly or wholly fail, or even prove to be altogether impracticable), on the other hand never embraces the whole content of Action and sometimes strikingly falls short of it; and this fact also lends colour to the appearance that actions sometimes "grow" out of antecedent desires and speculations without the intervention of true decision or willing (see note 2) in a sort of haphazard rambling or vegetable continuity.

12 See Kenny, *op. cit.*, p. 88, note 4. Anscombe misleadingly writes (*Intention*, p. 22), that Plato's example of a master refraining from beating a slave who has deserved punishment lest he should do so from anger shows that we can choose our motives. Kenny points out that we can indeed choose our actions and so far can choose between doing something from a certain motive or not doing it ("actualise" a motive or not, I would say with Sir David Ross) but, having once decided to do something (from whatever motive), we cannot then on top of it choose the motive from which to do it. I submit that if Plato's model shows anything at all it is precisely this inability of ours to choose our motives as such. The master felt that he ought to exercise an act of "retributive justice" but, being in a dudgeon, also felt that he could not help doing it with anger and therefore could not be sure that he would not do it from anger as well (which he considered an improper motive). None the less, Anscombe has a point in so far as, through deciding our conduct, we can indirectly curb or, as Joffre did in the reported case, strengthen the operation of our motives.

13 Cf. notes 3 and 4.

14 See Melden, *op. cit.*, Ch. IV: "How does one raise one's arm?"

15 Skinner's (*op. cit.*, p. 468) common sense is quick to notice what unsound enthusiasts and misinterpreters of freedom, such as most Existentialists, are apt to forget: "...that we seldom concern ourselves just with making a choice, but almost always with making the best choice, whether it is best from the point of view of our own comfort or pleasure, or from the moral point of view, or from the aesthetic point of view, or from the purely practical point of view of choosing a means to achieve some particular end." For the view that "counter-suggestion" (i.e. my doing deliberately the opposite of what I know somebody has predicted that I am going to do) fails to prove free-will, see Pears, *op. cit.*, p. 97.

16 Professor J. L. L. Aranguren, *Ética*, Madrid, 1958, pp. 62–6 and 72. He borrows this basic distinction from X. Zubiri, whose disciple he professes to be. Morality as structure is inherent in man's character as an agent; morality as content represents the moral standard and man's possible conformance to it. The distinction is obviously akin to, but not identical with, that between formal and material ethics and that between "metaethics" and the descriptive analysis of moral consciousness or the phenomenology of moral experience.

17 The concept of "unpredictability"—a distinctively English idiom only translatable into other languages by some equivalent of "inconstancy" or "capriciousness"—bears an adverse moral sign which, however, is barely more than marginal. It plainly means something far different from "non-predictability" which, taken descriptively, simply refers to free-will, and, taken evaluatively, would point to a rich and complex nature amply endowed with "inner freedom". But neither is

"unpredictability" a synonym of "unreliability". It is the attribute, not of a person whose promises cannot be trusted, but of a person whose presumable commitments, practical "maxims" and policies cannot be safely built upon or expected to operate.

18 The expression is Professor G. P. Henderson's (see "Predictability in Human Affairs", in *The Human Agent*, Royal Institute of Philosophy Lectures, I, 1966–7, London: Macmillan; and New York: St. Martin's Press, 1968, pp. 1–19), meaning, unless I have misunderstood him, the presence of free-will which can always be felt in agency and made conspicuous in salient cases but which is inextricably embedded in the network of psychological determinations.

19 Kenny's (*op. cit.*, p. 214) proposal to use the technical term "volition" as a portmanteau word for all emotive strivings and tendings that may issue in "willing" proper, and especially his bold attempt to make up for the absence in English of an ordinary, idiomatic form of "to will" as it exists in most languages (the Greek *ethelein*, as well as *velle, vouloir, wollen*, etc.) by introducing the ill-sounding technical term "to volit", is open to manifold criticisms but reveals a deep-seated need in man to "integrate" his being in certain "whole-hearted dedications" comprising his free-will and his psychological infrastructures alike. Paradoxes like the Christian quasi-commandments "Thou shalt love (God, thine enemies, etc.)", or the feeling of "guilt" for things one is not actually responsible for, or the ancient experience of "sin" that "happens to" the person and yet is somehow "sin" and "soils" him, are of course closely relevant here. So much is certain that, while—as we have seen—freedom of choice is not as such a moral category at all, moral evaluation, on the other hand, as distinct from deontic moral demands, applies to many features of character and behaviour outside the range of free choice, and moral achievement clearly depends on such factors also: e.g., to a large extent, "fortitude" and some other classic "virtues".

20 In the discussion following the reading of this paper at the Royal Institute of Philosophy, a speaker (unknown to me) made the most interesting remark that, in ordinary language, an "agent" meant somebody acting on behalf of another or of others and that something of this aspect also survived in the philosophic concept of agency. I entirely agree with that suggestion. My volitive and responsible, choosing and "decreeing" or "policy-making" ego is representative of the world of concerns, interests, wants, etc., compacted in my person as a whole; and in some sense also representative, in relation with these, of the macrocosmic world of facts, forces, standards, persons and institutions that surrounds me. I believe that the institutional presuppositions of "agency" and "will" have in fact been discovered or vaguely surmised by a number of sociologically interested authors. Cf. Mr B. Mayo's analysis of agency in terms of "playing a part", in "The Moral Agent", *The Human Agent*, Royal Institute of Philosophy Lectures, I, 1966–7, London: Macmillan; and New York: St. Martin's Press, 1968, pp. 47–63.

21 A. Farrer, *The Freedom of the Will*, London, 1958, p. 106. With several other trains of thought of this pithy but somewhat diffuse book I feel to be in substantial agreement.

The Indispensability of Philosophy

AUREL KOLNAI
1947

(Translated from the Spanish by Francis Dunlop)[1]

I

Man needs philosophy because he cannot stop thinking, just as the art of cooking is indispensable because he cannot do without food. In the latter case, the only possible choice is between eating well or badly; that is, his nourishment will depend on a culinary art that is rudimentary or developed, debased or perfected—not to mention variations naturally brought about by climate, custom and individual taste. Thus, the neglect of philosophy will not result in a simple, practical life deprived of a luxury which one might indifferently acquire or do without, but in philosophical error and a life subject to erroneous ways of thinking. But because the themes of philosophy are universal and all but inescapable, and above all because truth is incompatible with error, philosophy does not allow the same diversity of *styles* as cooking and the arts in general, including the fine arts. Without denying the usefulness of free discussion or the apparent insolubility of certain of its controversies, we require thought to be just in a stricter sense even than that applicable to the arts. Certainly not all thought is "philosophical"—taking the word in its narrower sense. Again, there need be no special discipline called philosophy, or philosophers in the sense in which there are musicians, cabinetmakers, mathematicians, historians. We are not all cooks or domestics, but, since we all need to eat, we depend on the work of these useful companions and fellow-citizens. The place of philosophers in society is more modest; their number is necessarily more restricted; the benefit or harm brought about by their work reaches those it affects in a less direct and obvious way. On the other hand it is more pervasive and makes itself at a more elevated level of human consciousness; it penetrates the character and destiny of men much more profoundly. In fact, whatever else it does, man's thinking expresses, and at the same time changes, his inmost being; it exercises a vital influence on all his multifarious desires and decisions; and within the limits of nature

---

1 Kolnai wrote this paper in English, at the suggestion of Manuel Mendoza, who was studying at Laval University, Quebec, and attending Kolnai's lectures. It was published in Mexico in Mendoza's translation as "Necesidad de la Filosofía", *Estilo* (San Luis Potosí), VII, 3, 1947, pp. 151–64. The original text does not survive.

and grace, it determines his destiny. Philosophy, then, is in some way to thought what thought is to the whole of man's soul and to his conduct. If we cannot live without thinking, we cannot live without doing philosophy. The same need for the universal, the same irresistible tendency towards abstraction and generalisation, the same dependence on a conceptual hunger which drives us to reflect at the moment of action (if not always before acting), to reason about the situations that surround us, to interpret the actions of others, in a word, to permeate our practical life with speculation—all this equally compels us to reflect on the very foundations of thought, the validity of its methods, the reality of primary data, the legitimacy of presuppositions, implicit or explicit.

Even if we are not philosophers we often find ourselves impelled to convince our adversary, companion or interlocutor by means of arguments or proofs. Here begins the philosophical problem of the validity of reasoning. Sometimes we venture to affirm that such and such an action of someone who does not please us is an offence against human dignity. Thus there may arise a need to justify our criticism. Perhaps we shall have to tackle philosophical problems for the first time: What is man? In what does his dignity consist? Is such and such conduct condemned as immoral? Still, it might cause pleasure in this case, or result in a definite advantage. What, then, is the fundamental meaning of the pejorative term immoral? Perhaps a moral judgement that contradicts our desires is an irrational prejudice? If not, why not? And anyway, what is an irrational prejudice? So we habitually respect certain divine commandments? Certainty about God's existence and his having spoken to us would still not by itself justify the term "immoral". We are told, in fact, that God prescribes the Good for man. This gives rise to the philosophical problem of intrinsic good, the need to understand (even in a rudimentary form, limited to the most essential points) what is the good in itself without resorting to divine authority. Then again, how are moral obligation and the disinterested desire to study reality to be harmonised with the ordered world of physical nature and the demands of biological life? Here are purely philosophical questions that arise not from the brains of philosophers with nothing much to do, but from the lives of men as such because they have many other things to do (often without knowing how to do them), and because they find themselves overcome with remorse after doing them, suffer misfortunes or are afflicted with troubles. The discovery of the limits of philosophy, of its sterility and ineffectiveness—though this is a matter of degree—is itself a philosophical discovery, though perhaps the least fruitful of all. For a long time we have believed that there is no place for the discussion of tastes, and yet they are still discussed. The ignoramus who openly proclaims: "I am no philosopher, I merely act in accordance with..." (interest, common sense, feelings, or else, let us suppose, as a patriot, scientific worker or faithful party member would) is, in spite of himself, a philosopher of utilitarian, materialist, sceptical, traditionalist, formalist, intuitionist or some other persuasion; and in some respect or other he will rarely be free from serious philosophical error. There can be no doubt that philosophy is difficult. And in a certain sense not everyone can be a philosopher—although again it is just as true to say that nobody can cease to be one.

Let us hasten to reinforce this argument for the indispensability of philosophy by making a point of the greatest importance. The fact that philosophy is a particularly hard discipline and that its study *demands* very considerable, and at the same time highly diverse, mental powers, makes it very easy for the understanding to be seduced by crassly erroneous philosophies which are extremely dangerous for most people. It is not that man is inclined to follow error rather than truth. The point is that false philosophies (whether one-sided, simplistic, naturalistic or pseudo-sublime) are easier to grasp, and at the same time flatter comparatively uneducated spirits who are ambitious or eager for knowledge with an appearance of precision or profundity, with an *illusion* of intellectual superiority, with the lure of knowing how to unlock mysteries without too much trouble. Unless special care is taken it is a priori likely that these sophistical philosophies will flourish. If philosophical culture is neglected and matters are left here to take their natural course the result will not simply be mere deficiency—that is, an intellectual culture deprived of explicit and formally acknowledged philosophical orientation—but the growth of false philosophical doctrines, more or less worked out and more or less efficacious. The typical case will not be the man who is full of good sense though lacking the intellectual adornment that philosophical culture provides, but the man whose good sense has been weakened and diminished, if not seriously corrupted, by this or that erroneous philosophy. Pure common sense is vulnerable to attack by thinking that is formulated, considered and erected into reasoned formal doctrine, unless it can be opposed by armaments as powerful as those of the opponent. In a state of confusion, error will overcome truth if it is expressed in more exact and elegant terms; in the same way it is easier to learn to manage erroneous simplifications with a kind of formal perfection than to express common sense through rigorous and coherent reasoning. This is why, in a society whose means of communication and diffusion of ideas have been very extensively developed, we see so many individuals whose common sense is crippled; and so many others whose effective inner convictions still partly resist the specious and obnoxious doctrines they openly profess, in such a way that their souls and conduct remain superior—because they preserve a fund of badly articulated wisdom—to their reasoned thought in the strict sense. But common sense, once reduced to uncertainty by the dissolving force of ideological reflection and conceptual eloquence, cannot return to its original state of pure imperturbability. The remedy consists not in freeing it from the philosophical pretensions that have disturbed it, but in giving it the help of a true philosophy which can rehabilitate, explicitly formulate and defend it against the prestige of the sophistries that war against the essential wisdom it contains. For mere abstention from thought does not remove the temptation to think badly; the only way out is the strenuous path of rational discourse, which, as well as being just and reasonable, stays in vital contact with the main points of that thinking which is distilled in common sense and preserved in our heritage of sound traditions.

Let us now review some of the reasons why the need for philosophy is so often forgotten; or, in other words, let us look at some of the considerations adduced by those who are inclined to deny this need.

II

1. One argument against the indispensability of philosophy arises from the fact that the number of philosophers, or rather of those who receive a serious philosophical training, always remains very small in comparison with the community as a whole. There certainly are many ordinary people who have never studied philosophy, either in formal courses or in their free time, and who do not live less well on this account. It might be concluded that the discipline has never been more than a luxury confined to an unimportant élite; a luxury that society can take or leave without serious consequences. Priests, doctors, technicians, etc. are also tiny minorities, but their work interests ordinary people directly, while that of philosophers only concerns themselves and a rather insignificant number of writers and other intellectuals.

This may be so, but these intellectuals are read and listened to by large numbers of people, to whom they transmit their own ideas which contain a certain amount of philosophical reflection, even if not the actual doctrines taught them by professional philosophers. Nevertheless, this reflection is aroused and stimulated, restricted and modified, directed or to a greater or lesser degree influenced by the contact these intellectuals maintain with philosophy proper. The universal influence of philosophy on the life of men (through their own thought, and through that of the men who inspire, direct and nourish it) is no less weighty through being much more indirect than, for example, the effect of literature, or even of science itself. We certainly admit that a plain man may dispense with philosophy without serious consequences. He will have religion, the steady tradition he finds himself living under, common sense and the natural rectitude he is born with to help him in many things. But not everyone is a plain man; moreover, when things change, the plain man can easily be corrupted. There is no need to trouble him personally with philosophy, without some special reason; but, since some ideological (and hence philosophical) influences can affect him, we should provide for their not being exclusively pernicious. Most of the things that society—or man in general—needs are not absolutely indispensable to every single person; there are very many things that many people do not need in the least; but the lives of these same people depend more or less on the accessibility of these things. The same goes for the resolute *petit bourgeois*, for example, who does not feel any kind of need for philosophy and who is not thereby prevented from being honourable, or happy, or pious, or all three. However, the philosophical orientation of many groups of people—his neighbours, his friends, his professional organisation, the social strata of the people who have authority over him, etc.—will very probably make its influence felt on the conditions of his life and the environment to which his conduct has to be adapted. Thus the argument is defeated.

2. A more definite objection is that religion and not philosophy determines man's moral being and spiritual environment. From the believer's point of view it will suffice to make stronger and more enduring the impression made by the faith on men's souls, by all practical means possible; a healthy philosophy will only play its part in this programme as part of the professional training of the clergy. But we do not live today in a society that is *ex officio* Catholic—far from it. On the other hand, as history shows, even a Catholic society is vulnerable to destructive influences, both internal and external, and above all in the intellectual sphere. It cannot be doubted that man needs the faith more than he needs philosophical thinking, but the faith itself needs the latter, and not only in the minds of the clergy. To limit ourselves solely to religious or political *action* on the part of the church would be to give over to one heresy after another the greater part of the more active intelligences among us without striking a blow, since their Catholicism is not firmly anchored in principle—those who do rest on a principle would soon cease to do so through lack of intellectual armour, in spite of the institutional presence of Catholicism! In any case, we cannot allow ourselves to be indifferent to the way non-believers think. Not only because the light of Catholic wisdom may prevail with them, in some cases; but also because, even supposing they remain unbelievers all their lives, their ideological orientation will be important both because of its repercussions on the condition of the body of Catholics themselves, and also for reasons of a more general kind, such as charity and patriotism. Their mental environment will either be more or less consonant with ours, or it will be antagonistically incompatible; the philosophy prevailing in their culture will be relatively healthy—without being part of the Scholastic tradition—or, on the contrary, it will violently oppose the philosophical presuppositions of Christianity and poison healthy discernment. It is an ill-conceived piety (or in some cases a straightforward political attitude) that wishes to replace a philosophical education with measures favourable to the church or with actual religious propaganda. It is rather like wanting medicine to take the place of hygiene, or theoretical

biology to take the place of the other two; it originates in the dangerous illusion according to which the only important actions are those that have an immediate effect over a wide field.

3. It may now be objected that no philosophical system has ever changed the world. Many have been constructed, but human misfortune and human wickedness have not sensibly diminished. In general terms this is certain, and it is also true of science, education, industry, perhaps even morality. But the question is not rightly posed in these terms. The issue does not concern the re-creation of the world, but living in it—and living in a fuller sense than merely staying alive. Well then, wanting to live without philosophising amounts to an artificial impoverishment of existence, just as a life spent philosophising badly is a much more corrupted life than it need be. No philosophy will ever take the place of prudence—the art of moral and wise conduct—either in the particular case or in principle; but to be content with prudence alone, that is, with good practical action, is unworthy of man's spiritual greatness and implies a narrowing of consciousness that will not be slow to have repercussions on prudence itself. Apart from that, philosophy will do much to illuminate and guide practical reason, and a great deal to divert, undermine and destroy it. Medicine, in spite of its various notable triumphs against certain epidemics and against infant mortality, has not yet been able to extend the limits of human life imposed by nature, or to improve the anatomical or physiological constitution of the human organism. But this is no reason for suppressing medical schools. If this were done we would not only experience an immediate spread of human disasters brought about by illness as such, but also a formidable growth of charlatans and the enormous dangers attending on them. The task of philosophy is not to revolutionise existence or to redeem the human race; it is to answer man's noblest intellectual need, to contribute, above all indirectly, towards the satisfaction of some of his practical needs, and to repress the tendency towards intellectual and moral perversion inherent in his rational nature, since his reason is very imperfect and vulnerable to the attacks of pride and concupiscence. In sum, we should engage in philosophy not in order to change our life into a kind of angelic life, but to keep it at a certain level which, though possible, is not easy to reach.

On the other hand it is true that the teaching of philosophy cannot be directly and infallibly assessed, as can, for example, that of technology, or in general any kind of technical instruction. A man may have studied the rules of logic without using them fruitfully, that is to say without thinking logically on the important questions that force themselves on our lives; our knowledge of good and bad criteria does not necessarily make us competent in the discipline; to have memorised or even analysed metaphysical beliefs may not assist us much towards a profound understanding of our own nature or that of the things that surround us; it is also possible to be instructed in the rules of morality without applying them well. The teaching of philosophy is in this sense a more prodigal and less economical proceeding than any kind of technical training—though this does not mean there is less need for it. A director or manager of some kind must also have assimilated more knowledge—much of which he will never apply—than a manual labourer; this clearly does not imply that a society does not need bosses or that it can be exclusively composed of labourers. That which is essentially more indirect, more fortuitous, more fraught with elements which can remain lifeless, less concentrated on what is indispensable, in a word less immediately applicable, is not for this reason less important. We need not only what is of everyday and, so to speak, primary use, but also that reserve of knowledge and intellectual habits to which we can recur when pressed by less predictable situations. Does that mean that the number of true philosophers graduating from philosophy departments will be very small? Less, in proportion, to that of good engineers trained in the technical departments? Without a doubt; but those who rate efficiency above everything else—seeing it as a favourable balance between money or energy invested in an enterprise and the yield or profit that results—will end by stripping life of all nobility and charity. Thankless tasks, such as that of combating a dangerous sickness which demands a very difficult and costly treatment, and which rarely spares the patient, are not inferior or insignificant in human terms. If the teaching of philosophy in one country has made possible the development of a dozen considerable speculative talents in the course of one generation; if, during the same period, it has preserved a few hundred active intelligences from falling into pernicious errors—and thus neutralising the deadly influence of those pseudo-philosophic styles or doctrinal perversions very directly applicable to real life—it has sufficiently justified its existence. We should not expect from such teaching the mass-production of Platos and Aristotles, or the endowment of society as it exists with a platonic or other kind of utopia. Besides, philosophical culture can be of considerable use even to those fleetingly exposed to it. To know how to judge well in any class of activities where thinking is essential, one needs to keep one's intellect at a high level through the attitude of rigorous reflection characteristic of philosophy, which is the abstract science of objects inserted just as they are in reality. There is another attitude of rigorous thought no less necessary for the training of high-level understanding, characteristic of mathematics, the science of objects reduced to pure quantity and extracted from their real locations. Without a mathematical preparation, it is not possible to acquire the habit of exact thought; without preparation in philosophy it is impossible to apply this habit to reality without losing one's way in arbitrary constructions which do violence to reality while appearing to explain it. Neither can be a substitute for the other. The gift of rigorous thought reveals itself more gloriously in mathematics; in philosophy it is more integrally invested with its character of seriousness.

4. Lastly, we ought to consider a more general and profound counterargument: a fashionable sophism which says that all products of thought are powerless before real life and which supposes that all men are naturally and exclusively obedient either to their interests, which smother all ideals, or to their feelings or inclinations, which rebel against any rational influence.

It is obvious that these two varieties of Naturalism contradict each other. In fact, if a man governs himself in everything by the calculus of interests, he acts with the help of reason and not at the mercy of blind passion or emotional prejudice; on the contrary, if he is not capable of resisting the immediate impulses of sensual or passionate desire, he would not be able to pursue his interests, since this presupposes the inhibition of immediate desires and a mutual adjustment of wants in the light of reason. This does not prevent one of the two theories being true, or the possibility of working out some sort of compromise between them, based on the principle they have in common. This common principle, this point of convergence between the two versions of Naturalism, is as follows: we always obey the impulses deriving from our vital instincts; in the numerous cases where they conflict, it is the stronger impulse which prevails; some very constant and well-established impulses work prospectively through the intelligence and constitute interest-types—such as the material interest, a classic example, which represents the instinct of preservation and is actively present even in those moments when we are neither hungry nor cold—which change in their turn into permanent impulses. This has led to the conclusion that man, at least, does not possess a truly rational nature: his movements do not result from objective consideration and appraisal of things, but from compulsive desires, among which are those recurring ones moulded into interest-types. The result is that he cannot be influenced by logical argument, rational discussion, objective considerations, or by the philosophical clarification of those problems— purely technical matters of the choice of means, where the end is fixed beyond any dispute, and which admit of and demand rational argument—but by seductive promises and sonorous and picturesque propaganda. As for the truths of philosophy and the values of morality or culture, these simply amount to ideology, slogans and rhetoric which disguise interests and express desires in words more dignified and impressive than the simple formulae "I desire this" or "I want that".

The attractive thing about this perverse doctrine resides in the satisfaction it affords to pride and the thirst for power. The idea that we have unmasked the true motives of human conduct and reduced the spiritual complexity of man to a mechanism of interests or a bundle of animal desires, that the world and human nature itself are, as it were, at our feet—all this is really very agreeable to our pride. The claim to manage the human material from behind the scenes, as it were, as though we could determine the functioning of some apparatus whose secret we possess, is equally a way of fashioning for ourselves an illusion of omnipotence.

Like most perverse theories, this one is also not unrelated to certain real facts which seem to justify it. These facts can be summarily reduced to three kinds: (i) It is certain that our animal needs are, up to a point, imperious and urgent, and that they have a kind of primacy over more refined wants. If a man is oppressed by hunger, he can only think about finding food, since if he does not get it he is certain to die very soon. His need to understand things, on the other hand, can be long denied satisfaction without occasioning such serious disorders. Hence the piece of sophistry that we can do nothing else at bottom than look for food and drink, at least in order to secure our future survival and perhaps that of our children. (ii) It is equally true that our choices in general do not allow for the methodical application of a single scale of philosophically systematised values, and that they can obstinately resist the philosophical arguments which seem to demonstrate their lack of foundation. Hence the erroneous belief in the omnipotence of feeling and the sovereignty of prejudice, inaccessible to all reasoning and irrefutably triumphant over discussion and argument. (iii) In the third place, it is no less true that ideologies frequently conceal egoistic interests and irrational intentions, or motives that are in general alien to the reasons put forward to support them. In the same way, if I show myself indignant at some injury to my person, it can be that my anger was really caused by the conduct of someone who, though disagreeable to me, has not offended against a single one of my legitimate rights. This everyday occurrence is the origin of the diabolical claim that all rights are merely convenient fictions for those who profit by them and that the very concepts of objective good and evil are merely words we use to give more force to our preferences and to impose on others what pleases us and prevent what we find displeasing.

The classic reply to this naturalistic heresy appeals to the same phenomenon as it finds itself obliged to admit by implication—the imperative need man feels to *justify* his conduct and beliefs in objective terms. The human imperfection we are fully conscious of is a sign of the rudimentary perfection of which we are capable; abuse presupposes legitimate use; deception claims the esteem possessed by virtue. We are weak, beyond any dispute; but this very fact demonstrates the existence in us of something more than mere weakness which is the cause of our discontent. Generally speaking we do think badly, but we do think, and it is only a certain possibility of doing it well that allows us to discover the degree to which we are inclined to think erroneously. We are always ready to identify our own cause with the objectively just cause: yes—precisely because it can be a just one; our claim is not necessarily false, and even if it is, the just cause is not necessarily that of our adversary!

We have already shown that the very existence of interests is a proof of man's fundamental rationality. It is clear that when rationality does signify "interests"—this is its strict and classic meaning—it simply refers to the choice of technical means in the service of fixed and permanent ends. But ends and means cannot be completely separated; a particular mean, once chosen, acquires the status of intermediate end, while every concrete and definite end is, in its turn, a means to some superior end which is more constant and more universal—a series culminating in the end that is the "good life", or "perfection". Thus rational thinking in our lives does not stop short at means—in which case it would fail to exercise any intrinsic influence over our wills; the directive influence of reason over appetite necessarily transcends the sphere of mere technique. This remains true in spite of the evident fact that reason alone does not as such determine any of our ends; it is desire, not reason itself, that moves me to acquire purely speculative knowledge. On the other hand, the power of our immediate desires and impulses of feeling, in the broad sense of the term, continually proves itself master of our long-term interests, and these latter really come to form a minority among the things that move us. In fact, when we come to consider the social character of our existence, together with the enormous variety of our social relations, we find it practically impossible to define our interests without having recourse to various motives that go beyond the sphere of interests, considered as aspects of self-preservation: in this further sense there are Catholic interests because there are Catholics, Irish interests—for example in the United States—because there is a group of people who bear such a quasi-national identity, and so on. None of these factors of identity, cohesion, grouping or division, even when they give rise to systems of interest, can be reduced to biological or economic interests in the strict sense of the word. But again, the tremendous range of our impulses, feelings, desires, passions and prejudices demands the ordering function of reason: we could not live without a certain mutual confrontation of our motives, predilections and judgements of value; this implies the necessity of second-order judgement—confirming, justifying, inhibiting, sanctioning, revising, condemning, putting out of action, as the case may be—from a higher level, like that of reflective reason. Nor do we first blindly follow our various affective promptings—a kind of primary matter that issues from some hidden cavity of the subconscious without the intervention of reason—and then all at once submit them to rational purification. On the contrary, our sentiments and predilections, erroneous and wicked though they can sometimes be, find themselves from the beginning more or less clearly directed by our rational activities. It is certainly true that reason is ordained to the satisfaction of many of our appetites, even though they come from our animal nature; but taken together—and in fact in every individual case at least to some extent—our appetites presuppose thought, since our nature is not only animal but also rational. It is precisely this that gives rise to a large number of the injustices and mistakes, errors and inconsistencies, that are part of our impulsive and affective lives. These are not the product of an animal nature which lacks reason, but of the abuse or clouding of reason by the violence of passion and of quasi-animal and quasi-vegetable habits such as intellectual sloth itself.

Let us take an example. There is someone we detest. It will be very hard for us to avoid thinking of him in abusive terms, describing him, as the case may be, as a bad lot, a traitor, knave, egoist, fool, vulgarian, and so on; even the vague term "disagreeable" suggests an objective disvalue present in him, which goes beyond anything that can be verified from the subjective *fact* of our current aversion. It may then turn out that all our accusations are objectively mistaken and that we really dislike the man because he rightly prevented some project we were about to bring off, or because he accidentally reminds us of some other disagreeable person or situation. Even in this case our attitude is not simply an animal one; it implies an aspect of misused and corrupted rationality, which makes it particularly false and reprehensible. Yet this fact also makes it in some way modifiable by right reason, either through personal reflection after the event, or through the counsels of a third party. Reason *can* lead us to moderate or even subdue our hostility towards this man, or to hate him, at least in silence, without the false solemnity of indignation or the active will to injure him. This alone would point to a considerable victory. On the other hand it could also be that the terms we use to express our dislike of the man are objectively unjustifiable, and at the same time we have a sufficient reason to despise him, but one that is too complex or difficult to express adequately in the moulds of current usage. Our conceptual or verbal apparatus does not approach the level of our good sense, or our instinct, or even our powers of apprehension, which nevertheless presuppose an impressive store of reason condensed and active, if imperfectly articulated: reason functioning soundly, but weakly and feebly. Some intellectual illumination, almost approaching the level of formal philosophy if you will, would be of enormous value in such a case. While it is morally permissible to hate a man—and in a certain sense praiseworthy, since it is good to hate what is real, in so far as it is the incarnation of evil, even though this is never true in an absolute sense—we are now doing so in full consciousness of our motive. This is now expressed in terms which are intelligible, communicable and convincing, in a steadier and perhaps more effective way, without falling into unjust exaggeration or exposing ourselves to valid objections which would confound us and probably drive us into an attitude of unhealthy hatred, which would be the more stubborn the less likely it would be to awaken the sympathy and approval of sensible people. It is nonetheless possible that this intellectual clarification of the situation brings us to a rational discussion of the matter with the person of our example, and by its means to clarify our hostility once and for all: if, for example, it is a matter of a definite error which we are in a position to formulate with justice and precision, it may be that we shall attain our end of convincing him of it. This would be the best outcome, since truth itself, like every good and every virtue, is ordained to charity, though this does not at all mean that evil ought to be denied or excused.

The analysis of this hypothetical case could be continued in its ramifications and more subtle aspects, or more examples could be adduced. This would not alter, but rather confirm, the one conclusion that interests us here: whether we like it or not, we are thinking beings—to wish for the falsity of this would be an evil in itself—hence we are constrained and called to improve and to cultivate our minds, which are the scene of many kinds of activity which go far beyond the sphere of rigorous philosophy but which necessarily include it. We are neither free to lower our condition so far as to refuse to follow objective truth and to try to bring reason into our practical attitudes, nor can we in the least, by simply renouncing our intellectuality, withdraw ourselves from the temptations of error and the traps to which the natural weakness of our thinking—increased and exploited by our moral corruption—exposes us at every step. We must try, as a consequence, to heal our intellectual powers and keep encouraging ourselves by soundly affirming our knowledge of things and our search for their interrelations. The function of a systematic and explicit philosophy, which is rooted in an organic tradition of teaching, without excluding certain freer marginal activities, is as follows: to keep in living contact with the philosophical elements of the other disciplines and the life of culture; to rest, above all, on the Christian tradition and on the inexhaustible wisdom which, though insufficient and ill-equipped for controversy, is contained in common sense. Philosophy will never rank with this good sense, nor with the faith and the tradition which contains it. Nevertheless, even if philosophy were only of use in arming those values with the weapons they could not forge for themselves, it would still perform an indispensable function.

II. PAPERS ABOUT KOLNAI'S WORK

1. Introductory

Kolnai's Mature Political Philosophy

LEE CONGDON

I

On November 25, 1940, Aurel and Elisabeth Kolnai boarded an American ship in Lisbon and set sail for the New World. They were to pass the ensuing four and a half years in New York and Cambridge, Massachusetts. "I was", Kolnai subsequently observed, "a misfit in America", in part, no doubt, because he was so pitifully unsuited for gainful employment. Eventually he did secure some translation commissions from the Office of War Information, but it was largely due to Elisabeth, who sewed buttons on military uniforms, designed goods to be sold in handicraft shops, and laboured in factories, that they were able to eke out an existence.[1]

There was, however, a deeper reason for Kolnai's discontent with life in the United States, namely his distaste for the American religion of Democracy. This came as something of a surprise to him, for he had long considered himself to be a democrat, even a social democrat; indeed, he had joined the Austrian Social Democratic Party in 1930 and expressed enough optimism with regard to the Soviet "experiment" that the Left Book Club made *The War against the West* one of its selections. Living in America, however, had convinced him that it was constitutional liberty, not equality, that he valued, and that democracy as egalitarianism tended

> to react adversely on constitutionalism, in that it undermines the qualitative, intellectual and moral foundations of rational and responsible citizenship, and thus invites demagogic tyranny and popular dictatorship, which we may or may not choose still to call 'democracy'.[2]

Nor did "the machinery" of checks and balances help much, for it operated in a society too indifferent to custom and too susceptible to popular pressures to serve as a suitable matrix for constitutional liberty.

That liberty, Kolnai concluded, depended upon

> the pluralistic idea of a hierarchical, manifoldly organised society, in which the central power, preferably Monarchy, has a strong substance of its own but is neither spiritually sovereign nor omnipotent in its action.[3]

This conception, it did not take him long to recognise, brought to mind the Habsburg Monarchy during its more constitutional moments. Toward the end of World War II, therefore, he began to lobby for a post-war "Danubian Federal Empire" modelled after old Austria–Hungary, writing in the Colorado-based *Journal of Central European Affairs*:

> That Austrian symbiosis of nationalities amounted to an experiment in supra-national government *after* the awakening of national consciousness which was, though less successful, far more interesting and possibly of greater spiritual importance than the British, the Swiss, or the Soviet one. For it lacked the comparative linguistic homogeneity of the British Commonwealth; its scope was very much larger and the task involved very much more delicate than is the case with Switzerland; and instead of resting on a foundation of totalitarian dictatorship it was undertaken in a sphere of considerable, though not complete, constitutional liberty.[4]

The notion of a resurrected monarchy failed to impress Oszkár Jászi,[5] the Hungarian-born left-liberal whom Kolnai revered as a father figure and model of intellectual and moral integrity. Having accepted a position at Oberlin College in 1925, Jászi could appreciate his devoted follower's disappointment with democracy in America, but he could not approve of his move to the political Right. He was particularly chagrined to learn that by setting a moral example he had contributed to Kolnai's disenchantment with the Left.[6]

To be sure, Jászi conceded that he, too, dissented from many particulars in the contemporary leftist creed and that on numerous points he stood closer to Kolnai than to his political friends. But he made it clear that he could muster little sympathy for a political outlook that was rooted in Catholic dogma. Although, he wrote to Kolnai, he too believed in eternal and absolute values—he was a proponent of Natural Law theory—he did not think that any man or institution could lay claim to being their permanent depository. "That is, I reject every possible conception of papal infallibility. I am not willing to sacrifice my freedom of conscience to any man or any institution!"[7]

Jászi was mistaken in his belief that Kolnai had sacrificed his intellect on the Church of Rome's altar. It was true, however, that in America he had become a more emphatic Catholic—and for a simple reason. In the 1940s, Catholics were more likely than other Americans to offer some resistance to mass democracy and to the cult of the "Common Man", he who lacked any particular distinction and yet had no betters. Such a Man was self-assertive because he took Humanity to be himself writ large; his needs were those of all men, his will the General Will. There was no objective natural or moral order to which he considered himself to be subject;

he would obey only his own subjective and arbitrary will as it was revealed to, and imposed upon, him by a state power which embodied it.

The Common Man's will, in its identity with the General Will, was absolute; it was, so to say, the will of God. Such a Man, Kolnai was later to write, was Man Deified—"Man above whom is set no Order, no Power, no Being essentially different from him, impervious to his reason, independent of his will".[8] But that was only another way of saying that the Common Man was self-enslaved Man, Man living under the most thoroughgoing form of despotism.

Clearly, then, life in the United States had converted Kolnai "to a creed of conservative constitutionalism or a conservative conception of Liberty as distinct from Liberalism or Progressive Democracy".[9] What he hoped to see conserved, that is, was the right-wing liberalism of Burke and Tocqueville—a liberalism that differed from the left-wing variety in that it was anti-democratic and securely tied to the traditions of Christian civilisation.

Kolnai left no doubt that his conception of liberty was Burkean rather than Benthamite or Millian in character. In his view, liberty was not secured by a few clear laws or simple principles, but by a densely complex society in which power was divided and jurisdictions overlapped, where the habits of liberty, disciplined by a respect for objective moral law, were deeply engrained, where hierarchies proliferated, and where privilege was the token of a limited state authority that made no claim to be the executor of a uniform and tyrannical General Will.

II

Kolnai always insisted that political philosophy should not be confused with moral philosophy. He did not mean, of course, that those who exercised political power were somehow relieved of ordinary moral responsibility; quite the contrary, in fact. They could not justify immoral actions by appealing to some vision of a world made perfect. "No vision of an ultimate good or goodness or perfection of mankind", he wrote, "can be justified in blurring the standards of good and evil as applicable to the intrinsic quality of my actions."[10] The politician's first duty, like that of the non-politician, was to obey the moral law.

Morality, then, set limits to political *means*, but it did not prescribe political *ends*, except perhaps in such general terms as "the well-being of members of the community". Political purposes were practical in nature and although they sometimes involved moral issues, they related most often to non-moral matters, including the mutual adjustment of conflicting interests. Conflicts of interest did present difficulties, but they constituted an ineradicable part of an imperfect, a finite, reality. Political wisdom therefore resided in a recognition of the inevitability of human imperfection and an ability to distinguish it from evil. "Imperfections resented as evils",

Kolnai warned, "will be interfered with too much, and this means that the comparative importance of existing genuine evils will be underrated, and, worse, that new and greater evils will recklessly be wrought."[11]

It was precisely, Kolnai argued, the refusal to tolerate imperfection or to accept the basic structure of reality that typified the "utopian mind". Like Michael Polányi, whose work he read with care and profit, he maintained that utopianism was a product of extravagant moral demands, a fierce determination to compress Is into Ought, Value into Reality, until they became one and the same. Just as revealing, utopians did not direct attention to the moral perfection of individuals but to that of "society". Individuals working for the cause were absolved for violations of the moral law on the ground that the end—the once for all elimination of imperfection—sanctified any means. And then, once heaven had been brought to earth, morality would simply collapse into practice; everyone would automatically act in morally perfect ways, by definition as it were.

Such a utopian attitude found its fullest contemporary expression in Communist totalitarianism. According to Kolnai, Communists in particular misjudged human imperfection as intolerable evil and remained ignorant of the fact that moral values were phenomenologically given in reality. The overturning of reality in its totality did, as Burke noted, "remove some grievance",[12] but Marxist-Leninists were then left without any moral guidance but Party dictation. In the effort to achieve perfection they destroyed the many goods that made life, despite its limitations and imperfections, worth the living.

It was for that reason, Kolnai argued in a 1957 article he published in Spain, that Hungarians took up arms in 1956. They did not have a new political doctrine to propound; they were not trying to replace socialism with capitalism or to restore monarchy. Theirs was a great rejection, a negative movement against the evils of utopianism. "The uprising against Communist oppression stands against tyranny and for 'normal life'. It was not against the existence of the state or the 'deviationist' or 'treasonous' executors of the Communist utopia; no, it fought against the Communist utopia itself."[13] In sum, the Hungarian rebels recognised what elsewhere he called "the thematic primacy of moral evil".

Like W. D. Ross, whose moral philosophy he much admired, Kolnai regarded the duty of "non-maleficence" as theoretically and existentially primary.[14] He did so because he had concluded that moral experience was "in the first place an experience of evil and of the 'signposts', 'taboos' or 'interdicts' which warn us of its presence".[15] The moral consciousness dwelt far more on an evil done than on a good left undone; it did not suffer loss of sleep because its possessor was not a saint, but it did endure feelings of guilt when its possessor broke a promise, betrayed a trust, or uttered a lie. The latter evil, as Aleksandr Solzhenitsyn has argued convincingly, corrupted personal as well as political life in Communist states.

III

To be sure, Communism was not the only form taken by the utopian mind. Though less totalitarian in outlook, Karl Mannheim's theory of planning struck Kolnai as tainted by utopianism. And so did the Christian-left ideas of his old friend and interwar mentor, Karl Polányi.[16] Nor, for that matter, were all *soi-disant* "conservatives" free of the contagion. Kolnai distanced himself from those whom he characterised as "reactionary utopians", those who glorified a past time and place to such an extent that they regarded all criticism as sacrilegious. He even found fault with so judicious a conservative thinker as Michael Oakeshott, who, in his judgement, failed

> to notice the point of kinship between the sham rationality that attaches to the reckless impatience and the infatuation for mechanical models of the "progressive" rationalism against which he inveighs, and the sham rationality no less inevitably produced by retrograde and self-insulating traditionalism anxious to hold its own against the corrosive action of the critical spirit.[17]

The conservatism that he himself wished to defend was critical and reformist. It was to political philosophy what British intuitionism and Austrian/German material value ethics were to moral philosophy. Like those approaches to ethics, political conservatism, rightly understood, regarded reality as good enough to bear within it a vast array of moral values, but poor enough to require critical scrutiny and reform. Differently put, true conservatives had first to accept reality as the bearer of tradition, just as moral intuitionists accepted the "moral consensus" that crystallised the collective moral wisdom and insight of people in all times and places. At the same time, they had to subject tradition to rational criticism, just as intuitionists had to deploy conscience against discreet aspects of the moral consensus. The reciprocal relationship between tradition and rational critique paralleled that between moral consensus and conscience.

> That [moral] consensus [Kolnai wrote] is not accurately or exhaustively represented by any specified system, creed, person or collective. It is laid down in the universe of moral intuitions, traditions and codes, which are necessarily incomplete and fraught with ambiguities and inadequacies, and are therefore in need of being interpreted, supplemented, re-stated and re-emphasised by Conscience.[18]

Not surprisingly, Kolnai listed as critical conservatives such right-wing liberals as Burke, Tocqueville, Wilhelm Röpke, and Raymond Aron.[19] All of them accepted the traditional order without succumbing to an uncritical obscurantism; all of them professed the "conservative conception of reform" that Kolnai had first discovered in the work of G. K. Chesterton, who brought him to see

> that change cannot be evaluated, nor, consequently valued, except in the framework of permanent standards; that progress not only demands a setting of conservation historically but presupposes it logically; that an active work of reform depends less on intellectual innovation than on intellectual constancy; that discontent sustained enough to be operative requires patience, which is to say, content at a deeper level.[20]

Interestingly enough, Kolnai discovered in Karl Popper, who stood to his political left, a persuasive and important exponent of a "critical tradition".[21] He may well have met the Austrian during the interwar, at Karl Polányi's Vienna flat; he did meet him at the London School of Economics in the early 1950s. At that time, Popper reproached him for seeking a haven in Roman Catholicism but described *The War against the West* as a "great book".[22] More important, he wrote a remarkably strong letter on Kolnai's behalf to the grant-awarding Society for the Protection of Science and Learning:

> I have the highest opinion of him both as a thinker and as a person of the highest integrity. He has also great personal charm—for me, at least... He is a very original thinker, and an extremely unusual one, and for this reason also an unusual person... My main point is that I personally think I could learn more from Kolnai, by way of stimulation, than from any other thinker in the field of political philosophy alive.[23]

For his part, Kolnai thought Popper too much the humanist and democrat but admired the famous philosopher's "radical rejection of totalitarianism" and "theory of piecemeal reform".[24] In particular he agreed with Popper's admonition to "work for the elimination of concrete evils rather than for the realisation of abstract goods",[25] for that was the political expression of the thematic primacy of moral evil. All in all, Popper seemed to him to understand, far better than most left-wing liberals, the importance of tradition as well as of a critical engagement with it.[26]

NOTES

1 Aurel Kolnai, *Political Memoirs*, ed. Francesca Murphy, Lanham, Maryland: Lexington Books, 1999, pp. 194–95.

2 *Ibid.*, p. 203.
3 *Ibid.*, p. 204.
4 Aurel Kolnai, "Danubia: A Survey of Plans for Solution", *Journal of Central European Affairs*, III, 4 (1944): 452.
5 Oszkár Jászi's letter to Aurel Kolnai, September 24, 1942, in "'Sorai ismét választ követelnek': Jászi Oszkár és Kolnai Aurél levelezéséből", *Világosság*, XXXVIII, 5–6 (1997): 84–85.
6 Aurel Kolnai's letter to Oszkár Jászi, September 15, 1942, in ibid., p. 79.
7 Oszkár Jászi's letter to Aurel Kolnai, September 24, 1942, in ibid., pp. 84–85.
8 Aurel Kolnai, "The Meaning of the 'Common Man'", *The Thomist*, XII, 3 (1949): 318.
9 Kolnai, *Political Memoirs*, p. 208.
10 Aurel Kolnai, *The Utopian Mind and Other Papers: A Critical Study in Moral and Political Philosophy*, ed. Francis Dunlop, London: Athlone, 1995, p. 121.
11 Ibid., p. 111.
12 Edmund Burke, *Reflections on the Revolution in France*, Harmondsworth: Penguin Books, 1969, p. 374.
13 Aurel Kolnai, "Gondolatok a magyar felkelésről egy év távlatából", *Világosság*, XXXVIII, 5–6 (1997): 116.
14 See W. D. Ross, *The Right and the Good*, Indianapolis: Hackett Publishing Company, 1988, p. 22.
15 Aurel Kolnai, "The Thematic Primacy of Moral Evil", *The Philosophical Quarterly*, VI, 22 (1956): 27.
16 Aurel Kolnai, "Konservatives und revolutionäres Ethos", in Gerd-Klaus Kaltenbrunner (ed.), *Rekonstruktion des Konservatismus*, Freiburg: Verlag Rombach, 1972, p. 111n. English translation in Daniel J. Mahoney (ed.), *Privilege and Liberty and Other Essays in Political Philosophy by Aurel Kolnai*, Lanham, Md: Lexington Books, 1999. The reference is in note 15, pp. 161–62.
17 Aurel Kolnai, "Rationalism in Politics", *Philosophy*, XL, 151 (1965): 69–70. Also in Daniel J. Mahoney (ed.), p. 169.
18 Aurel Kolnai, *Ethics, Value, and Reality: Selected Papers*, ed. Francis Dunlop and Brian Klug, London: Athlone, 1977 and Indianapolis: Hackett Publishing Company, 1978, p. 19.
19 See Kolnai, "Konservatives und revolutionäres Ethos", p. 100n., and trans. in Mahoney (ed.), note 5, p 159; *The Utopian Mind*, p. vii.
20 Kolnai, *Political Memoirs*, p. 114.
21 Kolnai, "Konservatives und revolutionäres Ethos", p. 107 n., and trans. in Mahoney (ed.), note 11, p. 160.
22 Karl Popper's letter to Aurel Kolnai, January 5, 1954, Aurel Kolnai Papers, in the possession of Dr. Francis Dunlop. I am grateful to Dr. Dunlop and to Professor David Wiggins for allowing me to quote from the Kolnai Papers.
23 Cited in Gábor Palló, "Kolnai Aurél és Karl Popper", *Világosság*, XXXVIII, 5–6 (1997): 48n.
24 Aurel Kolnai's letter to his cousin, George Lányi, December 1952, Aurel Kolnai Papers.
25 Karl R. Popper, *Conjectures and Refutations: The Growth of Scientific Knowledge*, London: Routledge and Kegan Paul, 1963, p. 361.
26 See Popper, "Towards a Rational Theory of Tradition", in *ibid.*, pp. 120–35.

The Ethical Theories
of Aurel Kolnai

JOHN D. BEACH

Apart from those who knew him personally, it is doubtful that many attribute to Aurel Kolnai the importance that the penetration and fineness of his thought merited. To a degree this may have been the case because he lacked, by choice and by chance, an enduring group identity—doctrinal, ideological, cultural and national. Born in Budapest of Jewish parents in 1900, he was throughout the Great War strongly pro-Ally. Following the war he went to the University of Vienna, where he earned a D. Phil. from both the philosophy and history faculties (Schlick, Gomperz and von Mises were among his teachers). Later, he studied under Edmund Husserl and Martin Honecker in Freiburg. In the mid-twenties, influenced by G. K. Chesterton (whom he saw as a phenomenologist) and the German Phenomenological School of Philosophy, he was converted to Catholicism. Despite numerous philosophical publications, both books and articles, until 1945 he chose to be a writer and journalist rather than an academic. His writings dealt with many matters, ranging from political events in Germany and Austria, the thoughts of Belloc and Chesterton, and the "rule of money" in democracy, to the relationship between Fascism and Bolshevism, the ideology of progress, and the meaning of racial obsession. His approach was frequently polemical. After years of effort (one locale of which was a Vienna coffeehouse frequented by Austrian Nazis), he completed and saw published *The War against the West*, a brilliant study of Nazi doctrines and policies. Up to the end of the thirties he was, politically, sympathetic toward democratic socialism, but, among other things, the proclamation by a "progressive" association of French *lycée* teachers that the West did not have the moral right to defend itself against Hitler's Germany caused a change of view, and he became what today would be called a neo-conservative, that is, a supporter of a liberal, capitalist, and, institutionally at any rate, democratic society. During the war, after internment in France and escape through Spain and Portugal, he and his wife Elisabeth found refuge in America, where he worked in journalism and for the Office of War Information. From 1945 to 1955 he taught in the Faculty of Philosophy, Laval University, after a short time as *professeur agrégé*. At Laval, reasonably enough, his thought took on a Thomistic cast, although he was critical of the approach to St. Thomas prevailing there. A resident of London from 1955 until his death in 1973, he was Visiting Lecturer in Ethics and Political Philosophy at Bedford College. During this period his philosophical endeavours acquired an "analytic" style, this being facilitated by a perceived agreement in theme between phenomenology and the British analytic school. From 1945 on he contributed an abundance of articles in philosophy to various journals in America, Canada and England, and on the Continent, in English, French, German and Spanish, all of which, in addition to Hungarian, he spoke and wrote with distinction and native adeptness. He frequently read papers in England and abroad, and was Visiting Professor of Philosophy at Marquette University in 1968.

In 1977 there appeared a volume of his papers, most previously published, edited by two former students of his at Bedford College, Mr. Brian Klug and Dr. Francis Dunlop, with a preface by Bernard Williams of Cambridge and David Wiggins of Bedford.[1] Its purpose was to achieve a better balance between his accomplishments and public appreciation of them. The selections cover only his London period, but they are representative works of someone who was, above all and at all times, an unyielding foe of those who would debase the central features of human existence. The themes of the collection are many. A pervasive one is the perversity in assigning a near-divine status to human appetite. Another, closely related, is the wrong-headedness of egalitarianism, though he acknowledged its underlying moral urges. A third, also related to absolute humanism, is the threat posed by utopian dogmas. Yet another is the error of a wholly rationalistic conception of ethics, the belief that one can and ought to demonstrate the basic tenets of a consciously moral life. Each of these points is found, openly or implicitly, in the conclusion to part I of the volume's most important work, "Morality and Practice", here published for the first time. Speaking of the inevitable failure "to cope conclusively with the question 'Why should I be moral?'", he holds that such a failure

> may make the philosopher sensitive to a rationalistic-naturalistic misdirection always latent in ethical speculation: the mirage, that is, of a necessary goodness of Man—or of every Will—and of evil as a mere appearance. Behind the claim of "proving" to me that I "should" be moral there is at work the fond hope, self-contradictory and Utopian, imbued with an atmosphere of all-goodness and all evil in its implications, of demonstrating that I *cannot but* be moral even though some of my operations are ill-conceived and harmful owing to error, inadvertence or technical disability. The practical conclusion to which this speculative schema would point is excessive mildness in dealing with immoral conduct and boundless tyranny in dealing with people, that is, the policy of cleansing the world from evil and fashioning it in a

moral mould once for all, by a comprehensive plan of coercion, need-gratification, indoctrination, training and selective elimination.[2]

Clearly, Kolnai did not see as a product of chance the co-presence within today's dominant totalitarian systems of a rationalism run amuck in the structuring of society, the toleration, indeed state-sponsorship, of life-destroying personal behaviour, the coercion operating at the social level, the purges of those who resist, and the offering of a future in which the gratification of spontaneous human desires is the culminating condition of the cosmos.

Kolnai also sets himself the task of probing and judging existentialist conceptions of ethical being, principally those of Sartre and Heidegger. One target is what he terms the Idol of Authenticity, the insistence that a person must unqualifiedly shape himself, never submitting to "objective" values, even those of his own making. The difficulties that he finds within the Sartrean formulation of this scheme are several:

> If I am free, my craving to evade freedom and sell myself into the bondage of "thingness", to forge myself a mystifying network of objective goods, values, rules, standards and determinants of all kinds, also springs from my freedom. And if, apparently, freedom does not take kindly to itself, why not allow it the freedom to undergo limitations and indulge its thirst for solidification and reification?…Further, what is wrong with shams, dodges, ungenuineness and artificiality? Why not choose these freely, rather than seek with desperate monotony to display my untainted freedom by an endless string of "gratuitous" choices, that is, by trying always to obey one vacuous principle instead of actually choosing x for being a greater good than y, and then z because it is an obligation, or *non-q* because q is evil? And if insincerity *is* wrong, is it wrong because my freedom has so decreed? Hardly. But why then assent just to this one moral intuition or divine commandment or deduction from the utility principle or socially established standard, and not to others as well? Should it be simply because Sartre has so chosen *pour les autres*, including me? But are not all general and immutable principles a fake, and might he not (perhaps ought he not to) choose anew and differently at any moment?[3]

However, the basic objection that Kolnai has to these thinkers' doctrines is found here:

> Sartre's exposure of the modes of "bad faith" and Heidegger's analogous critique of *das Man*, that is, of man's ordinary consciousness thriving in the medium of civil society, while rich in pertinent insights and, beyond psychology, relevant also to ethics, breathe the sterile

spirit of nihilism in that they ultimately attack, not so much an erroneous doctrine or a specified kind of morally inferior conduct, as
human existence itself—which in its main body is first and foremost,
unalterably, everyday existence—and aim at invalidating the moral
demands which arise *in the context* of that existence.[4]

A related flaw is also to be discerned. While they would claim "that the
whole treasure of decencies and loyalties" that often guide men is "no better than a homogeneous fabric of sham", the "authentic" act can at best
embody the standard principles of moral action:

> the extraordinary, "marginal", heroic and "gratuitous" feats of authen-
> ticity, apart from being in strictness impossible—for the "freedom"
> man is doomed to is empty and unsubstantial, since he can neither
> attain to divinity nor be sanctified by a non-existent God—themselves
> depend, for such meaning as they may be credited with, on tradition-
> ally approved principles and concerns, like sincerity, benevolence,
> courage and the welfare of mankind.[5]

Kolnai has no more favourable a view of conventional relativism. In the
paper "Erroneous Conscience" he calls attention to the fact that advocacy of relativism precludes devotion to any one set of values. In his words,
"the philosophical relativism of 'several moralities equally justified' is
incompatible with actual adherence to one of *these* alleged moralities".[6]
One reviewer has questioned Kolnai's claim here, but its soundness is not
difficult to grasp. Relativism asserts that no moral doctrine or judgment is
simply valid, that is, that none expresses an intrinsic value that is objectively given. On the other hand, adherence to a particular ethic is to
declare that a value is so given. The inconsistency of the two positions is
thus evident. The attempt to dissolve the inconsistency through recourse
to a qualifying "it is so given *to me*" would amount to the admission that
it is not so given, that you now realize the subjective or culture-bound status of the moral datum that in a less controlled spirit you overlooked, and
so abandon the ethic to which you had carelessly subscribed.

In another paper Kolnai argues at greater length against the creed of
relativism. Its title is "Moral Consensus", and its major points are that,
one, there is substantial agreement among men on moral questions; and,
two, without such agreement we would very likely succumb to a radical
disorientation. The first point naturally calls for a consideration of its
doctrinal denial. This denial, he insists, is at its

> crudest...prone to confuse the prevailing *practice* of men with their
> prevailing moral *appreciations.* It would only accept the fact of moral
> consensus if it saw the terrestrial world superseded by a uniform heav-

en of saints (or perhaps a uniform abode of the damned, under the sign of either *Lasciate ogni speranza* or *Evil, be thou my Good*). It tends to identify moral decay with a "new morality" and *mores* with morals.[7]

He also observes that the corollary of the position, cultural determinism (like relativism, it stems directly from the understanding of an ethic as an expression of a given culture's genius), precludes understanding of a common and highly relevant state of affairs, namely the existence within a society of those who, on moral grounds, condemn its practices.

> Its favourite belief in homogeneous (and mutually alien) "epochs", "cultures" or "societies" makes it overlook the potent presence of the Jeremiahs, Juvenals, Bossuets, Burckhardts and similar critics of their own societies.[8]

Another error of relativism is the claimed identity between a society's moral code and its selective emphasis upon this or that specific value.

> [R]elativism is guilty of confusing morality with *ethos*, that is, the variable and particular vividness of moral *emphasis* as displayed in locally and chronologically differentiated ideals, idols, and ideologies, traditional code-phrasings and fashionable slogans, whose moral tenor is intimately amalgamated with the indefinite multeity of non-moral concerns, particular interests and aspirations, self-loves and selective sympathies.[9]

It would be rather unreasonable to claim that the Latin stress upon warmth, or the Germanic devotion to thoroughness, or the Jewish emphasis upon intellectuality, constitutes a moral value unique to that culture.

Finally, relativism overlooks the fact that disagreements in non-moral matters far surpass those in the moral sphere:

> [H]ow much more striking is the discordance between the factual beliefs of men, their religions, their para- or non-religious outlooks, not to speak of their dominant individual and collective interests, than between their moral beliefs all over the world and along its history! To become aware of this contrast in its full proportions should suffice to establish the fact of Moral Consensus.[10]

While granting that they will involve "modulations and differentiations", and that they will be codified "with simplifications and irksome omissions", he insists on a "consensual perspective of feelings, insights, views" to the effect that

benevolence is good and malice bad; that veracity is right and mendacity wrong; and similarly with the contrast-pairs of courage and
cowardice, self-control and intemperance, respect for others and arrogant self-assertion, yet on the other hand self-respect and servile self-
surrender, adulation or pliancy, dignity and meretricious cynicism,
magnanimity and cruelty, chastity and lust, honesty and dishonesty,
fidelity and treachery, loyalty and treason.[11]

The list is an impressive one; indeed, a convincing one. It has, however, a
dominant feature that is, in the context, somewhat puzzling. An account
of transcultural moral concordance ought, it would seem, to focus on the
matter, the content, the specific values, of human life—on such things as
the various forms of friendship, the activities of the mind, and self-deter-
mination or autonomy. Instead, in the above we are offered the human
responses, virtuous or vicious, to the elements of life, without explicit reference to the values upon which these responses bear. This emphasis on
the state of the will faced with its objects is, we shall see, a major element
in the paper "Morality and Practice", which contains Kolnai's most developed original contribution to ethical theory. There, however, we find a
balance between the will and its object, one which, without diminishing
the decisive role of the will and its responses, does assign a definite priority
to the object.

In "Morality and Practice" Kolnai seeks to develop an adequate
account of human goodness. He begins the project proper by noting and
distinguishing two ways in which we use the word "good".

When we speak of the good the agent is pursuing (perhaps efficacious-
ly, with the appropriate means, and successfully) or of the "good of
man", and when we speak of the goodness of conduct or of a "good
man", we mean by "good" sharply different things, whatever relations
we may on closer inquiry discover between them.[12]

The first, the "good of man", embraces the "desirable, satisfying and valuable...what I hold in high esteem...what is known to be desired by or
useful for people in general or a category of people."[13] Among such goods
in this sense, then, would be the possession of wealth, or status, or power,
and, more important by far, the *perfections* of man's specific being, those
forms of existence toward which he is inclined by his nature, those
stressed in the Aristotelian natural law ethic.

Man's *goodness*, on the other hand, is found in his self-directing but
self-detached devotion to value, a devotion, that is, involving "a relinquish-
ment of the 'John's good' point of view, a decisive step beyond the John-
centric system of coordinates, a radical change of perspective".[14] Such a
change of perspective will be signalled by a desire to be a good person:

At a certain level of moral virtue, that is, if he is really "good", John will be *concerned* about being virtuous, develop a sensitive conscience, and suffer whenever he has failed to follow its suasion.[15]

In such a case, for John "the goodness of his will has indeed become a precious part of 'his good'", though of course it is "his good" in a sense quite different from that in which, say, power is his good. Concern for his own virtue

> means a *reception,* into the structure of his wanting, of a *claim on him* as contrasted to the autonomous unfolding and pursuing of *his desires* as such and a readiness to renounce frequently, at the cost of pain and effort if necessary, "his good" in the direct, perhaps fully experienced and often even very comprehensive sense of the word, and to check his pursuit of it.[16]

What is the target of these characterisations and distinctions? Quite simply, the view that through the fulfilment of his root urges, inclinations, and desires, through the acquisition of further actuality, the acquisition of ontologically richer modes of being, man, by that fact alone, takes on a kind of grace, that is, moral goodness in its proper nature. Concerning what he calls Aristotle's Metaphysics of Good, he states:

> His point of departure lies in the conception of good as *perfective* of the thing whose good and, basically, the object of whose striving, it is. Good is inconceivable without a reference to its power of attraction; but that attraction is thought of as consequent upon the objective *need* on the part of the attracted thing for having its being *perfected*—sustained, accomplished, enhanced—by "its good"…Good thus becomes a concept subordinate to that of perfection of being…*qua* the kind of being.[17]

In a clear reference to G. E. Moore's Naturalistic Fallacy, Kolnai terms the above Aristotle's "metaphysical naturalism", and he will have none of it:

> It may well be morally good to promote the "perfection" of self and of others in any meaningful sense of personal perfections, but neither does this in any way define or comprise morality nor is it true that a man is morally better for being more perfect in any, however basic and desirable, non-moral sense.[18]

He then adds, in a definite paradox that we shall specify later:

> Man's being distinctively human or fully developed *qua* man cannot be the criterion of his morality, for what distinguishes man from the "brutes" is his being morally *accountable*.[19]

What is the proper response to all this? That, largely, it is both valid and adequate. Let it be granted that we naturally seek to be knowing, free, and loving, and that these states are in some deep and experienced way perfective of our being, our existence as human. This does not mean that our possession of them is one with our virtue, our moral goodness. A person is not moral because he is knowledgeable and wise, self-determining and, to cite the most evident instance, "in love". He is, however, morally good in *seeking* these states—in seeking them as cognisant of their worth, thus seeking them for himself and for others.

At this point we come to something not found in Kolnai's accounts of the good offered above. Clearly it is not in the deliberate seeking of just any desired object that we take on the quality of moral goodness. This means that we have need of what, in another passage, Kolnai calls an "intermediary" concept of good,

> the further concept of an *intrinsic* but not in itself moral good which is not, then, a quality or characteristic but (along with "goods") an *object* of the agent's pursuit, yet at the same time endowed with autonomous validity and a standard or measure of the quality of that pursuit rather than a function or consequence of it.[20]

Accordingly, man's pursuits and man himself will acquire moral goodness if it is to objects that have intrinsic worth that he deliberately directs himself. And what are these? Interestingly, they are for Kolnai, as, presumably, they are for the rest of us, those mentioned more than once, those that Aristotle would see as naturally sought by man, those that he would see as perfective of man as such—namely, the forms of true friendship, intellectual operations, and autonomous behaviour. A reading of certain passages given above and of many others scattered through the papers of this collection would reveal that. True, it is not because they are naturally sought, not because they are perfective of our nature, that the pursuit and the pursuer take on the quality of goodness, but because of their *specific* characters and because we see that such modes of being are what we ought to acquire. Our view of them thus should be akin to the view that we have of our own virtue: something that we seek for ourselves, indeed, but in a spirit of subordination to what has worth quite apart from its possession by us. The upshot of this is that the good intermediary between the good of man and man's goodness tends toward man's goodness, without, of course, directly having that quality, which by its nature is a *response* to the moral imperative. The quasi-union between the goodness of man and, for want of a better word, the goodness found in nature, has an important function. Human virtue is more readily acknowledged if we grant the existence in nature of that which, having intrinsic worth, compels and measures our choices:

Moral self-detachment may itself become more understandable, more credible, as it were, if seen in the context of somehow analogous objectivisations than if regarded as an isolated miracle.[21]

This means, as Kolnai sees it, that there is "some sort of congruity between the natural and the moral good", and that "being in its manifoldness and coherence and the functioning of nature *must* be 'good'".[22]

The claimed harmony takes another form. We saw that in the passage where he rejects the view that "being distinctively human or fully developed *qua* man" is the standard of morality, he adds that "what distinguishes man from the 'brutes' is his being morally accountable". Paradoxically, this is to say that man's distinctive being is at its core *moral*; that, further, to be developed *qua man* is to be virtuous, for to that state is moral accountability ordered. We might also note that both accountability and the ability to have a detached yet feeling response to value are rooted in man's intelligence, will, and freedom. In rejoinder, though, Kolnai could stress that whatever its ground, virtue is a *non-natural* quality and that nothing he holds commits him to what he rejects in others, that is, the identification of an acquired natural mode of being with moral goodness.

And here we are brought back to Kolnai's underlying concern: the defence of the characteristically human; above all, the defence of that uniquely human mode of existence, the moral, against all forms of reductionism, all confusions between it and the non-moral. He would hardly be bothered by the claim that the moral is *human* in origin. To the contrary, he would insist that, in our experience, it is with man that the moral is inserted into existence. But this is far from justifying the inference that the moral is illusory or subjective in its status. Speaking of moral opinions, as he might also have of moral feelings, habits, or actions, he observes:

> The point is that [there] are *moral* opinions, that *all* moral opinions are facts, and these facts are the only data on which any analysis and interpretation of morality, and not of something else arbitrarily substituted for morality, can be based.[23]

It could of course be brought out in seeming or partial rebuttal that the above does not wholly answer the question which has always followed any formulation of the Naturalistic Fallacy: since the Good is not a natural mode of being, what precisely is it? In so far as Kolnai answers by designating that manifestly non-natural state of the human psyche that we term the moral, fine. But what of its claimed analogue in nature, that which he sees as congruous with the moral, indeed as the measure and standard of moral goodness? There, what does "the good" signify?

The question is surely both fair and difficult. Still, reversing the order established by Kolnai, we might say that the *goodness* of a natural mode of being becomes more understandable and credible if seen in relation to its somehow analogous objectifications in the human spirit that we call moral goodness. Further probing of moral goodness might thus enrich our understanding of the good in nature. Probing the undeniable instances of the natural good—knowledge, love, and freedom—might also help. Not only are they intimately related to moral goodness, but they, too, have fallen outside the notion of Being favoured by the radical monist; they, too, have been the objects of an attempted reduction to Being, that thick and throbbing but essentially homogeneous and indifferent stuff with the concept of which, in the manner of the ancients, contemporary thought is comfortable.

NOTES

1 *Ethics, Value and Reality: Selected papers of Aurel Kolnai,* London: The Athlone Press, University of London, 1977, and Indianapolis: Hackett Publishing Company, 1978. All references are to pages in these volumes.
2 *Op. cit.* p. 94.
3 "Existence and Ethics", p. 124.
4 *Ibid.,* p. 128.
5 *Ibid.,* p. 129.
6 "Erroneous Conscience", p. 20. *See* also this volume, p. 77.
7 "Moral Consensus", p. 156.
8 *Ibid.*
9 *Ibid.,* p. 157.
10 *Ibid.,* p. 158.
11 *Ibid.,* p. 154.
12 *Op. cit.,* p. 66.
13 *Ibid.,* p. 65.
14 *Ibid.,* p. 68.
15 *Ibid.,* pp. 68–69.
16 *Ibid.,* p. 69.
17 *Ibid.,* p. 74.
18 *Ibid.,* p. 77.
19 *Ibid.*
20 *Ibid.,* p. 71.
21 *Ibid.,* p. 72.
22 *Ibid.,* p. 83.
23 "Moral Consensus", p. 151.

2. Politics and Utopia

The Democratic Subversion of Political Liberty and Participation

JOHN P. HITTINGER

Aurel Kolnai made a significant contribution to political philosophy through a series of articles in which he unmasks the ideological core of modern liberalism, retrieves the basic principles of an authentic "conservative" political philosophy, and defends liberty and constitutionalism. He fruitfully develops the notion of political "participation" from a metaphysical perspective in order to unveil those tendencies of democratic ideology which in fact subvert the possibility of political participation and liberty itself.[1] This metaphysical perspective is not that of an *a priori* system, nor is it a detached abstract system which he brings to bear on politics; rather, we find in Kolnai a unique ability to observe and reflect on the political events of his time, so as to arrive at some essential core principles of political life. In a statement of method, Kolnai said that his was a "phenomenological temper...averse to speculative dogmatism but in revolt against the tyranny of the positivistic, monistic, and naturalistic outlook".[2] Kolnai's political philosophy is well grounded in human experience and aided by careful analysis of precise meanings. Yet it is also a bold and daring attempt to view political life in its metaphysical depth. Kolnai's concern resembles that of Tocqueville, although Tocqueville is more diffuse and sociological, while Kolnai is more direct and phenomenological.

The core of Kolnai's philosophy may be stated in two broad statements. The first is that political liberty and the democratic ideal require a respect for various forms of "privilege" for their own endurance. Indeed, "Privilege is a rampart of liberty—not the liberty of 'the privileged' only, but of all classes of the people, of the whole multitude—because it expresses and safeguards the existence of relatively independent persons.." (PL 94). And, further, privilege inextricably entwines both natural and artificial excellence: "There is no 'natural' distinction which is not the fruit of various 'privileges', and none which is not generative of privileges" (CM 289). Kolnai seeks to demonstrate, not the need for aristocratic government, but the appreciation of diverse pockets of excellence, many of which have been sheltered in the folds of social privilege. Kolnai's second basic thesis is that the hatred of privilege and hierarchy is the bridge to a totalitarian form of democracy (PL 66, CM 272). A political movement which excoriates privilege and seeks its elimination must resort to a centralised "consciousness" and will. Such centralisation then absorbs or destroys any independent sector of initiative, wealth, or value standing in the way of equal justice. Kolnai had direct experience of both Bolshevism and Nazism; he had the courage and hope to resist Communism and he foresaw the eventual demise of the Soviet scourge; but he warned of a similar threat of political danger to liberal democracy from within. The ideology of the common man, or what Kolnai also calls "progressive democracy", uses the resentment against privilege to destroy all vestige of hierarchy and the very notion of transcendence. In a way, progressive democracy is the mother of all totalitarianism, not fascism or socialism.[3] A "dialectical chrysalis is hidden from the outset" in modern political liberalism, which is "ready to develop while feeding, by virtue of that original kinship of stuff, on the flesh of its host, until it may assume full life and cast away the carcass of its devoured relative" (PL 86). At stake is the "metaphysical substructure" of a sound political order of liberty and the contrast of a "metaphysical subversion" (PL 75) of the highest order which comports not simply with a Hitler, a Lenin, or a Mao, but an "inherent tendency towards anti-constitutional, monistic, totalitarian types of power", which tendency may be discerned in America, Britain, or Germany (CM 317). In fact, Kolnai thinks that American political life may well generate the most insidious forms of the "ideology of the common man".

The ideology of the common man is a complex, conditioned by at least three interrelated movements of thought and action. They are (i) reduction of the good, (ii) uniformity of reference, and (iii) centralised consciousness and will. By way of contrast, a sound political order, according to Kolnai, requires (i) a notion of hierarchy of value, (ii) analogy of being, and (iii) structural pluralism. Partly as a result of new interpretations of nature and the search for a lowest common denominator, the good comes to be defined in terms of desire- and want-fulfilment. Rights become means for protecting one's conception of the good life, however defined; and freedom, perhaps, a means for ensuring comfort. Society loses an objective axiology, and good is readily defined in terms of appetite and satisfaction (CM 327–28; PL 94).[4] Kolnai thought that the rhetoric of Roosevelt, his idea of "freedom from want", signalled the transformation of freedom as a high good, a constitutional value for limited government, to the idea of freedom through government (PL 82). Government must do something to make me happy, equal, free etc. So too the desire for comfortable self-preservation sets the dynamic for what Tocqueville calls a "soft despotism".[5] Kolnai says the common man "craves security, comfort, and the bliss of never being denied a need" (PL 82). This facet of progressive democracy Kolnai calls the "immanent sovereignty of human needs". The loss of objective value reference is but the first step in the totalitarian impetus of progressive democracy.

Second, the "more recondite" notion in democratic self-understanding derives from a denial of analogy of being; this "carries us straight to the core of the matter" (PL 67). The common good must be interpreted in terms of "sameness of reference, use, enjoyment, and immediacy". This very thesis is hard to grasp at first, yet it "has farther reaching implications" than mere egalitarian jealousy (PL 68). The core notion is the thesis that "no man must hold more or be more than his fellow-man", and if he does happen to

> hold more or represent more, this must be…on behalf, in the name of, and under the jurisdiction of Society as an actual Unit of Consciousness, an actual Subject of Will entirely contained in the collective thoughts, moods and decisions of the Moment. (PL 68–9)

It is the notion of "the common man" that captures this notion of fundamental sameness of reference and provides the rationale for centralisation of power. The common man is more than a plaintiff, nor simply a victim of spoliation; the common man is the construction of a preferable type of man, indeed "a hero, if not a new god" (CM 279). The notion of the common man embodies the modern aspiration to overcome limitations and contingency; to become the master and owner of nature; to be free in the most radical sense of free from limitation by nature and God. Thus Kolnai claims that the "war against nobility" (hierarchy and privilege) is "in truth an essential and metaphysical rebellion levelled at something that towers infinitely above kings, dukes, barons, squires, factory owners, generals and admirals, fops or usurpers" (CM 302). The common man must be the generator of value, not submissive to any higher value. The tribunal of the common man, so constituted, must lead to the utopian goal of abolishing alienation and must rely on the means of centralising a mass consciousness and will.

It may be important to compare the notion of the "common man" and the "plain man", as Kolnai does. The "plain man" has a centre of gravity in "his practical concerns" but is attached "by firm, if somewhat elastic, ties to things 'higher than himself'" (CM 310); the plain man is embedded in a particular background; the plain man may be distrustful of élites; he may be indifferent to the concerns of higher culture. As such, Kolnai says, the plain man is necessary as a corrective and supplement to the "higher" or notables of society (CM 309). The common man, on the other hand, is what philosophers now call the "unencumbered self"; Kolnai says this "anyone" implies a standard without the implication of either mature personal judgement or a particular creed or tradition which most members of a community happen to share. It is precisely this foundation of an empty humanistic "universality" in the sense of "any-oneness" upon which *this* "creed", the cult of the Common Man and the mentality bred by that cult, is erected. (CM 323)

He is indeed not a notable (without distinctions of wealth or social position) but can be "any man". Any particular commitment or perspective is a limit to his commonness. He is not only distrustful of power, but is intolerant and covetous of the higher ranks. He cannot "appreciate...the meaning of any 'ideal' point of view not assimilable to...his welfare'" (CM 310).

According to Kolnai,

only superficial critics can believe that the quasi-religious impetus of Total Equalitarianism draws on no deeper forces than envy and jealousy, competitive self-assertion, the need to overcompensate for one's inferiorities, and the craving for material comforts. (CM 281)

In fact, the Common Man is

Man Divine as "mere man"...Man above whom is set no Order, no Power, no Being essentially different from him, impervious to his reason, independent of his will; no social authority, therefore, either, which symbolises, expresses, and fructifies, illuminating its various aspects and corollaries, this fact and this sense of metaphysical subordination". (CM 318)

Tocqueville also connects the vehement hatred of inequality or privilege with a divinisation of man and its concurrent trend towards centralisation.[6] Indeed, Kolnai sees the political power of the common man become "the ensemble of human consciousness moving and decreeing in complete unison throughout all individual minds" (CM 319); or again, the common man must represent "humanity pure and simple, sheer humanity" such that "all particular determination must be broken up (as) it implies Man's *creaturely limitation*" (CM 281). If hierarchy and privilege stand for the "submission of man to what is highest in man", that is, participation, then equality

proclaim(s) the equal and joint sovereignty of men (and) speak(s) the idiom of Identity, (which) taunt(s) man with the mirage of "positing" and "generating" reality, including his own, of absorbing the infinite into one human Consciousness, of supplanting or, indeed, "creating" God. (PL 73)

The true goal of the regime of the common man must be the utopian goal of overcoming alienation. What becomes irksome is the sheer otherness, alterity, of social reality, that is, its contingency and dividedness. It is not masterable or controllable by the immediate reason and will of the common man. Therefore, the ideology leads to an "active suppression" of what is alien to self; this suppression may involve branding the other as an outcast or pariah, or an "immature" section of mankind in need of re-education. We now use such terms as fundamentalist, fanatic, or "mediaeval", or perhaps we elaborate a more refined instrument of uniformity called "public reason".

Hierarchy and privilege are most irksome to the common man in their claim to represent a value higher than private satisfaction or human creation. They are reminders to society that human good is fragile and possessed only in a partial and tentative way. The superior or higher must be brought down and neutralised; that is, whereas the "plain man" may register some indifference or avoid contact with the higher claims, the common man must either eliminate them, or better yet "annex" and "remodel them", thereby bending them to "the measure of his 'requirements', with the pretension of thus enhancing and intrinsically 'improving' them" (PL 70, cf. CM 311). The institutions of religion and education are particularly vulnerable to the process of annexation and remodelling.

The idea of the common man as just "anyone" means that "any human subjectivity as such is—equivalently to others—a judge of truth, and, similarly, any human need an immediately sovereign determinant of the good" (PL 76). The rampant spread of subjectivism and relativism in ethical thought reflects this trend—"Who is to say what is right or wrong?"— since anyone's judgement is as good as another's; and so too the notion of a therapeutic society places any felt need as a *prima facie* right to be reckoned with. Kolnai perceptively notes that unity becomes a "self-contained *theme* of society"; no longer is it "a function of the convergence of minds towards a transcendent Cause, Measure and End" (PL 77). Thus religious differences do not require true civility and dialogue, but rather such differences are suppressed as divisive or remodelled along the lines of a New Age substitute for religion, a generic unifying spirituality that takes the place of divided, particular faith traditions.[7] The very claim for truth or a claim for divine privilege is attacked as the source of division and fanaticism. The utopian goal is that of a "tensionless common subjectivity" (CM 320), and this means the destruction of any "objectivisation", be it religious, philosophical, juridical or social. It was with good reason that Kolnai found that the very mildness of its methods rendered progressive democracy more "insidious" than Nazism or Communism: it could assimilate "under the deceptive verbal cloak of liberalism and tolerance, the thinking, moods and wills of everybody to a wholesale standard of the 'socialised' mind".[8]

The contradiction of progressive democracy cannot be hidden or contained. The quest to overcome alienation leads to a super-alienation, it requires an all-powerful central consciousness which can overcome dividedness and otherness, thereby rectifying the injustices of privilege and liberty: "[an] omnipotent levelling power itself needs a distinct supremacy over the power of 'common men' as such" (CM 289). How else shall we secure truly equal conditions; who shall cleanse "the tissue of society from power relationships—from relations of dependence and from 'vertical' principles of articulation"? We must concentrate power in the hands of

> "One Subject" of consciousness and will: the subjectified, totalitarian Collective; to make all social order dependent on the decrees of one human Agent supposed to incarnate the "rational will" of "us all". (PL 95)

Kolnai is amazed at the ultimate willingness of the citizens of liberal democracy to be directed by the central consciousness; it amounts to a self-enslavement of man. The real object of hatred is the idea of

> a concrete natural order of Society's life; of an artificial texture of social relationships and appreciations reposing on a receptive incorporation of "natural" data of value rather than on the opinion and will of an omnipotent collective Subject. (CM 300–1)

This tendency towards centralisation is something more than a sociological trend or fact; it is part of the logic of the common man. Thus Kolnai thinks that the liberal has become virtually totalitarian in the war against privilege in the common man's name.

How can such a movement be resisted or reversed? Kolnai's understanding of a sound political life is centred on the presence of social hierarchy and various forms of "privilege". He shows the vital dependence of political liberty on hierarchy and privilege. "*Normally*", he claims,

> that is, given a certain amount of division, equilibrium, control and manifoldness of social hierarchies, positions of authority, power, rank, prestige, wealth, etc. deserve being respected and honoured not because they warrant personal excellence but because they stand for a vital necessity of social order and are conducive to the recognition by and *in* society of the hierarchical distinction of values...[9]

The noble is a "notable"—one who is known and is not anonymous (CM 297) and therefore exists and acts with a degree of independence. Notables are members of the higher middle class, the urban patriciate, the

Church organisation—as well as found in "military, academic, and even trade union milieus" (CM 299). Such notables have a claim to social prerogative or leadership in virtue of a "value intrinsic, distinctively qualitative, pervading the essence of its bearer" (CM 298). Yet the sense of hierarchy does not as such mean the noble persons are higher morally, or even metaphysically better than another; but they do serve as "a stimulus and a gross *provisional* measure of value" (CM 294). The noble represents a higher value; there is an exemplariness—such as the general of conspicuous courage, the scholar's devotion to truth, the monk's dedication to prayer, the union leader's commitment to justice etc. The idea of "exemplar" reveals the depth of the metaphysical substructure of a well-ordered society. Kolnai says that nobility simply means

> the reception...by society of a structural principle of order that is not of its own making or positing but originates in a supra-social, quasi-"entitative" human value. [...] (It is) a recognition of what(ever) is higher and better than its own "thesis", "volition", or "appointment" may be. (CM 299)

This notion of participation means that we receive the good; we hold it precariously and tentatively; we are stewards, if you will, of the good.[10] The notion of participation implies analogy—that is, diverse modes of fulfilment of the value, with various sets of primacy and secondary modes of fulfilment and responsibility. Hierarchy and participation mean that

> a certain *personnel*, by virtue of its very constitution and in a sense penetrating its distinctive "being", as it were, is *primarily ordained* to actualise and to cultivate a certain set of higher values; to attend to, and to serve, certain aspects of the common good. (PL 72)

There are higher values—indeed the noble stands for the idea of

> Man's participation in values higher than those universally and actually attainable for man, and with it, for Man's *bondage* to an objective order of natural being which essentially and metaphysically surpasses his power and outranges his sovereignty. (CM 302; cf. PL 73)

Kolnai considers the denial of otherness and the utopian projection of unity to be an "impossibility on the border of the 'analytic' and empirical"—it violates the "basic constitution of man" and leads to an "incurable self-contradiction".[11] The violation of human nature involves the very requirement of an object for the human activities of "love, fight, curiosity, understanding, virtue, possessions, rank, equalisation, conquest, adaptation"; and, further, "alienation constitutes a fount of pleasure, thrill, happiness, vitality, a sense of being alive".[12] Alienation is a condition for human adventure. As Kolnai explains it:

> By claiming Identity we estop ourselves, as it were, from Participation; by asserting man's absolute and all-comprehensive Actuality we foil the manifold real potentialities in man which can only thrive in spheres remote from a totalitarian concentration on the "evident needs of the Moment", and prevent them from actualisation; by "emancipating" man from the "divisions", "tensions", "contradictions", *Verdinglichungen* and "alienations" that are inherent in his natural status, we isolate, "divide" and "alienate" him *integrally* from his proper humanity, set him against whatever represents the reality of freedom and dignity—of nobility and sovereignty, of virtue and wisdom, of perfection and progress—*within* him (and that can never be simply *he*, any more than *his*) and reduce him to a mere abject Thing while inflating him into a self-styled Deity. (PL74)

At the end of the day

> we are merely creatures and "guests" of God even on earth, not in any sense "claimants" on Him…[and] we are also, ineliminably and most fortunately for us all, beneficiaries and benefactors, servants and masters, pupils and teachers, imitators and exemplars of one another… always in a more proper sense as receivers and followers than as "privileged" spenders or leaders. (PL 70)

Response, not fiat, is the primary gesture of man.

Patience and respect for privilege stand at the heart of a sound political order because

> Privilege means the social projection, the institutional recognition, the traditional embodiment of the essentially insurmountable dividedness, imperfection and subjectivity (in the face of a transcendent Object and Good) of Man […]

and a correction of our smallness and fallenness. Those who have achieved something in some limited respect may make it possible for "others (to) reach out beyond their own immediate possession or proper nature and enrich themselves…" (PL 69). What Kolnai has in mind here by privilege would be something like privilege of rank, privilege of attaining a social position like that of a tenured faculty member, member of the bar, or physician; or alternatively students at a college, traders in a market, etc. They are able to carry on their business or profession without external interference and to gain access to the information, tools, etc., which they need to perform such activities. It is their independence of the actual will or appetites of society which enables the privilege to serve such an enriching function in society. Privilege is an established positional value in society relatively independent of the will of society, yet fundamentally in tune with it. Privilege allows "a pattern of concrete and specialised 'points of interblending' between the private and the common good". It implies intermediate groups, classes, bodies with their own "perspectives, insights and devotions, virtues and loyalties, responsibilities and vocations, standards of honour and accumulations of values" (PL 93).

Privilege serves as a rampart to liberty; again because of its social role and because of the metaphysics of participation and the dispositions it cultivates in a social body. The historic root of political liberty lies in Privilege and its extension. There were privileges of the barons against the crown; or privileges of universities from political and ecclesiastical control; so citizens' rights are in some way "geared to and dependent upon the subsistence of certain 'exemplary' privileges...necessarily limited to a minority" (PL 89). In this way, then,

> Privilege is a rampart of (the) liberty...of all classes of people...because it expresses and safeguards the existence of relatively independent persons as quasi *finite* parts of society, as "principles" of the community. (PL 94)

A free society will "be a society rich in privileges, affording manifold means of redress and opportunities of ascent (*not* devised in the spirit of *effacing* the framework of privileges) to the 'underprivileged'" (PL 96).

It should be a balanced society involving a plurality and limitation of all social powers and political prerogatives, and an ordering "in deference and in reference to a Power radically beyond and above Man in his social reality, in his political dignity and in all manifestations of his 'will'" (CM 274). Such is the meaning of "liberty under God".

Aurel Kolnai considered himself to be a conservative. But he was well aware of the special illusions, shortcomings and exaggerations to which that political side might fall prey.[13] He qualified his own "conservative" position as follows:

> What we have in mind is not, of course, a proposal to substitute for (Western) Democracy, along with its ideological biases, a fancy system of Conservative Constitutionalism, nor a "return" to this or that specified stage of the past, but a suggestion to *displace the spiritual stress* from the "common man" aspect of Democracy to its aspect of constitutionalism and of moral continuity with the high tradition of Antiquity, Christendom and the half-surviving Liberal cultures of yesterday. (CM 274)

Kolnai did not want a reactionary return or conservative utopia; his sights were trained on the liberal democracies of the West as high historic achievements requiring support. He championed Democracy, first against Fascism and Communism, and then against itself. His main concern was the preservation of liberty against the ideology of the common man. As a "conservative", Kolnai did not have in mind an aristocratic, let alone an oligarchic, defence of privilege. The best arrangement for liberty lay in a mixed regime, first recommended by Aristotle. The form of mixed regime Kolnai had in mind is of course a popular democracy in which broad strata of society are enfranchised and participate in the political process. It is a society that most of all reflects balance; political checks and balances as well as division of social power. His own best formulation runs as follows:

> [W]hat has made the concrete reality and duration of liberal democracy, with its manifold compromises and elements of sanity, possible and practicable has been the Conservative—the Christian, hierarchic, pluralistic, and realistic: as it were, "finitistic"—substance of our civilisation... (PL 87)[14]

Indeed, Western liberal democracy shelters in itself, and "has...guarded against utter peril and extinction, the traditions of civilisation and fragments of liberty...which its destruction by *any* opposing force would wipe out, beyond repair..."[15] Because progressive democracy rests upon an "ineliminable" dualism between the utopian ideal and the givenness of human reality, there will be an incompleteness in its totalitarian trends. The liberal democratic order reposes on pre-liberal axioms, conventions and traditions which limit the excess of individual liberty and popular sovereignty; one cannot rely solely nor primarily upon the automatic mechanisms of constitutional order.[16] The

> *Liberal* conception of society...cannot support and protect liberty except in a precarious and self-contradictory fashion, [because it must] rely[ing] on Conservative values unofficially tolerated yet continually harassed and eaten away by the immanent dialectic, the "law of evolution", of liberal democratic society as such. (PL 86)

In that breach between the utopian ideal and the historic reality and achievement of liberal democracy, Aurel Kolnai stood to fight and engage the philosophical issues surrounding democracy.

Kolnai was a spirited defender of liberty, rights and liberal democracy, not their opponent.[17] Some conservative writers today see the very idea of human rights as one of the chief culprits in our political confusion and decline. For example, Robert Kraynack, in his book *Christian Faith and Modern Democracy*,[18] chastises Jacques Maritain and John Paul II as "Christian Kantians" whose political theory of rights decisively undermines the true defence of liberty. Yet Kolnai accepted the historic reality of rights, a "concrete element of the democratic tradition", which serves as a bar to totalitarian manipulation, alongside the rule of law, checks and balances, and independent ownership (PL 91).[19] In fact, he accounts for rights as an extension to many of the "exemplary privileges" of the few (PL 89). He affirmed the historic achievement of liberal democracy and did not seek to radically question its compatibility with Christianity; in fact, he seems to think that liberal democracy derives from the "finitistic substance" of the Christian notion of creation. Many liberal thinkers derived their philosophy from this Christian heritage. Political rights are not a "Kantian" reading of politics, but rather Kant borrowed from the tradition a notion of human dignity and human freedom. With good reason did Nietzsche call Kant the "great delayer". He wanted human freedom and dignity without the metaphysical substructure. But the issue, for Kolnai, was not the presence or absence of reference to human and civic rights. The problem was, rather, how to interpret those rights. He sought not a "fancy system" of conservative constitutionalism, but merely to "displace the spiritual stress" away from the ideology of the common man. Perhaps his phenomenological realism preserved him from the folly of re-founding political philosophy in opposition to a notion of rights. Ironically, Kolnai has much in common with Jacques Maritain and perhaps less with contemporary writers who denounce the very notion of rights, such as Robert Kraynack. Although Kolnai was harsh with Maritain, he affirmed the fundamental point of agreement between them—the stress on "social pluralism".[20] He rightly pointed out that Maritain did not fully appreciate the conservative implications of this fundamental facet of political life. But unfortunately Kolnai overstated and distorted Maritain's sympathies with "progressive democracy", as Kolnai defined it. Maritain also criticised just this notion of democracy as derived from Locke and Rousseau.[21] And as Kraynack finds reason to criticise the discourse of rights in John Paul II, I believe that Kolnai would have found in John Paul II a deep affinity. Both range beyond traditional Thomism and take an interest in realist phenomenology; both were raised in a Catholic culture in Eastern Europe; both are linguists who appreciate the real diversity of human beings and culture; both are scholars and teachers who lend an urgency to their study beyond the merely "academic" enterprise. Thus Aurel Kolnai and Karol Wojtyla both developed a deep appreciation for the political reality of Western liberal democracy, and a deep disdain for its totalitarian rivals. But, their orientation to the "sovereignty of the object", their trust in the pull of Truth, and their subordination of human action to Providence,[22] prevented both a conservative quibbling with the long tradition of human rights as unfolded in the West, and a liberal inflating of the rhetoric and ideology of expansive rights. In sum, the full Catholic vision of reality framed their reflections upon man in society. The root of the modern crisis is that men have forgotten God. Kolnai said:

> Man has chosen to "progress" on the wrong track; and he will contin-
> ue doing so as long as he dreams of "controlling moral and spiritual
> forces"…instead of surrendering to the moral and spiritual Reality
> outside and above him.[23]

The idea of human rights, like that of federalism, separation of powers, universal suffrage or many other proud achievements of modern political systems, is not in itself either the marker or the obstacle to human progress. Rights lie scattered like so many iron filings to be tossed aside or heaped in a meaningless bulk until such time as they are arrayed in line with the sovereign point of attraction, God. In Kolnai's writing the phrase "liberty under God" is the most adequate and true expression of political order. Perhaps the greatest challenge to contemporary readers of Kolnai is the ease with which he refers to God and the transcendent. He follows the way of faith and reason, being neither a fideist nor a rationalist. In fact, as I have compared Kolnai to Tocqueville, I believe that the comparison to John Paul II is even more fitting. The ultimate remedy for social and political disorder is the recovery of the true God as a counter to the God of the common man. For a student of Kolnai the following passage should be seen as a fitting capstone and statement of Kolnai's political philosophy par excellence:

> By formalising, restricting, relaxing and refusing his allegiance to Him
> Who Is, man has set himself at war…with Being as such and con-
> demned himself to seek satisfaction in the dissolution and reduction of
> all Substantiality and Nobility. By "emancipating" the Image from its
> Exemplar, the privileged Creature from its sovereign Creator, he has
> virtually destroyed his very humanity. He will recover his humani-
> ty…as soon as he truly and integrally reasserts the greatest and most
> vital of his needs, ignored and maimed and stifled by humanitarian-
> ism: the need for a meaning of his life which points decisively and
> majestically beyond the range of "his needs".[24]

The case against the ideology of the common man could not be more suc-
cinctly made, nor could the root of participation and political liberty be more aptly stated. John Paul II, in his encyclical *Faith and Reason*, also traces the crisis of our time to the lack of meaning and the implicit nihilism of much modern thinking.[25] Quick to see the political implications of the search for meaning, John Paul II challenges philosophy to recover its sapiential dimension, affirm the reality of being, and follow the

bold range of reason in seeking knowledge of the highest things. I would suggest that Aurel Kolnai, in all of his writings, but especially his political philosophy, belongs in that group of philosophers esteemed by John Paul II for the integrity of their reason in the context of faith—Jacques Maritain, Etienne Gilson, John Henry Newman and Edith Stein.

NOTES

1 The series of articles includes: "The Meaning of the Common Man", *The Thomist*, July 1949, pp. 272–335; "Privilege and Liberty", *Université Laval Théologique et Philosophique*, V, 1, 1949, pp. 66–110; "The Humanitarian versus the Religious Attitude", *The Thomist*, October 1944, pp. 429–57; and "The Cult of the Common Man and the Glory of the Humble", *Integrity*, VI, 2, 1951, pp. 3–43. The first two are included in Aurel Kolnai, *Privilege and Liberty and Other Essays in Political Philosophy*, ed. Daniel J. Mahoney, Lanham, Md.: Lexington Books, 1999. The former will be referred to as "CM" the latter as "PL". Pagination refers to the original publication sources. See also his book on Nazism, *The War against the West*, London: Gollancz, 1938, and New York: Viking Press, 1939. See my articles exploring Kolnai's political philosophy: "Approaches to Democratic Equality", "Maritain and Simon's Use of Thomas Aquinas in the Justification of Democracy", and "Aurel Kolnai and the Metaphysics of Political Conservatism", in John P. Hittinger, *Liberty, Wisdom and Grace: Thomism and Democratic Political Theory*, Lanham, Md.: Lexington Books, 2002.

2 "The Concept of Hierarchy", in Aurel Kolnai, *Ethics, Value and Reality*, ed. Francis Dunlop and Brian Klug, introduced by Bernard Williams and David Wiggins, London: Athlone, 1977, and Indianapolis: Hackett Press, 1978, p. 167; he also says "Phenomena, especially such as play a great and manifold part in man's mental and practical life, after all *do exist* and cannot be explained away as '*mere* appearances' or *reduced to* more massive and more universally indubitable data of experience...", p. 166.

3 "Three Riders of the Apocalypse: Communism, Nazism, and Progressive Democracy", *Appraisal*, II, 1, 1998 (ISSN 1358-3336): pp. 4–11. Reprinted in Mahoney, *op. cit.*, pp. 105–18. "Progressive democracy is *the* Rider of the modern Apocalypse", p. 118.

4 The connection between liberty and moral relativism may be found in Hobbes and Locke. See John P. Hittinger, "Why Locke Rejected an Ethics of Virtue and Turned to an Ethic of Utility", in Hittinger, *op. cit.*, note 1.

5 *Democracy in America*, ed., J. P. Mayer, trans. George Lawrence, New York: Doubleday Anchor, 1969, vol. 2, IV, 6, "What Sort of Despotism Democratic Nations Have to Fear."

6 Ibid., vol. 2, IV, 3, p. 672. Tocqueville discerns the same fundamental metaphysics as Kolnai—see, for example, his analysis and denunciation of "pantheism" as the typical democratic religious framework, vol. 2, I, 7, p. 451.

7 On the issue of religious indifference and toleration, see Kolnai's "Cult of the Common Man ...", pp. 36–37.

8 "Three Riders of the Apocalypse", Mahoney (ed.) p. 108, *Appraisal*, II, 1, p. 5.

9 *Op. cit.*, note 2, p. 185.

10 For a metaphysical treatment of participation see Norris Clark, *The One and the Many*, Notre Dame: University of Notre Dame Press, 2001, and John F. Wippel, *The Metaphysical Thought of Thomas Aquinas*, Washington D.C.: Catholic University of America Press, 2001.

11 "Utopia and Alienation", in Aurel Kolnai, *The Utopian Mind and Other Papers*, ed. Francis Dunlop, London: Athlone, 1995, p. 178.

12 *Op. cit.*, pp.176–77.

13 See PL 66 on "reactionary aestheticism and fascist hysteria", and PL 99 on Platonist and romantic misconceptions of social hierarchy; as well as "The Moral Theme in Political Division", *Philosophy*, XXXV, 1960, pp. 234–54, reprinted in Francis Dunlop, ed., *op. cit.*, note 12, on right-wing hypocrisy, inertia, and dangerous "holism".

14 See "The Humanitarian versus the Religious Attitude", pp. 429–57. *See* also "The Cult of the Common Man and the Glory of the Humble", pp. 1–43.

15 "Three Riders", Mahoney (ed.), p. 118; *Appraisal*, II, 1, p.11.

16 Cf. George Grant, *English-Speaking Justice*, Notre Dame: University of Notre Dame Press, 1985, on the role of theological traditions that supplemented the threadbare philosophy of social contract of Hobbes and Locke.

17 Interestingly, his harshest judgement is often reserved for fellow Catholic intellectuals, such as Jacques Maritain, who would sometimes exhibit an excessive zeal for rapprochement with progressive liberalism. *See* Kolnai's review of Maritain's *Man and the State*, "The Synthesis of Christ and Anti-Christ", in Mahoney (ed.) (who gives a different subtitle), pp. 175–81. I compare and contrast Maritain, Yves R. Simon and Kolnai in the articles cited above.

18 Robert P. Kraynack, *Christian Faith and Modern Democracy*, Notre Dame: University of Notre Dame Press, 2001.

19 Cf. PL 69, 86.

20 Review of *Man and the State*, Mahoney (ed.), pp. 178–79.

21 See my "Maritain and Simon's Use of Thomas Aquinas in the Justification of Democracy", *Liberty, Wisdom and Grace...* For ref. *see* note 1.

22 Kolnai's phrase from "Three Riders", Mahoney (ed.), p. 118; *Appraisal*, II, 1, p.11.

23 "The Humanitarian versus the Religious Attitude", p. 457.

24 *Ibid.*

25 Pope John Paul II, *Faith and Reason*, Boston, Mass.: Daughters of St. Paul Press, 1998, §85 and passim. *See* my "John Paul II and the Exorcism of the Ghost of Descartes", in *Liberty, Wisdom and Grace*, first published in Timothy L. Smith, *Faith and Reason: Notre Dame Symposium of 1999*, South Bend: St. Augustine Press, 2001.

Liberty, Equality, Nobility: Aurel Kolnai and the Moral Foundations of Democracy

DANIEL J. MAHONEY

"If society exists for the sake of anything at all, it exists for the sake of itself and thus for the sake of its ruling, leading and tone-giving members, and for the sake of the distinctively valuable, eminent, virtuous, ingenious and creative members emergent in its midst, and, last but not least, for the good of its members pure and simple."[1]

INTRODUCTION: KOLNAI, CRITIC OF "PROGRESSIVE DEMOCRACY"

The Hungarian-born moral and political philosopher Aurel Kolnai (1900–1973) was among the twentieth century's most philosophically minded conservative critics of "progressive democracy". In his writings in political philosophy, he was an independent, even idiosyncratic thinker, indebted most especially to the broad spirit of classical and medieval thought, and to the phenomenological school's desire to "let the phenomena speak", to recover the "sovereignty of the object". He particularly identified with "conservative-liberal" thinkers such as Burke and Tocqueville (and a host of lesser-known nineteenth- and twentieth-century critics of mass society) who recognised the ultimate dependence of modern liberty on premodern traditions and supports. In his *Political Memoirs* (1955) he states that these conservative-liberal thinkers helped him arrive at the "insight that, if the technical elaboration of the *Rechtsstaat*—constitutional government and society regulated by law—had been largely a work of Liberals, its historical basis and spiritual presuppositions were eminently Conservative: tied, that is, to a habit of stable civilisation and an intrinsic concept of moderate and plural authority" (PM 210).[2]

Kolnai's occasionally intemperate polemics against progressive democracy sometimes convey the impression of a cranky, backward-looking thinker, an aristocratic liberal who saw democracy as the deadly enemy of liberty properly understood. But this is far from the case. In the spirit of the best conservative-liberal thought, Kolnai defended "the constitutional design of public power, the validity of the universal moral Law, the protection of general human and civic rights, and the plane of Christian equality among men" (PL 49). Kolnai, to be sure, fiercely denounced a "'common man' conception of democracy"[3] which reduced the inherent plurality of individual and collective life to an understanding of man as "nothing but man", "unencumbered by culture and possessions" and "unfettered by dogma, tradition, and presupposition" (CRE 142). As John Hittinger has noted, Kolnai was a critic *avant la lettre* of contemporary liberalism's celebration of the unencumbered self.[4] Kolnai believed that such a reduction of man to the lowest common denominator of "pure humanity" undermined the dignity and individuality of all men, including the "nobleness" inherent in the ordinary human being as such. The "common man" conception of democracy was incipiently totalitarian because it presupposed a unitary and "arbitrary human will", a "prideful identitarianism" which was coextensive with the "self-sovereignty" of man (PL 44).

Kolnai believed that true liberty was inseparable from privilege. This language hardly reassures dogmatic democrats but it is not evidence of anti-liberal or anti-democratic intent on Kolnai's part. He never defended the right of an aristocracy or oligarchy to rule by nature or independently of the just claims of ordinary citizens. Instead, he envisioned a rich, pluralistic, and balanced society that respected the dynamic interplay of "relatively independent" persons and groups. In his view, radically egalitarian or "identitarian" democracy transforms free persons into "anonymous molecule(s) of society", the individual into nothing more than an "*infinitesimal* entity of the political calculus" (PL 47). It is therefore essentially anti-democratic, despite its extravagant claims made on behalf of the "sovereignty" of the people. In contrast, a pluralistic, conservative democracy accepts the reality of "privilege and countervailing privilege" but also the "finiteness and limitations" (PL 47) of all privileged claims. It affirms "liberty under God" (PL 39) rather than the self-sovereignty of man. Kolnai's point is inseparably political and metaphysical: "It is only because *some* people, in different manners and different respects, *weigh* something in the scale as against state power that the 'individual' as such, the 'plain man' who is not in any sense a 'master', may also 'count for something' and make an active contribution to the life of the state" (PL 47).

In essays such as "Privilege and Liberty" and "The Meaning of the 'Common Man'"[5] Kolnai repeatedly affirms that democracy has "manifold positive manifestations" (PL 44) and therefore cannot simply be identified with its most radical or pernicious tendencies. He insists that a decent society, one that affirms and attempts to embody the common good, must place a special emphasis on the "*participation*, at various levels, of the broad strata of the people in shaping public policy (MCM 87). The ordinary or plain man, with his legitimate claim to participation in the body politic, is a constant reminder to the "privileged" (that is, to everyone with a stake in the social order) that their prerogatives are subordinate to a common good that respects the civic and human rights of all of society's members. In a Chestertonian manner,[6] Kolnai even affirms the superiority of the judgement of the plain man, the "democrat" with common sense, to the specialist or refined intellect, "the man enslaved to one definite pursuit or preoccupation" (MCM 87). Kolnai did not share the reactionary's, or revolutionary's, aesthetic disdain for ordinary human beings. While refusing to make an idol of the all too human "plain man", Kolnai goes so far as to insist that "it is indisputably true that a system of government in which the 'plain man' as such 'has a say' is *intrinsically* better than government by an esoteric caste of public officials, no matter how well bred, 'cultured' or 'public spirited'" (MCM 87). Kolnai, the Christian conservative, rejects the "Platonic" defence (however qualified) of the right of the wise or the few to rule by nature, not to mention the insidious Nietzschean distinction between "master" and "slave" morality.

Kolnai is careful, however, to root his defence of the democratic claim in a capacious consideration of the common good rather than in any notion of individual or collective sovereignty. Kolnai upholds what the nineteenth-century French statesman François Guizot called "the sovereignty of reason" over will, and what Alexis de Tocqueville called the primacy of "humanity, justice, and reason" over the pretensions of an omnipotent majority.[7] Even more radical than Kolnai's politically incorrect defence of privilege as a prerequisite of liberty is his denial of the self-sovereignty of man in any form. He defends the "privilege" that protects individuals and groups against the abuse of state power and the sense of creaturely limitation that makes both privilege and power compatible with the common good.

Kolnai remarks that one of the sources of the relative moderation of Western democracy, at least in comparison with totalitarian regimes of the Left and the Right, is the way its formal acceptance of the sovereignty of man is moderated in practice through its acceptance of the countervailing claims of the sovereign individual. Two versions of "self-affirmation" keep each other in check and hence "constitutionalise" the theoretically unlimited pretensions of modern sovereignty (PL 38). This fruitful conflict between the "individual will" and the "general will" helps keep liberal democracy relatively *liberal* despite the totalitarianism implicit in its formal claim that man is sovereign over himself. Kolnai's rejection of "progressive democracy", with its acceptance of the totalitarian principle of human "self-sovereignty", should not be confused with a rejection of democracy based on other moral and metaphysical presuppositions. In "The Meaning of the 'Common Man'" Kolnai instead calls for a new *emphasis* or *stress* in the defence and articulation of Western democracy against its totalitarian critics (Kolnai was writing during the coldest period of the Cold War). Kolnai believes that the conservative prerequisites of balanced, pluralistic democracy, those features which keep it free and decent, need to be stressed in any theoretically or practically sound defence of Western democracy. Kolnai writes:

What we have in mind is not, of course, a proposal to substitute for (Western) "Democracy", along with its ideological biases, a fancy system of Conservative Constitutionalism, nor a "return" to this or that specified stage of the past, but a suggestion to *displace the spiritual stress* from the "common man" aspect of Democracy to its aspect of constitutionalism and of moral continuity with the high tradition of Antiquity, Christendom and the half-surviving Liberal cultures of yesterday. In other words, instead of emphasising the "ideal" of "Democracy", which is a bait held out by the Enemy as well as a current emblem of our own world and of that which makes it go round, we should shift the emphasis within "Democracy" from the fabric of ideas and tendencies symbolised by the "Common Man" onto whatever the "Rule of Law" stands for—a Balanced Society, that is, and the finiteness of all human power even on the level of human relations; the plurality and the limitation of all social powers and political prerogatives; the ordering of society in deference and in reference to a Power radically beyond and above Man in his social reality, in his political dignity and in all manifestations of his "will". (MCM 64)

KOLNAI AND TOCQUEVILLE

This quotation confirms Kolnai's debts to and affinities with conservative-liberal thought, including the greatest, most balanced and perspicacious of conservative-liberal thinkers, Alexis de Tocqueville. In fact, one of the strengths of Kolnai's work is that it gives theoretical depth to some of Tocqueville's most profound, but naïve and "untheorised" observations. As John Hittinger has suggested, Kolnai provides more "conceptual and phenomenological clarity" than Tocqueville, and philosophises where Tocqueville relies on his powerful observations or on historical or sociological generalisations.[8]

Nonetheless, the affinities between the two thinkers are quite striking. Both agree that the cause of liberty and human dignity is not strengthened by striving to maximise democracy at every turn. Both recognise the salutary dependence of democracy on what Tocqueville called "aristocratic inheritances" and on what Kolnai called "axioms, conventions, traditions, and habits (whether they be expressly held or tacitly respected) which transcend the liberal-democratic framework itself and impose certain 'material' or 'objective' limits on both individual liberty and popular sovereignty" (PL 38). Both thinkers feared that these pre-democratic inheritances or traditions would be eroded by the gradual democratisation of society and by the dogmatic application of the principle of popular sovereignty. They feared that everything would come to be judged in the light of the imperative of individual and collective consent. Tocqueville and Kolnai both appreciated that democracy was a meta-political as well as a political phenomenon. They knew that democracy "democratises" aspects of life such as the family, religion, and the intellectual life which were once considered to be natural and hence, in crucial respects, beyond politics.

Both were committed to the idea of "a regulated and orderly freedom, controlled by religious beliefs, mores, and laws" as Tocqueville put it in his *Recollections*. Yet at the same time these wary partisans of liberty appreciated the discreet but deadly tyranny that democracy was capable of exercising over the human mind and soul. They knew that under the democratic dispensation, when push came to shove there would be no resort to anything outside the collective judgement of the people, or the ubiquitous claims of "public opinion". Tocqueville went so far as to state that he did "not know any country where, in general, less independence of mind and genuine freedom of discussion reign(ed) than in America".[9] Kolnai, for his part, was convinced that there were totalitarian premises lurking in democratic ideology. Democracy all too readily degenerated into a "religion of progress" and was defenceless against more consistent forms of historicism and materialism. The dream of a "world of Man as such...unencumbered by the 'ballast' of prejudice, bias, dogma, tradition and taste" was nothing less than an inhuman utopia, in his view (PM 200). To be sure, "Utopia, in America, displays its more moderate face; but the protest of human nature against Utopia is most effectively silenced there" (PM 201). In different ways, Tocqueville and Kolnai oscillated between a recognition that revolutionary despotism was the gravest threat to political liberty and human integrity in modern times (although Tocqueville did not live to see the ideological tyrannies of the twentieth century but only the anticipation of totalitarianism that was Jacobinism) and a belief that a mild, democratic despotism was a far more subtle, invidious and dangerous threat to the integrity of human nature.

In any case, Tocqueville and Kolnai shared the conservative-liberal insight that democracy is undermined by its flatterers or "excessive friends". Its true friends refuse to succumb to the "democratic dogma". They have the spiritual independence to recognise the limits of democracy. In Pierre Manent's felicitous words, they know that "to love democracy well, it is necessary to love it moderately".[10]

In his remarkable 1972 essay "Conservative and Revolutionary Ethos", Kolnai writes admiringly about the insights of Tocqueville into the political and spiritual condition of modern man. His remarks are worth quoting at some length:

> The great conservative-liberal thinker de Tocqueville could not have known Marx's febrile dream of a "realisation of the human race"—the real totalitarian ideal—or the "historical necessity" of this operation, or of the Marxist vision, as highly revolutionary as it is reactionary, of the

future abolition of the division of labour. Yet he saw, with piercing vision and fearful foreboding, the danger that the demand for "equal rights", with which he completely sympathised, leads with almost logically unavoidable necessity to the demand for an equal level of culture and welfare; and that this, if only because of the need for a *measure* of equality, leads to an unimaginable impoverishment, flattening and despiritualisation of life, as everything becomes increasingly *homogeneous* and human beings more *similar*, proletarianised and *uniform*. (CRE 142)

Kolnai saw Tocqueville as the discerning analyst and critic of what Pierre Manent has called the "pantheist dream of democratic man", of man as "the self-contained Whole".[11] Tocqueville had the greatness of soul to anticipate that this "realisation of the human race", of man as such, could only lead to "an unimaginable impoverishment, flattening and despiritualisation of life". He also understood that the just claims of democratic equality could only be appreciated or adjudicated in the light of a standard which could not be provided by the democratic ideal itself. It is precisely this insight that Kolnai develops in his writings in political philosophy. Kolnai's two greatest essays of Christian conservative political reflection, "Privilege and Liberty" and "The Meaning of the 'Common Man'", powerfully dissect the pantheist dream of democratic man. In "Privilege and Liberty" Kolnai highlights the subversive effects of "Atheist Humanitarianism". Atheist Humanitarianism proclaims Humanity as a heroic project, but its view of the "common good" is utterly *indeterminate*. It lacks any criterion, end or means by which to judge the actions of men. Its denial of an order of things or an entity or law above the human logically gives rise to the pantheistic delusion of collective human self-sovereignty and thus to the essential "self-enslavement" (PL 34) of man:

There being, by supposition, no Entity and no Law *above* man, no definite and subsistent good *outside* man to measure and to direct his corporate action, the concept of ultimate values and obligatory principles is confined to what is assumed to be "self-evident" to everybody and anybody: which amounts to saying that any human subjectivity as such is—equivalently to others—a judge of truth, and similarly any human need an immediately sovereign determinant of the good; hence, anarchy cannot be averted except by the actual sameness and fusion of human thoughts and volitions *as such*; unity, no longer a function of the convergence of minds towards a transcendent Cause, Measure and End, becomes a self-contained *theme* of society; whoever questions the evidence of the "self-evident" or fails to fit in with the "typical" constitution of "needs" places himself (virtually at least, but perhaps with massive consequences) outside the bounds of recognised humanity. (PL 29–30)

NOBILITY AND DEMOCRACY

Kolnai is the twentieth century's most articulate and philosophically penetrating critic of the "religion of Humanity"—and of the radical "enmity
to Being" underlying the project to "emancipate" man from deference to
"what is highest in man and higher than man but claiming his attention"
(PL 26–27). Against the partisans of liberation or emancipation who
advocate a conception of human Identity, which destroys pluralism, individuality, and any coherent notion of the Common Good, Kolnai defends
the modest but humanising understanding that he calls *participation* (PL
23–30). In this perspective, human beings participate in an order that
they do not make. Participation "is another word to express man's affirmation of—or loyalty to—Being, Form, and Limits" (PL 26), and his
trust in God and appreciation of creaturely limitation (CRE 154). Against
the delusion of collective self-affirmation, the proponent of participation
acknowledges that "*response*, not *fiat*, is the prime gesture of the human
person" (PL 26). In Bertrand de Jouvenel's complementary formulation,
"The wise man knows himself for debtor, and his actions will be inspired
by a deep sense of obligation."[12]

Kolnai thus gives *theoretical* expression to the Tocquevillian critique
of pantheism.[13] Like Tocqueville, his critique of the prideful self-affirmation of democratic man is at the service of human greatness rightly understood. In agreement with Tocqueville, Kolnai insisted that the democratic
conceit of human omnipotence was the enemy of true human greatness.
He defended pluralism, "privilege", inequality, and nobility against the
leveling claims of democratic ideology. No doubt Kolnai's evelling defence
of inequality is less rhetorically deft than Tocqueville's and must offend
some decent democratic sensibilities. To speak so brazenly of privilege is
bound to offend democratic peoples who associate privilege with merely
conventional inequalities and thus with injustice. But as we have already
suggested, Kolnai was no enemy of equality properly understood. He
instead defended the necessity for a standard to judge equality, one that
could affirm its rightful role as well as its intrinsic limits within a decent
human order.

In many ways, Kolnai's critique of the "common man" conception of
democracy and his metaphysical and political defence of nobility are a
theoretical refinement of Tocqueville's earlier, commonsense distinction
between "a manly and legitimate passion for equality that incites men to
want to be strong and esteemed", a passion that "tends to elevate the
small to the rank of the great", and the "depraved taste for equality in the
human heart that brings the weak to want to draw the strong to their level
and that reduces men to preferring equality in servitude to inequality in
freedom".[14]

As we have seen, Kolnai calls this depraved sense of equality, which is the enemy of nobility as such, the "common man" conception of democracy. In "The Meaning of the 'Common Man'" he observes that, despite the absolutely crucial differences that separate Communist totalitarianism from the decencies of liberal democracy, the "common man" ideology serves as a "common denominator" between the two regimes, at least in the sense of "paralysing our resistance to Communist Imperialism" (MCM 63). The Harry Hopkinses, Henry Wallaces, and Eleanor Roosevelts of the world could see in the land of Gulag only impatient efforts at equality and social justice. Stalinism was, as Hopkins put it, merely "the New Deal in a hurry". But Kolnai's objections to "common man" ideology go beyond the now irrelevant question of how to respond to the Communist threat. Kolnai believed that the assumptions underlying progressive democracy undermined any "sane" view of democracy (PL 40, MCM 87) and risked nothing less than the self-enslavement of man. It is certainly the case that the phenomenological dissection of Communist utopianism was Kolnai's deep and abiding theoretical and practical concern. He spent the last two decades of his life working on his posthumously published masterpiece *The Utopian Mind*. This work exposed the utopian effort "to overcome or conceal at any price the classic scissures which characterise human being" (UM 160). He showed that revolutionary ideologies are defined by an absolute *negation* of both prudence and conscience. In aiming to put an "end to History" they undermined the very preconditions of moral and political responsibility and gave free reign to the inhuman lie. But the ancillary critique of democratic ideology is also central to Kolnai's conservative defence of privilege and liberty. What totalitarian and democratic utopianism have in common is the absence of a standard that grounds and limits egalitarian claims (however just) and that challenges human pretensions of absolute sovereignty.

"Common man" democracy may be defined, in fact, as a perverse form of equality, one which refuses to acknowledge any purpose or end that guides the choices of, or relations among, men. It is, strictly speaking, a "privative concept", one which considers Man "stripped of all specific excellence, distinction, superiority; of all inherent pretension to be another's 'better'" (MCM 66). It ignores the dialectic of equality and inequality that defines the human condition and celebrates Man "decapitated" (MCM 69). This decapitation of man is the precondition for his transformation into the "Superman" (MCM 69)—into the Lord of History and Society. The "common man" ideology sees in the degradation of man to the lowest common denominator, the "Naught" (MCM 69) which lies beneath every distinction or claim, the precondition for the unleashing of mankind's collective power.

For the advocates of progressive democracy, it is only by becoming nothing that man can become everything and thus overcome his all too human humanity. The price is exorbitant, entailing nothing less than collectivist conformity, "the uprooting of man's moral substance" and, most significantly, "the sacrificing of man's intrinsic freedom to the fetish of his unlimited power" (MCM 103). The cult of the common man sacrifices everything that is human, including that most representative type, the "plain man", to the cause of Humanity as a self-subsisting Whole that in principle knows no intrinsic limits to human self-affirmation. The freedom and dignity that belongs to man as man is sacrificed to the delusion of unlimited human power—an emancipatory delusion that haunts the modern project from its beginning.

Kolnai insists that the manifold plurality of the human condition must be defended against those who would sacrifice man to this idol. The idea of nobility must be recovered both for its own sake and for the sake of authentic democracy and liberty. Nobility reflects man's deference to what is highest in man and the subordination of everything human to what is above man. This "meta-political" understanding of nobility requires a social articulation or embodiment in the multiple privileges that define a vital, pluralistic, and free society. The recognition of privilege or nobility in no way entails a denial of the fundamentally equal dignity of human beings. Yet despite the moral equality of man under God and the law, the human world is necessarily "pregnant" (MCM 75) with inequality. Whenever humans recognise different "'types of virtue'—'models' or 'ideals' of public validity, such as the monk or the hero, the entrepreneur or the scholar, the artist or the artisan—[they] have assented to Inequality" (MCM 75). There is a "hierarchical tension" (MCM 75) inherent in social reality. Kolnai insists that social embodiments of nobility are not identical with personal moral or intellectual nobility; "nevertheless, its *existence* is indispensable for the *existence* of such nobility: indispensable as a stimulus and a gross, *provisional* measure of value" (MCM 77). Nobility, in its social embodiments, discloses the "knowability" of the noble as an "'intelligible' and 'identifiable' primary 'factor' of society" (MCM 80). Nobility needs social "references" or "resonances" as palpable signs of quality or "value intrinsic" (MCM 80). Just as the freedom and property of the ordinary man depends upon the acceptance of privilege *in general,* so the nobility of the plain man depends on recognition of quality, nobility, or distinction *in principle.*

Despite his resort to the quasi-aristocratic language of privilege and nobility, Kolnai's defence of social nobility as acknowledged quality or value also has a democratic import. He defends a legitimate equality, Tocqueville's "manly and legitimate passion for equality", that recognises the nobility inherent in the people and the partially conventional character of merely social nobility. Like Tocqueville, Kolnai sees that the uprooting of nobility in the name of social levelling will not enhance the nobility of the people. "By taking away their nobility from the 'nobles' we cannot 'ennoble' the 'people' but merely annihilate a large part of the 'nobleness' present in the 'people' themselves" (MCM 78). Egalitarian levelling does not and cannot "raise the 'people' to the level of the wealthy and the highly 'educated', nor even lower the 'ruling classes' to the level of the people, but depress[es] *everything* to a *new* 'common' level which, in the most important respects, will be decisively *inferior* to the old level of the 'people'" (MCM 78–9). Just as inequality is rooted in difference as such, so nobility is present in any social body that represents qualitative superiorities. Social nobility is thus not reducible to the social categories of premodern or aristocratic societies but is present in any differentiated social order that respects individual differences and qualitative human achievements. Capitalist entrepreneurs, the urban patriciate, and even the élites of "certain military, academic and even trade union milieux" (MCM 81) represent a kind of "nobility". Even in a formally democratic society, qualitative differences need a social resonance: there can be no natural aristocracy without its quasi-natural, quasi-conventional social counterparts. Kolnai thus rejects Jefferson's famous, seemingly clear-cut but finally utopian distinction between a good natural aristocracy and an unjust conventional aristocracy. Kolnai defends the integrity of a corporate or intermediary realm between the state and the individual as the *sine qua non* of liberty, and believes that such social bodies can never simply be "voluntary" in character. Democracy, too, needs inherited "spiritual bodies" that provide a buffer against monistic state power and that remind democratic citizens of the purposes and ends of human freedom.

KOLNAI AND THE RHETORIC OF INEQUALITY

I have, for the most part, emphasised the affinities between Tocqueville's and Kolnai's analyses of democracy and equality as well as their shared critiques of pantheistic and identitarian thinking. But the differences between these two thinkers are not insignificant. To be sure, Kolnai's insistent defence of nobility is quite Tocquevillian in character, as is his recognition of the dependence of liberal democracy upon aristocratic inheritances. Yet Kolnai does not follow Tocqueville's rhetorical lead in baptising as "democratic" those institutions and practices that are aristocratic in origin but necessary for the health of democracy, for example municipal self-government. Tocqueville stresses that municipal self-government is an inheritance of an older liberty but also the most perfect and salutary embodiment of the "sovereignty of the people".[15] Tocqueville's political science is rhetorically more democratic than Kolnai's, and for that reason more likely to persuade decent democrats who cannot abide aristocratic categories. And while never conflating moral, intellectual, and qualitative nobility with social inequality *per se*, Kolnai sometimes seems to suggest that liberty is essentially aristocratic and can survive only incompletely or *analogically* in democratic times. His political reflection is open to the criticism that he does not sufficiently recognise the inexorability of what Tocqueville called the "democratic revolution" and hence the progressive assault on social privilege as a bulwark against tyranny. Yet the weaknesses of Kolnai's approach turn out to be more rhetorical than substantive— perhaps the result, as Pierre Manent has suggested, of the relative isolation in which he pursued his remarkable reflections on the political condition of modern man.

THE DEFENCE OF THE "PLAIN MAN"

Despite the aristocratic tone of his rhetoric, Kolnai did not hesitate to defend the fundamental decency of the "plain man" against the pretensions of "common man" ideology (MCM 83–91). The plain man is a "representative" human type, generally sane, commonsensical, and by no means the reflection of man in his "nakedness". He is the furthest thing from the unencumbered self. He is, in his own way, colourful and distinctive, and much more likely to defend inequality or distinction than most contemporary intellectuals. The plain man has eminently practical concerns but is capable of respecting what is highest in man and higher than man. He does not judge everything by the criterion of how it affects his welfare. He is most assuredly not his "own paramount theme" (MCM 86). He is not easily fooled by demagogues or tyrants who speak in the name of the people, and looks warily at political or ideological movements that want to make the people everything (MCM 86)—and therefore nothing. At his best, the plain man "*presupposes* Distinction, in the broadest sense of the term. He embodies a complementary relation to it" (MCM 89). In Kolnai's view, the plain man was a reminder of the "relativity and transitoriness" of "all human scales of rank" (MCM 89) and of the subordination of the claims of both the people and the few to an order of justice that accommodates both the fundamental moral equality and the qualitative distinctions that define the human condition.

KOLNAI, TOCQUEVILLE, AND "AMERICA"

Aurel Kolnai, then, aimed to do justice to what is just in democracy. It is true that he sometimes wrote as if liberal democracy posed a more invidious threat to human freedom and spiritual integrity than full-scale totalitarianism. But in general he saw Communist totalitarianism, with its desire to overcome all divisions, conflicts, and human limitations, as the gravest threat to human freedom and to the very notion of an order of things that respects conscience and moral choice. He hated the Communist Lie infinitely more than he disliked the mass conformity of a democracy such as the United States. Nonetheless, he believed there was something unreal in the American defence of the common man who aimed to live without reliance on tradition or dogmatic beliefs. He stated his critique of the democratic conceit more boldly and a bit more contemptuously than Tocqueville. Tocqueville wrote sympathetically about the poor Americans who unknowingly embodied Cartesian premises and thus were vulnerable to conformist pressure from the crowd. Kolnai was, in contrast, rather horrified by the way America, despite its considerable economic and social dynamism, seemed frozen in time. He never felt comfortable in the United States during his years living there as an exile during World War II. In his view, Americans were disciples of the abstract, mechanical, and rationalist philosophers of the eighteenth century—"prisoner(s) of that locus in the history of ideas which is more or less mapped out with the names of Locke, Rousseau, Jefferson and Franklin" (PM 202). To be sure, he admired American liberties, America's determination to resist Communism, "the most sinister of public evils", and the attitude of benevolence that marked America's attitudes toward "humankind in general" (PM 202). In the end, however, he was bewildered by a nation that was completely devoid of European-style utopian fanaticism yet was blind to the defects inherent in the "kingdom of the Common Man" (PM 200).

Kolnai was temperamentally much more attracted to English constitutionalism, to the remnants of aristocracy within its "democracy", and to monarchy as a symbol of national continuity and tradition. Without a doubt he would be pained today by New Labour's assault on Old England, its modernist celebration of "Cool Britannia", its emphasis on people's England, and its determined efforts to reform, if not mutilate, the inheritance which is the British constitution. In Britain, the idol of the common man seems to be winning out over the good sense of the plain man, while in plutocratic America the kingdom of the common man seems to meet real and enduring resistance. Perhaps Kolnai underestimated the practical solidity of those abstractions to which America, as a liberal democracy, remains obstinately dedicated.

Conclusion

Aurel Kolnai is one of the most profound and least appreciated political philosophers of the age. His critique of the mendacity inherent in Communist theory and practice anticipated Solzhenitsyn's and Havel's dissection of the Communist Lie, and his critique of dogmatic egalitarian ideology—of the cult of the unencumbered self—challenges the most cherished assumptions of contemporary liberal political philosophy. His generally sober insights were expressed in what is perhaps an excessively traditionalist idiom. But his courageous dissent from democratic dogma renewed the Tocquevillian insight that true democracy is always "formal"—and that the effort to maximise democracy in every nook and cranny of life leads to the death of liberty and equality alike. In this sense, Kolnai boldly proclaimed what Tocqueville merely intimated: liberal democracy, whether it knows it or not, whether it admits it or not, is "aristocratic" in that it presupposes qualitative moral, intellectual, and even social distinctions. In the best conservative-liberal tradition, Kolnai reminds us that the truth of the human condition is a mixture of aristocracy and democracy, equality, and inequality. Democracy, at its best, is a mixed regime that reflects the mixed character of the human soul. Kolnai's writings provide powerful impetus for a conservative defence of democracy that emphasises humility as the true source of human greatness.

The greatness of man is located not in his individual or collective power but in his patient acceptance of an order of things that he did not make and cannot ultimately command. Nobility is a constant reminder both of the objective and hierarchical character of value but also of the transitoriness and finiteness of every merely human rank and claim. Kolnai is able to do justice to both pagan magnanimity and Christian humility by showing that they stand or fall together against the fanciful claims of "common man" ideology. Kolnai thus provides a genuinely radical challenge to relativistic, radically egalitarian, and postmodernist interpretations of democracy that dominate contemporary political theory. The effort to defend democracy on the basis of an indeterminate conception of the common good is a prescription for collective suicide. As Tocqueville lucidly foresaw, it leads to the pantheistic negation of both liberty and true individuality. Kolnai reminds us that sensible democrats need not abandon the quest for "the truth about man". It is up to us to take up Kolnai's challenge and rethink, in a genuinely open way, the entire question of the moral foundations of democracy.

NOTES

1 Aurel Kolnai, "The Concept of Hierarchy" (1971), reprinted in *Ethics, Value and Reality: Selected Papers of Aurel Kolnai*, ed. F. Dunlop and B. Klug, with an introduction by Bernard Williams and David Wiggins, London: Athlone, 1977.
2 Titles of Kolnai's works cited in the text are abbreviated as follows:
PM: Aurel Kolnai, *Political Memoirs*, edited by Francesca Murphy, Lanham, MD: Lexington Books, 1999.
PL: "Privilege and Liberty" (1949), in *Privilege and Liberty and Other Essays in Political Philosophy*, edited and with an introduction by Daniel J. Mahoney, with a foreword by Pierre Manent, Lanham, MD: Lexington Books, 1999.
MCM: "The Meaning of the 'Common Man'" (1949), in Daniel J. Mahoney (ed.).
CRE: "Conservative and Revolutionary Ethos" (1972), in Daniel J. Mahoney (ed.).
UM: *The Utopian Mind and Other Papers*, edited by Francis Dunlop, London: Athlone Press, 1995.
3 Kolnai's phrase is clearly a reference to the one-time American vice-president Henry Wallace's evocation of "The Century of the Common Man" in a book of

that title published in 1943 and translated into twenty-nine languages. In that book, Wallace castigated inequality and imperialism and celebrated "progressive", "forward-looking", and egalitarian thinking. It is no accident that the same Wallace wrote cheerfully about what he saw on a visit to Soviet Asia in 1944, including the so-called Gulag camps which he mistook for American-style public works projects. He was a populist demagogue and naive "political pilgrim" all wrapped into one. See Geoffrey Wheatcroft, "The prince of Wallese", *The Times Literary Supplement*, November 24, 2000, pp. 28–9.

4 Cf. John Pollard Hittinger, p. 31 of "Kolnai and the Metaphysics of Political Conservatism", *Appraisal*, II, 1, pp. 26–36.

5 Both essays originally appeared in American Catholic philosophical journals in 1949.

6 Kolnai was a great admirer of the English Catholic defender of common sense, although not of his "distributism".

7 *See* Tocqueville, *Democracy in America*, trans. Mansfield-Winthrop, Chicago: University of Chicago Press, 2000, p. 380.

8 *See* Hittinger, pp. 29–30.

9 *See Democracy in America*, p. 244.

10 Pierre Manent, *Tocqueville and the Nature of Democracy*, Lanham, MD: Rowman & Littlefield, 1996, p. 132.

11 *Ibid.*

12 Bertrand de Jouvenel, *Sovereignty*, Indianapolis, IN: Liberty Fund, 1998, p. 317.

13 *See Democracy in America*, vol. II, pt. 1, ch. 7.

14 *See Democracy in America*, p. 52.

15 *Ibid.*, pp. 57–66.

Aurel Kolnai: A Political Philosopher Confronts the Scourge of Our Epoch

PIERRE MANENT

*(Translated by Francis Dunlop
and David Wiggins)*

As early as the middle of the eighteenth century, it was possible for Adam Ferguson to write that we had entered "the age of separations".[1] Ferguson's is one of the first and most striking formulations of an idea that has become a commonplace to us, and conveys as much satisfaction as disquiet—satisfaction at the advance of knowledge, which makes possible the division of labour, especially intellectual labour; disquiet at the impossibility of a synoptic grasp of the scattered elements of human learning. There are many separations. If there is any that arouses more disquiet than satisfaction, it is the long-standing division between political and moral philosophy.

A political philosopher—or a *political scientist,* as we now have to call him—who describes shrewdly the workings of the body politic, or issues judicious suggestions for the improvement of these workings, will habitually do this without concerning himself with the question of the kind of human being who inhabits or will inhabit it. Such a theorist is anxious not to let a value judgement escape him, lest it spoil the scientific nature of his work. The moral philosopher, on the other hand, examines minutely the perplexities of the moral agent, but normally without attending to the fact that these perplexities may be intimately bound up with the political regime in which the moral action unfolds. His fear is of obscuring or sullying the specificity and the purity of his field of enquiry.

Among the reasons for this remarkable divorce between moral and political philosophy, there is one we should mention immediately. Over the last two centuries, at points widely separated on the political spectrum and on the basis of divergent and even contradictory analyses of the nature of modern society, there has emerged a single conception of political action. This conception rests on the assumption that as soon as a certain rational arrangement of our institutions has been achieved, the whole human problem will be essentially solved—or that whatever remains problematical in human affairs will not affect the essential and definitive validity of the political structure. The happy contemplation of a certain institutional automatism, the servo-mechanism that is supposed to guide the body politic on its way to being what it ought to be, excludes all fundamental questioning about the motives of man in society or about the ambiguities and tensions that characterise the relation between man and citizen. This idea of an ultimately infallible "political mechanism" may be given a liberal or a socialist content, and it can prompt initiatives with very different practical consequences. But it retains one single essential characteristic—that of being *utopian*.

Aurel Kolnai is one of the philosophers of the twentieth century who have given most attention to the growing power of the utopian mind, the spirit which both expresses and aggravates the loss of meaning in human action—our loss of any relation to values. Kolnai belongs also among those thinkers who have given most attention to the "ideologising" of modern politics. From the moment when the conviction grows—however justifiable within certain limits—that man can and ought to change society by making it conform to his ideal, there looms the risk that, paradoxically, the content of the ideal will become less and less desirable as its form—its *ideal* character—is embraced with increasing zeal. There is the risk that in the name of utopia the legitimate search for social improvement will be perverted into an exercise in destruction. Thus the seductive power of utopia is owed not so much to its value content—the social, moral and philosophical ideas which give it an intelligible outline, or the passions and aspirations which first attract its zealots and enthusiasts—as to its promise of a certain formal perfection, which will infallibly and definitively reconcile *reality* and *value*, reconcile the *is* and the *ought*. Kolnai's study of modern society and politics convinced him that the utopian mind is an object *sui generis*, quite distinct from the political stances or sociological ideas that it will engage as its ministers. The utopian mind deserves philosophical study on its own.

At this point two caveats suggest themselves. The first caveat is this. It may well be true that the utopian mind works more spontaneously in the social and political ideas of the Left; yet, as Kolnai himself remarks, the utopian mind has no analytically necessary connection with ideas of the Left. For the same leftist sociological ideas (the idea which sees the emancipation of the working class as a central requirement of modern society, for instance) are just as susceptible of commonsense presentation (reformist, moderate) as of utopian. In the second place, we must note the existence of what could be called "rightist" utopias. There are the moderate utopias of the moderate Right. Economic liberalism, for instance, according to which market mechanisms can by themselves solve the problems of social man, has an incontestably utopian stamp. But there are also the extreme utopias of the extreme Right. These come in two kinds: (1) reactionary utopias, common on the Continent until quite recent times, which see a glorified *ancien régime* as the natural order of human society, or as the order required by Christianity; (2) subversive utopias, like Nazism, which attract those whom they attract by a particularly murderous vision of racial purity. In short, if Aurel Kolnai's approach in this book[2] may be called conservative—in a sense we shall have to clarify—it would be a grievous error to see in his critical analysis of the utopian mind a conservative attack on, let us say, socialism or democracy.

The second caveat to be entered here concerns the impression of excessive generality created by the idea of the utopian mind. The idea of utopia is much more determinate than the idea of "modernity", for example. Yet the idea of modernity has long had the freedom of the philosophers' city, if only by virtue of the flamboyant criticism that was directed at the modern world and modern ideas by such writers as Nietzsche and Heidegger. The idea of the utopian mind is still less imprecise than the idea of political rationalism, the target of Michael Oakeshott's sharp—if not mortal—barbs.[3] Above all, we should not charge the analyst with the abstraction that is apparent in the *object* of his study. It is not in Kolnai but in Marx that one comes across ideas as abstract, emphatic and vague as that of the "reconciliation of man with man and with nature". The extreme generality of the idea of the utopian mind is not something with which one might justly reproach Kolnai. Excessive generality is the reproach that Kolnai himself wants to make against utopian thinking.

It appears that what first drove Kolnai to his study of the spirit of utopia was his dissatisfaction with the usual criticism of utopias: that they are "unrealisable", "too beautiful" ever to exist in this world. Such criticism is obviously true in one sense. The state of complete human satisfaction envisaged by Utopia is indeed unrealisable. But such criticism is superficial, because it leaves out what is special about Utopia. It is precisely its unrealisable character, or the particular nature of its unrealisability, that provides the motive power for attempts to realise Utopia, and is responsible for the peculiarly destructive effects of these attempts.

Utopia is not unrealisable in the way that a barefoot ascent of Everest is unrealisable. It is impossible in empirical fact for the human body to harden itself to the point where it could surmount those icy slopes barefoot, but no essential contradiction of human nature, or of the laws of gravitation, is to be found here. Kolnai emphasises that what singles out the utopian project is precisely its being unrealisable *a priori*—that is, its being *contradictory*, or *unthinkable*. The reproach one can and ought to make against the political utopian is not that of wanting to realise what is not realisable, but that of wanting to realise—or at least of claiming to want to realise, and acting as if he truly wanted to realise—what is not even thinkable, what neither he nor anyone else can completely think out, without contradiction. The man who gives himself unrealisable but thinkable objectives, such as climbing Everest barefoot or conquering the world, incurs ridicule; or, like Alexander the Great, he commands the admiration that we will accord to one who fails nobly because he has undertaken too much. One who gives himself objectives which are unrealisable *because* they are unthinkable destroys or corrupts, both in himself and in those he seduces or subdues, the natural relationship between ideas, motives and values on the one hand, and human action on the other. What he attacks is the internal constitution of the human world.

In Kolnai's eyes this "unthinkable" or "contradictory" character of the utopian project is immediately apparent from its claim that the new order of humanity must be attained by the conscious and deliberate actions of an enlightened group that is in full command of the direction in which they are headed, fully aware of each stage on the way, *even* as the new order itself nevertheless represents perfect spontaneity or total freedom. On the one hand there is the artificial, the self-conscious, the preconceived; on the other, there is the natural, the spontaneous, the unforeseen. These will mingle, support or hinder each other, yet be inextricably entangled in ordinary society; in the utopian project they are at the same time violently divorced and totally confounded. During the phase of "constructing" the new order they will be violently divorced. But then it seems they will be totally confounded in the new order that is realised. The distinction between two phases—of before and after the institution of the new order—does not remove the contradiction. For even during the phase of construction, the utopian group or sect *simultaneously* desires sovereign mastery over nature or history *and* docile servitude under it.

This contradiction is especially characteristic of totalitarian utopias. In the Bolshevist project, for example, the organisation and action of the Party are kept rigorously apart from civil society, and even apart from the working class that they are thought to represent. Yet at the same time, this organisation and action are identical with the irresistible spontaneity of the historical movement for which society provides the location and the instrument. (That is the basis of their legitimacy.) The emphasis differs in the project of National Socialism. Here, deliberate political action is the servant not so much of history—though Nazism did itself claim to be borne along by the wave of history—as of nature, the nature which precedes and transcends every human project, a purely biological or animal nature, lacking all specific human characteristics. The superhuman is claimed and constructed in the name of the subhuman. Though it uses the language and the disguise of a distorted "biological science", it represents the same, familiar utopian contradiction. In every case the totalitarian project simultaneously affirms the absolute sovereignty of man—his triumph over necessity through his own efforts and his ushering in of the reign of liberty, or else his creation of the superman—and his absolute enslavement, either to historical necessity or to blood and race.

Kolnai's analysis, of which I have here been able to give merely the bare bones, has the considerable merit of defining clearly the concept of totalitarianism. This idea once attracted considerable attention, largely as a result of Hannah Arendt's work,[4] but today it has fallen somewhat out of favour, at least in Anglo-Saxon countries. But whatever totalitarian regimes may have in common with dictatorships and despotisms, their specific characteristic—the one that most markedly affects their functioning and their impact on the societies enslaved by them—is their utopian logic. It is in this utopian kernel that the explanation is to be found of the strange yet absolutely central role of terror in these regimes. The totalitarian organisation or Party must not only show that it is still the only victor in the political struggle, the one and only sovereign; it must also make people understand and feel that a new reality has replaced yesterday's shabby and corrupted world. Yet, according to the theory, this new reality will be realised only when the totalitarian organisation has withered away and the new man has been left to his spontaneity. To get over this contradiction, the regime compels society—that is, the old society now overturned through its violence—to *say* that it is the new reality, the new world transported with happiness; it compels it to acclaim its total subjection as a complete liberation. Thus it is the office of terror both to affirm and to deny the distance between the surreal world of utopia and the real world.[5]

The reason why there is such a temptation to consider totalitarianism as simply an extreme version of ordinary or perpetual despotism is, as we have just seen, precisely the element of unthinkability that resides in its specific project or proper essence. How, then, can the unthinkable be thought? The analyst or interpreter must force himself, let us say, somehow to think objectively what cannot be thought subjectively. If he wants to render the temptation harmless, he must show how this subjectively unthinkable, contradictory end is none the less objectively possible. The better he can show how the utopian project helps him to escape from his condition, the more he is obliged to show how such an aberration is possible, how it has its origins, and the conditions of its possibility in the shared human situation.

On this point Kolnai establishes, with a great wealth of psychological analyses, the continuity of the utopian mind, even in the extreme form of totalitarianism, with mental attitudes that are commonly encountered among ordinary people and in ordinary society. He carefully distinguishes the different varieties and gradations of perfectionism, and of what could be called the utopian mind in its moderate form. This is responsible for what Kolnai calls departmental utopias, which relate to a limited sphere of human life. Above all he shows how the utopian mind is born of a perversion—something which, if not natural, is at least intelligible—of our relation to values. It is natural to desire the incarnation, or realisation, of positive values. In this sense, for every significant theme of human action and for every value, it is natural to desire a coincidence between the *is* and the *ought*. But in ordinary, non-utopian life, everyone is aware, despite this desire, not only of his own inadequacies and of human inadequacy in general, but also of the tension between different positive values (not to speak of the ambiguity and indeterminateness of every one of them), of the way in which urgency can shift value priority, of the weight of necessity and the role of contingency. Departmental utopianism, then, selects a *single* value and claims that its realisation will lead infallibly to the realisation of all other values, or at least the main ones. For example, it is supposed that morality will bring prosperity, health and happiness. But extreme or totalitarian utopianism—that is, utopianism *par excellence*—allows itself to become obsessed with, or infatuated by, the evident desirability not just of a particular value, or even all of them together, but of the coincidence of *is* and *ought* as such. It will experience a burning desire for resolute action—so that this coincidence may be effectively guaranteed. By a subtle but decisive displacement, the idea of "evidence" is transported from the intellectual to the volitional sphere. Since it is far from evident to the intellect what would count as such a coincidence of *is* and *ought*, the will takes its place and conceives the desire for that which it cannot conceive—while making the intellect believe that it conceives it. But then, in reaction, there is an inevitable rebound, and the feeling of contingency and freedom emigrates from the volitional to the intellectual sphere. Cut off by the will's decision from all authentic contact with the real world, the intellect feels an intoxicating licence to justify and motivate whatever actions the utopian will dictates. Thus the respective places in the human economy of theory and practice, intellect and will, are interchanged.

To see these diagnoses of utopianism as metaphysical subtleties would be a great mistake. As Kolnai deploys them, they make a powerful contribution to our understanding of certain particularly strange features of totalitarian action. Take Bolshevism. This is characterised by an astonishing formal rigidity of ideological framework, coupled with an almost incredible arbitrariness in the ideas that form the immediate accompaniment of action. (Thus, simultaneously, the Party is always right: yet, between one day and the next, such and such a hero of the Revolution becomes an inveterate enemy of the people.) The rigidity of the ideological framework certifies the absolute legitimacy of the totalitarian organisation and the self-evident desirability of its action. Since the will is thus guaranteed and strengthened in its self-evidence, revolutionary action enjoys absolute freedom in its choice of means and measures, and in their justification. And whereas the ideology affirms that "socialism is achieved", action—that is to say, terror—is justified by the claim that many individuals, even within the Party, even among the companions of the supreme leader, are busy day and night in the work of re-establishing capitalism. Thus, the ideas which constitute or go to formulate the utopian project are not there to create a bond between the agent and values, to guide his action or inform his will; on the contrary, their function is to liberate the will from all rules, from any mental content whatsoever, and to protect the agents of utopia from all spontaneous and personal contact with values.

For all its intrinsic aberrancy and the destructiveness of its practical implications, this inversion of the roles of theory and practice has been, if not directly caused, then made possible at least by an intellectual development which seems quite innocent and even salutary—it is one with which we are, in any case, perfectly familiar—namely, the virtual disappearance of "practical reason" from the political thought of the last three centuries. It is a commonplace that political philosophy has traditionally been conceived, largely under Aristotle's influence, as a practical science. But now it has tended to become pure theory. (The almost complete substitution of the idea of political theory or science for that of political philosophy is the linguistic expression of this noteworthy fact.) The social or political scientist tends to regard the body politic as a "system" or "structure" whose functioning he endeavours to describe, while as far as possible ignoring the motives or ends that lead men to act in this structure or system. That is to say, he refuses to take account, as philosophy once did, of what links him, the observer or thinker, to the object of his study. He refuses to take account of what makes both of these human. For the most part he is content to rely on what is a virtual tautology—that men act in accordance with what he calls their interest. Since "interest" is defined here as what the agent himself thinks it is, the political scientist's assumption amounts to this—that men act as they desire to act, or desire to act as they act.

The rationale of a development such as this seems to me to be the following. An Aristotelian analysis of human conduct in terms of motives or ends—in terms, that is, of *our* motives or *our* ends—seemed to lead almost inevitably to a *ranking* of these motives and ends and the subsequent elaboration of a dogmatic philosophy of human nature or human good. This conception of human nature and human good leads to the conception and promotion of a political regime "in conformity with the nature" of man. But this in its turn seems to endanger the liberal idea of a political power which is neutral between various conceptions of human life or between various world-views. It is clear that the transformation of political philosophy and its practical knowledge into a political science which is *value-free* is closely bound up with the development of liberal and representative political regimes. Thus, in so far as it rests on the dwindling of ideas of practical reason and the hypertrophy of theory or science, the utopian or totalitarian temptation is bound up with an intellectual development that is inseparable from the progress of our civilisation. How, then, can we triumph over this temptation without reintroducing a dogmatic idea of human nature which would conflict with our liberalism, besides being heavy with the threat of reactionary utopia? It is as an answer to this question that Aurel Kolnai's conservatism is so important.

We are not obliged in ordinary life, or in the political arena, to act in the light of any clearly defined image of human nature—any thick concept of human nature. To do so would involve us once again in those arguments I have just mentioned over the definition of the "highest good", from which our fathers escaped with such difficulty when they conceived of a State which would confine itself to guaranteeing the external conditions of free action and abandon any pretension to tell us what our good is. We are born in and act in a world *already* structured by institutions, models, achievements, traditions—by traditions, moreover, which do not force us to be "traditionalists", precisely because we have the good fortune to be heirs to the tradition of rationally criticising traditions. We do not have to construct an alternative world, an alternative society, as the utopian mind supposes—a construction for which we should find ourselves forced to borrow features of the world and society that we already have. (Separated from other features that complete and correct them, these would lose their value and even their meaning.) Rather, our task is quite different. It is to explore our world phenomenologically, and thence to derive our concepts and motives. Any legitimate reason for transforming the world will arise from the world as it reveals itself to this kind of enquiry. I have just alluded to the phenomenological outlook. Although Kolnai hardly mentions phenomenology in this work,[6] he was a student of Husserl, and his fundamental inspiration certainly came from that quarter. It is perfectly possible to "bracket" the ultimate categories once beloved by metaphysics and their claim to capture all that there is of nature or history. A scrupulous description of the framework of thought through which we express our humanity is enough, if not to guide all our actions, at least to provide a sound orientation for our thinking and living.

In order to define this "phenomenological conservatism" more clearly, it is well worth comparing it with the conceptions of two writers to whom Kolnai thought himself closely allied: Karl Popper and Michael Oakeshott. Like Popper, he believes that reforming activity presupposes a fixed— hence traditional—framework, without which the reform cannot even be thought and appraised. In order to assess what changes, we must have something which does not change.[7] Like Oakeshott, he holds that the human world is structured by "idioms of conduct", and that human life, as Europe has come to savour it, finds its mainspring and its happiness in an attentive fidelity to the immanent meaning—and thus, for the most part, to the traditional procedures—of each of these idioms, whether culinary, scientific, or political.[8] But in fact Kolnai also sets himself firmly apart from these two authors. He thinks that Popper's conservatism is too exclusively epistemological, too much concentrated in the value of a traditional frame of reference, for the progress of knowledge and the appraisal of reforms:

that Popper is not sensible enough of the *intrinsic* merits, both moral and vital, of a conservative attitude. In the last analysis, Popper puts too much faith in the reformatory ideas of the age. As for Oakeshott, Kolnai thinks he goes too far in his criticism of "rationalism", and puts reason itself in jeopardy; that he exaggerates the virtues of "immanence", of "habitual" and "unreflective" absorption in a traditional "idiom of conduct"; that he fails to see both the necessity and the possibility of the mind's acknowledgement of objective rules formulable in universal terms, such as moral laws, and even of its striving, within certain limits, to define something resembling a human nature, albeit in sketchy and tentative fashion. If Popper's political philosophy is tainted with "progressivism", Oakeshott's is tainted with "obscurantism", with the conviction that it is possible to be a conservative and nothing else.[9]

A second and fundamental objection Kolnai raises against Oakeshott's moral philosophy is that it gives no place to *conscience,* through which a human being is able to bring his conduct into living contact with the universal rules of morality; nor to that splitness, that interior dialogue, by which one is reminded of the irreducible distance between what one does and what one ought to do, what one is and what one ought to be. This is also one of the main objections Kolnai makes to the utopian mind. According to Oakeshott's extreme conservatism, morality consists in spontaneous conformity to the moral idiom of our civilisation and to the habits it has developed—or ought to have developed, had it not been in part overlaid by reflexive and abstract conceptions of morality. But the utopian mind empties conscience even more radically. In its contemplation of a future state of humanity in which reality and value, *is* and *ought,* coincide, it contemplates a human condition in which conscience will have no function and no meaning. The man of the future, man *par excellence,* is a being without conscience. It follows that what is given to us as conscience in our present state is, in the utopian's eyes, merely social man's dissatisfaction with our actual and provisional condition, a dissatisfaction which will naturally come to an end when utopia is realised.

Thus, whereas Kolnai judges Oakeshott to display a kind of aestheticising extremism in his striving to be a conservative and nothing else, the distinctive mark of Kolnai's own conservatism could be said to be its giving so large a place to conscience, understood as the capacity and the duty of every person to judge situations, actions and human beings (himself included) not only in the light of the idioms of conduct implicit in our civilisation, but also in the light of explicit and universal rules. Certainly conscience, as such, is not conservative. On the contrary, since it judges— wisely or unwisely—in the name of a moral absolute, it can easily become the principle of a revolutionary attitude if it is left to run on its own. That is why, in practice, totalitarian undertakings find so ready a support among sincerely conscientious people who are indignant at the misery of the poor, say, or at national humiliation—moving them to place their moral energy in the service of a conception which destroys the very idea of conscience. But this is the point. It is because there is a natural and necessary tension between the conscientious and the conservative attitudes that the prudent man has to learn how to combine them, to learn that the relative weight of each depends on circumstances and on the agent's ability to compose and harmonise, judiciously and even stylishly, the various legitimate themes of free conduct. A conscience with a lively sensitivity to universal moral demands, but also well aware of political constraints, of ambiguities and conflicts of values and the uncertainties attending action; a conscience which, while it is at odds with the world, does not hurry to condemn the world but takes time to consider the adversary's reasons; in short, a conscience informed and armed with a conservative political philosophy—here, says Kolnai, is the rock on which the totalitarian temptation, and the more general utopian temptation, will founder.

Kolnai's criticism of the utopian mind is pertinent and convincing, and his phenomenology of the social world contains a wealth of suggestions. Nevertheless, it seems to me that there is an important question that he largely ignores: what is it that has brought about the devastating spread of the utopian spirit in modern times, especially the twentieth century? As I have already pointed out, one can only admire Kolnai's demonstration of how the utopian illusion rests so naturally on the human relation to values and to the desirable, yet goes on to falsify and pervert it. But is this psychological genealogy enough? The real theme of Kolnai's investigation is not so much the utopian mind as such, which is always possible and present to some degree in every age. It is the modern, extreme, form of the utopian mind: namely, totalitarianism. Kolnai does show that there is a legitimate place for a study of the social, political and spiritual circumstances which have favoured the development of totalitarianism, and among these it would seem that he accorded central importance to the mechanisms of mass society. But he does not enquire more deeply into them.[10]

Certainly the utopian mind displays more than enough striking and clearly defined characteristics for it to be treated as a kind of essence. The fruitfulness of Kolnai's analysis amply justifies singling out this mentality for study. Not only that—there is even a danger of blurring the sharp outline of totalitarianism by concentrating on an enumeration, however erudite and discerning, of the circumstances which have favoured its development. But between the uniqueness and solidity of the essence on the one hand, and the multiplicity of circumstances to which the analyst seems free to refer or not as he sees fit on the other, there seems to be too great a hiatus. Something is still wanting in the analysis. I am led to think that the missing link we are looking for, between the essence and the circumstances, can be found only in the study of ideas. Is the utopian mind an ever-present possibility for the human relation to values as it is actualised under particular circumstances? Perhaps this is so, but if these circumstances are to set in motion such a radically new historical phenomenon, with the consequence that this natural possibility should be realised and stabilised in an essence as prodigiously effective as that of totalitarianism, then the explanation has to lie in the working of some intellectual system that can make what is in fact unthinkable apparently thinkable, or present a contradictory project of the will as a positive scientific theory. From time to time Kolnai does recall the theories that seem to him to be particularly suggestive of the contradictions of the utopian mind, especially the theory of Rousseau. But it seems to me that Kolnai is insufficiently attentive to the actual workings of intellectual mechanisms and systems of ideas—not only in what makes all sorts of totalitarian projects possible but also in the development of modern politics more generally.

In my discussion of the dwindling of practical reason and the enlargement of the theoretical point of view, I have already pointed to what seems to me to be one of the intellectual preconditions for the existence of the totalitarian attitude. To this, as it were, negative condition, I should like to add a positive one.

Let us remember that Kolnai sees the central contradiction of the utopian project in the fact that man is given two strictly contradictory roles. The utopian wants man to be responsible for a radically new social world, yet thinks of him as the passive product of the society which precedes him. He is thus at the same time the omnipotent master of society or history, and its raw material or docile creation. He is both sovereign maker or sovereign artificer, and mere matter. How can one avoid thinking here of Thomas Hobbes, who, in his *Leviathan,* presents us with social man in precisely this double role, described in these very terms?[11] Certainly Hobbesian absolutism has hardly anything in common with modern totalitarianism. But I would like to suggest that certain fundamental categories of the modern politics whose framework Hobbes did so much to determine—especially the categories of "sovereignty", of "representation", of the "artificial" body politic—are pregnant with the possibility of the development or dialectic whose study might shed a strong light upon the genesis of totalitarianism. In this way—thanks to our making room for this third term, which is the workings of a system of ideas—might one not articulate more completely and adequately the study of particular historical circumstances with the general phenomenology of the human world?

This is only a suggestion. Whether or not there is the need that I suppose there to be, this does not in the least impair the essential validity and importance of Kolnai's study of these matters. After all, we have plenty of judicious historians of modern political philosophy. Only very rarely do we come across thinkers like Kolnai, with the nerve to link political reflection with a phenomenology of the human world, to meet a historical emergency with their gaze fastened on the invariants of the human condition, and with the nerve and the capacity to assume the role of a political philosopher.

NOTES

1 *See* Adam Ferguson, *An Essay in the History of Civil Society*, 1767, IV, 1.
2 Pierre Manent's essay was written in 1993 as the introduction to *Aurel Kolnai: The Utopian Mind and Other Papers*, ed. Francis Dunlop, London: Athlone, 1995. [Editor's note.]
3 *See* Michael Oakeshott, *Rationalism in Politics, and Other Essays*, London: Methuen, 1962.
4 *See* Hannah Arendt, *The Origins of Totalitarianism*, New York: Harcourt Brace, 1951. Revised edn., New York: Meridian Books, 1958.
5 On these points Kolnai's analyses are very close, though he could not have known them, to those developed by Alain Besançon in his great work *Les origines intellectuelles du léninisme*, Paris: Calmann-Lévy, 1977; English translation *The Rise of the Gulag*.
6 [Ed.: *see* note 2.]
7 *See* Sir Karl Popper, *The Poverty of Historicism*, London: Routledge & Kegan Paul, 1957; also "Towards a Rational Theory of Tradition", in *Rationalist Annals*, London, 1948.
8 *See* Michael Oakeshott, *On Human Conduct*, Oxford University Press, 1975; also *Rationalism in Politics*.
9 Kolnai wrote a noteworthy review of *Rationalism in Politics*: *see Philosophy*, XL, 1965, pp. 263–64.
10 [Ed.: Pierre Manent could not have known that some of Kolnai's plans for the book show that he intended to deal at length with this topic, though he never actually did so.]
11 [Ed.: Kolnai himself pointed, incidentally, to the utopian aspects of Hobbes. *See* the translation of "La mentalité utopienne" on p. 155 of *The Utopian Mind*, etc. Ref. in note 2.]

Aurel Kolnai and Utopia

DAVID WIGGINS

1. The familiar criticism of utopias is that they are wildly impracticable; or, slightly more interestingly, that the pursuit of utopias, however wildly impracticable each utopia may manifestly appear, constantly deflects people into unwise, ruthless or extreme courses of action they might never, in the absence of utopian thinking, have undertaken. Thus Thomas Nagel, in his book *Equality and Partiality*, sees the evil of utopianism as the twin of the evil of hard-nosed realism.[1]

Kolnai would not have disagreed with the observation that the idea of something that is in fact impossible can all too easily have practical and sinister effects. (That was something he had often said himself.) But he would not have been prepared to see the evils of utopianism and hard-nosed realism as symmetrical. For Kolnai's own criticism of utopianism was not in the first instance practical but conceptual. Specific schemes for the piecemeal improvement of people's health or wealth or recreation or education or whatever (even schemes for the amelioration of the lot of mankind) can often be thought about coherently. They can be conceived— or they can be imagined, rather, without any claims to predictive accuracy—to almost any degree of detail that one might wish. In someone's visualising such improvements, the motivation for the proposed improvement need not be lost. With utopias, little of this applies, or so Kolnai held. With utopias of the kind that he was concerned with—in a moment we shall delimit this kind—the wonderful possibility that seems to be envisaged and desired cannot be coherently thought through or coherently embraced, even as an ideal. In so far as the pursuit of some particular utopia attains for some person or group of persons (despite this incoherence) the status of an active ideal, and in so far as the ideal then conditions some aspect of their whole being, the evil that then presents itself is of an altogether different order from that of hard-nosed realism. It will subvert value, thought and practice in a way in which they could never be subverted by ordinary world-weariness, ordinary apathy, or ordinary cynicism.

2. Kolnai's writings on these matters have been around for a long time. Indeed, his doctrines of moral emphasis and value pluralism, which led

the way into his critique of perfectionism and of utopianism, are prefig-
ured in the *War against the West*,[2] Kolnai's book about Nazi philosophy
and Nazi ideals. He saw as the product of a pathologically exaggerated
emphasis on some human values at the expense of others. That book was
written and published in the 1930s, two full decades before the appearance of the published writings of the late 1950s that Francis Dunlop collected alongside the unfinished book *The Utopian Mind*.[3] Nor was
Kolnai's stance a completely solitary one. There is some convergence,
I understand, between the insights and diagnoses of Kolnai, those of
Raymond Ruyer in *L'Utopie et les utopies*,[4] and those of Alain Besançon in
Les Origines intellectuelles du léninisme.[5] But the truth is that diagnoses
such as these have scarcely impinged at all on the steady flow of present-
day moral and political philosophy—or on social psychology for that matter. No doubt this has some connection with the fact that so little has
been done in America and Western Europe to measure up to the full
import (the whole philosophical, political and psychological significance)
either of the rise or of the collapse of Communism; and the further fact
that in Eastern Europe so many philosophers and political scientists now
think that the only forward-looking thing they can do is to waste not
another moment before they engage with Anglophone models of justice
and democracy.

3. The conceptual insouciance that Kolnai complained of in utopian thinking is worth illustrating. I shall mention two examples.

Richard Rorty is a writer philosophically so squeamish and/or so canny
that he rejects all philosophical notions of essence, nature or truth. He
rejects philosophical conceptions of the difference between appearance and
reality, between relative and absolute, between how a thing is in itself and
how it is in relation to human needs, and between objective and subjective. He avoids all reference to human nature, to essence or to correspondence. But, despite this fastidiousness, Rorty uses over and over again,
without any perceptible self-consciousness, such phrases as "our chances
of achieving a democratic utopia" and "scenarios that were supposed to
culminate in an egalitarian utopia". Over and over again, he reiterates sentiments such as these: "So far as I can see, nothing theoretical that we
have learned since Mill's time, and in particular nothing we have learned
by deconstructing the metaphysics of presence, or from Freud or Lacan,
gives us reason to *revise*, as opposed to supplement, our previous descriptions of utopia. Neither Foucault, Derrida, Nietzsche nor Lacan can
make obsolete the old-fashioned utopian scenario, the one that leads to a
global society of freedom and equal opportunity."[6]

That is America in 1999. In England and in the same year, John Carey,
a learned, astute and sometimes acerbic critic of English literature, published *The Faber Book of Utopias*.[7] Carey makes a point of including and

commenting upon numerous "dystopias" (in full cognisance of the solecistic etymology of such an antonym of "utopia"). But he does not address the conceptual question. Perceiving and lamenting this, I sent to him photocopies of various Kolnai pieces. He replied that he was making something of the wonderfully concise essay Francis Dunlop recently retrieved and supplied for Daniel Mahoney's edited collection, *Aurel Kolnai: Privilege and Liberty and other Essays*. Something had clicked. But, in the week when I was thinking what to say here in Budapest, I turned on the wireless to hear Carey still quoting, as if in summation of his own position (though radio programmes allow little time, I know, for anyone to set forth their whole position), Oscar Wilde's dictum, "A map of the world that does not include Utopia is not even worth glancing at, for it leaves out the one country at which humanity is always landing... Progress is the realisation of Utopia."

It goes without saying that Kolnai used the same citation. He had a vivid sense of the indispensability to the human condition of human ideals and unfinished projects. But he would say that it is precisely the indispensability to us of ideals that enforces both our attention to that which we make the object of our ideal and some measure of self-consciousness about the sort of emphasis we prepare to place upon such an object.

4. Now that the relevant writings of Kolnai are published, thanks to Dunlop and Mahoney, one possible way forward is for his admirers and critics to try to spell out the conceptual critique that Kolnai wanted to make of Utopia—of utopias as such—and to do so in English so ordinary, or (if necessary) so professional and analytical, that Anglophones cannot say that they do not understand what is being said. Then, in whatever way they choose, our contemporaries can respond. I shall take the first step or two. Then I hope others will help me.

5. First then, what are we talking about? Kolnai's working definition is as follows: "Utopia is the conception of a perfect condition, envisioned as real, of men (or of a superhuman kind of being evolved from men), which is free from painful tensions and from the awareness of any presence of evil."

For a pedestrian Anglophone, this rushes things a bit. There is the conception and there is what the conception is of—its object—and we need each of these. Moreover, we need to start with the object. So, following the definition that Kolnai quotes approvingly from the *Encyclopaedia Britannica*, let us begin as follows: "A utopia is an ideal commonwealth whose inhabitants exist under perfect conditions." From John Carey let us catch up the sentence: "To count as a utopia, an imaginary place must be an expression of desire. To count as a dystopia, it must be an expression of fear."[8] From all this let us distil, first, something like this: "A utopia is a place, commonwealth, or state of affairs where human beings (or persons evolved from them) exist under perfect or ideal conditions—conditions that do not dispense with any intrinsic good or compromise any intrinsic good for some other intrinsic good, still less for evil." And let the word "Utopia", so capitalised, stand for the genus of such imaginary states of being.

What then of "utopianism"? I suggest we let this denominate not the mere impulse to conceive of some utopia (this, that or the other variant of Utopia), nor yet the mere desire for its coming into being—that is John Carey, but it is too faint for our purposes—but the properly serious entertaining of that utopian state of being (either everywhere or in some whole department of human affairs) as a *significant and compulsory reference point* for practical thinking.

The central case of utopianism, so understood, is the simple, wholehearted embracing of the projected state of affairs as one of a person's active concerns. Here, though, we may discern two variants, the first being more common than the second and the second presupposing the first. One who indulges in the commoner kind of utopianism will simply tend to attach great significance to the imperfection of any actual arrangement. He will be strongly disinclined to consider the real possibility that all alternatives to it are imperfect also. He will be reluctant to suppose that an existing arrangement with existing defects might yet be the best possible. In its least malignant form, this sort of utopianism represents the outlook of an ordinary progressive democrat (also bringing to mind, though, the warning that Kolnai cites from Jakob Burckhardt—"Keeping everything persistently subject to discussion and change, democracy will end up with a host of irreconcilable contradictions"[9]).

That is the more common but less pure form of utopianism (dangerous chiefly where ignorance, philistinism or lack of education that take pride in themselves commandeer the democratic process). In a stronger form, however, utopianism leads the way into something altogether more formidable, namely the utopian mind or the utopian mentality. In Kolnai's treatment, this mind or mentality amounts at least to this. It is the mentality of one for whom the ideal of some utopia *either* takes up his whole sky *or else* competes actively with all rival motivations and ideals for any and every part of his whole sky. Either in some whole sphere or else limitlessly he embraces in its totality the idea of some utopia. Here at last we arrive at the mental state whose typical bent it is to pursue and/or uphold through thick and thin some totalitarian political order. Here we catch up at last with the *utopian will*.

Back now to utopias in philosophy. It seems reasonable to let Utopianism be the philosophical position that defends utopias, defends the genus Utopia, defends utopianism and exempts the utopian mind or mentality from all other faults than those of precipitancy or impracticality. It does not see incoherence in Utopia, nor does it see in the utopian mind any inevitable subversion of value (as such) or practical reason (as such).

6. Let me make it clear that I am not trying to improve on Kolnai or to reorganise his position: I am only preparing to spread out in front of you explicitly, and at an artificially leisurely pace, one of his several arguments about Utopia (arguments not always distinguished by him with antiseptic clarity) and to do so in such a way that an Anglophone philosopher could not, in 21st century, dismiss the result as unintelligible. In preparation to do this, the next thing is for me to paint in two or three of Kolnai's own observations about utopias as so far characterised.

Utopias are man-made. Their every detail is either deliberate or deliberately acquiesced in. Nothing is left to chance or (in that sense) contingent.[10] Moreover, utopias are cut off from alteration or contamination by that which is non-utopian.

> The purity, exclusiveness and isolation of the utopian dream-world proclaim the negation of the [actual] world, that is, of the world of division, of mutual awareness of alterity, with the ever-renewed demands of adjustment, of frictions, compacts, and compromise.

I quote here from the published version of the short essay "The Utopian Mind", to be found in Daniel Mahoney's collection *Aurel Kolnai: Privilege and Liberty and other Essays in Political Philosophy*.[11]

Secondly, there is the *content* of the utopian vision. Because the *"streamlined perfection"* of utopias implies

> wisdom, insight, all institutions perspicuous and carrying their justification on the face of them, eugenics flourishing, medical and biological advances of all kinds, fascinating regularities, bodies and buildings resplendent with beauty, a boundless and fully deserved trust of men in one another and in their common medium…[precisely for that reason] *criticism and opposition*, split and tension in any sense, *no longer have a point of application*. There is nothing to provoke them and they are uncalled for, they have no motive to thrive on—and are *a limine* impossible…[12]

For in a utopia all conceivable values are fully realised together. And this is to say that values and advantages do not, in a utopia, need to be set in the context of "evils, renunciations, and necessities of choice". They are not "subject to the permanent necessity of being weighted against and tempered to one another". There is no need to experience them "according to a *mode of imperfection*".[13]

7. The effectiveness of Kolnai's critique will depend on at least two things. We need to be reassured (but this I leave largely to others) how exactly utopianism lies at the root of (all or most) totalitarian political thinking and how integral it is to all so far recorded subversions of constitutional order. But it has also to be shown—and this is my chief concern—what utopia's *conceptual incoherence* is. What prevents, what *logically* or *conceptually* prevents, a place, country, commonwealth or state of affairs from embracing all intrinsic goods and dispensing at the same time with all Kolnaistic compromise—either the compromise of good by bad or the compromise between the demands of one intrinsic good and the demands of another intrinsic good? Let us begin with Kolnai's own words:

> A cat can be all black, all white, all grey tiger, and so forth, or black and white, or parti-coloured in various ways, up to the bizarrerie of a tortoiseshell with white and striped ginger patches; but the selfsame cat cannot possess all the peculiar loveliness of, say, an all-black *and* that of an all-white, an all-blue, an all-ginger and an all-tortoiseshell fur. It is easier to dream of a perfect state of man incorporating both complete determination and pure spontaneity. Even in personal projects of life, highly strung utopianism is quite possible. A man may jointly pursue several ambitious goals which are in fact incompatible with his circumstances, and also intrinsically inconsistent: thus social grandeur with the corresponding display of high living, and sovereign spirituality along with high thinking. Whatever the outcome may be, it will be widely different from the proposed aim, which cannot consistently be thought out, let alone achieved.[14]

> Utopianism rejects the commonsense *submission* to the human condition and "pursuit of the good" *on its* [the human condition's] *terms*, erecting in its place the idol of a perfect human condition which would not be a human condition and which demands the *self-surrender* of man to an alien, unreal and (as to its actual features) inconceivable construct of his abstractive mind. Linked therewith is a mirage of the all-comprehensive perfect good, discontinuous and out of tune with man's actual pursuit of value achievements in the framework of a reality which is not identical with the Good but logically inseparable from any meaning man may attribute to it [i.e. the Good].[15]

8. In the face of these claims of Kolnai's, an opponent may arise who will make the following objections: "Kolnai is a pluralist about the Good, as are you and the others who follow in his footsteps (or Aristotle's footsteps). For you people, goods are not variations on a single theme or simple determinations of some specific determinable (compare *Nicomachean Ethics* 1096b.21ff.). For you, intrinsic goods, as you follow Ross in calling

them, have separate and intrinsic characters corresponding to attachments and discernments that are separately and diversely rooted. Why then should not *all* these distinct kinds of good coexist in some set-up?"

My reply to that is that it does not follow from the separateness and diversity of distinct intrinsic goods that the *demands* they place upon the circumstances or things that are to satisfy them in the actual world are causally or logically disjoint from one another. If you have to give as much as it demands to one kind of good, then that will trespass on the space you needed in order to make room for some *other* good thing. Examples ought to suffice to show this.

Consider Richard Rorty's global society of freedom and equality of opportunity. Such a society will need to emphasise deliberately the particular goods that it designates as important among the larger plurality of intrinsic goods. If so, how well will freedom and equality of opportunity so designated cohere with another goal—namely that there should not be too great an inequality of *outcomes*? Or, passing across to something that is less controversially intrinsically evil, how irrational is it for one to fear that emphasis on equality of opportunity will not only entail the institution of procedures that restrict freedom (intentionally or unintentionally),[16] but also bring progressive immiseration of those who make too little of the opportunities furnished to them? Again, is it a simple accident or contingency that in England the public's preoccupation with equality of opportunity, and with every last detail of what that (as the public interprets it) requires, now promises to deform universities' admission procedures to a point where "reverse discrimination" will crowd out some of those who are better equipped for the subjects that they apply to pursue? If the long-term effect of this last is to endanger the cultivation of disinterested learning itself, will that too be a mere accident? There is equality of concern and there is disinterested learning. Each is intrinsically good, but it may be impossible for there to coexist at one and the same time as much as *society thinks it desires* of this equality *and* of this learning.

It may be insisted that these problems and difficulties are only contingent. I am not sure that that is true. But in any case there is in this area a necessary truth. Name any plurality >1 of intrinsic goods. Then, in the presence of a set of laws or law-like tendencies that are the actual laws and tendencies in operation, the pursuit of any one good will limit the possible ways of pursuing any other intrinsic good. If any one good is pursued *à outrance*, that rules out the maximal pursuit of some other(s). Even if we imagine the causal connections and exclusions of the actual world being varied, that is not to imagine a world without causal connections. It is to begin to imagine a world with different causal connections and exclusions. It is surely a conceptual necessity, no less, that there be some such. It is not a matter of what Nicholas Rescher calls, in a related context, the "harsh realities of a difficult world".[17] If you call the actual world a difficult world simply on the strength of its having causal connections and exclusions, then every conceivable world will have to count as difficult.

9. At this point, a philosophical utopian may say that Kolnai and his allies are confusing *intrinsic goods* and *prima facie intrinsic goods*. The important thing, the utopian will say, is to understand better the causal connections and exclusions just mentioned and then make the right choice. A simple analogy from cooking may be invoked here. In making a sauce béarnaise or a sauce hollandaise, one needs to get as close as possible to the right proportion of ingredients. It would be absurd to think of the proportionalities involved in sauce-making as compromises between the separate claims of egg yolk, of vinegar, of salt, of butter, of lemon juice... In a sauce, one is not aiming to have as much egg as one may, as much butter as one may and as much lemon juice as one may. The correct mixture in cooking is not a compromise at all. Still less is it what Kolnai called a "mediation".[18] Analogously, then, it may be said that that which practical reason pursues in the case of each *prima facie* intrinsic good, and pursues for its own sake, is the right compound or the right measure. That is the real intrinsic good.

To this I should make three replies, of which the first is independent of the other two.

The first reply has the shape of a doubt concerning the very idea of an overwhelming argument or consideration that could provide a unique answer to the question of the right choice between the whole plurality of intrinsically good things. Here, my own philosophical allegiance lies with William James:

> In this solid and tridimensional sense, so to call it, those philosophers are right who contend that the world is a standing thing with no progress, no real history. The changing conditions of history touch only the surface of the show. The altered equilibriums and redistributions only diversify our opportunities and open chances to us for new ideals. But, with each new ideal that comes into life, the chance of a life based on some old ideal will vanish; and he would needs be a presumptuous calculator who should with confidence say that the total sum of significance is positively and absolutely greater at any one epoch than at any other of the world... There are compensations: and no outward changes of condition in life can keep the nightingale of its eternal meaning from singing in all sorts of different men's hearts...[19]

Of course, one in Kolnai's position will refuse to treat the Christian epoch as an epoch just like any other. But his reasons for that lie off the page (off these pages), and they do not suffice to distinguish one Christian period from all others. The substance of James's point is still available to him.

Secondly, I should insist that the idea of *prima facie* intrinsic goodness does insufficient justice to that which reasonable agents value. What they value for itself is not simply the life that brings together, so far as possible, equality of opportunity (say) and disinterested learning. Rather, they value disinterested learning itself (for itself) and whatever else (for itself)—as well as the life that contains both.

Thirdly, I offer an observation on a recent exchange between Ronald Dworkin and David Miller, where Dworkin seeks to uphold his claim that conflicts between distinct values are "illusory":

> If liberty or community or respect for merit really did conflict with equal concern for all, then the only acceptable result would not be a compromise of equality but the total defeat of the rival value.[20]

Here, one who is more or less persuaded by Kolnai's view will be bound to wonder how such a head of steam could build up behind "equal concern for all" (interpreted as Dworkin interprets these words) that it could inflict this kind of defeat. It is one thing to find the proper accommodation (here, now, in these circumstances) and another thing to say that this is the *only thing* here to be treated as an intrinsic value. Maybe the point is meant to be that "equal concern for all" is meant to roll up everything that is desirable intrinsically. (How?) Even if that were possible, what could prevent intrinsic values from importing conflicting demands within the determination of the content of equality of concern?

10. The time has now come for Kolnai's next move. Suppose someone has looked about him, has found wanting every actual human arrangement about him, and has reacted to this not in a spirit of improvement or emendation, but in a spirit of utopianist dissatisfaction. Suppose that, in the face of imperfection which he confuses with rank evil, he looks around him for something altogether better; and suppose some radical alternative presents itself to him, first as a reference point for the criticism of current institutions or practices, then as the ratified object of his utopian will. Once this happens, Kolnai will say, this utopia will

> not be understood as a mere lavishly stocked grange of goods, a superabundant *collection* of values, advantages, achievements and satisfactions. Rather, these are merely so many facets of the selfsame unique perfection, logically necessary manifestations of a unique happy "*solution*" of the puzzle.[21]

The utopian world (or un-world) is not perfect because it is good in every respect, the criteria being, as it were, taxatively enumerated. It *cannot but* be good in every respect, *because* it is *utopian*. The ordinary world, with most of its evils reformed out of existence or confined within narrow limits, and with most of its values improved to the point of excellence, would still fall short of any approximation of utopia, and would essentially amount to nothing greatly better than before: its accomplishments might as well not exist, and, being contingent, would be perishable and thus intrinsically below the standard of perfection. To put it differently again, what utopia purports to be is not the fulfilment of so many tasks but the solution of *the* puzzle. From the principle of perfection on which it is built everything else derives; and *that* they so derive makes all these particular achievements valid and inseparable one from the other... Utopian perfection can be *read* in terms of universally accepted values (i.e., self-evidently confirmed by outside "observers"), but it expressly and defiantly refuses to *submit* to the test of ordinary, universal outside standards.[22]

The next phase then, after the fiat of the utopian will, is the terrifying confidence and ruthlessness of the utopian will—sustained at just one remove by the selective blindness and unscrupulous optimism of the philosophical utopian. At the critical point where a utopian commits himself to this or that utopian alternative, the decisive consideration for him, and the reasons for his choice, will be as various as the perfectionist creeds themselves. Nazism, Bolshevism, pure laissez-faire, anarchism are simply the more visible among a whole multitude of possibilities. But what, then, tips the balance? What magnifies the imperfections of the actual set-up and distracts attention from the risks and the costs of implementing some total alternative? What makes the unknown alternative seem compulsory?

Kolnai's answer is that, at the crucial point, the chosen utopia comes to be seen as the *answer to the puzzle*. Hence the lifelong effort he made to show that, in the absence of any even thinkable answer to the puzzle, an absence philosophically entirely intelligible, the puzzle is *itself* fraudulent. There is nothing in the logic of value predication or the logic of practice (see here Kolnai's lecture notes for his London intercollegiate course on phenomenology, preserved in the Nachlass), and nothing in the logic of mixed evaluations and prescriptions, to subvert the fundamental truism that, everywhere and anywhere, over and over again, we have to compromise and mediate, with some right emphasis, between the demands of independent intrinsic goods. The proper response to the needless misery of mankind is not to start from zero, but to persist in the renovation and repair of that which is. The renovation and repair of that which is, undertaken in the light of the good towards which our workaday ethical practices and notions point immanently, offers almost limitless scope for the human ideals without which most of human life and striving would lose its meaning. The aboriginal and indispensable impulse to the utopian perversion—the impulse to that perversion of personal idealism which first attacks imperfection as intolerable but in the end justifies evil as "transitory" and "inevitable"—deserves a better object than some alternative state of being that is simply *unthinkable*.

NOTES

1 *See* the passage quoted on pp. ix–x in my preface to Aurel Kolnai, *The Utopian Mind and Other Papers*, ed. Francis Dunlop, London: Athlone Press, 1995.

2 London: Gollancz, 1938.

3 *See* note 1 for reference.

4 Paris: Presses Universitaires de France, 1950.

5 Paris: Callman-Lévy, 1977.

6 *See Philosophy and Social Hope*, Harmondsworth: Penguin, 1999, pp. xiv, 230, 236, etc.

7 London: Faber & Faber, 1999.

8 *Op. cit.*, p. xi.

9 Kolnai, ed. Dunlop, *op. cit.*, p. 37.

10 Rather, nothing is left to chance unless it is *deliberately* left so—as in certain images Kolnai might also have wished to count as utopian or as *derivatively* utopian. Compare an observation of Michael Oakeshott's about Hayek:

> [T]he informality of English politics...enabled us to escape, for a long time, putting too high a hope on political achievement—to escape, in politics at least, the illusion of the evanescence of imperfection... [T]hat resistance has now itself been converted into an ideology. This is perhaps the main significance of Hayek's *Road to Serfdom*—not the cogency of his doctrine, but the fact that it is a doctrine. A plan to resist all planning may be better than its opposite, but it belongs to the same style of politics.

Michael Oakeshott, *Rationalism in Politics*, London: Methuen, 1962, Essay One, text adjoining note 28.

11 Daniel J. Mahoney (ed.), Lanham, MD: Maryland: Lexington Books, 1999, p. 124.

12 *Op. cit.*, pp. 124–25.

13 *Op. cit.*, p. 126.

14 Kolnai, ed. Dunlop, op. cit., p. 91.

15 *Op. cit.*, p. 101.

16 Cf. Burckhardt: "...the social demand imposes on the state an inconceivable load of tasks, which cannot be solved except by means of an equally unheard of plenitude of power", quoted by Kolnai in Dunlop (ed.), *op. cit.*, p. 37.

17 Nicholas Rescher, *Ethical Idealism*, University of California Press, 1987, p. 54: Even a rule ethic can make room for the conception of an obligation that is not destroyed by mere infeasibility—and can thus permit of "impracticable ideals". An ethic of rules is not inherently antithetical to one of ideals, precisely because it itself provides for an ideal that is in fact unrealisable *amid the harsh realities of a difficult world*—that of a person who altogether "lives by the rules". The moral enterprise is fundamentally committed to the never fully achievable task of making a place for the ideal in the *hostile environment of the world's realities*.

18 Compare Ronald Dworkin's engagement with Judge Posner, reprinted in *A Matter of Principle*, Oxford: OUP, 1986, pp. 237–66, to which I am indebted for the analogy with cooking. In this dispute Dworkin prevails, but he prevails, I think, because the values that are at issue are justice and efficiency, and efficiency is not a good candidate for an intrinsic value.

19 William James, *Talks to Teachers on Psychology: and to Students on Some of Life's Ideals*, London: Longman, Green & Co., 1899, pp. 299 and 301.

20 *Times Literary Supplement*, December 1, 2000, p.15.

21 Mahoney (ed.), *op. cit.*, p. 125.

22 Mahoney (ed.), *op. cit.*, p. 126.

3. Ethics

Aims in Games and Moral Purposes

LORÁND AMBRUS-LAKATOS

In "Deliberation is of Ends",[1] Aurel Kolnai argues against what he takes to be a fundamental doctrine of Aristotle's ethics, that deliberation is of means, of means for the attainment of the supreme final end, which in turn could be glossed as happiness.[2] But there is no such final end. Deliberation is, instead, of the "conspectus" of autonomous ends that might be more or less permanently present in our lives.[3] Concerning the ethical "side" of this issue, Kolnai claims that "morality turns on cherishing one sovereign right end", that is, the virtuous man desires to lead a morally good life (DE 56).

If there were one overarching end that is not strictly speaking moral, then morality would be debased to the level of instrumentality. If, on the other hand, there were a single ultimate end and this were taken as that of being moral, then there would be no room for practices that are morally neutral. However, the pursuit of the moral end cannot encompass all the worthy and autonomous pursuits we might have:

> [E]ven a man endowed with the keenest sense of honesty does not as a rule make business transactions from the motive of practising the virtue of honesty, and the rules of honesty tell him no more in what business transactions he should engage than the rules of chess tell the player what moves he should make in order to win the game. (DE 57)

Several questions remain. Suppose it is a matter of choice whether the main moral aim is included in the ensemble of ends we pursue. To allow this possibility, it seems, would also amount to lowering the status of morality. Take also into account that, according to Kolnai, while ideals are chosen instead of being imposed by rational evidence, the main moral end is not an ideal. Then if we ineluctably respond to the demands of the main moral end, and if deliberation is of ends, that is, of which ends we are to regard as our own when faced with the necessity to make choices, why and how do we deliberate about it? Also, can there then be a serious conflict between pursuing the moral end and seeking our non-moral ultimate ends?

Both of these questions could possibly be answered by stating first that the moral end is not monolithic; it has an internal structure. However, if, for instance, its pursuit consists in obeying a set of rules, as the above quotation actually suggests, it is still hard to see what role deliberation can play in moral practice. Either there is a supreme moral principle or the moral agent has to seek consistency between the various rules, and the thesis according to which deliberation is of ends is still hard pressed, irrespective of which of these alternatives is adopted.

In this paper I seek to present a view on Kolnai's conception of the main moral end and of moral deliberation.[4] My starting hypotheses are that indeed for him this aim is complex and that it has to reflect the structure of the moral demands we have to face. Section I introduces Kolnai's analysis of games playing, in the framework of which his conception of how and what aims are pursued in certain important essentially social practices can be presented. Section II describes his position on how our moral purposes fit into this conception, and section III examines critically this position. Finally, section IV offers an account of how Kolnai thinks of the structure of moral demands, and proceeds to discuss how these ideas relate to the understanding of what our moral purposes are and what their structure is.

I

Kolnai's main task in his essay "Games and Aims"[5] is to present a philosophical analysis of the social practice of games playing. At the very beginning of this work, after considering two opinions on the importance of this subject, he quotes approvingly this passage:

> The theory of Games is never likely to provide a calculus of Morals; but it may well provide models on which to sharpen our logical teeth and develop our moral sense.[6] (GA 103)

This quotation then introduces another theme: what lessons for moral philosophy can be derived from a study of games, from the phenomenology, as it were, of what it is to play them? However, the theory of games that appears in this quotation is obviously that of von Neumann and Morgenstern, and Kolnai does not seem to be interested in discussing the relevance of this theory for ethics. Instead, he describes a conception of games that is his own. Thus in order to understand how the analysis of games as such may contribute to the development of our moral sense, this conception has first to be examined. Nevertheless, it might be helpful to consider it in contrast with what is generally known as game theory.

While what Kolnai proposes to deal with is games playing itself, game theory, as is well known, is about something else. It is an obvious misnomer, as its subject matter is strategic interaction.[7] In strategic situations agents cannot assume that the consequences of their actions depend only on their decisions and on the workings of chance. Rather, what others in the same situation do also affects the outcome. John von Neumann thought that games provide excellent models for such situations, but the problem that motivated the development of his and Morgenstern's theory was a then unsolved puzzle in economic theory, namely, the behaviour of firms in markets where they could neither dictate prices nor take as given the ones generated by other market participants.[8]

In Kolnai's analysis, chess is the paradigm of games, as it "presents, to a degree nearest to perfection or bordering on it, the characteristics of the Game situation as such" (GA 107). The possibly most important feature of chess, and thus of games, is that its "operational field" is constituted by a set of artificial rules. What one does in a game cannot be performed outside the game; one cannot commit one's fifth foul, as the rules of basketball define this act, outside a basketball game. Another crucial feature of games is that their course can be represented by a "denumerable sequence of moves"; the moves of the players can be conceived of as separable from the "psycho-physical reality" surrounding the players. In contradistinction to, say, billiards or golf, chess can be played by correspondence. Next, Kolnai also posits that games are detached from serious practices, and a completed game can produce nothing real for the players. A "serious" practice like participating in a two-bidder auction for oil-tract leases is not a proper game, despite the fact that it could be played by correspondence. Chess, the paradigm of games, has only two players, and the rules ought to allow only three sorts of outcome, a player either wins or loses, or attains a tie. So in the terminology of game theory it can be taken, as Kolnai also notes, as a two-person zero-sum game (GA 108). For von Neumann and Morgenstern chess is of course not the paradigm game, as there is no such thing. The paradigm in game theory is a canonical model consisting of a collection of mathematical objects (such as sets or probability distributions)[9] which, together with assumptions that further specify the model, should be able to represent strategic aspects of various sorts of social situations. Kolnai thinks that the common denominator of the characteristics of chess is the idea of the greatest possible abstractness (GA 108); the canonical model of game theory is as abstract as one can get.

Again, games in game theory—that is, models of strategic situations—are detached from serious practices only in the sense that they have to represent them, but they are meant to engage with these practices in virtue of the advice the theory can issue about how to behave within their confines. (Ironically, game theory can provide only vacuous and potentially misleading advice about how to play chess.) There is another important contrast. The rules of chess cannot of course prescribe the aims pursued in them, but naturally call for adopting the aims of winning or at least of not losing the game. In game theory, it is taken for granted that the players have to play the game, and its rules are conceived of as completely independent of the objectives of the participants within the game. The players are assumed to have the objectives attributed to them, and this is the maximisation of the expected value of their payoffs (in the several outcomes they may reach given a chosen action or course of actions). Now are these differences significant?

An obvious motivation Kolnai has in making chess the paradigm of games is to point to a paradox. While winning might seem at first sight as the natural goal in chess, it is not the only goal the players pursue. There is also an aim that is (in a sense) prior to that, that of playing the game at all (GA 112–13). Even if it is natural to suppose that one plays chess in order to provide a certain sort of entertainment for oneself, chess is played for its own sake. Playing a game is an essentially eirenic activity; he who plays chess does so in concert with the other, the two pursue a shared aim. But as he also aims at winning the game, or at least of not losing it, he has to participate in an agonistic context. This other aim can be attained only at the expense of the other failing to reach his corresponding goal. To rephrase the paradox, players co-operate in order to defeat each other; and also strive to outdo each other in a framework of collaboration. Indeed, Kolnai's paradigm is designed to bring out this tension, as the several kinds of races, or contests like drawing competitions, also exhibit game-like features, but they are not altogether agonistic. Similarly, due to the possibility of coalition-building in the course of playing them, many card games also fail to fit into the above pattern. By setting chess, or more generally board-games that can be described as zero-sum games, as the paradigm, the theme of co-operation appears only at the level of playing the game.

Rational deliberation in game theory[10] is a matter of finding out what one should do given one's objective.[11] The main difficulty concerns what reasonable beliefs can be formed about the course of action one's counterpart will adopt. As the objectives are ascribed to the players,[12] this deliberative problem is not sensitive to whether they are foolish or immoral. The only more or less eirenic feature is the need to co-operate with the other, in certain specific interactive settings, to attain an outcome that would be rational for each to reach, despite the fact that standard procedures of rational deliberation in game theory might not assure, and might even foreclose, its attainment. These settings include, among others, the well-known Prisoner's Dilemma game and the so-called "pure co-ordination" games. In the latter, the evaluation of the outcomes is identical for each player, and it could still be a problem for them to implement the one they regard as the best. Here the theory faces the well-known challenge of articulating the aim of co-operating with the others and of articulating the reasoning about the fulfilment of this aim. This articulation is problematic since the players are taken as having no shared aims, and since participating in an interactive situation is, again, not regarded as a matter of having any aims.

II

As it ascribes one aim to the players, that of maximising their expected pay-offs, game theory cannot capture Kolnai's paradox. It might even be the case that its problems with motivating co-operation, when this emerges, upon analysis, as a reasonable resultant or derived objective, could only be explicated by pointing to inevitable tensions between agonistic and eirenic aims in social interaction. But this is hardly what Kolnai thought of as the lesson the study of games can offer for moral philosophy. In fact, he writes that he is concerned "not so much with games of all kinds as with the peculiar structure of the standard 'self-contained' game situation, seen in its relation to the structure of willing in 'actual' or 'serious' practice" (GA 110). For the explication of this structure, we are to turn to his analysis of how the two aims pursued in the practice of playing chess are related to each other.

Can their relationship be described in standard terms of teleological analysis? These may be listed as follows. Something that is pursued for its own sake is an end in itself. Something that is pursued for the sake of something outside of itself is to be referred to as instrumental; it is a means to achieve an end already adopted. Clearly, a given activity, say, can be both an end in itself and instrumental at the same time; a standard example is that of playing basketball. If an end does not refer to another end, it is autonomous. A system of activities could be organised around one autonomous end, in which case it is a one-track system. Or it could have parallel ends. These, in turn, could be independent, or complementary to each other. According to Kolnai, the aims of chess players cannot be characterised by any of the teleological categories sketched out above. While it is true that aiming at winning is instrumental to playing, winning is not in a proper instrumental relationship to the end of playing the game, as an instrumental activity properly so called can serve its end only if there is a need for it being successfully accomplished. But winning is not necessary for playing a satisfactory chess game. And the two ends are certainly not independent, as one could not make sense of the aim of winning without conceiving the aim of playing the game; and, in turn, in normal cases one does not play it without being aware of the aim of winning. Finally, the aim of winning is not complementary but subordinate to the aim of playing, as one cannot aim to win in chess if one does not play it. Kolnai proposes to call the relation between the two aims a paratelic relation (GA 116), and I propose to call it, below, an enveloping relation. The secondary or enveloped aim of doing well in the game is described as the lateral implicate of the primary or enveloping aim of playing the game at all. [13]

Even if it is but rarely recognised that there are activities, embedded in serious practices, that could be best understood as serving two (or more) aims in an enveloping relation, they are, according to Kolnai, very widespread. For example, various academic endeavours, trials or lawsuits, even agricultural shows, all feature both overarching aims—gathering knowledge, finding out the truth, or developing suitable techniques—and also local goals, such as doing just a little bit better than our peers. In all these contexts competition for honours, promotions and other distinctions may even be guided by a co-operative spirit (GA 118–20). Indeed, we do well in viewing politics in a pluralist constitutional order as conducted within the confines of sufficiently game-like rules (GA 124–28). Now is it the case that we can find enveloping relations between ends only in contexts that are sufficiently game-like, or was chess only a convenient example by means of which this relation could be properly explicated? We need to note that the conclusion of the argument presented above about the relation of the two aims in chess points to a set of formal requirements which characterise any aims in an enveloping relation. Let A be the primary aim and B the secondary aim. First, B is not to be instrumental to A; just trying to achieve the former suffices for serving the latter. Next, B is to be an autonomous aim. Third, A and B cannot be independent of each other; they cannot be conceived independently of one another. Finally, there must be a relationship of subordination between them; B cannot be pursued if A is not pursued at the same time. It follows that whenever the pursuit of an activity involves two aims that meet these requirements, we are entitled to regard them as being in an enveloping relation. It is still reasonable to suppose that when an activity is pursued in a game-like context, we should be prepared to see an enveloping relation between the aims pursued there. While the question whether a certain practice is more or less like a game is determined by the degree to which it conforms to the strictures of the paradigm game of chess, to interpret it as a kind of game may serve to emphasise that its practitioners have to adopt both co-operative and conflict-involving aims.

For Kolnai, one can discern enveloping relations between aims not only in certain practices, but in general practical deliberation as well. The particular practical purposes pursued at any one time, recurrently, or almost always, are thus related to "permanent and paramount" aims (GA 122). Now what about activities that have moral significance, activities with "moral emphasis"? Kolnai states that a kind of enveloping relation

> may be seen between a moral agent's general and comprehensive aim of 'being righteous' (or 'virtuous'), that is, leading a morally good life, and his implied and subordinate, but autonomous, aim of doing his duty in each morally significant situation and endeavouring to achieve the concrete purpose entailed by that duty fulfilment. (GA 122)

In justifying this statement he refers to the formal criteria of an enveloping relation. The two sorts of moral aims are not independent, as to do right "derives its meaning from the 'blanket' aspiration of moral goodness". And a particular purpose of carrying out one's duty is not in an instrumental relation with the aim of securing one's moral worth, "it is also given body and determined at the level of actual reality by the diversified intention of obeying the moral commandments in a way appropriate to the given situations or necessities of decision" (GA 122). Now according to Kolnai morality is neither a department of practice in general, nor is it the sum total of non-moral practical activities (ME 102).[14] They are superimposed on these practices. So the above two characterisations do not exhaust the possible relations there could be between practical aims. Accordingly, he points to a third kind of enveloping relation, that between pursuing ultimate non-moral ends and keeping to moral rules:

> Success in "the game of life" (the Aristotelian "hitting of the target") will at least to a high degree depend on…"playing the game", *scil.* the game of morality, and single practical gains, or successes in life, would appear to be deprived of value if obtained outside the framework of the moral game and in disrespect of its constitutive rules. (GA 123)

III

Our starting-points were Kolnai's view that we have one overarching moral end, and the claim, which still has the status of a supposition, that everyone has to have that end. This led to the question: What then is it to deliberate about that end?

In "Deliberation is of Ends", deliberation is presented as the reaffirmation or restructuring of our more or less permanent ends whenever we are confronted with a serious choice. In setting about to adopt an end here and now, we have to refer to higher ends with which this particular end could be compatible or contradictory, so we work on achieving a relatively consistent array of autonomous ends, that is, again, a set of ends, none of which can be regarded as means to any further end. "It is the choices, confrontations, inner dialogues, hesitations and new engagements implied in this process that *primo loco* constitute the field of deliberation" (DE 52). The statement that our non-moral practical aims are in an enveloping relation forms an important supplement to this account, as it explains why we do not always have to be in the business of considering our ultimate ends whenever we act purposefully, and why the purposes we adopt are not necessarily means to further or higher ends. The statement about the relation between non-moral aims and the moral end also explains in what sense the latter is primary with respect to the former, without overwriting the autonomy of either. It could seem, also, that there is room for moral deliberation, since, while we do not deliberate about the comprehensive moral aim, which we just have to have, we do have to deliberate about how the performance of at least some of our duties relates to this general moral purpose, even if fulfilling them is an autonomous task.

Accordingly, in order to see whether the answer to our question has indeed been found, let us focus on the thesis according to which the primary moral aim, that of leading a morally good life, is in an enveloping relation to secondary aims, to be glossed as fulfilling particular duties when this is called for. Is it true that this thesis holds because activities with moral emphasis are sufficiently game-like? Of the core characteristics of games in Kolnai's account, many certainly cannot be those of morality, as morality is undoubtedly a serious issue and can be conducted by correspondence only in marginal cases. Still, activities with moral emphasis might be taken to be constituted by rules.

Indeed Kolnai writes that moral worth or status, the attainment of which is the primary moral aim, is defined by moral rules. However, for him the sum of practices cannot be constituted by moral rules, given the relationship between practice and morality.[15] Indeed, notwithstanding the text of the quotation which ends §II (GA 123), there is no proper analogy between the rules of games and moral rules. This is because keeping the moral rules is itself a specific and potentially difficult task, whereas keeping the rules is not part of the game once a player is familiar with it. It is not particularly hard in chess to make a move with the knight in a legitimate way. Also, ordinary moral practice frequently exhibits debates, arguments, and so on concerning the acceptability of the moral demands or precepts that claim our attention. In contrast, challenging the rules of the game should never be part of playing it (GA 121).

Further, its being constituted by rules is neither necessary nor sufficient for a practice's generating aims in an enveloping relation. For sufficiency, consider that if a player knows what his winning strategy is, there cannot be a difference for him between the aims of winning and of playing, respectively, unless it is insisted that the very striving to achieve the internal, enveloped aim, no matter what level of intensity it needs to reach, makes it an autonomous aim.[16] For necessity, consider Kolnai's Wittgensteinian example of a man who may induce himself to swim just by jumping into the water. That is, entering a practical context is likely to "generate purposes, or one paramount purpose, appropriate to that context" (GA 116–17). But there are no constitutive rules that stipulate what it is to swim ashore, in that adopted context. Another relevant example is the relation between the aim of the artist to develop a given theme and his possible permanent aim of "self-expression" (GA 123–24). Here there are clearly no constitutive rules in the background. Chess appears, then, as a special practice, where an enveloped aim happens to be partly generated by submitting to a set of public and constitutive rules. So none of the characteristics of games proper are shared by activities with moral emphasis. Therefore the thesis that there is an enveloping relation between the primary moral aim and the enveloped moral aims is to be evaluated on the basis of the formal criteria to which this relation has to conform.

For such an evaluation, it has to be specified what the primary moral aim is. There seems to be ample textual support, in the relevant places of "Games and Aims", for the view that the primary moral aim is to keep to a set of more or less consistent rules or principles; "being moral" or "being good" is defined by adherence to these rules. Then the secondary aim seems to become that of keeping to these rules on each occasion when this is called for. If this were the case, one could object to the thesis of enveloping aims by the following argument. If carrying out secondary moral aims, like fulfilling one's duty on a given occasion, amounts to obeying a set of rules which are more or less determinate, then this aim cannot be autonomous, as the enveloped aim is part of the encompassing primary aim. If I aim at keeping to the rule of playing basketball each week, then my aim of playing basketball this week, while not independent of the general aim and not a means to its fulfilment, and subordinate to it, is still not an autonomous aim. If true, this fact undermines the thesis examined now by pointing to the violation of one of the formal criteria of an enveloping relation.

One could attempt to respond to this objection by referring to Kolnai's insistence that keeping to the rules of morality demands a great deal of thematic attention, or "diversified intention…appropriate to the given situation or necessities of decision". Now what could this mean? What could hinder the straightforward application of moral rules in concrete cases, and why does this generate autonomous local purposes? Consider some version of the game of billiards which can be played alone, and suppose that we conceive that in order to do well in it one just has to keep to a set of rules. In principle at least, one can then specify what actions have to be taken in order to get closer to this aim in at least the vast majority of the situations that can arise in the course of the game. Still, inherent difficulties of playing well in billiards include the necessity of acquiring outstanding dexterity and the like. At the same time, the view according to which the physical implementation alone always stands in the way of applying moral rules straightforwardly, or generates autonomous local aims, is quite implausible.[17] The same holds for prudential, that is, nonmoral preparations related to the implementation of moral tasks.

Or it could be proposed that what could hamper the application of moral rules in particular situations is the inevitable presence of other agents, since morally motivated actions, just like playing chess, tend to take place in social contexts. Assessments of what the others' future actions might be feature in reasoning about what to do; but one cannot, generically, make moral rules sensitive to these assessments. Suppose that two agents

are engaged in a Prisoner's Dilemma game and that its Pareto-optimal outcome is also morally warranted (because, say, the evaluation by the players
of their payoffs adequately reflects their well-being). Consider the claim
that no matter what putative moral rule is followed, it cannot be assured
that that outcome is reached. However, that someone acts upon a moral
rule here does not imply that that rule has to call for the achievement of
some specific outcome. In the Prisoner's Dilemma game in question, one
may be called upon to choose the action that is merely conducive to the
attainment of the supposed morally warranted outcome. One should not
propose that the presence of others necessarily stands in the way between
moral rules and their applications.

Consider, next, the claim that it is partly the complexity of chess that
is responsible for the fact that winning in it is an enveloped aim. It can
then be suggested that what "thematic attention" glosses in the argument
for the autonomy of the secondary moral aims is overcoming some "intellectual difficulty". According to this proposal, doing well in a problematic
moral situation often requires the solution of an intellectual problem, that
of finding out, even deducing from the moral rules, what morality requires
us to do in that situation. Compare addition. Even if one has a sure grasp
of how to do it, adding many very large numbers could be difficult and
may require the employment of some suitable supplementary techniques.
Further, rules of addition might not be applicable when very large numbers or very many of them are to be dealt with, and a search for additional techniques, suited to these cases, could be called for. But how does this
help us in thinking about the autonomy of the secondary aim? Suppose a
person tries to solve a mathematical puzzle, which is to find the proof of a
challenging theorem. Proving theorems presupposes doing mathematics.
Let us then grant that one can prove a mathematical theorem only by
keeping to a range of rules which characterise the practice of mathematics.[18] Now the aim of this person certainly seems to be an autonomous
aim. However, it is probably too extravagant to think, and correspondingly too misleading to suggest, that carrying out particular duties is analogous to proving new theorems. So suppose next that the proof of the theorem is already known. Is solving the puzzle still an aim which is different
from that of doing mathematics? It is not clear what one should say. Nevertheless, it might be proposed as a general answer to the objection that,
if the primary aim is that of following moral rules, the secondary aims are
not autonomous, that the presence of at least one of the above factors
(including overcoming difficulties in the physical or tactical or strategic
implementation of a given duty, or the presence of intellectual challenges)
will make the aim of duty-fulfilment autonomous.

Against this way of settling the issue, the following argument could
be suggested. Suppose the person who works on the proof in the above
example has already once proved the theorem, but has forgotten how she

did it; yet she refrains from looking up the proof in a book on the shelf behind her. (Here and now, she thinks that only by proving the theorem herself can she gain a real understanding of it, or can truly master the mathematical field she is interested in.) Or consider the next variation of the case, in which the proof is not especially difficult, but she still somehow wants to figure it out herself. This sequence of cases might show that doing mathematics may generate internal aims irrespective of the complexity of particular puzzles, in virtue of the very endeavour to solve them. Indeed, let us recall at this point Kolnai's claim that the significance of pointing out that aims can stand in an enveloping relation in at least one practice is that it highlights the structure of willing in human practices; and also his remark that inducing oneself to swim by jumping into the water amounts to making oneself willing to swim. In "Deliberation is of Ends", he writes that ultimate ends are to be chosen, instead of accepted on rational grounds, and choice "reveals the affirmation and exercise of our free will" (DE 54). So we may say that it is our willing to deal with the problems posed by secondary moral aims that make them autonomous, and we can further add that the importance of the various difficulties enumerated above is that we have to will to overcome them, no matter what form they take.

Nevertheless, we can continue the above series of cases and turn next to one in which the person engaged in mathematics wants to prove an elementary theorem; followed by yet another case in which she has to add three and four. It would be strange to say that her very willing to deal with them makes these tasks autonomous. On the other hand, think of a mathematician who solves even complicated problems easily and almost without effort: are we ready to say that the absence of the need to mobilise his volition makes his task different from the task of those who have to struggle to deal with them?

I turn now to another objection to stating that both the enveloping aims thesis and the claim that the primary aim is that of obeying moral rules can be true at the same time. Consider that, for a range of cases where the presence of an enveloping relation between two aims has been acknowledged, the primary aim provides criteria for what it is to accomplish the enveloped aim. The rules of chess determine when one player has won the game; there are criteria for what it is to have swum ashore; it can be checked whether a putative proof is really a proof. Suppose, however, that a putative primary aim does not provide clear criteria for what the achievement of the secondary aim is.[19] Then the two aims appear to be independent of each other, and this violates one of the requirements an enveloping relation has to meet. But it can be added that moral rules cannot be conceived of as altogether determinate, therefore they do not issue clear-cut criteria for their fulfilment. So the two sorts of moral aims cannot be in an enveloping relation. Note that this objection does not also challenge the non-instrumental relation between the two sorts of aims, as it would be fallacious to equate the need for an agent to achieve her aim with the criteria specifying what that achievement amounts to. Also, difficulties in carrying out the secondary aim do not correlate with the presence of criteria for achieving it.

The two objections examined, then, might make us conclude that the enveloping thesis and the claim that the primary aim is that of obeying moral rules cannot be held together. But as we are interested in the thesis itself, as part of the characterisation of moral deliberation, we are to explore what other formulations for the primary aim could be found.

IV

In order to understand Kolnai's conception of the main moral aim better, it might be advisable to turn to his account of the general moral demand. As an agent who is concerned with morality has to meet its demands, the structure of his aims has to reflect the structure of this demand. I will seek to lay out a schematic, although hopefully not oversimplified, model of this structure, based mostly on the essay "The Moral Emphasis".[20]

A central characteristic of the moral demand is that it points to the requirement to fulfil our duties—expressed in terms of prescriptions or imperatives, therefore in terms of rules. The main bulk, as it were, of these duties is negative, in the sense that they express prohibitions. One should not kill, one should not steal, one should not tell lies. These prohibitive rules are relatively determinate. Further, murder, theft or lying ought to be avoided no matter what other practical concerns are also pursued. The moral demand attached to the negative duties intrudes, as it were, into any kind of practice; negative duties are saturated with the theme of morality. They have a special urgency, generated by the primacy of the need to avoid evil.[21] A moral agent can understand the stringency of the duty not to steal by being confronted with the evilness of robbery, theft, and so on. We also have positive duties. These also can be couched in the form of imperatives, but these are rather exhortative than prohibitive. For example, one has to provide help to members of one's family, to one's friends, and to one's colleagues; one has to execute one's work with care. Fulfilling these duties requires creativity and possibly innovativeness; the way we help our friends is important.[22] These duties are also relatively less determinate. They have only an implicit reference to morality; acting on them can generate broad practical concerns that tend to merge with other, only implicitly, moral activities in life. Being proficient and well settled in such endeavours, then, gives rise to potentially difficult tasks of deliberation.[23]

[This] means primarily the creation and emergence of objectively valuable human realities, such as a fine character or a well-ordered and
noble pattern of interpersonal relationships, or a kind of work that connotes moral significance: in a word, the presence of something exquisitely
positive. (ME 113)

Now moral imperatives proper are embedded in a constitutional frame, as
it were, that is based on a fundamental fact, that of "the intrinsic relevancy of rules and their content for the life of personal beings (in the context
of the human condition...)" (ME 113). It is also a moral demand to relate
ourselves to this constitutional frame, cast not as an imperative but as a
statement. Kolnai does not invoke, in the first place, the idea that the
moral imperatives are justified by this declaration, but points to the question of the authority conferred on them by the sovereign authority of the
constitutional frame. It might be said that for the non-religious or for the
theist *qua* moral philosopher,[24] the authority of the rules is derived from
"the fact of consensual moral valuation and its pressure on men's individual and joint lives as manifest in the phenomena of conscience, responsibility and the moral critique of collective behaviour" (ME 114).

Before considering the question of how the authority of the consensual
moral evaluation could be established, let us first relate this model to the
thesis of an enveloping relation between the primary and secondary moral
aims. The main moral aim, for Kolnai, appears, then, as the very submission to the authority of moral demands and this is not, in itself, a demand
for following any rules. But "being well established" in this aim has to be
taken to mean that its content is well understood. And then it has an immediate implicate, the comprehension of the non-negotiable importance of
moral imperatives. Moral worth is indeed defined thus by moral rules in
the sense of accepting the requirement to implement them. Then fulfilling our negative duties is a more determinate task, situations laden with
moral dilemmas and occasional calls for serious sacrifices notwithstanding. On the other hand, the aim of fulfilling positive duties is vaguer and
needs to mesh with the pursuit of other, necessarily manifold, practical purposes. The enveloping relation between the primary aim and that of fulfilling duties on particular occasions is partly generated by the thematic
attention, right willing and care the latter tasks demand; and partly by the
fact that the primary aim is not altogether that of following rules. This is
a decisive difference between the practice of games-playing and morality.
But moral deliberation means something else as well. Fulfilling positive
duties is a matter of creativity; rules specifying a positive duty, like the
duty of fidelity, exhort to "something existent and life-pervading" (ME
115). Carrying out these demands necessitates weighing up various practical ends and concerns, and in this sense we do indeed deliberate about eth-

ical ends just as we do about other ends. That is, as in the passage quoted at the very beginning of the paper, a man may often, indeed, have to deliberate about what business dealings he should engage in, but moral rules, though they always apply, will not fully guide him on these occasions.

The authority of the primary moral aim would be almost completely undermined if the statement of the fact that we have to relate to the moral demand was not, immediately as it were, followed by laying out a set of imperatives. As indicated above, these rules themselves might be taken as available in the form of a consensus. Indeed, Kolnai claims that while seeking to meet moral requirements, while experiencing them, we are guided by moral evaluations. Moral evaluation, in turn, relies on evidence that is not as such factual, neither is it logical; so disagreements about the validity of moral claims needs recourse to specific standards. When we are confronted with disagreement in evaluation, we seek consensual confirmation.[25] Morality is interdependent with social co-operation, and moral experience involves the experience of reciprocity and mutual responsibility. Kolnai writes that "a consensual attunement between claims and the recognition of claims constitutes, I do not say a definition, but a focal characteristic of moral emphasis and meanings" (MC 147). Suppose that the consensus itself is available to us in the form of moral codes and traditions, and that it is sustained by communication in various modes. Recall, however, the observation made while drawing the contrast between the game of chess and activities with moral emphasis, that moral dissent, and calls for moral reform, are themselves moral phenomena. Consider also that while seeking out the terms of moral consensus we have to assume that it is couched in rational terms (ME 114). Moral dissent challenges the prevailing ethos in a community; dissenters perceive a divergence between that ethos and true morality. Granted that moral reforms are sometimes legitimately called for, and are sometimes successfully carried out, just conforming to the actual consensus in our community is not a fulfilment of the moral demands on us. However, the terms of what we may call the true moral consensus might not always be straightforwardly available in human communities, neither to moral reformers nor to moral zealots nor to ordinary persons.[26] Kolnai emphasises that it may be hidden from view and overshadowed by "immoral idols" and traditions, by various prevailing fashions, and moods. Nevertheless, rebellion against the moral *status quo* has to be on behalf of morality, not against it. The true task of moral reform is to reinstitute moral consensus (MC 163). So let us note that, in light of this amended explication, the two characteristic moral aims may appear, then, as the search for the terms of what the moral consensus dictates, and the aim of acting according to one's best understanding of what these dictates are. Nevertheless, the stringency of the moral demand is expressed by its being almost inevitably formulated in terms of imperatives. This account of the dynamics of moral reform has to involve not only the view that there are criteria for finding out what moral rules we are to follow, where these rules specify our duties, but also that there have to be criteria for what it is to carry out at least some of these duties. Still, again, negative duties are more likely to have these second sorts of criteria attached to them.

Now can the moral imperatives be explicitly justified? If one accepts that the terms of the moral consensus are given, and if we have to submit to them even if their contents are not altogether available to us, then one could also accept that they are already justified. In this view, it certainly cannot be the case that our very agreement concerning them can justify them. However, the question might still be asked: If obeying imperatives is an overarching aim as well, should not there be an explication of their attractiveness or inherent appeal? Kolnai does indeed refer to a pre-moral social order, the preservation of which is closely related to the main moral theme of shunning the attitude and conduct of those who oppose that order (AG 83–84).[27] It is explained that "interpersonal relations are primordially—more naturally and more rationally, one may venture to say—friendly and eirenic than hostile and agonistic" (ME 108), nevertheless "the concerns of life and nature...form no self-contained and self-sufficient unity and, while destined to the attainment of good, are also essentially generative of evil in their operation" (ME 114). The moral demand is not to be derived, then, from considerations of the goodness of creating and sustaining this pre-moral order (AG 84–85, ME 104). At the same time, the implicit and positive aspects of morality can be understood in reference to this order (ME 115). So in one sense, morality has primacy over the various practices of men and women; it is sufficient to say that the moral consensus manifests the authority of the moral demand. In another sense, the practical concerns of mankind have a primacy over morality (ME 110), but this does not mean that the latter can be justified in terms of the former. This thought could also be expressed in the following way. Whatever a person wants or desires and so on is his good, and we are even entitled to refer to his true good in so far as what he pursues is ratified by others as truly good for him. On the other hand, moral goodness, which can only be assessed from a perspective that is not solely the person's own, is a matter of keeping to the moral imperatives (AG 68). But this goodness cannot be derived from the goods of the person or persons so evaluated.

Morality is, then, like a game (like chess), in that submitting to its demands and standards is a matter of obeying rules, and in that the justification of these rules is not called for, their authority is taken for granted. Although it is possible to think of an aim that is served by the aim of being moral, that is, leading a morally good life, for Kolnai the latter has to be conceived of as an autonomous and primary aim.

NOTES

1 Aurel Kolnai, "Deliberation is of Ends", in Francis Dunlop and Brian Klug (eds.), *Ethics, Value, and Reality: Selected Papers of Aurel Kolnai*, London: Athlone Press, 1977, pp. 44–62. References in the present text to the page numbers of this essay are prefixed by "DE".

2 David Wiggins has argued against this reading of Aristotle in "Deliberation and Practical Reason", in *Needs, Values, Truth*, Oxford: Clarendon Press, 1998, pp. 215–38. He insists, in "Truth, Invention, and the Meaning of Life", *op. cit.*, p. 122, that his account of this problem is similar to Kolnai's.

3 Cf. Bernard Williams, "Internal and External Reasons", in *Moral Luck*, Cambridge: Cambridge University Press, 1981, p. 104; and Harry Frankfurt, "On the Usefulness of Final Ends", in *Necessity, Volition, and Love*, Cambridge: Cambridge University Press, 1999, pp. 91–94.

4 Although the terms "end", "aim", and "purpose" have different meanings, I will regard them below as more or less synonymous.

5 Aurel Kolnai, "Games and Aims", *Proceedings of the Aristotelian Society*, LXVI (1965–66), pp. 103–128. References to this paper are prefixed by "GA".

6 The quote is from John Lucas, "Moralists and Gamesmen", *Philosophy*, XXXIV, 1959, p. 11.

7 R. Duncan Luce and Howard Raiffa, *Games and Decisions*, New York: Dover Publications, 1957, ch. 1.

8 John von Neumann and Oskar Morgenstern, *Theory of Games and Economic Behavior*, Princeton: Princeton University Press, 1947, pp. 9–15. About more recent developments, see David Kreps, *Game Theory and Economic Modeling*, Oxford: Clarendon Press, 1990.

9 *See*, e.g., Martin Osborne and Ariel Rubinstein, *A Course in Game Theory*, MIT Press, 1994, pp. 11–13 and 89–90.

10 There is a distinction in game theory between non-co-operative and co-operative games. In the former, agents are presumed to have to act without knowing what their counterpart(s) will do; in the latter, the participants can not only agree on a joint course of action but can also assume that such agreements will bind the other(s). In the text, I refer to rational deliberation in the non-co-operative context, the context of playing chess.

11 The conduct of chess players, for Kolnai, is also "wholly in the mode of effective rational operations" (GA 111).

12 Cf. *op. cit.*, note 7, pp. 104–106.

13 Kolnai refers to ends in themselves as autotelic, to means to further ends as heterotelic, to one-track systems of activity as orthotelic, and to systems in which independent parallel ends are pursued as syntelic. Concerning the relationship between the two aims in chess he writes: "I propose to call it the *paratelic* relationship, seeing that the internal or thematic aim—'winning' or 'mating', or short of that 'enforcing a draw'—may be looked upon as a lateral implicate of the enveloping or primary aim of 'playing' *etc.*", and adds, "if some looseness of terminology be allowed, I would also call the aim of winning a paratelic aim, and the activity displayed *in* the game a paratelic endeavour or pursuit" (GA 116). I think the term "enveloping relation", and the distinction between enveloped and enveloping aims, adequately convey what Kolnai wishes to express here.

14 Aurel Kolnai, "The Moral Emphasis", in Francis Dunlop and Brian Klug, *op. cit.*, note 1, pp. 94–122. This essay is part of the unfinished project "Morality and Practice". References to it will be prefixed by "ME".

15 John Rawls comes close to stating that they are, in "Two Concepts of Rules", *Collected Papers*, Harvard: Harvard University Press, 1999, pp. 20–21; but *see* also p. 43. John Searle might also have held the same view at the time of writing "How to Derive 'Ought' from 'Is'", in Philippa Foot, ed., *Theories of Ethics*, Oxford: Oxford University Press, 1967, pp. 101–14, but later he states, concerning institutional facts, only that they exist exclusively within systems of constitutive rules; *see*, e.g., *The Construction of Social Reality*, New York: Free Press, 1995, pp. 27–29.

16 Suppose two persons are engaged in the following game. They play on a board of round shape, each has an infinite amount of round pieces at his disposal, and these are much smaller than the board (let us say that each could put at least seventeen pieces on the board). One of them has white pieces only and the other has black pieces only. The one who has the white pieces starts with putting a piece on the board and then they take turns in putting further pieces down. The criteria for "putting down a piece" are these. Pieces cannot overlap (especially as they are three-dimensional, say) and they have to be strictly within the boundary of the board. The party that cannot any longer place a piece on the board loses. In this game, as is well known, the first mover has a winning strategy; furthermore, this winning strategy is easy to carry out.

17 Thomas Nagel observed that not managing to save a child from a building on fire due to clumsiness has moral relevance; see his "Moral Luck", *Mortal Questions*, Cambridge: Cambridge University Press, 1979, p. 25.

18 I do not wish to involve here sceptical arguments about our ability to follow rules. As Frederick Schauer pointed out, this issue is mostly irrelevant for the analysis of prescriptive rules: *Playing by the Rules*, Oxford: Clarendon Press, 1991, pp. 64ff. Note that the context of John McDowell's well-known discussion of the importance of this matter for ethics is the problem of ascribing values: "Non-Cognitivism and Rule-Following", *Mind, Value, and Reality*, Harvard: Harvard University Press, 1998, pp. 198–218.

19 There is nothing controversial in the claim that rules may be indeterminate; indeed Schauer regards limited specificity as an essential feature of prescriptive rules; cf. Schauer, *op. cit.*, note 18, pp. 82–84. He does not discuss, however, the issue of criteria for successfully complying with a rule. This is no doubt due to the correlation between the specificity of a rule and the criteria for meeting it: the rule that we should carry out our work with care has limited specificity and vague criteria of what its accomplishment means. Nevertheless, rules guiding mathematical proofs (of theorems, say) are not maximally relevantly specified, but it is (normally) clear when a proof has been accomplished.

20 For the reference, *see* footnote 12.

21 Cf. J. L. Mackie, *Ethics: Inventing Right and Wrong*, Harmondsworth: Penguin Books, 1977, pp. 139–40 and 165–66.

22 Joseph Raz, in his study of the normative force of rules, recognises only rules that require certain actions to be performed and rules granting permission, cf. *Practical Reason and Norms*, Princeton: Princeton University Press, 1990, p. 9 and chs. 2 and 3.

23 This is not just a matter of interpreting what the rules, through which positive duties might be conveyed, demand us to do; on interpretation of rules see Gidon Gottlieb, *The Logic of Choice*, London: George Allen and Unwin, 1968, pp. 91ff.

24 The authority of moral rules may be derived from the declaration that they are issued by God; indeed the Decalogue itself displays the threefold structure of moral demands (ME 115).

25 Aurel Kolnai, "Moral Consensus", in Francis Dunlop and Brian Klug (eds.), *op. cit.*, note 1, pp. 144–64. References to this paper are prefixed by "MC".

26 David Wiggins emphasises this feature of Kolnai's conception of moral consensus in many places; see, e.g., *Needs, Values, Truth*, Oxford: Clarendon Press, 1998, p. 32, also p. 162.

27 Aurel Kolnai, "The Ambiguity of Good", in Francis Dunlop and Brian Klug, *op. cit.*, note 1, pp. 63–94. References to this paper, the first chapter of the projected work "Morality and Practice", will be prefixed by "AG".

Kolnai and Kant on (Human) Dignity

ZOLTÁN BALÁZS

I INTRODUCTION

The concept of human dignity is one of the most frequently used and widely applied moral concepts in contemporary Western political discourse. Rightists and leftists, believers and non-believers alike rely on it, on the assumption that its core is undisputed and commonly accepted by every mature human person. But a lack of dispute may well turn out to be a lack of reflection. In fact, the concept of *human* dignity *is* quite often defined and circumscribed, but the concept of dignity is not, though, obviously, the former concept must be derived from the latter.[1]

Kant's contribution to making the concept of human dignity one of the prevalent ideas of our moral philosophical tradition is huge. But the fact that he nowhere explains exactly what he means by dignity, though he has very elaborate views on a closely related, yet distinct, concept of sublimity, calls for explanation. Although it is impossible to enlarge upon the enormous literature on his moral theory in such a short essay, I shall try to suggest an answer to the question whence this curious unevenness arises.

Contrary to Kant, Aurel Kolnai has an explicit account of dignity. In his essay, simply entitled "Dignity", he distinguishes what he calls "dignity as a quality" from human dignity. The paper was republished in 1995 to provide the conceptual introduction to a distinguished collection of papers on human dignity.[2] Yet the editor does not seem to be aware of the irony hiding in the fact that Kolnai thinks that the concept of human dignity is *deeply problematic.*[3] His moral theoretical sympathies lie with personalism, a conception into which human dignity can easily be inserted, but his axiological approach to the realm of values or qualities, which includes dignity, does not unequivocally support such a conception.

I shall proceed in the following manner. First, Kolnai's account of dignity as a quality will be summarised, after which his brief account of human dignity will be analysed. If his account of dignity is correct, then human dignity is only a very imperfect and partial instance of dignity, similar to the dignity of, for instance, some animals or even inanimate objects, and thus it can hardly uphold the entire edifice of our enlightened moral intuitions. Secondly, Kant's analysis of the sublime will be summarised, and his views on human dignity cited. It will be argued that his account of the sublime, which is itself heavily influenced by his moral intuitions, establishes the concept of *human sublimity*, but not of human dignity. Obviously, the concept of human sublimity is too artificial and counterintuitive, and this deficiency is aggravated by the problem that sublimity lacks reciprocity, the idea of mutual respect. Dignity has it, and this explains its increasing importance in Kant's arguments. However, Kant nowhere shows how the concept of dignity can be meaningfully applied to every human being.

II. DIGNITY

(i) Kolnai's phenomenological account of dignity

Kolnai does not *define* dignity in a rigorous manner. His approach is phenomenological, making a survey of related concepts, and suggesting analogies, metaphors, linguistic connotations, both positively—explicating dignity; and negatively—explicating un-dignity, distinguishing them from similar concepts and contrasting them with opposed ones. Dignity is described as a phenomenon clearly discernible within the realm of values.

In what sort of persons might we recognise the traits of dignity? Here is a condensation of Kolnai's most telling observations.[4] A person with dignity is a person who is calm, reserved, self-controlled; who has integrity, autonomy, a centre of gravity, independence, a certain sense of invulnerability; whose conduct is reliable, predictable, not capricious; who is able to keep distance, to avoid unruly intimacy, yet who is serene and patient, though not passive or resigned; who leads a morally integral, virtuous and principled life; and, most importantly, who is able to accept and put up with the tension between value and reality, with external disorder, with the perpetual change and fickleness of other people. Briefly, such a person has *weight*. It is important to realise, however, that as the various aspects of dignity might be present in different degrees in different persons (not to speak of the plurality of occasions, ages, contexts in which a particular person may be said to act, speak, etc. with dignity in different degrees), dignity itself is present in different degrees.

Kolnai's way of circumscribing dignity is to offer new insights about dignity in various contexts (e.g. by penetrating the "feature-world" of un-dignity). Despite the lack of a clear-cut categorisation of its features, there seems to be a virtual structure among these features.[5] Kolnai himself notes that dignity is neither a purely aesthetic, nor a purely moral value, yet its "descriptive content" (252) is dominated by aesthetic and moral aspects. To this a third kind of aspect, the intellectual, may be added. How does Kolnai apply these three categories to dignity as a quality?

First, to some extent, dignity seems to "enter into the category of the aesthetical" (254). Thanks to genetic or environmental influence, or as a result of their conduct and way of life, some people have a manifestly dignified appearance. Others may be born with a more patient, tranquil, sanguine, reserved nature. Sometimes incumbents of high social rank may acquire such character traits through its exercise, as a result of having to meet general expectations. Reserve, weightiness, solidity, non-monotonic simplicity of this kind are the features that make dignity often appear as an aesthetic value. It is in that sense that material objects (landscapes, buildings) as well as certain plants and animals may be said to have dignity, or at least to have something dignified about them. In this aesthetic respect dignity may properly be contrasted with and distinguished from similar, but distinct, aesthetic categories like nobility, grace, or elegance.

Secondly, some features of dignity as a quality may be attained by conscious and deliberate social and moral education, even if, as Kolnai observes, dignity as such can hardly be its direct aim. Unlike justice, veracity, moderation or temperance, but like humility and modesty, dignity is a virtue that cannot be deliberately *exercised*. On the other hand, it can work as a principle or desirable feature or a demarcating line in and for one's moral and non-moral behaviour. In other words, whereas it is rarely a matter of deliberative decision to *act* in a distinctly dignified *manner*, it is a matter of choice to *do* or not to do *what* is dignified.

The distinction just drawn reflects a deeper difference. Kolnai points out that dignity is related to morality, as a matter of course, yet in two different ways. On the one hand, it may be pertinent to one's personal moral character and be called a *virtue*. Kolnai discusses its connection with modesty and exactingness, pride and humility. A dignified *character* is usually modest, yet exacting, devoid of hypocrisy, sincere, serious, serene, has self-control in all areas of life, and is thus capable of a "personal response to impersonal standards" (267). This is the character which most contemporary theorists call "autonomous" or "integral", which explains in what sense the person of such a character is "intangible, invulnerable, inaccessible to destructive...interference" (253). As a virtue, dignity could be an object of desire and a fruit of conscious (self-)education.

On the other hand, it would be a "fatal misunderstanding of Dignity as a Quality" to place it "in an antithesis...to plain deontic morality" (270). Thus, though dignity may be linked with other moral virtues, it is at the same time related to the observance of one's duties and moral commitments. Dignity *is* in a deep sense a consummation of one's moral character traits, and not merely a component of the character. Kolnai ponders a case in which he first resists the temptation of being bribed, but, as the sum offered is increased, he gives in. This is a simple case of doing an immoral action, amounting to a loss of dignity by both the briber and the bribed. Dignity can be lost or lessened as a result of plain immorality, since the dignified person "is felt to be *penetrated*—rather than merely commanded, controlled, governed or interested—by Morality to the point of being *personally inseparable* from it" (270, Kolnai's italics). Hence, acting in a morally right way, doing what is right, tends to make the actor dignified.

Thirdly, some features of dignity appear to relate it to another value category, which Kolnai calls cognitional.[6] Personal values of intellectual excellence, as well as objective values of truth, knowledge, memory, imagination, might be said to belong to this category. Such values are less directly valuational, or preference-related, and more objective, in a natural sense. Describing the opposite of dignity, Kolnai makes the following observation: "The core of Un-Dignity…is constituted by an attitude of refusal to recognise, experience, and bear with, the tension between Value and Reality; between what things ought to be, should be, had better be or are desired to be, and what things are, can be and are allowed to be" (262).

Kolnai does not dwell much on this assertion, but, for the purposes of this essay, it is worth spelling out in more detail. For his contention is not merely a variant of the familiar claim that dignity is partly constituted by independence, invulnerability, resistance to change. In itself, being independent or invulnerable may amount to a sort of indifference (albeit not to disinterestedness) toward all contingencies in and of the world. The detached, disengaged observer's standpoint is, however, not a dignified one. As a matter of fact, his position has *no weight* whatsoever. Only if one enters the world may one gain weight. Dignity has an emphatic presence in, and an intrinsic relation to, the world. It is not a passive attitude of enduring the tension between value and reality, nor is it a hedonistic celebration of the plurality of values, nor a sort of intellectual laziness, or despair, at the sight of this tension. Rather, dignity as an attitude toward the world and to the tension between reality and value must somehow be a reflection on and participation in, rather than a reaction to and rejection of, this tension. A person who possesses this intellectual feature of dignity is, therefore, both aware of the antinomies of value and reality and their ultimate ineradicability, and in his own personal life, practices and attitudes he is capable of reconciling them. This feature of dignity is preeminently person-dependent, in other words, it is attainable by education, reflection on experience, and perhaps the intellectual aspect of the moral virtue of humility.[7]

(ii) Responses to dignity—and sublimity

To be *in* the world, but not *of* it, is a relation best described as having weight. This is the central metaphor Kolnai uses. However, he also says that "our experience of Dignity is centrally an experience of 'Height'" (252). Though the two metaphors are not straightforwardly contrary, they stand in contrast to each other, and this requires some explanation. For this, one should consider what happens when one encounters dignity.

The experience of dignity supervenes on the phenomenon of dignity. However subjective the experience is, it is necessarily dependent on the phenomenon being experienced. Further, the response that the object elicits is an essential part of the experience. The reaction or response to dignity does not come after a sort of reflection, but is elicited by dignity. In Kolnai's words, our rough and immediate response to dignity is "emphatic respect, a reverential mode of response...a 'bowing' gesture" (252). This implies verticality, an appreciation of hierarchy, and thus the notion of height.

However, Kolnai immediately qualifies this judgement, as a result of a comparison drawn between dignity and *sublimity*. Their difference is revealed by attending to the difference in the responses they elicit. Whereas the experience of dignity does not crush, but, rather, tranquillises us, "our response to the sublime has something awestruck about it" (253). It is the central metaphors of weight and height that help us hold the two qualities separate from each other. Dignity is eminently an experience of weight, whereas sublimity is more tightly linked with height. Dignity entails participation, involvement in the world and its affairs. It is one of its essential features that it should have a relation toward the world. On the other hand, what is sublime is, in the first place, above the world, not contingent or dependent on it in any sense. Briefly, while it is crucial that the world have a relation to the sublime, it is not crucial that the sublime have a relation to the world. Weight is something that we encounter *within* the world, while height, the epitome of sublimity, is something we experience as being *above* the world.[8]

Where it is appropriate, our response to dignity is not merely an appreciative, but a value-creating act: it will confer dignity on the perceiver or make him aware of his *own* dignity. But it must be stressed that this awareness of our own dignity is not the result of our reflection on ourselves, but on something that we find dignified *in the world*. The awareness of our own dignity emerges out of our encounters with things and persons that bear the mark of dignity. In other words, a recognition of our own dignity presupposes a knowledge of dignity based on experience.

To sum up: dignity is a quality with aesthetic, moral and intellectual aspects. It is also clear that dignity can be a distinctive quality of *certain, but not all* human beings (who, moreover, possess it in different degrees). Therefore, when we speak about the dignity of a landscape, of an artistic style, of an office, of an idea or principle, and so forth, our description is an application of the complex notion of dignity. However, extending it in this way entails narrowing or reducing it to one or more of its features or aspects, and hence using it in a metaphorical sense.

III. Human Dignity

(i) Kolnai's account

Kolnai introduces his own account of human dignity by means of a brief discussion of human rights. Whereas dignity, he has argued, is a quality, a descriptive notion which has, nonetheless, normative implications, rights are either prescriptive or ascriptive notions. Rights are entirely relational; if human dignity were an instance of dignity as a quality, it would have to exist independently of recognition. Therefore, the two notions are logically different. But human dignity is different from dignity as a quality, and similar to rights, in as much as it is ascribed to "persons as such, independently of their distinctive virtues, modes of bearing, and mental levels and attitudes" (258). It is, hence, a *"quasi-*quality" (ibid). Yet although human dignity is not "a matter of more or less" (ibid), "there still seems after all to be some rudiment of a 'more or less' about [it]"(259), in so far as even human dignity may be diminished, or it may altogether vanish, as a human being approaches the condition of loss of personhood, "mainly" as a result of "powers alien to us" (260). Hence, the interpretation of human dignity as a minimum level of dignity, present in every human being, is not self-evident. Human dignity as a quasi-quality is not only logically different from dignity as a quality, but "behaves" in a different way. The relationship between dignity as a quality and human dignity is, therefore, not a relation of more and less, of the same thing. To sum up, Kolnai's views about human dignity may be condensed into three assertions. First, human dignity refers to a quality less real than dignity, more ascriptive, as rights are; yet secondly, in so far as it may grow or lessen, it is similar to dignity; but thirdly, it is essentially different from dignity as a quality, even though it must be related to it.

Neither the comparison between human dignity and human rights, nor that between human dignity and dignity as a quality, contribute much to a description of the *content* of human dignity. True, Kolnai refers to a sort of essential "alterity of others" (257), or to the "humanity" (258) of each human being, but these terms hardly mean anything specific. Simply to assert its existence will not do; human dignity must reveal itself directly to consciousness. Unless one can tell in what human dignity consists, or in virtue of what it subsists, one must conclude that *there is no such thing as human dignity.* Kolnai's own arguments support this conclusion.[9]

Even if it were possible or conceivable that every human being possesses something in common to at least a minimum degree, it is very questionable whether it can be meaningfully related to dignity as a quality. All that can be done about "human dignity" is to examine *how strong the metaphorical link* between it and dignity proper is.

(ii) The link between dignity and human dignity

First, aesthetic features. Strange though it may sound, one could outline an argument for the aesthetic value of "human dignity". For it may be argued that there is something attractive about human biological, physical, emotional, cultural, psychic, social, etc. complexity.[10] And to anticipate a later argument, even Kant's conception of human dignity is heavily influenced by an aesthetic evaluation of humanity. The trouble is that complexity, sophistication, dynamism are features not very congenial to the aesthetic feature-world of dignity (in which simplicity prevails).

Again, notwithstanding the many vices and immoralities of many human beings, it could perhaps be argued that no one is entirely without virtues. Even historical figures who have deserved the epithet of "satanic" did possess certain virtues. The difficulty with this view is the irreconcilability of dignity as a moral virtue and a sign of moral integrity with wrongdoing, despite the presence of certain virtues. The fact is that while certain persons do outrageous acts, others do heroic acts.[11] Is there anything dignified about people doing the former? Interestingly, Kolnai seems to make a concession to such a view. He writes that uncontrolled passions (perhaps not of any kind: his examples are lust, avarice and fear) are "not an incarnation of Un-Dignity" (264). Milton's Satan, the paradigm example, has something dignified about him. Yet contrary to Kolnai's suggestion, and perhaps more in accord with his general perspective, uncontrolled passions, like natural forces, are much more (imperfect or queer) examples of *sublimity* than of dignity.

Finally, intellectual features of dignity. It may be suggested that as even the most villainous criminals possess certain virtues, so utopians who refuse "to recognise, experience, and bear with, the tension between Value and Reality" (262), are able to do so only because they are aware of this tension, have grasped its range and significance, but having been shaken by it, devote themselves to overcoming it entirely. In other words, as they have *human dignity,* they know this tension, but in as much as they refuse seriously to face it, they lack the intellectual aspects of dignity. The problem with such a view is, not surprisingly, identical with the one found in the preceding paragraph. If dignity presupposes the acknowledgment of the sovereignty of the Object over Reason, then intellectual pride is closer to something sublime (in a distorted way, of course), than to something dignified.

It might be argued that both our moral and our rational *faculties* have something dignified about them, without their being actually used. A single good moral action may be considered as revealing something about man's capacity to make the world better. This is a capacity, however, that only human beings possess. Similarly, even though there are differences in how certain human beings use or abuse their intellectual capacities, being able to discern value, to distinguish it from disvalue and from reality, is a faculty with which all persons are endowed. This view adumbrates, again, Kantian ethics.

Now although capacities to act morally and with reason lack any value in themselves,[12] there is a sense in which the existence of such capacities may be, after all, associated with dignity. This link can be explicated by way of recalling the key metaphor of "weight". Anything in the world that takes responsibility for itself or for its own existence, refusing to live a wholly opportunistic life,[13] must be treated as having weight. Being a human being means possessing weight. There seems to be, again, a deep truth behind the contradictory claim that possessing human dignity is reconcilable with possessing the ultimate degree of un-dignity that stems from a life entirely devoid of autonomous willing: an obstinate refusal to enter the world on one's own account *is possible* only if it is clear at least to the person himself that he has some true weight to lie about or hide. Thus, even those who are unwilling to take any moral or intellectual responsibility for their actions and thoughts may have some responsibility for their unwillingness. Their ensuing opportunism is a single, coherent, lifelong lie about their inner selves. The consequence could be moral or intellectual death, long before their biological passing away. But this, nonetheless, is a *sui*cide. This is not, of course, the type of suicide Kirilov commits in Dostoevsky's *The Possessed* as a proof of his divinity. This is the very opposite type: living in such a way that makes no difference to the world. If human dignity may consist in our capability to dissipate our own weight, so much the worse for human dignity. For it is, in this sense, just the opposite of dignity.

IV. KANT ON THE SUBLIME

Although contemporary discussions about human dignity almost unexceptionably rely on Kant, there is very little about this concept in Kant's writings. This fact may not necessarily trouble the champions of human dignity, since they may simply declare, as Dillon does, that "...for Kant 'dignity' is a technical term referring to the unique worth possessed by an end-in-itself..."[14] But can any theory be taken seriously whose central concepts remain unexplained, especially in a case when the method of the theory is just the critique of common sense (i.e. practical reason)? Given the extent of Kant's analysis of the sublime, one has yet another reason to expect him to devote a similar space to dignity. But he does not do so. The most reasonable approach is, then, to recapitulate Kant's main ideas about the sublime and see how they can be related to his scarce references to dignity.

(i) The analysis of the sublime

A substantial part of the *Critique of Aesthetic Judgement* is devoted to the analysis of the beautiful and the sublime.[15] The structure of the critique is, however, not easy to follow. In paragraph 5 Kant suggests that there are three basic types of objects that please us: the agreeable, the beautiful, and the good. The highest aesthetic pleasure is connected with what is beautiful. In paragraph 29, however, he introduces the idea of the sublime. Since it is discussed within the confines of aesthetics, and marked off from the non-aesthetical pleasure found in what is agreeable or good, the sublime seems to be an aesthetical category. However, it is not as purely aesthetical as the beautiful is. In contrast to the latter, the sublime is, in the first place, the experience of quantity (which is not necessarily beautiful), and not of quality. Further, there is no such thing as "the most beautiful", and the beautiful resists being captured in rules and concepts. On the other hand, the idea of the "greatest thing" *is* meaningful. "*Sublime* is the name given to what is *absolutely great…in comparison with which all else is small.*"[16] By implication, there can be no measure of the sublime except itself. In an almost Anselmian way, Kant argues that the greatest conceivable thing is that which is capable of making sense, or grasping the idea, of absolute greatness. Thus, what is sublime in the most proper sense of the word is the capacity of human reason to transcend "*every standard of sense*".[17] Thereby sublimity, the concept of infinite greatness, is discovered in every human being, elevating all to a supernatural level. Kant concedes the point that the mind can develop the idea of the sublime only after perceiving *something* in nature that is sublime (infinite, immeasurable, mighty), and even that this perception is mediated properly not through our intellectual but our aesthetic "estimation of magnitude".[18] But he insists that the true locus of the sublime is the human mind. Nature, or natural forces, may thus be called sublime only improperly, though legitimately.

Despite the brevity of this summary, the essential difference between Kolnai's approach to the quality of dignity and Kant's approach to the quality of the sublime is, I hope, clear. For Kolnai the object impresses us, elicits certain reactions proper to it, and, as in the case of dignity, it may make us aware of its presence in us. But it retains its sovereignty, or autonomous existence. For Kant, in Lazaroff's words, "the aesthetical character in general of a judgement or representation is determined by its reference to the subject as opposed to the reference to the object".[19] And there is even more at stake with the sublime than mere reference. "Whereas judgements of taste have one object which is called beautiful, judgements of the sublime can be said to have two objects… The external scene in nature is like the indirect object in that it only occasions this judgement, whereas the realm of rational ideas which transcends nature is the direct object of the sublime."[20] But it is apparently wrong to call a *feeling* or *awareness* (of our own sublimity) an aesthetical *judgement*. Thus, it is not a purely aesthetical judgement.[21]

(ii) Response to sublimity

As was argued, the adequate response to sublimity is a more emphatic respect than that due to dignity, a sort of respect mingled with awe and fear, making the encounter with the sublime both a positive and delight-ful, and a negative, painful, experience. Kant agrees on the duality of the feeling of the sublime, but he makes a curious *exchange*: we are dissatis-fied *qua* small and finite beings, compared to the infinity implicit in the sublime; yet satisfied as being able to grasp the infinite (absolute great-ness) conceptually, that is, by reason. Considering the fact that only human beings can do that, the genuinely sublime must be said to reside in us. Thus, on the ultimate balance the response elicited by sublimity cannot be fear or trembling. It is a respect most properly due to our-selves, or, more precisely, to our rational and moral faculties, "which we attribute to an Object of nature by a certain subreption".[22] Kant acknowl-edges that fear has also a legitimate place in our response. But even man's relation to God, the ultimately sublime, cannot consist in mere fear and helplessness.

Thereby Kant rejects the classical, commonsensical appreciation of our response to the sublime which is dominated by fear and awe,[23] and suggests a concept of sublimity to which our response is that sort of respect which was found most appropriate to *dignity*.

V. KANT ON HUMAN DIGNITY

The logical step for Kant, then, would have been to celebrate *human sub-limity*. Indeed, when each human being is said to be capable of making universally valid laws within the moral realm, such a lofty position can in fact be associated with sublimity. As the *Companion to Aesthetics* observes, for Kant the category of the sublime is supposed to bridge the gap between "the moral realm where action accords with principle and the aesthetic realm where there is perception and feeling but no principle... An action has moral worth only if the agent is moved by respect for the moral law."[24] But Kant does *not* exactly do that. The bridge exists on paper only. Kant does not celebrate human sublimity; rather, his exclamations on the unique worth of every human being echo the concept of *human dignity*.

He had sporadically used this concept in his pre-critical period, and it appears in crucial passages of the *Groundwork* and the *Metaphysics of Morals*. In the former he writes that "the dignity of man consists precisely in his capacity to make universal law."[25] In the *Metaphysics of Morals* he first talks about the *dignity of mankind* present in human persons, but later says that "man regarded as a *person*...is exalted above any price, for as a person...he is not to be valued merely as a means to the ends of others or even to his own ends, but as an end in himself, that is, he possesses a *dignity* (an absolute inner worth) by which he exacts *respect* for himself from all other rational beings in the world."[26]

Kant's position is apparently ambiguous. Considering the citations in the order implied by the preceding passage one may detect an implicit move *from* the notorious conception of human dignity *as* the sublimity of the supreme legislator *to* the conception of human dignity *as* the uniqueness of each human being, *via* the conception of human dignity *as* the dignity of mankind.

It is the final version of human dignity that is most widely and approvingly cited. It is usually summed up in Kant's own words, saying that human beings are *ends in themselves*; or that human beings have an "absolute, incomparable, unconditional worth".[27] Modern commentators have been at pains to develop this line of thought towards a more systematic account of moral autonomy which does not stop at the universal-noumenal self but includes much of the practical identity, personality, personal relationships of individuals—briefly, their particularities. Human dignity is said to rest on autonomy, particularity, individuality, humanity, irreplaceability, and the like. Human persons are ends in themselves, not because they are sublime, as Kant thought, but because they are dignified, or have an inner worth, which is but another expression of the same thing.[28]

I shall not undertake to evaluate these revisions here. Nor is it necessary to repeat the arguments, reviewed above, which seriously question the tenability of human dignity thus conceived, though it is worth remembering that Kant himself admits that a liar is less worthy than a thing, and loses his or her dignity altogether. Thus Kant's position anticipates that of those who struggle with the equivocality of the concept of human dignity: first, that it cannot grow or diminish or be lost; and second, that it can grow or diminish or be lost.

Why Kant made these highly debatable moves must, however, be answered here. The chief reason seems to be the following. He must have had to realise the untenability of his view on *respect* as being the adequate response to sublimity. Even though, for obvious reasons, fear and awe are detached from sublimity conceived as a category most objectively exemplified by human persons, sublimity requires a peculiar type of respect (reverence, deference), which is *essentially one-sided*. Thus the idea of human sublimity does not do. The bridge from the realm of aesthetics to the realm of morality cannot be built in this way. For morality is a *joint* business of all human persons. It cannot be one-sided. In other words, what sublimity and the response due to it lack is just the aspect of *reciprocity*, which is indispensable for morality. It is present in our experience of dignity, but not in that of sublimity. Thus, dignity must replace sublimity, for only dignity implies an adequate sort of reciprocity, embodied in the idea of respect.[29]

The advantages of the notion of dignity are evident. It was circumscribed as something representing weight, yet as having something reciprocal about it. The idea of reciprocity follows from involvement and participation in the world, without giving in to the disorder, conflict and antagonism that prevail in the world. The sublime is something basically different. It was associated with height. What is sublime is something above the world. At least as a first approach, Kant agrees with that: the sublime is what no "standard of sense" can match, and it is, in his terms, related to greatness, not to weight or weightiness. But reciprocity is distinctively missing from our relation to the sublime. It is present in dignity, however, and just in the required sense.

Dignity elicits respect, which works both ways: toward the dignified, and toward the subject. Respect is, *pace* Kant and neo-Kantians, *infectious*. Once it is elicited, it begins to spread out and create the Kingdom of Ends. This is what makes it appear extremely valuable and attractive, and suitable to become the foundation of morality.[30] But the notion of respect has to be interpreted convincingly in such a way that it does not imply any morally, intellectually, or aesthetically positive evaluation of the person. It should merely prescribe that he or she should be given due attention, taken seriously; or at least it should exclude certain kinds of treatment. In general, respect should not simply be morally or pre-morally relevant. Its relevance must override the relevance of any other normative claim.

Such a conception of respect needs thorough argumentation; it cannot be taken as self-evident. For instance, respect might not be shown to be "infectious" in the required sense; it might not be easy to separate from evaluations; and it might not override any other normative claim. But even if these claims can be validated, the *sine qua non* condition of respect, that human dignity is a solid or thick concept, that is, more than a weak metaphor, cannot be provided.

NOTES

1 Without any reason offered to justify his method, one of the most distinguished philosophers of human dignity proceeds in the reverse way in his essay on dignity as a virtue (Michael J. Meyer, "Dignity as a (Modern) Value", in *The Concept of Human Dignity in Human Rights Discourse*, D. Kratzmer and E. Klein eds., The Hague etc.: Kluwer Law International, 2002, pp. 195–207): "In the analysis to follow I will take the 'virtue of dignity' to have its conceptual home within the notion of

'human dignity'" (p. 196). Of course, one *may* begin with human dignity and proceed to dignity, but this does not change the simple logical fact that human dignity is a *narrower* concept than dignity, and the former must be placed within the confines of the latter.

2 *Dignity, Character and Self-Respect*, R. S. Dillon (ed.), New York and London: Routledge, 1995.

3 As he puts it, Kolnai's "chief concern" is dignity in the sense in which it is restricted to those who best "comport" themselves; Dillon, introduction to *op. cit.*, R. S. Dillon (ed.), p. 22.

4 Page numbers given in the text without further references always refer to the first publication of "Dignity" in *Philosophy*, 51, 1976, pp. 251–71.

5 When describing dignity as a quality or value, Kolnai has various ways of proceeding. Dignity has different features that it "connotes" (254), or that "may be empirically ascertained to cluster round" it (252). It has "aspects" (254) and "senses" (256); it is both a "moral virtue" (269) and "connotes a specific trait of 'ontological value'" (256); and its core "is constituted by an attitude" (262).

6 A. Kolnai, "Aesthetic and Moral Experience", in *Ethics, Value and Reality*, F. Dunlop and B. Klug (eds.), London: Athlone Press, 1977, pp. 187–210.

7 A. Kolnai, "The Sovereignty of the Object: Notes on Truth and Intellectual Humility", in *op. cit.*, note 6, pp. 23–43.

8 Hence, in Kolnai's words, "the dignified connotes the idea of *verticality* in a more discreet fashion than does the sublime, and connotes, at the same time, a certain idea of *reciprocity*" (253, original emphases).

9 Again, let me quote R. Dillon. He interprets Kolnai as saying that the differences between persons in terms of dignity have "much to do with how they regard their human dignity. Human dignity is, *of course*, the familiar Kantian notion, involving the ideas of the inherent and inalienable value of being a person..." (*op. cit.*, p. 22, emphases added). That is too fast, to say the least.

10 It is noteworthy that Robert Nozick (*Philosophical Explanations*, Cambridge, Mass.: The Belknap Press of Harvard University Press, 1981) builds his ethics on aesthetic experiences, adding to this the claim that "the degree of organic unity is the basic dimension of intrinsic value" (p. 418), thus emphasising a feature of life that has a significant role among the features of dignity. On the other hand, Kolnai also surmised that "our response to Dignity" may be "the purest 'value response' (*Wertantwort*) as such" (253).

11 Here is Kant's own judgement about the liar: "Lying is the...obliteration of one's dignity as a human being. A man who does not himself believe what he says to another...has even less worth than if he were a mere thing"; *Metaphysics of Morals*, Cambridge: Cambridge University Press, 1993, pp. 90–91.

12 David Statman frankly admits that if the very low level of the basic moral and rational capacities is said to be the basis of human dignity, then there is hardly any sense in which human dignity can be hurt or offended, and thus its protection is not a very important moral duty at all. He wrestles with this dilemma in vain. See D. Statman, "Humiliation, dignity and self-respect", in *op. cit.*, D. Kratzmer, E. Klein (eds.), pp. 209–27. Others, like Thomas Hill, do not see this at all. Hill wholeheartedly accepts the view that even the worst criminals possess human dignity, and on that basis he argues that those who reject this view are moral snobs, inferior in a sense to the worst criminal. Hence, the lowest sense of human dignity has a moral strength superior to the greatest moral excellence. This absurd conclusion is a result of a desperate attempt to endow the concept of human dignity, based on the lowest common denominator, with an irresistible moral power. *See* Th. E. Hill Jr., "Social snobbery and human dig-

nity", in *Autonomy and Self-Respect*, Cambridge: Cambridge University Press, 1991, pp. 155–172.

13 Such as the character "Selig" in Woody Allen's movie.

14 R. Dillon, introduction to *Dignity, Character and Self-Respect*, R. S. Dillon (ed.), New York, London: Routledge, 1995, p. 21.

15 This was in conformity with the philosophical tradition, whose classic work was Edmund Burke's treatise on the beautiful and the sublime. Much of what Kant says about the experience of the sublime is a compendium of examples commonly used in his time.

16 I. Kant, *The Critique of Judgement*, Oxford: The Clarendon Press, 1992, pp. 94 and 97, original italics.

17 *Ibid.*, p. 98, original italics.

18 *Ibid.*, p. 103.

19 Allan Lazaroff, "The Kantian Sublime: Aesthetic Judgement and Religious Feeling", p. 357, in *Immanuel Kant: Critical Assessments, Volume IV: Critique of Judgement*, R. F. Chadwick and C. Cuzeux (eds.), London, New York: Routledge, 1992, pp. 356–77.

20 *Ibid.*, p. 362.

21 It is, however, worth recording that Kant has another essay on the sublime and the beautiful, written in his pre-critical period, which anticipates his later view about the essential link between morality and sublimity, even about human dignity, or the dignity of human *nature*, but is much more phenomenological in its approach and thus more entertaining and thought-provoking. In it, the beautiful is associated with the sanguine mentality, sublimity as an aesthetical category with the choleric mentality, whereas sublimity as a moral category with the melancholic type. The phlegmatic type is not related to any of these values. Whatever one thinks about the soundness of these observations, they are at least telling observations, less burdened with monistic philosophical speculations. *See* I. Kant, *Vorkritische Schriften bis 1768, Werkausgabe II*, Frankfurt am Main: Suhrkamp, 1996.

22 I. Kant, *The Critique of Judgement*, Oxford: The Clarendon Press, 1992, p. 106.

23 Lazaroff's criticism of Kant (*op. cit.*, p. 367) amounts to the same: "...sublimity contains a unique element which is not aesthetical at all but religious. It is the feeling of the numinous. Though the judgement of the sublime has basic characteristics which are aesthetic, these converge with an equally basic feeling which is numinous." Thus, contrary to Kant's view, sublimity is closer to aesthetics and religion than to morality. Or, alternatively, in Kantian moral theory "man is the direct object of the religious feeling" (*ibid.*, p. 368).

24 David Whewell, in *A Companion to Aesthetics*, David E. Cooper (ed.), Cambridge: Blackwell, 1992, p. 411.

25 I. Kant, *Groundwork of the Metaphysics of Morals*, New York, etc.: Harper and Row, 1964, p. 107.

26 I. Kant, *The Metaphysics of Morals*, Cambridge: Cambridge University Press, 1993, p. 230 (original italics).

27 R. Dillon, introduction to *Dignity, Character and Self-Respect*, p. 14.

28 On this, *see* William K. Frankena, "The Ethics of Respect for Persons", *Philosophical Topics* 2, 1986, pp. 149–167.

29 Contrary to dignity, respect has been extensively discussed by philosophers. The notion that Kant himself uses in his moral writings (*Achtung*) is not fully identical with the English "respect", which therefore needs clarification. "Regard", "consideration", "recognition", "respect" have been proposed by various philosophers. *See* Robert L. Arrington, "On Respect", *Journal of Value Studies*, 12, 1978, pp. 1–12; Carl F. Cranor, "On Respecting Human Beings as Persons", *Journal of Value Inquiry*, 17, 1983, pp. 103–17; Robert Darwall, "Two Kinds of Respect", in

Dignity, Character and Self-Respect, R. S. Dillon (ed.), New York, London: Routledge, 1995, pp. 181–97. Few observe, or consider it important, however, that the original notion of respect was strongly related to power and might, and was less reciprocal than it is today. J. Feinberg does note this, and says that respect has retained the idea of power but has been "purged of the element of fear"; *see* Joel Feinberg, "Some Conjectures about the Concept of Respect", *Journal of Social Philosophy*, 4, 1975, pp. 1–3. But in an interesting article, S. Buss argues that "Shame is respect in its primitive, pre-reflective mode" (Sarah Buss, "Respect for Persons", *Canadian Journal of Philosophy*, 4, 1999, pp. 517–50), p. 537. Hence, even today, moral education aiming at making us respect other persons is based partly on shame, which is pretty much the same as any other form of experiencing power and might. In that case, however, respect and shame ought to be reconciled. This seems to be an extremely difficult task.

30 Christine Korsgaard's interpretation of Kant's moral theory hinges precisely on that: from the Formula of Universal Law we are carried to the Formula of Humanity. In terms of the present essay, we are to turn from human sublimity to human dignity. *See* Christine Korsgaard, *Creating the Kingdom of Ends*, Cambridge: Cambridge University Press, 1996.

Kolnai's Dissertation *Der ethische Wert und die Wirklichkeit:* A "Completion" of Scheler's Value-Ethics

FRANCIS DUNLOP

Readers of Kolnai's ethical writings cannot fail to notice the charge of "immoralism"[1] which he frequently levels *en passant* at various kinds of ethical Naturalists and some other kinds of moral theorists. This habit of Kolnai's derives from his early conviction that ethics cannot be a purely theoretical activity. As he says in the introduction to his dissertation: "The man who tells me what is good awakens some of the powers at work in me and urges them on; in the last analysis he does nothing else."[2] Then, in the "Concluding Remarks", he argues that false theory and immoral practice are intrinsically connected.[3] These claims are closely linked with what he calls the "two ultimate data" of ethics: "the moral need and the *moral intuitions actually current in society*".[4] The first is explained as the presence in us all of "life-directing motives that are not 'biological', or subservient to vital interests" (though could easily be led astray); it reveals itself—here we have the second "fundamental datum"—in even the most hardened villain's use of the common language of moral discourse, either to justify his own faults, or to show that he himself is no worse than his neighbour. Kolnai goes on to stress the importance of the moral philosopher's becoming thoroughly familiar with all aspects of the moral vocabulary, especially the language of moral value; since positive ethical concepts all signify aspects of the moral Good, sustained attention to them, undistorted by abstract theory, cannot fail to have some positive moral effect.[5] The moral philosopher is, in fact, engaged, willy-nilly, in the struggle between Good and Evil.

The background to the dissertation is, then, a conviction that ethics must be able to show the moral agent how he may contribute to the more effective realisation of the Good, a task which the best-known ethical writers had done, at best, very patchily. Most of them, in Kolnai's opinion, had been content to set forth a universal moral principle or set of principles, and leave it to others to show exactly how such "abstract" things could be "applied" to the real details of the moral life. But this cannot be done, says Kolnai, without understanding that, just as ethical value influences reality through human conduct, so reality influences what is of ethical value in particular situations. The moral philosopher who neglects to study the latter form of influence has "only done half his job".

There is a great deal in Kolnai's dissertation, as in his later work, which links him with Max Scheler, and Kolnai presents his own work as a "completion" of his.[6] Scheler's great achievement was his defence of the objectivity of "material", or non-formal, values as the focus of all moral judgement and conduct. Values—the qualities of acts, persons, processes, situations, in short, of all possible kinds of objects, in all their hierarchically graded kinds from "hedonic" to "religious"—are, then, in some sense "there" for us, as persons. Once we have clearly felt the nature of, say, justice as a quality of the real or imagined conduct of a moral agent, we cannot go on living in total disregard of this knowledge. Scheler also held that the morally good act was one in which, for example, the value of promise-keeping is given precedence over that of amusing oneself by reading a thriller. Moral values thus emerge "on the back of" preferences for the higher value (in this case the spiritual value of a just act is put before the hedonic value of self-entertainment); the moral value is a resultant of this preference.

Kolnai accepted much of what Scheler had to say about the ordered realm of values.[7] But, like most commentators, he rejected Scheler's account of the moral value of conduct. He thought that it could not possibly be simply a practical expression of the agent's "preferences" between values, as Scheler seems to make it, since the moral agent frequently has to choose between values of equal rank, and can only do this in the light of the "undifferentiated" Good; in addition, the moral agent must always have some self-awareness in moral conduct, which Scheler dismissed as Pharisaism. The "will to serve the good" and the "will to be good", as Kolnai puts it in "The Structure of Moral Intention",[8] to which readers of the dissertation are referred, will seldom be prominent in the intention, but they must at least be present as background elements. Besides them, the moral agent must have somewhere in the forefront of his attention five distinct things (exemplified here by one of Kolnai's examples, "reading aloud to my uncle, who is ill in bed"):

(a) particular ethical values (Kolnai suggests "family solidarity");
(b) moral rules or principles observed (perhaps "help those in need");
(c) "object-goods" concerned in the action (here, the person concerned);
(d) some good result intended (raising his spirits);
(e) non-moral motivations which can be harnessed to ethical conduct (perhaps my enjoyment of reading aloud).

The relative importance of these elements varies from case to case. But they are all more or less morally significant for the assessment of conduct.

Another major Kolnaian disagreement with Scheler concerns what

Kolnai sometimes calls "objective tensions". The link between awareness of value and appropriate practical response, especially where moral obligation is involved, is always a problem for a value-ethics. Scheler, partly reacting against the Kant-inspired overextension of the idea of duty, manifestly slurs over the problem. Kolnai takes the tension of moral obligation (only relaxed when the right thing is done), together with the moral values on which it is based, as moral objects (that is, phenomena present to consciousness which cannot be wished away): "There is, above all," he writes, "a series of values marked by the note of *urgency*: above all values of cleanness[9] and correctness".[10] Some of these relate primarily to the person of the agent, as when a teacher, say, detects in himself a malicious pleasure at the prospect of (justly) punishing a particular pupil, followed by the felt demand to get rid of this defilement.[11] Others relate more directly to our treatment of other people, when there is a temptation to treat them with, say, injustice. In the latter type of case, says Kolnai, the value (or disvalue) comes before us with a note of *compulsoriness*; we feel we "must" not commit this injustice, and, perhaps, that others might justly prevent us.[12] In other cases, certain, usually positive, conduct comes before us with the note of something to be *expected* (not to act accordingly would be to "let them down"), or *hoped for* (it would be a pity if we did not act thus). Other conduct would be *welcomed* (as something others would be glad of but "have no right to expect"), and so on up to the saintly acts which would call for *veneration*, "with a decreasing level of specificness and fulfilability and an increasing level of 'richness'".[13] In all these cases *something like* the tension of obligation is felt by the agent, but increasingly only by certain types of people (cf. *noblesse oblige*).

What I want to do now is to focus on the key concepts which Kolnai *added* to Schelerian value-ethics. For, apart from his disagreements with Scheler's phenomenology, which we have sampled, he saw that Scheler himself had largely neglected the reality problem and was himself almost an "abstract" theorist, along with the Kantians and Utilitarians. When he was old, Kolnai used to say that all his subsequent philosophy was contained in germ in his dissertation. There can be no doubt about this, despite its many obscurities. The key to understanding it is given with this statement of intention: "My purpose", he writes, "is…to bring to light some of what seem to me to be essential phenomena of the ethical *concern with reality* and of the gradations of emphasis."[14] Since the original title of the work was "Limitation and Gradation in Ethics", it will not be inappropriate to centre our exposition on these ideas.

The second chapter is about the necessary limitation of value-claims. As its title, "The Limits of the Ethical End", implies, it is about the active pursuit of the Good, rather than the avoidance of Evil, with which most "everyday" morality is concerned. It clearly owes a great deal to reflection on the utopian governmental decrees of the Hungarian Bolsheviks and their associates in 1919, which they attempted to justify with moral arguments, and contains the germ of his mature anti-utopianism. In his expansion of Scheler's idea that value is first apprehended *in* real or reality-derived objects, Kolnai argues that this implies that we should approach reality as a kind of totality, good but with "substandard parts" often not clearly detachable from their environment. The adoption of ethical ends thus always amounts to the decision to alter the world (existing value-reality) in ways that cannot be entirely foreseen. But some "parts" clearly indicate that change is desirable; Kolnai likens the truly moral programme to an Aristotelian *entelechy*, or further unfolding, of the already existing Good.[15]

In the first section Kolnai expounds two necessary conditions for the adoption of a morally approvable end. The agent thirsting to improve things must ask himself whether the moral resources are, or will be, really available for achieving the desirable end, or whether they are only sufficient for some inferior result. Moral impulses, the vague desire to "do good", even moral zeal, are not enough. Positive moral achievements require sustained moral energy and determination. Where these are not likely to be forthcoming the concrete project has no moral value. The second principle relates to the kind and degree of resistance the envisioned changes are likely to arouse. Opposition is always likely to react back on the agent and change him for the worse. But compulsion will be inevitable in certain circumstances: indeed, the refusal to contemplate it alienates the will from reality. Kolnai suggests two principles for its employment: opposition is normal; compulsion must be regarded as "barely justifiable". He also illustrates this issue in regard to private life, where one party tries to win another's friendship through frequent or expensive gifts. Another case (not Kolnai's) might be the attempt to change the lives of certain old and isolated people "for their own good". The section ends with an extended example of "displaced value-emphasis", where someone sets out to make money in order that he may use it for philanthropic purposes, but is so changed himself in the process of getting rich that his philanthropy becomes distorted.

In the section "Ideal and Reality", Kolnai again engages with the *extent of the real foundations* on which the would-be beneficent project is based. Images of valuable states of things cannot provide lasting motivation if they are merely fantasies and have no real foundation in experienced reality. He then sums up these observations with the idea of a *"Provisional and adjustable 'goodness of the world'"*, with *"substandard parts"*, inviting us to think of the morally significant world as divided into the following provisional classes:

(a) "emphatic variants", which are those parts of reality requiring improvement, and manifesting "objective tensions";

(b) "unemphatic variants", like the spheres of technology and the economy;

(c) "emphatic constants", which include the "value-essence, existence, rights and need-structure of persons" (and the basic moral rules which protect these things), and the existence and character of social unities;

(d) "unemphatic constants", such as psycho-physical make-up and "the laws of nature".[16]

The adoption of ethical projects must, then, always respect emphatic constants (persons and social unities) and take account of unemphatic constants.

The third section, "The Ethical Suppression of Need", argues that we should only contemplate a radical suppression of specific human needs or affective tendencies for the sake of some lofty spiritual goal, since it is our needs that first direct us to values. A section on ethical reform then spells out certain principles of political activity. The final section of this chapter on limitation, where Kolnai draws the more important threads together, emphasises once more the principle of "the genuine presence of moral need", which rules out any arbitrary or "experimental" attitude to "moral ends", and the danger of confusing moral need with forms of moral *ressentiment*.[17] As in other parts of the book, he here stresses the importance for the moral life of absolute clarity about the values and states of mind that underlie moral conduct. He continues:

> But since the ethical need is never simply to pass judgement on "external" states of things (including states of one's own self), but always includes the judgement of *conduct* relating to them, and since moral energy is naturally channelled into the determination of willed activity, we can also put it like this: the selection of ethical ends should only comprise those states of things *which are kept in being by human decisions or the continuous support of human wills*.[18]

The less this is so, the more must the "ethical response" confine itself to a merely critical role. Once criticism becomes an end in itself, having lost touch with its genuine moral roots, "we have something immoral or at any rate ethically mistaken".[19]

Chapter three introduces the idea of graded moral emphasis, which is not only a prominent *leitmotiv* of the work, but the one that—certainly as regards its detailed working out—gives the expositor the most trouble. In the first section of the chapter Kolnai takes up Scheler's claim that values are given in an order of values, graded according to value-height, and transforms this into an order of values graded according to moral emphasis, in response to reality. He begins thus:

> The application of a value-concept…extends over a range of situations, at the heart of which it occurs with the greatest emphasis; towards the boundary its emphasis diminishes and dies away as respect for relative constants takes its place.[20]

We can exemplify this as follows: truthfulness is self-evidently and emphatically required in most cases where we assert something, but much less obviously so (i.e. with "diminished" emphasis) in others, where relative constants, such as the value of human existence or welfare, or some principle protecting them, strikes us as equally or more important in the immediate situation. This shows that values limit each other. Attempts to evade this through the universal and indiscriminate use of a single value, like justice, can do a great deal of harm. It follows that a prime requirement for the moral thinker is a "complete relation to value", from which all partiality has been firmly banished.

"One implication of the order of values, taken in this sense", he continues,

> is that no value may be accredited with the power to command us come what may, but that every single one needs some continuous and determinate connection with the Good as such, the Good as yet unanalysed into individual values.

This need for a continual background reference to the Good receives additional support when we consider the relationship that exists between values:

> Justice only strikes us as a fully-fledged value when it is something more than a merely geometrical or aesthetic feeling for symmetry, and its bearer reveals himself as an upright man in general.

What is more, we can see in Justice

> a feeling for the related values of "truthfulness" on one side, for "peaceableness", a natural accompaniment of justice, on the other; moreover a complete indifference to the consequential value of human welfare, whose furtherance is the point of just judgements and decisions,[21] would completely undermine the appearance of justice… Thus the order of values can only be understood as an order of values valid in themselves and qualitatively independent, yet in each particular case in need of completion, mutual reference and complementarity, and inclusion in something greater [the Good].

"This means", Kolnai goes on, "that every value implies other particular values, which have a watered-down and, as it were, peripheral presence in our image of the first value".[22] If justice is the most emphatic moral value in a situation, the values peripherally present or implicit in it will have much less importance, but still a far from negligible one. This is one application of the idea of "graded emphasis".

Before we look further into the idea of gradation we need to ask what exactly Kolnai meant by "moral emphasis".

> "Emphasis" in ethical conduct [he writes] is…to be understood in terms of…devotion to value, of exalting the claims of value [...], of feeling the presence of value in one's own action, or some moment of it. The feeling can issue…in a variety of evaluative stances, recognitions, decisions or projects—in feeling the value of the objects or ends one has in mind, in feeling obliged to do something, in feeling the urgency of some matter, and so on. All ethical phenomena of this kind have a common source in the fundamental fact of emphasis.[23]

Thus, as he also says, moral emphasis has an "integrating" function.[24] Kolnai also invites us to compare and contrast moral emphasis with the emphasis of "social utility", which is, in general, closely allied.

> For example, "untrustworthiness", "murder", and a "disorderly sexual life" are all both immoral and socially harmful, yet the condemnation issuing from the two points of view is concentrated on different features... From the point of view of purity of heart, moral steadfastness, gentleness, love or cleanness the judgement of particular cases will be very different from that reached on the basis of the maintenance of the social order or the survival of society.[25]

Kolnai also insists that moral emphasis is

> objectively verifiable, right down to a remnant which cannot be derived without contradiction either from the subject's opinions or from what he does; it never ceases to yield to the application of objective criteria.[26]

Again, he claims,

> The ethical meaning ascribed by the onlooker to the subject's conduct and to its individual features will conform exactly to the underlying structure of emphasis, if we discount the shift of perspective necessarily brought about by their differing points of view.[27]

Kolnai is not claiming here that, in every individual situation, it is always possible to reach agreement about right and wrong, but that if we know enough about the moral situation in which the agent acts, including the agent's own moral character, we can agree about what values are morally emphatic, that is, what features are morally important or relevant, in that situation. But there are no universal criteria for this: hence, "the theory of emphasis belongs to moral phenomenology".[28]

Where the maximally emphatic values (one must not forget that emphasis characterises the value[s] of some element of actual or possible conduct) are values of urgency, or compulsoriness, which is virtually always the case with what Kolnai variously calls "obligatory values", or "everyday morality",[29] the moral agent's conduct is usually morally determined, at least in a negative sense (certain things must not be done). But a value can be "very highly emphatic", Kolnai says, "yet its detailed determination and realisation may have nothing to do with the subject." The value in this sort of case will, it seems, be that of one of the ethically emphatic constants, which have, in general, only a "background emphasis" and do not require any specific conduct. Here "the relation between devotion to value and the value-bearers concerned can...be of an essentially different kind, not varying with the degree of emphasis."[30] The long passage that follows is not easy to comprehend in detail because of its metaphorical abstractness and lack of any really clear example, but it is introduced as an illustration of this claim that emphasis does not necessarily prescribe conduct. What emerges from it is that a person's particular situation or moral character (which are both elements of reality) can "actualise" a special emphasis, which can be integrated into the general system of emphases. The obscure passage begins with a brief reference to someone whose life makes him especially sympathetic to the suffering of animals. This "compassion for animals" is qualitatively different from compassion for suffering human beings (Kolnai says a specific "feeling for nature" is required), but can itself lead the mind, or heart, towards it along a "line of gradation", as can equally well happen in the opposite direction, when, perhaps, a person helps an animal out of pity when he is unable to offer relief to a suffering human being. Kolnai calls this kind of thing the "embedding" of special and individual emphases (here compassion for animals) in the "highest and permanent ones" (compassion as such).[31]

The rest of the section can be summarised as follows. Since moral emphasis can only be "felt", the boundary between minimal moral emphasis and some other kind of practical emphasis is virtually impossible to establish. It is therefore possible for an individual's "devotion to value" to bring into his moral sphere all sorts of actions and concerns which are normally regarded as extra-moral. The important point is that we should be able to see or to feel what Kolnai calls the "real presence" of the moral Good in these new activities.[32] An example might be that of an individual who adopts a wide-ranging project of cultural value which, after a time, gives rise to expectations on the part of others which he now feels morally bound to meet. Kolnai shows that the idea of the moral Good is wide enough to cover all such cases, which are further examples of the "embedding" of special emphases in general and permanent ones.

The important thing for Kolnai about these extensions of the moral sphere, which might be said to belong to the sphere of moral supererogation, is that, although they depend on something "subjective"—that is, devotion to value, though this is itself a development of the universal "moral need"—they are guided by aspects of reality, or "value-reality", some of which are, of course, psychological facts. As he says in connection with the idea of the "actualisation of emphasis", that is, the here and now emergence into moral prominence of some aspect of value, it occurs both in response to the objective situation (as when I come face to face with a person in need) and also when the individual's "conduct has taken up a direction". The effect of his claims is to rule out of court any attempt to carve out some distinct bounded category of "basic" or "everyday" morality, with which a complacent individual agent might be satisfied. His idea of the "complete relation to value", which is a consequence of devotion to value, or "the Good", is a necessary part of morality.

In order to fill out a little more Kolnai's idea of graded moral emphasis we should briefly look at one or two other of the examples he gives. The third section of chapter one starts as follows: "Moral experience teaches us that all aspects of conduct contribute to its moral value and disvalue, but that the degree of their moral emphasis varies from case to case."[33] I have already listed some of the features of the "moral intention" above. Kolnai specially mentions here some other dimensions of conduct. Its consequences can be divided into those vaguely foreseeable and those intrinsically bound up with the nature of the action. The circumstances of the action (nature and situation of agent) are relevantly distinct from the consequences of the conduct. Again, there is an important difference between subjective intention (what is more or less consciously willed) and the objective results of conduct. Lastly, there is the difference between aspects of the intention relating to oneself and those relating to others. Kolnai's point is that some moral importance attaches to all these elements, but that the degree, or grade, of value emphasis varies according to the nature of the reality "on" which one is acting. Different "lines of gradation", or series of elements of diminishing moral importance, will start out from the different points of view from which the conduct can be examined. There is no abstract schema for assessing particular items of conduct which can be generally "applied"; no absolute boundary between what is moral and what is not.

An interesting example comes in chapter five, in the very valuable discussion of the "exclusion experience".[34] Kolnai begins this account of the most fundamental way the moral intention grasps reality as follows:

> There are modes of conduct, manifestations of "life" in general, which will have nothing to do with any kind of moral consciousness whatever, phenomena whose presence calls radically in question the very survival of ethical value-reality.[35]

He goes on to classify these "vicious states of mind", which must at all costs be "excluded" from our lives, into three main groups: malice, uncleanness and baseness. The need to keep these aspects of reality out of ourselves is absolute. Hence there is no gradation of emphasis, which implies "more" and "less", in the proper sense. Nevertheless, there are other elements of reality, such as feelings of hostility or sensual pleasure which, while of no moral significance in themselves, become so when closely associated with, say, forms of self-abandonment or exclusive pursuit of one's own interest, which are at least morally questionable. Hence the exclusion-experience, as Kolnai puts it, "sets up gradations" in the sphere of the morally indifferent in response to real circumstances.

Another example concerns what he designates the "incorporation experience" of reality, which occurs whenever "ethical valuation concerns elements of reality just as they actually are". This

> comprises both the incorporation of the elements in question in a value-reality to be constructed, and also the incorporation of the psychological bond with these elements in the general devotion to value.[36]

The values concerned are those of "achievement" and "love" in their widest senses. The gradation series of morally significant loving acts goes as follows: the most moral importance attaches to the objective values (which do not have to be *moral* values) of the achievement or the object loved; then comes the value of the conduct itself; then the connection between the object and the value-tendencies of the subject; and lastly subjective features of the object which reflect the subject's taste.[37] The point here is that all these elements of value-reality may have some relevance in a moral assessment, and may have the maximum emphasis in some situations or for some agents.

Kolnai's employment of the idea of gradation is an essential aspect of his reality-related conception of morality. In his main theoretical account of this[38] he contrasts his conception with that of what he calls the two main forms of "normative dualism". The first, whose prime representative is Kantianism, he calls "the ethic of duty or law with no overview". "In so far as an ethic is possible" on the basis of the Categorical Imperative,

> its purpose is simply a rough external ordering of certain layers of reality, *as if* these were themselves emphasised, although really only the norm [or imperative] itself has value-emphasis, as though it were the epiphany of some higher being.

"The idea of graded emphasis", he goes on,

> presents the greatest possible contrast to this. Here every element of reality has some value-emphasis through the hierarchical interweaving of different kinds of emphasis in different proportions.[39]

The other kind of normative dualism, utilitarianism, or plan-ethics, he calls "the ethic of law…combined with an overview". "Here also we find only a *single* emphasis, but now every element of reality has a direct share in it; everything becomes determinable."[40] So the agent must proceed as if everything he meets were emphatic.

"Both forms of normative dualism utterly fail", writes Kolnai,

> because of the inner contradiction between the assumed neutrality…of all concrete reality and the fundamental ethical data of seriousness, responsibility and reference to what is concrete and real.[41]

The monstrous "as-if emphasis" they both share "is bound to lead to vacuous ethical speculation out of all touch with reality and to unethical violation of reality".[42] He is especially scornful of the "overview" aspect of plan-ethics. In his own conception,

> the agent moves in a system of scales of emphasis, whose link with the highest emphasis is real, not a construction for the purpose of calculation, and which have an intimate, not arbitrarily alterable, relation to the real situation in which the action takes place, including the agent's own character. It is then the real experience of the values of concrete reality which limits the overview, since emphasis cannot be externally assigned or transferred, but only—with corresponding changes—pursued in the form of devotion…if it is really to remain emphatic.[43]

Another quotation may help to make this conception clearer.

> *The ethical transformation of reality proceeds through an inward and graded permeation of reality by value, not through a dualistic field of tension between the two.* The former is the case when I do my duty (as duty!) with

a cheerful heart and with understanding of its origin; or when I love a person with an ethical love, that is, love him in such a way that as a result, or, better, *in* the very act, I affirm and develop his value-essence.[44]

The reader who steps into the stylistically clearer air of the *Sexualethik*, which was published three years after the dissertation, will find no trace of "lines of gradation", let alone "counter-gradation" (which I have not introduced), and very little about the gradation of emphasis at all. Kolnai the university student, inhaling the atmosphere of academia and being constitutionally interested in the "structural" aspects of things, seems to have felt the need to engage in ethical theory. Since he was already by then convinced that there could be no moral theory in the "abstract" sense in which the Categorical Imperative, or the principle of the Greatest Happiness, are theories, he had to cast about for "logical 'lines'",[45] or logical aspects of his subject. But there was, perhaps, something factitious about the lengths to which Kolnai takes them, as he implies in a sentence of his memoirs. The context of this is Husserl's judgement on him after his term at Freiburg in 1928: "You have still a long way to go, Mr Kolnai: you can do description well, but you are as yet far from being a phenomenologist."[46] Recalling this, Kolnai adds:

> No doubt Ernst Mally's finely chiselled criticism in a German review, of my *Ethical Value, etc.*, emphasizing that my advertence to logical structures was not in proportion with my capacity to observe and describe shades of moral accents, pointed in the same direction.[47]

The important point to make in conclusion is that the value of the dissertation is the fruit of Kolnai's "capacity to observe and describe shades of moral accents", and is not eclipsed by the relative obscurities of the structural analysis. The general idea of gradations of value, as the chief indication of reality's influence on value, remains. That in any moral situation there will be many different things of moral significance, that some will be more important than others, that even slightly different configurations of reality will make a valuational difference in the situation, and that some systematisation is worth attempting here—these and similar principles are surely of lasting importance. The effect of them is to reinforce the idea that there can be no moral theory in the traditional "abstract" sense; that, on the other hand, it is well worth investigating the very large number of principles, or considerations (some of them amounting to "compulsory" rules), in the light of which one's claim to act morally may be justified. To some thinkers, Kolnai may almost amount to an anti-philosopher; but, if so, he is one who succeeds in systematically illuminating many odd corners of the moral world which philosophers have largely ignored or over-

looked. The dissertation's value lies here. I hope that I have given sufficient indications of this in exploring some of the more prominent features
of the work.

NOTES

1 *See* "Erroneous Conscience", reprinted in this volume, p. 70, for a definition.
2 *Der ethische Wert und die Wirklichkeit*, Freiburg i. Br.: Herder & Co, 1927, translated (as "Ethical Value and Reality") by Francis Dunlop, in *Early Ethical
Writings of Aurel Kolnai*, Aldershot: Ashgate, 2002. All references in the notes
are to the translation (EVR), with references to the German original (EWW) in
brackets. So the present ref. is: EVR 12 (EWW 2).
3 Especially EVR 165–67 (EWW 166–68).
4 EVR 17 (EWW 7).
5 Hence his qualified affirmation of the Linguistic Analytic approach to ethics in
later life—despite its relative "sterility".
6 I have had to ignore here the work of Dietrich von Hildebrand, though Kolnai
also sees his work as a development of Scheler's.
7 It is this fact which most clearly prevents the Kolnai of EWW (EVR) from being
classified as a "naturalist", despite his insistence on the reality connection. Kolnai's
general position on values is set out in ch. 2, §2; *see* the notes to this section for
some of his reservations about Scheler.
8 *See Early Ethical Writings* (ref., note 1), pp. 169–81. The original is "Der
Aufbau der ethischen Intention", *Philosophisches Jahrbuch der Görres-Gesellschaft*,
XLI, 1, 1928, pp. 1–16.
9 *See* EVR 124 (EWW 123) for these values. They denote freedom from the various forms of malice, uncleanness and baseness, which threaten to destroy personal life altogether.
10 These include "truthfulness, honesty, justice, objectivity, consistency, genuine-
ness, openness, loyalty (to oneself, to what one has consciously chosen)", EVR
130 (EWW 130).
11 My example. This work of Kolnai's suffers from the paucity of examples.
12 See note 10.
13 EVR 25 (EWW 16).
14 EVR 124 (notes) (EWW 122).
15 EVR 20 (EWW 11).
16 EVR 39–40 and 57 (EWW 31 and 50).
17 Kolnai often says later that utopian reformers are motivated by resentment against
reality as such.
18 EVR 56 (EWW 50).
19 EVR 57 (EWW 51).
20 EVR 59 (EWW 52).
21 The last clause should not lead anyone to think that Kolnai ever suggests that
justice is *merely* a means of securing human welfare.
22 EVR 60–62 (EWW 53–55).
23 EVR 63–64 (EWW 57). Cf. "Morality and Practice" (p. 100), printed for the first
time in *Ethics, Value and Reality*, Francis Dunlop and Brian Klug (eds.), London:
Athlone, 1977, but written in the early 1960s: Moral emphasis is "the peculiar,
sharply characterised tone attaching to every experience of what strikes us as moral-

ly relevant, a tone of warning, urging, vetoing and commanding with an 'absolute' and 'unconditional' ring of ultimate gravity about it". A little further down on the same page he says that it is "the basic subject matter of ethical enquiry". The strange thing about the earlier description is that, whereas the later passage concentrates on the objects of experience ("the...tone..."), the earlier includes what is surely contributed by the subject, or moral agent ("*devotion* to value, the *investigation* of value-claims", etc. (my emphases). This also contrasts with the stress on objectivity which comes in the next paragraph of my text. On the other hand, Kolnai's frequent recourse in the dissertation to the (foundational) moral *need*, which the moral agent can "activate" so as to bring into the moral sphere all sorts of conduct which might not otherwise be called of moral importance, together with echoes of the Schelerian conception of morality as an expression of the love of God, does suggest a way in which the subjective and objective can here be reconciled.

24 EVR 64 (EWW 57).
25 EVR 64 (EWW 58).
26 EVR 65 (EWW 58).
27 EVR 64 (EWW 57).
28 EVR 65 (EWW 59).
29 These will mostly concern the values of "cleanness" and "correctness". *See* notes 8 and 9.
30 EVR 65 (EWW 59).
31 EVR 67 (EWW 61). "Morality and Practice" (for ref. *see* note 22) prefers to use the terms "moral relevance of some kind" or "moral connotation" to characterise the kind of case in question. By this time Kolnai was far more concerned to distinguish "Thematic" from "Implicit" morality (*see* pp. 48–54 of this volume) than to argue that moral emphasis was extendable by activation of the moral need.
32 EVR 67 ("really...present"). The German (EWW 60–61) talks of "reale Gegenwart".
33 EVR 23 (EWW 14).
34 This type of value-experience is essentially concerned with the values (and of course disvalues) of "cleanness".
35 EVR 124 (EWW 123).
36 EVR 135 (EWW 135).
37 EVR 139 (EWW 139–41).
38 EVR (and EWW) ch. 3, §2.
39 EVR 68 (EWW 62).
40 *Ibid.*
41 *Ibid.*
42 *Ibid.*
43 EVR 69 (EWW 63).
44 EVR 67 (EWW 61). The "value-essence" is taken over from Scheler, and denotes a quasi-metaphysical, ideal, state of the person (or any other object), attainable through love.
45 The phrase is Ernst Mally's, from his favourable review of Kolnai's book. *See* note 47 for reference.
46 *Political Memoirs*, Dr Francesca Murphy (ed.), Lanham, Boulder, New York, Oxford: Lexington Books, 1999, p. 137.
47 The review appeared in *Blätter für deutsche Philosophie*, III, 1, 1929, Berlin. Much of it is translated in my introduction to *Early Ethical Writings of Aurel Kolnai* (*see* note 1 for ref.).

The Nature and Scope of Ordinary Morality: Some Reflections in the Spirit of Aurel Kolnai

M. W. F. STONE

*"There is a solid bottom everywhere. We read that the traveller asked the boy
if the swamp before him had a solid bottom. The boy replied that it had.
But presently the traveller's horse sank up to the girths and he observed
to the boy, "I thought you said this bog had a solid bottom." "So it has,"
answered the latter, "but you have not got half way to it yet." So it is with
the bogs and quicksands of society; but he is an old boy that knows it."*

Henry David Thoreau, *Walden*.

After many decades of unwarranted neglect, the seminal ethical writings
of Aurel Kolnai are finally receiving the attention they merit. Due to the
selfless efforts and estimable tenacity of his literary executors, and the long-
standing patronage of a select band of prominent thinkers in the field of
contemporary ethics, Kolnai's sophisticated body of work can now be
used as a stimulus to further reflection on a broad range of topics of human
interest. As far as the current orientation of moral philosophy in English-
speaking countries is concerned, Kolnai's salutary proposal that there is
neither a pressing nor a self-evident need for a fixed codification of moral
reality and practice stands out as especially relevant to a philosophical culture that appears all too accepting of the idea that a complete theory of
moral thought and action is a much needed desideratum. Given Kolnai's
genius as a cartographer of moral reality, and his enviable ability to bring
to bear illuminating powers of description on those opaque and transparent forces that govern our thought and actuate our behaviour, there is much
to be learned from his exacting treatments of a wide range of moral phenomena. In his doctoral dissertation *Der ethische Wert und die Wirklichkeit*,[1]
and in later essays such as "Erroneous Conscience", "Deliberation is of
Ends" and "Moral Consensus", as well as in his unfinished monograph
preserved in the transcript "Morality and Practice I and II",[2] Kolnai provides sagacious commentary on many issues that are essential to any philosophical consideration of practical deliberation, moral value, and the problems of conscience. Even though these themes no longer command the
attention of a philosophical constituency in the manner in which they once
did—due no doubt to the pervasive influence of various strands of ethical
naturalism and the further relegation within professional moral philosophy of anything like a traditional moral psychology—Kolnai's work offers
to modern ethicists a means of recasting their subject by offering a return

to a much more speculatively unprejudiced and phenomenologically attentive study of the assorted problems of human life.

In what follows I propose to set down several considerations which
will take their impetus from Kolnai's ideas and writings. I will argue that
an examination of the content of so-called ordinary morality, that is, the
web of belief and thicket of varied yet competing values that constitute any
agent's existing or pre-theoretical and inherited opinions, is of vital importance to any meaningful study of moral philosophy. My reason for advancing this claim issues from a view which I share with Kolnai and others,
that philosophical reflection on evaluative beliefs and practices is often
contaminated and enervated by the imposition of antecedent ideals and
notions which do not always have a fixed or plausible basis in our ordinary moral consciousness, and which furthermore prescribe in advance
what the scope and point of such reflection should be. One has only to
peruse the current state of contemporary English-speaking moral philosophy to observe that this tendency is shared by practitioners of seemingly
different approaches to ethics, such as deontological theorists, conse-
quentialists, contractualists, and self-styled virtue theorists. Significantly,
what all these thinkers hold in common is an aspiration that it is possible,
albeit in varying degrees, to discover an underlying unity or foundational
coherence to morality which then can be used as a subsequent starting
point on which a theoretical account of moral philosophy can be grounded.

A quality which all these approaches lack, and one which is found in
abundance in Kolnai's corpus, is the ability to describe, simply and without preformed assumption, the assorted beliefs, intuitions, convictions,
dispositions and principles that typify our various responses to objective and
subjective values, as well as our attempts to instantiate our moral convictions at the level of action. There is a blatant disregard of phenomenology
in contemporary moral philosophy, and such general disinterest in advancing relevant descriptions of ethical phenomena has had the consequence
that so many aspects of practical deliberation and evaluative appraisal are
reduced to parsimonious explanations that rarely capture the richness
and salience of the moral phenomena they purport to explain. Kolnai's considerable prowess as a moral phenomenologist provides us with a stout
and timely example of how ordinary morality can be philosophically clar-
ified and assessed, if only we take the trouble to describe our consciousness of the multiple values that inhere in the assorted principles we seek
to instantiate at the level of practice.

The view that ethics is primarily concerned with the description and
examination of our existing moral beliefs and practices, rather than with
their substantive reform or rejection, has a long history within moral philosophy. Aristotle, for example, thought that *politikê* (a branch of practical
enquiry that includes ethics and politics) is concerned first with the project of sorting through the intuitions and beliefs agents already have about

the nature of human action, and second with an attempt to preserve those existing beliefs and opinions about action which can be demonstrated to be internally consistent. Thus in book VII of the *Nicomachean Ethics* he writes:

> We must, as in all cases, set down the appearances [*ta phainomena*], and after first working through the puzzles, go on to prove, if possible, the truth of all the common beliefs [*panta ta endoxa*] about these experiences or, if this is not possible, of the greatest number and the most authoritative [*ta pleista kai kuriotata*]. For if we both resolve the difficulties and then leave the opinions (*endoxa*) undisturbed, we will have proved the case sufficiently.[3]

A related commitment to describe and examine the content of our existing moral opinions and beliefs about action, albeit from a quite different philosophical perspective, is also to be found in the work of Immanuel Kant. Throughout his ethical writings, Kant repeatedly announces that the moral principles he intends to put before his reader are to be reached through a descriptive analysis of what "common human reason" (*die gemeine Menschenvernunft*) holds to be true. In his *Grundlegung zur Metaphysik der Sitten*, for instance, the reality of a pure moral philosophy is declared to be "self-evident from the common idea (*gemeine Idee*) of duty and moral laws".[4] Similarly, when the categorical imperative is first introduced in that same work, Kant is quick to state that "*Gemeine Menschenvernunft* in its practical judgements agrees completely with this and has this principle constantly in view."[5] In this respect, Kant's "supreme principle of morality", the categorical imperative, is, he argues, to be found "within the moral knowledge of *gemeine Menschenvernunft*".[6]

It is noteworthy that both Aristotle and Kant are here giving voice to the view that the discipline of ethics must always reckon on the fact that agents will already be heavily "moralised" to some recognisable degree. If this is correct, then it follows that the subject-matter of ethics will be both characterised and conditioned by that stock of everyday or existing ideas which agents entertain on the nature of value within human affairs and by their views as to how goodness and rightness are to be pursued at the level of action. Any success, then, that the subject of moral philosophy may claim to possess as a practical discipline will depend on its ability to explain, with accuracy, sympathy and fidelity, what Kolnai termed the "material" values of ethics, these being those morally significant qualities of persons, aspects of conduct and beliefs derived from reflection on artefacts and enduring human institutions, which constitute the content and force of our ordinary moral outlook.[7]

In more recent times, however, the view that ethics must either be answerable to, or even substantively restrained by, our common sense or existing opinions about morality, has been the focus of a great deal of philosophical debate and criticism. In particular, some philosophers, most noticeably those of a virulent consequentialist persuasion,[8] have argued that an approach to ethics that simply describes and documents our existing opinions will yield no more than a series of contradictory commands and conflicting directives in matters to do with practical conduct. Indeed, it is contended that moral philosophy ought to be suspicious of ordinary morality since it can be shown to be "self-defeating".[9] Further to this, it has also been suggested that a purely descriptive approach to the subject-matter of ethics will bring to light nothing other than a messy composite of half-baked moral convictions, mysterious intuitions and recalcitrant beliefs about action, and that the upshot of such an enterprise will mitigate against the putative ancient promise of moral philosophy to provide clear and consistent guidance at the level of action.[10]

What is interesting about these criticisms is that they all trade upon the opinion that whenever we subject ordinary morality to philosophical scrutiny, we will come to realise that it is unequal to the complex task of providing coherent and reliable guidance in action. In order that a modicum of order or "system" may be imposed upon our moral consciousness, those theoretically impatient with the seeming intractability of ordinary morality have advanced the view that moral philosophy ought to bring about the substantive "reform" of our ordinary morality (e.g. Sidgwick's call for "systematisation" and "correction" in note 8). Such a process of "reform" is thought to be facilitated either by the introduction of unequivocal methods for moral decision-making, or else by the postulation of priority rules, which have as their aim the resolution of the deliberative uncertainty that is thought to be caused by the conflicting directives which issue from our existing moral thought. Under both these heads, the "method" of those enamoured with such strategies is clear: what is sought, and in some cases antecedently desired, is a procedure by which philosophical analysis can attempt to smooth away the tousled edges of moral experience in order that consistency and coherence can be secured in practical conduct. The important issue, however, turns on whether we can ever decide that we have good grounds for arriving at this conclusion. I would contend that the legacy of Kolnai's important contribution to the study of value and moral action provides us with reasons to be sceptical that so-called ordinary morality is as "self-defeating" or deficient as its contemporary opponents are minded to suggest.

I intend, then, to advance some provisional reasons which I hope will begin to call into question the efficacy of the projects of "reform" and "correction" adumbrated above.[11] My aim is to examine whether we can always be sure that we possess sound reasons for supposing that the deliberative resources available to ordinary morality ought to stand aside and make way for "correctives" such as unequivocal decision procedures, priority rules and umpire principles. By way of examining this issue, I shall argue that the impetus for reform in so much recent moral philosophy is premature, since it rests on a partial and unnecessarily reductive understanding of ordinary morality. What is needed, I contend, before such issues can be decided, is a deepened appreciation of the phenomenology of those quotidian beliefs and basic intuitions that we bring to bear on our moral decision-making. This is where Kolnai's contribution to recent moral philosophy comes into its own.

A great deal, then, seems to rest on how we choose to characterise "ordinary morality". How might we make this rather daunting composite of variable beliefs and intuitions about action and value perspicuous? Departing from the letter of Kolnai's texts, while keeping within their spirit, one of the ways in which we might illuminate the substance of ordinary morality is to introduce a position which, following the work of John Rawls, the late Bernard Williams termed "methodological intuitionism". In his *Theory of Justice* Rawls defines intuitionism as a doctrine that embraces two features.[12] First, intuitionist theories consist of a "plurality of first principles which may conflict to give contrary directives in particular types of cases", and second, such theories "include no explicit method, no priority rules, for weighing...principles against one another." In this sense, the version of intuitionism before us is a methodological rather than an epistemological doctrine,[13] since it claims that an ethical view is intuitionist if it admits a plurality of first principles that may conflict, and further holds that there is no antecedent method for resolving the conflicts which may ensue from this state of affairs.

The pertinence of methodological intuitionism to our discussion can be brought out in the following way. On the basis of adopting a commitment to describe rather than to reform our existing moral consciousness, we might say that methodological intuitionism provides us with a convenient heading under which we can describe our actual deliberative experience of the content of ordinary morality. Thus, if we examine the numerous allegiances, requirements, directives, permissions and prohibitions we have inherited from the assorted forces and agencies that have conditioned our pre-philosophical understanding of morality, we will be powerfully struck by the fact that within our existing stock of moral judgements there are a plurality of values which may at various times come into conflict, and that our responses to such divergent axiological requirements invite us to consider the contexts in which we are required to act in very different ways.

Now, if methodological intuitionism can be said to account for a good deal of our ordinary moral experience, it follows that our lives will be variously subjected to occasions of significant moral choice even though it will still be an open question whether or not these choices are fully resoluble at the level of action. Such occasions may well take the form of having to override previously held values, or they might take the form of cases of conscience in which we are presented with situations in which we are required to choose between two mutually exclusive ways of acting. Since this account accepts such occurrences as an inevitable consequence of the existence of a plurality of competing values within our ordinary morality, we might expect it to be unable to afford us decisive deliberative assistance in those cases in which we are unsure as to where our duty lies or where our obligation might be said to reside. The issue here is that if we eschew all recourse to "correctives", as I have termed them (e.g. unequivocal decision-procedures, priority rules, or umpire principles), in cases of deliberative uncertainty, and simply rely upon the resources available to ordinary morality as described by methodological intuitionism, how can we then come up with anything but arbitrary resolutions to such cases?

In order to examine whether a neo-Kolnaian account of ordinary morality can meet this challenge, let us consider a particular case of conscience, this being the well-known example of the perplexed Student in Jean-Paul Sartre's famous lecture *L'Existentialisme est un Humanisme*.[14] One can appropriate this account without drawing the non-cognitivist conclusion favoured by Sartre, who argued that such cases prove that ethics is bereft of any objective means of resolving such perplexities. Sartre's example runs as follows:

> One of my students came to see me under the following circumstances: his father was estranged from his mother, and moreover was inclined to be a collaborationist; his older brother had been killed in the German offensive of 1940, and the young man, with somewhat immature but generous sentiments, wanted to avenge him. His mother lived alone with the boy, very upset by the semi-treason of her husband and the death of her older son; the youth was her only consolation. The young man was faced with the choice between leaving for England and joining the Free French Forces—that is, of leaving his mother—and helping her with the business of carrying on. He was fully aware that the woman lived only for him and that his departure—and perhaps his death— would plunge her into despair. He was also aware that everything he did for his mother's sake would be realisable, in the sense that it would help her to live, whereas every effort he made toward going off and fighting might flounder and prove completely useless. For example, on his way to England he might, while in transit through Spain, be detained indefinitely in a Spanish camp; he might reach England or Algiers and be stuck in an office at a desk job. As a result he was faced with two very different kinds of action: one concrete, immediate, but concerning only one individual; the other concerning an incomparably vaster group, a national collective, which for that very reason made that action appear more dubious since it might be frustrated en route. At

the same time he was vacillating between two kinds of morality: on the one hand a morality of sympathy, of personal devotion, and on the other a broader morality, but one whose efficacy was more dubious. He had to choose between the two.[15]

Having set out the example we have now to consider whether or not it is possible to find a method of reasoning which, building on the type of deliberative resources available to ordinary morality, can furnish us with a non-arbitrary settlement of this case. I shall argue that Sartre's Student could conceivably find a morally informed settlement of his conflict, or be led to the threshold of discovering such a practical conclusion, by engaging in a method of practical reasoning which I shall explain in terms of the *specification* of the principles that aim to take account of the values at stake in the case.[16]

Put very simply, this method consists in an agent's seeking to specify, and further specify, what he can actually grant or deny (both in his deliberation and at the level of action) to the objective values expressed within the opposing requirements that characterise his case. The activity of specification might be said to be "dialectical", since it involves the agent's construction of a deliberative dialogue between his antecedently existing moral values, recognised in the form of the principles that require a sure course of action, and the exigencies or opportunities of "the situation", where this is defined as the configuration of facts that demand his practical attention. Specification, in this instance, might be said to have two objectives: firstly, it seeks to refine an agent's understanding of the conflicting demands that characterise his case of moral uncertainty; and secondly, by truthfully and illuminatingly reconstructing what is involved in this, it aims to prompt the agent to identify the demand which he (morally) cannot bear to override in the light of what he is objectively required to do. Should we bring to bear the resources of this model of practical reasoning on the case of the Student, we might ask how the method could suggest a way forward for him. As mentioned above, the aim is to specify and further specify the heterogeneous elements that bear on an occasion of moral perplexity. Yet what, in this context, do "specify" and "further specify" mean? Before I can attempt to answer the first question, I shall need to answer this second query by making some further observations about how the Student's conflict is to be reliably characterised.

When we describe the principles which are at variance in a case of conflict we typically use the *language of deontology*. This is true in the present instance, as it seems obviously right to begin any characterisation of the Student's dilemma by employing deontological language in the headings "he ought to stay with his mother" and he has "a duty to join the Free French Forces". The principal reason why deontological language is useful here is that it provides a convenient way of talking about those obligations which have worked themselves out in such a way as to ensnare the Student in a situation of moral uncertainty. It is important to realise, however, that this characterisation can only be partial, for we need to spell out in further detail how the Student's actual experience of the conflict will influence his deliberation. In order to facilitate this task we need to turn to the *language of evaluation*.

The incorporation of axiological terminology into our characterisation of the Student's dilemma is warranted by the fact that the conflicting moral principles which compose the case are expressions of the Student's antecedently existing moral convictions. This last point is vital because the Student's dilemma directly concerns the conflict which has been created between the love and concern he feels for his mother and his desire to fight for France in order to avenge the death of his brother. What makes it such an agonising and pressing occasion of moral choice for the Student is the fact that circumstances have conspired to compel him to choose between two of his most treasured objective values, values which represent and express what he presently deems to be important within his existing stock of standing concerns. Because of the nature of his choice, the language of evaluation is needed to flesh out the substance of the conflict.

While deontological and axiological language both have a role to play in the characterisations of dilemmas and other cases of moral uncertainty, it is important to stress that axiological language is better suited for explaining the role of specification in these matters. For when we are confronted with a particular case and consider how we should act, we invariably appeal to those general moral principles which reflect our settled moral convictions and values. The reason why we make appeal to such principles is that they provide a framework in which we can bring to bear our standing concerns and values in the consideration of such cases. Yet in a case like a moral dilemma we shall often need to find more specific versions of these principles before we can understand just what and how much we are in a position to grant to each of the conflicting claims that are made upon us. Here lies the role of specification.

These points can be illustrated by the case at hand. Although the Student's conflict can be represented as a conflict between the general axiological headings "his love and concern for his mother" and "his desire to fight for his country", etc., what he needs, in order to understand better what he can do about the conflict in which he now finds himself, is to get behind these general headings and look to the claims which more specific formulations of the evaluative convictions expressed in these headings suggest. So, in the context of his ongoing discernment of what he must do in this situation, specification is the act or process through which the Student can identify just what is required of him by the values whose clash has orchestrated this moment of moral choice.

This last remark invites further explanation. When we specify in a particular case a highly general principle (P), for example "One ought to tell the truth and to avoid telling lies", a principle which expresses our axiological conviction that "veracity is noble and mendacity is vile", we do this by determining or supplying characteristics which attempt to make (P) more relevant to the circumstances in which we find ourselves. If we find ourselves in a situation in which our veracity will be put to evil uses, we shall want, when we come to specify the demand made by the original principle, to consider as many of the known details of our situation as possible, so that our eventual specification of the principle will take these details into account. The incorporation of these details in a specification of the general principle—for example, that any information that we divulge will aid and abet the torture and persecution of innocent people—is essential to our task of figuring out what we can morally grant or concede to the value of veracity in *this* situation.

Given this, the original principle (P) can then be specified to become (P1): "One ought to tell the truth and to avoid telling lies, but only in those cases in which one's veracity will not be put to evil uses." For (P1) is what becomes of (P) when we attempt to honour the original value expressed by (P) in this set of circumstances. Being a more specific principle, (P1) can then assist us in the task of getting clearer as to what we can actually give or deny to the objective value of veracity. The important point to note here is that when we describe our moral principles in terms of the language of evaluation, this language does not invite ready-made coinages for examining circumstances in the way that the language of deontology does. In this respect, the language of axiology will generate a lot of ideas about duty while the language of deontology will make it possible for us to act on those ideas.

When a principle like (P) is made more specific, however, its original formulation still stands; it is not invalidated. One needs to be precise here. When we are in the process of figuring out what we must do in these circumstances we do not consult (P1). Rather we consult (P); for (P1) is the result of consulting (P) in these circumstances. The point of specification, then, is to give the value expressed in the general principle its due by attempting to honour that claim for as long as circumstances will allow.

If this is what we do when we attempt to specify a general principle, what does it mean to give the value expressed in the original general principle its due? Moral principles of a highly general form like (P) are intended to have an application to all types of particular cases; in this sense they are designed to be "universal".[17] Yet what such principles can finally require of agents, in the sense of the doing or non-doing of certain acts in particular cases, can only be determined by the contexts and situations where these principles are applied. It is these contexts and situations which add the detail sufficient to enable us to arrive at a more specific and circumstantially nuanced understanding of the importance we attach to the value expressed in a general requirement. This means that the value or antecedent conviction expressed in a general moral principle is never in abeyance, even though the act that the principle demands of an agent will only become clear in the effort to take account of all the known details of a situation.

Having outlined what it is to specify a moral principle, we have now to illustrate how specification might work by returning to the case of the Student and considering the question: What is it within the Student's situation of conflict that needs to be specified? Sartre himself specifies the following features: the Student's uncertain understanding of the nature and limits of his filial and patriotic values and disvalues, his emotional response to his mother's despair, his initial awareness of the different practical efficacy of one option when judged against the other, his uncertainty about the nature of the authority behind the putative moral permissions and prohibitions he is confronted with, his desires for revenge, action and adventure, and, less explicitly, his recognition that he will end up denying his mother everything she asks of him if he chooses to indulge his desires for action and adventure.

I shall suggest that the Student can begin to specify and further specify his understanding of the competing demands under which he is placed by constructing *hypothetical narratives*. The purpose of these narratives is to enable him deliberatively to rehearse and explore the moral possibilities and impossibilities imposed by his occasion of significant moral choice. This means that in order to discern what he can do the Student needs to narrate, to tell different stories in which he can begin to work through the events which might ensue if he actually adopted one of the competing moral options he is forced to choose between. The purpose of these stories is to give expression to the nature of the principles at variance within the conflict, as well as to the moral requirements of the situation.

If, for the sake of discussion, the Student were to construct these hypothetical narratives, he might start by narrating to himself a possible sequence of events in which he has already joined de Gaulle's forces and is stationed in an army camp in England. During the course of a particular day he receives a letter from a family relative which has been smuggled out from France. The relative writes to tell him that his mother has had a severe nervous collapse and that her chances of a complete recovery are very slight. On reading this letter the Student realises—this is what he imagines—that his decision to leave for England has decisively contributed to this state of affairs. He then feels unbearable remorse for what he perceives to be his role in his mother's deterioration and eventual collapse. Further to this, he now feels completely helpless; there is nothing he can do for her. He cannot return to France to be by her side as it is still occupied by the Germans, and in being unable to visit her he cannot bring her the comfort she so obviously needs.

By narrating this hypothetical yet not unlikely sequence of events, the

Student has to begin to consider whether he could or could not morally bear to live with such news. Depending upon how he reflects upon this— and depending upon the outcome when he turns the narrative on its head and imagines how his mother would react to the news of his death—he may come, in turn, to determine what he can go through with and what he cannot. By determining the limits prescribed by the moral alternatives available to him, he will derive a clearer sense of the objective value of just what his mother's continued presence means to him. In this sense he is rehearsing the possibilities which inhere within his situation.

A second sequence of hypothetical events which he could narrate might focus on what would ensue if he opted to stay with his mother. In this narrative he is placed in a daily situation in which he is forever deferring to her needs. Knowing his mother as he does and the type of emotional demands she will make of him, he has to consider whether this is something he can willingly do, or, if he cannot willingly do this, whether he can sacrifice his own needs, desires and aspirations to his feeling of filial responsibility. If his relationship with his mother is already strained by the existing emotional demands she has placed upon him, he may then come to realise, having rehearsed this narrative, that he simply has to leave her for the sake of his own moral well-being, in spite of his love for her, since the requirement that he go to war is a more fitting moral response to the situation.

There is yet another hypothetical sequence of events he could explore. These events relate to what may come to pass if he opts to remain at home and does not offer himself for military service. Could he really bring himself to remain at home under such terms? By remaining with his mother he would certainly have to forsake any hope of avenging the death of his elder brother. Being so tied to the house and to attending to his mother's needs, he might lose all hope of heroically redeeming his family's name from the disgrace caused by his father's collaboration with the Germans. From the point of view of his desire to be of service, what would he be able to do in such a situation? Would he be able to leave his mother for periods long enough to enable him to become an active member of the local *Maquis*? And how would he feel if it should prove that he was one of the few young men who remained at home and did not join the army? Would he be able to rise above the inevitable accusations of cowardice or the taunts that he is still tied to his mother's apron-strings? Would he be able to suffer these moral indignities for the sake of his acting out of a sense of filial responsibility? If he cannot easily digest the thought that he will be away from the "action" and "adventure" of war, then the act of remaining with his mother will be unbearable.

My proposal, then, is that it is only by the effort of attempting to specify what we can actually give or deny to the objective values which are expressed within the competing principles that compose a dilemma or case of moral uncertainty, that it can be revealed whether it is possible for an agent to act on it. Directing these remarks to the Student, we can say that any practical conclusion to his conflict can only emerge on the basis of his dialectical consideration of the following points. In the first instance, he must ask himself what the values which are expressed in the conflicting principles require of him in the situation, and then he must ask whether they require him to do or to refrain from doing a certain act. In the second instance, he must ask himself how much he can morally suffer to give or to deny to the above values, and whether or not it is possible for him to do or not to do what the values require of him, so that he will be able to live with the sequel of doing or not doing what they require of him.

The useful point which specification can demonstrate is that a practical conclusion to the Student's conflict may well emerge, albeit slowly, on the basis of incremental advances in his moral understanding. One must be clear that the method of specification cannot be turned into a method of helping agents in moral dilemmas to arrive at definitive "right answers"— at least as this term is presently understood in the literature. Agents may or may not make deliberative progress as a result of reasoning dialectically. What the method does provide, however, is a synoptic outlook upon the process of decision-making in hard cases, which is useful in enabling agents to understand the different evaluative forces which govern their thought and condition their behaviour. What this outlook upon moral decision-making suggests is that important moral decisions can be arrived at by a detailed consideration of the nature of those antecedent convictions which one expresses in the form of general principles, and by a thorough scrutiny of the practical context in which one is to act. These processes are by their nature synergetic, for moral principles can only be effective if they can help us to interrogate situations reliably, and the scrutiny of situations can only have value if motivated by a desire to improve our understanding of the practical efficacy of our general principles.

A further lesson which might be drawn from reflecting on the example is that specification can help us to question the accuracy of a traditional view about the activity of resolving cases of conscience. According to this view, acting out of one's convictions in a dilemma represents the application to that situation of preformed principles, principles that an agent will have to fashion, as far as possible, in a way that renders them consistent and complete. Our discussion of the Student's dilemma, and our further description of the deliberative resources available to "ordinary morality", provide us with grounds to doubt this view; for the lot of the Student will not be improved by importing into his situation a new second-order principle or set of principles which will determine for him the stringency of the competing options between which he is forced to choose. What the Student does have need of, however, is a method of reasoning through which he can discover for himself the weight of the competing moral values: that is, the nature and extent of his love for his mother and what he can actually do or actually deny her in the light of this discovery, and the nature and depth of his feelings about going off to war.

It is here that we may see the suggestiveness (in the best sense of that term) which the method of specification might hold for the contemporary discussion of moral dilemmas and other cases of moral uncertainty. For it proposes that in cases of conscience of a certain type—dilemmas in which an agent is not faced with a micro-second choice (cf. the Trolley Problem, or Sophie's Choice)—an agent may be able to find out, or by a process of moral reasoning be led to the threshold of discovering, the thing he finds he can bear to live with by the standards of objective value. What will be important about such a discovery, if indeed such a discovery is made, is that it will be arrived at by the agent's scrupulous attention to what he already knows and is morally committed to. This suggests that a decision as to how to act in a hard case will be reached once an agent has specified and further specified what he can grant to the conflicting objective values of the case and their binding requirements.

What, then, does all of this show? Well, in one sense it reveals very little, except that ordinary morality deserves a fair and thorough hearing before it can be sent to the gallows. Yet in another sense—and this was an insight so valiantly upheld by the collective writings of Kolnai—it suggests something that ought not to be lost sight of, namely, that it is possible to describe valid and important methods of moral reasoning which resist "correctives" and other varieties of philosophical idealisation. Perhaps the only sensible conclusion to be drawn from this exercise is that we ought to resist making prior decisions on the status of ordinary moral reasoning, and instead devote greater time and philosophical labour to the more difficult enterprise of describing the direct and indirect relations which may or may not be said to exist between our antecedent convictions, beliefs and intuitions, and our ability to make decisions of moral principle. Here Kolnai surely shows us the way. For without the benefits of patient labour and incremental advance, both in our appreciation of what we already know morally and in our knowledge of so-called ordinary moral reasoning, we shall, like Thoreau's traveller, surrender to panic whenever we temporarily flounder "in the mud". Kolnai knew this; contemporary moral philosophy would do well to take heed of his intelligent advice.

NOTES

1 *Der ethische Wert und die Wirklichkeit*, Freiburg im Breisgau: Herder, 1927. This has now been magisterially translated by Francis Dunlop in the invaluable collection *Early Ethical Writings of Aurel Kolnai*, Francis Dunlop (ed.), Aldershot: Ashgate, 2002.

2 All these papers are included in *Ethics, Value and Reality*, Francis Dunlop and Brian Klug (eds.), London: Athlone Press, 1977.

3 1145b2–7; cf. *Eudemian Ethics* 1235b12–180.

4 Prussian Academy Edn.: *Kants Gesammelte Schriften*, Berlin, 1910 and ff. years, IV, 389/2.

5 *Op. cit.*, IV, 402/14

6 *Op. cit.*, IV, 403/15. Similar appeals to common human reason and to the necessity of philosophical ethics being constrained by it are made in numerous other Kantian texts (e.g. *Kritik der reinen Vernunft, op. cit.*, A 807/B 835, A 831/B 859; *Kritik der Praktischen Vernunft* 87–90, 105–09; and *Metaphysik der Sitten* VI, 376).

7 See Kolnai's observations in *Der ethische Wert und die Wirklichkeit, op. cit.*, note 1, pp. 86–96.

8 The obvious exception within modern consequentialism is Henry Sidgwick. While not initially hostile to common sense, he nevertheless thought of the history of moral philosophy as a series of inexact attempts to state "in full breadth and clearness those primary intuitions of Reason, by the scientific application of which the common moral thought of mankind may be at once systematised and corrected", see *The Methods of Ethics*, 7th edition, London: Macmillan, 1907, pp. 373ff. Sidgwick, however, takes it for granted that philosophical reflection will lead to revisions in our commonsense judgements. For a discussion of Sidgwick's methodology *see* J. B. Schneewind, "First Principles and Common-Sense Morality in Sidgwick's Ethics", *Archiv für Geschichte der Philosophie*, 45, 1963, pp. 137–56.

9 *See* the article by Derek Parfit, "Is Common-Sense Morality Self-Defeating?" *Journal of Philosophy*, 76, 1979, pp. 533–45. Parfit's more general observations about the nature of moral theory can be found in his *Reasons and Persons*, Oxford: Clarendon Press, 1984, pp. 3–52. For a quite different use of what amounts to the same type of argument against existing moral assumptions see Peter Unger, *Living High, Letting Die: Our Illusion of Innocence*, New York: Oxford University Press, 1996.

10 For an analysis of "ordinary morality" which argues for this perspective see Shelly Kagan's *The Limits of Morality*, Oxford: Oxford University Press, 1988. *See* also his more recent *Normative Ethics*, Boulder: Westview Press, 1998, pp.189–304 for a restatement of his antagonism toward ordinary morality.

11 My more detailed views on this subject will appear in *The Subtle Arts of Casuistry, volume 2: Ordinary Morality and Practical Reasoning*, Oxford: Oxford University Press, forthcoming.

12 John Rawls, *A Theory of Justice*, Oxford: Oxford University Press, 1972, pp. 34ff. Before Rawls, intuitionism in ethics was ordinarily considered to be an epistemological doctrine, which, in the hands of philosophers like H. A. Prichard and W. D. Ross, amounted to a view about the way in which ethical propositions were grasped or known. In the second decade of the twentieth century, epistemological versions of intuitionism came in for a great deal of criticism at the hands of Stephen Toulmin, *The Place of Reason in Ethics*, Cambridge: Cambridge University Press, 1950; R. M. Hare, *The Language of Morals*, Oxford: Oxford University Press, 1952; and P. H. Nowell-Smith, *Ethics*, Harmondsworth: Penguin, 1954.

13 For an interesting and insightful discussion of the relations between methodological and epistemological intuitionism, to which this discussion is greatly indebted, see Bernard Williams, "What does Intuitionism Imply", in *Making Sense of Humanity and Other Philosophical Papers*, Cambridge: Cambridge University Press, 1988, pp. 182–92.

14 Jean-Paul Sartre, *L'Existentialisme est un Humanisme*, Paris: Edition Nagel, 1970, first published 1947.

15 Sartre, *op. cit.*, pp. 39–42. My translation.

16 For a related, if slightly different account of specification, see Henry Richardson, "Specifying norms as a way to resolve concrete ethical problems", *Philosophy and Public Affairs*, 19, 1990, pp. 279–310; and his later book *Practical Reasoning about Final Ends*, Cambridge: Cambridge University Press, 1994, pp. 49–88. Like my account, Richardson's is indebted to Kolnai's article "Deliberation is of Ends", and to the writings of David Wiggins, especially "Deliberation and Practical Reason", *Proceedings of the Aristotelian Society*, 76, 1975–76, reprinted in his collection *Needs, Values, Truth*, Oxford: Basil Blackwell, 1987, pp. 215–38.

17 *See* Kolnai's important clarification of this term in "Are There Degrees of Ethical Universality?", first published in the present volume.

4. Feeling and Emotion

Is Love Intertwined with Hatred?

ANDREAS DORSCHEL

1. INTRODUCTION

1.1. Kolnai's "Versuch über den Haß"

In 1935, Aurel Kolnai published "Versuch über den Haß", "An essay on hatred", in the German periodical *Philosophisches Jahrbuch*.[1] The coincidence of author, subject matter, year and country of publication is remarkable in several ways. It is remarkable, to begin with, that two years after Hitler had been elected chancellor, a Jew[2] was able to publish at all in Germany—and not in some marginal journal but in what was, as it still is, considered one of the most distinguished philosophical periodicals. The reason seems to have been that *Philosophisches Jahrbuch* is edited by the Görres-Gesellschaft. It was the Catholic Church (with which the Görres-Gesellschaft was closely linked) which rendered possible a publication that was highly inopportune in Nazi Germany.[3] The publication must have been highly inopportune not least because of its topic. The emotion most obviously mobilised by the Nazis to get their rule going was hatred. When Heinrich Mann published a collection of his anti-Nazi essays in Amsterdam in 1933 he appropriately entitled it *Der Hass. Deutsche Zeitgeschichte*,[4] which in English is translated: *Hatred: Contemporary German History*. Hatred against the Jews and love for Germany: these two emotions were represented by Hitler as just two aspects of a single attitude.

1.2. Outline of the argument

Is love intertwined with hatred? This is the question Kolnai discusses mainly in the fourth section of his essay, and it is the question I will pursue here. Despite my historical introduction my interest in Kolnai is not historical, but systematic. I shall not merely report what Kolnai said; rather I shall use some of his ideas for what I hope is a reasoned answer to the question whether love is intertwined with hatred.

I shall try to arrive at such an answer by the following steps: to begin with, I shall make two brief remarks on the relevance and the methodical status of the problem (1.3.). That love is intertwined with hatred can be understood in two ways. Either that love and hatred are always present at the same time as *ambivalent* attitudes towards *one and the same* person or thing, or, alternatively, that they are always present as *complementary* attitudes towards *different* persons or things, persons or things that are opposed to each other, typically my friends and my enemies. I shall discuss the first interpretation of the thesis in the second part, and the second interpretation in the third part of my paper. In the second part's first section I shall give you an extended passage from Kolnai in free paraphrase—Kolnai's essay has not so far been rendered into English—a passage that conveys what is supposed to be meant by an intertwinement of love and hatred understood as ambivalence, not as complementarity. The fact that the passage is from Kolnai does not imply that he endorses the thesis of an intertwinement of the two emotions; he himself introduces the ideas expressed in the passage as a hypothetical view to be submitted to scrutiny (2.1.). My next step will be to consider some evidence which seems to be in favour of the claim that love and hatred are intertwined as ambivalent attitudes. The evidence derives from the observation that when love ceases, it seems to turn typically into hatred rather than indifference. I shall argue that this observation, while important, does not establish an affirmative answer to our question (2.2.). While the evidence from love turning into hatred is that of a mere succession of love and hatred, I shall, in the section which then follows, ponder evidence from a simultaneous presence of these two emotions: the case of what is sometimes called mixed feelings. I shall argue that the evidence from mixed feelings is not conclusive either (2.3.). It is further weakened by two features of hatred stressed by Kolnai: namely its centrality and its depth (2.4.). To end the second section I will examine whether the phenomenon of jealousy proves that hatred always lurks at the bottom of love (2.5.). The third part of my paper is concerned with the other interpretation of the thesis of intertwinement, the interpretation which says that love and hatred always go together as complementary attitudes towards different persons or things. As we shall see, the reasons for believing this are weak, and partly derive from confusing love and hatred with other attitudes (3.). Finally, I shall offer my conclusion (4.).

1.3. Relevance and method

Hardly anything could be more banal than the combination "love and hatred". Yet the question whether love is intertwined with hatred is clearly an important, sometimes even a pressing one (cf. p. 161). It is so in particular against the background of hopes to *abandon* hatred. Where political agitators of the type represented by Joseph Goebbels appeal to hatred, we are led to believe that we can live together peacefully only if we manage to get rid of hatred. But if the answer to the question whether love is intertwined with hatred is in the affirmative, then such hopes must be idle. For in that case to get rid of hatred would mean to get rid of love, too. But it seems just unimaginable that human beings could desire life without love.

Yet, however important our question may be, we need to know what kind of question it is. Almost mechanically we fall into the alternative: Is it a logical or a psychological question? I do not believe that this alternative is helpful here, and I doubt whether Kolnai would have accepted it for his phenomenological account of hatred. Psychological problems are sometimes in some ways logical problems. Our lives do not simply fall apart, they collapse in structured ways, and the fault lines are marked by our concepts. What we are interested in is of course the reality—the psychological reality—of love and hatred, and the language by which we are able to speak about these emotions is one important clue to their reality.

2. First Interpretation: Ambivalence

2.1. Statement of the view

What can be meant by the view that love is intertwined with hatred? Essentially, as Kolnai makes clear, it can mean two things. Either, first, it can mean that love and hatred are always present at the same time as *ambivalent* attitudes towards *one and the same* person or thing, or, secondly, it can mean that love and hatred are always present as *complementary* attitudes towards *different* persons or things, persons or things that are opposed to each other, typically my friends and my enemies.[5]

In his essay on hatred, Kolnai hypothetically, as devil's advocate, introduces a statement of the *first* reading of that view, as a starting point for examining it. I shall here paraphrase it liberally in English.

At the basis of all love lurks hatred, the proponent claims. All hatred, conversely, can be reduced to unhappy, disappointed, embittered love, or to love that was cut off before it came to expression, love that we did not avow to the beloved or perhaps even to ourselves. With all love of something, after all, goes the possibility of hating the same thing. For love brings about a close connection with what is loved. As a consequence, everything in what we love that in some way opposes our attempts to draw it towards us becomes a possible source of hatred. Of course it would not become so, if we could easily let go once we experience some resistance; yet since we love, we cannot easily let go. But, conversely, all hatred also builds on love. We do not just ignore and pass over what we hate; on the contrary we turn *towards* it, and that would not be feasible without an initial, though subsequently, as it were, aborted impulse of love. Again hatred, unlike contempt, takes seriously what it hates, and it does so not only as regards its physical force, but also its spiritual power. Hence it involves a kind of appreciation—something that would be impossible for hatred, did it not have love at its bottom. No hatred is more burning, more sharply personal than hatred towards a previously loved person who has frustrated the lover, a person who has, so to speak, punished the lover for his love now known to be "false", and has thus turned him into a hater. Frustration here does not need to, though it can, mean rejection of the love expressed. What we can perhaps pardon least is that *we* deceived ourselves in the primary infatuation about certain qualities we attributed to the beloved, and that she—inevitably, because she is like that—in due course turned out to be different from how we saw her.[6]

2.2. Love turning into hatred

Clearly, it is a complex picture that we get here. What we should do, I suggest, is to cut out pieces of evidence and examine them by themselves. While we do this we must not forget the larger picture, and for that purpose I will have to go to and fro at some points. But if we do not isolate points to some degree, we shall never arrive even at tractable questions, let alone answers.

So is love intertwined with hatred? Is there any evidence that these two emotions cannot be separated from each other?

It seems that there is such evidence. When a passionate love relationship comes to an end, when a marriage breaks up, the typical outcome is manifestly not that the man and the woman who are about to separate from each other solve their problems in a rational, businesslike manner. This happens, but it rarely happens, and we are rightly surprised when it does happen. We are not surprised, on the other hand, if animosity, enmity, hostility show up in such a situation, particularly when it is recent. We are inclined to say "Such is life", when in such a situation traits of hatred, malice and rancour are expressed, even though we know that these emotions are the opposite of love and even though we are convinced that the love between the two persons involved was honest and deep. Indeed, as Kolnai suggests, that love turns into hatred seems to happen only if that love was deep, and not merely a passing infatuation (pp. 157–58).

What is this phenomenon evidence for? It is, Kolnai points out,[7] evidence for believing that love is actually much closer to hatred than to indifference (*"Gleichgültigkeit"* [p. 172]). The evidence runs counter to the logically tempting simple idea that love and hatred are opposite extremes on a spectrum where indifference is in the middle. If that were true, we would always have to go through indifference when we start to hate someone whom we loved before. Again, this can happen, but it does so neither always nor typically. Rather, when love ceases, it can be transformed, and is transformed more typically, into hatred. This seems a plausible view. For love and hatred are both hot, while indifference is cool. And from heat we get into heat rather than into coldness, even though we know perfectly well we would be much better off staying cool when discussing the implications of our divorce for our insurance policies and bank accounts.

This is as far as the evidence goes. And we should add immediately what it does not show. It does not show, Kolnai insists, that love and hatred are intertwined in the sense of being there at the same time. They are not there simultaneously, but successively.[8] True, love turns into hatred, and it does so with an amazing immediacy—but the love has ceased once hatred is there. Hence love and hatred, at least as far as the evidence presented so far goes, are not as closely intertwined as some other things in the world. These are the things which we describe by *polar concepts*.

What is meant by "polar concepts"? The expression "polar concepts", it must be noted to begin with, is used as a technical term. For of course I do not wish to deny that in some sense of the word there is a polarity between love and hatred. Magnetic and geographical poles come in pairs, and, in the way we speak about emotions, love and hatred form such a pair, as do good and bad or good and evil respectively, in the ways we speak about values. In the more precise technical sense of the term, however, two concepts are polar if, and only if, it is impossible for an instance of one of them to exist without some corresponding instance of the other.[9] Thus "husband" and "wife" are polar concepts. Two persons must be in a certain relation, namely that of marriage, before one can be described as a husband. So whenever there is a husband, there is bound to be a wife, or, to put it in negative fashion, if I do not have a wife I cannot be a husband. "Form" and "matter" or "shape" and "stuff" are polar concepts. Whenever there is a form there will be some matter that has that form. And though the definition we are drawing on here is a stipulated one, it fits well the paradigm case of geographical poles. Two positions must be in a certain geographical relation in order for one to be north of the other, and so whenever there is a north there is bound to be a south. It is clear that this close conceptual relationship does not exist between love and hatred. If I say of myself that I love somebody, it is not logically required of me that I simultaneously hate the same person or some other person.

As I have already indicated, one of the crucial differences in the relevant cases seems to be that between simultaneity and succession. If something is supposed to be form, then there must be *at the same time* some material which it is the form of, whereas even if love were *always* turning into hatred—which it obviously is not—this would still be a mere succession.

2.3. Mixed feelings

But is it not possible for us to love and hate at the same time? It is obvious that we *can* love one person and hate *another* one at the same time. If we were even *bound* to do that—if we would need enemies to have friends—then love and hatred would be *complements*, an interpretation I shall discuss in section 3. Here our question is rather: Can we even hate and love *one and the same* person at the same time? Can there be mixed feelings—mixed, that is, of love and hatred?

If we imagine, says Spinoza in part III of his *Ethics*, that a thing which usually affects us with an affect of sadness is similar to another one which usually affects us with an equally great affect of joy, we shall hate it and at the same time love it.[10] So Spinoza allows for cases of emotional ambivalence which he calls "animi fluctuationes",[11] vacillations of mind. Explicitly he acknowledges that these are not cases of mere succession: describing the temporal aspect, "simul" is the word Spinoza uses in the passage I have cited. Spinoza sees such ambivalence as a result of a transfer of emotions which he calls "imitatio",[12] imitation. As the cited passage suggests, mixed feelings come about on the basis of resemblances between various possible objects of emotions. I may love my friend, but there are certain gestures which she makes that inevitably remind me of a teacher at school who used to harass me, and to that extent I hate her at the same time.

What does such a case show regarding our question? Even such a case does not show that love and hatred *are intertwined*. It merely shows that they *can coexist* when relating to different aspects of a person. While remarkable, clearly this is a much weaker claim. For one thing to be intertwined with another the connection would have to be a necessary, not merely a possible one.

2.4. The centrality and depth of hatred

Kolnai provides a consideration that further weakens the argument from mixed feelings (2.3.). We want to distinguish hatred from a mere dislike ("Abneigung", p. 148) or displeasure ("Mißfallen", cf. p. 162). Hatred is distinguished from the latter by what Kolnai calls, following an established usage in early phenomenology ("in phänomenologischer Sprache", p. 148), centrality ("Zentralität", p. 148) and depth ("Tiefe", p. 148). What is central is opposed to what is merely peripheral, and what is deep is opposed to what is merely superficial. A mere dislike can be directed to certain peripheral and superficial traits of another, but hatred is concerned with the centre and the depth—both of the hater and of the hated. We say that hatred comes from the heart, from the centre of the person; and at the same time it is also directed at the centre of the other person. If I have had a bad night, if I am therefore in a sour mood and make a few ill-humoured remarks at the first person that comes near me, then these are not an expression of hatred, though certainly of a dislike of the world as it is.

I believe that Kolnai is essentially correct here, though some additional clarification may be needed. Kolnai, the Hungarian Jew, was of course sharply aware of the anti-Semitic hatred of the Nazis which drove him out of Central Europe. But is this not an example of *superficial* hatred? Racists are concerned about colour of skin or the form of noses, surfaces of the human body—what could be more superficial than this? Now clearly there is a sense in which racists are superficial, treating a general feature, descent, as if it could possibly exhaust what a human individual is.[13] But in the sense Kolnai has in mind, racist hatred is also both central and deep. It emerges from the centre of the person—otherwise we could not understand the lifelong obsession that a man like Hitler had with the Jews. And it is directed at the centre of the hated other—racists would never be satisfied with changes in the surface of what they consider their enemy race, say nose surgery for Jews. The surface they constantly talk about is merely symbolic of an evil deep in the other. That is why racist hatred ultimately aims at no less than the other's annihilation.[14] The fact that racism is deep in the present sense is the real disaster. For if it were superficial, we would just have to wait until people got over that transient mood; but of course that is not how it is. Again, we tend to think of depth as essentially a good thing, a position closer to the truth than superficiality or shallowness: profundity, then, is a synonym. While that is one legitimate use of the word, it clearly is not the point of the technical term "depth" in phenomenology. Depth here just means something that emerges from the innermost traits that make somebody who he is—and if these are corrupt, then it is actually a bad thing if the person acts from such depth.

We have arrived on a somewhat toilsome path at a defensible interpretation of Kolnai's claim that hatred is always central and deep. As I said at the beginning of this section, this consideration further weakens the argument that an intertwinement of love and hatred is evidenced by mixed feelings. It does so, because the consideration forces us to revise the way in which we have described a case of mixed feelings. Let us reconsider our example (2.3.): I may love my friend, but there are certain gestures which she makes that inevitably remind me of a teacher at school who used to harass me, and to that extent I hate her at the same time. Once we have understood Kolnai's point, I think we are bound to replace "hate" here by "dislike". It is obviously a rather superficial similarity which guides my association. Hatred, Kolnai says, relates to a person as a whole ("Ganzheit", p. 148.); it seems that I cannot split up the other person, or indeed myself, into bits that I love and bits that I hate[15]—though it may be true that I like certain features and dislike others.

Perhaps "dislike" in some cases is too soft a word here. For what if a mannerism drives you crazy? But the distinction that I am driving at here by keeping "dislike" and "hatred" apart is not so much one of intensity, although that seems to be a connotation of these words. If a mannerism drives me crazy, my reaction is intense yet superficial; after all I could say to myself: "It's *just* a mannerism." Intense as my reaction may be, it lacks centrality and depth. We would therefore tend to say something like this: "It is just that quirk of his that upsets you—you should realise this doesn't mean that you hate him."

To love and to hate the same person at the same time—the famous "Odi et amo" that baffled Catullus[16]—then, is possible if, and only if, I manage to relate *via* these contrary attitudes to the depths and the centre of the other. I must represent her to me as having, as it were, two centres—a sort of schizophrenia, if we do not confine this word to psychiatric usage. Now, as Kolnai acknowledges (p. 173), such a thing can happen.

Again, an example may make things clearer. I might love somebody: I see myself as loving and loved, and so I see her. To that extent, I see the two of us as equals. Yet my love for her makes me depend on her. To that extent, if we suppose our case to be an extreme one, I see her as master and myself as slave: and I might *hate* it to see myself in this way—I might even hate her. In such a case love and hatred, taken as attitudes of both depth and centrality, coexist. In the relationship I see myself as equal and unequal, free and dependent at the same time, and this becomes a source of contrary emotions. Thus the coexistence of love and hatred is possible. It is, however, by no means necessary. For someone could love his dependence. The example, once more, represents a special case rather than a universal feature of love and hatred.

2.5. Jealousy

One of the weaknesses of the argument from mixed feelings was that it seemed to show only a possible coexistence, not a necessary intertwinement (2.3.). Considering the centrality and depth attributed to hatred by Kolnai, we have even questioned whether love and hatred can coexist, though not of course whether liking and dislike can (2.4.). But here is an attempt to show that love and hatred can exist together in the same heart and that, moreover, their connection is indeed a necessary, not merely a possible one.

The argument is this. If we really love somebody it seems that we must inevitably hate one thing: that person's loss. Such loss can be due to a number of circumstances: our beloved may cease to love us, or may be drawn away from us by a rival. The issue which comes up here is that of jealousy. Jealousy seems to be central and deep: the person as a whole and in the inmost core of his or her being is at stake—both the person I love and my own person. Spinoza has analysed jealousy as "animi fluctuatio orta ex Amore, & Odio simul",[17] a vacillation of mind born of love and hatred at the same time. Jealousy involves an element of hatred, and this element is, following our previous distinction, twofold: We hate the rival in so far as he or she draws our beloved away from us; but we also hate our beloved to the extent that he or she *allows* him- or herself to be drawn away. The question, then, is: Can there be love without jealousy? If the answer is "no", then love and hatred are intertwined.

Now it seems to me that jealousy is always possible. It is always possible that loved persons are not available to us and that they are (thought or felt to be) available to others. Their absence, then, will tend to be experienced as loss to a rival. Of course, jealousy is no inevitable reaction in such a situation. A Stoic might react with Stoic apathy. But if the reaction were such indifference, I believe we would be right in doubting that there was much love—love as a passion—in the first place. In fact, Stoicism is quite consistent in being equally opposed to hatred and to passionate love.[18] If a person does not feel jealous, or is incapable of feeling jealous, we tend to conclude that this person does not really care. Of course the jealous person does not just care about the other, he also cares about himself. In jealousy there is more self-love than love, says La Rochefoucauld,[19] and he is probably right; but he is also right in seeing *amour* and *amour-propre* here as both present in different degrees rather than as alternatives. Without interest not only in ourselves but in the other there will be no jealousy, but just a different, entirely self-absorbed and self-satisfied emotion.

As an upshot of the fact that we, or most of us, do indeed care about some others, jealousy, with its share of hatred, thus seems to be quite a normal, not a pathological reaction in a situation of feared loss. What does not seem to me necessarily true, however, is that love has to be in such a situation. I do not see, in other words, why two lovers could not be in a state where it does not even occur to them for a moment that there could be rivals around. While jealousy *can* be a sign of real caring and not merely, as has been maintained, of seeing the beloved as a property and thus as a thing, it is not a necessary sign of caring. Two lovers may be able to confer upon each other a feeling of perfect security and trust. And since I do not see any argument why that cannot be the case, I conclude that there can be love without jealousy and, to that extent, without hatred.

The case for the claim that love is intertwined with hatred, then, has not been made, as far as the claim's *first* interpretation goes. The first interpretation, as you will recall, said that love and hatred are always present as *ambivalent* attitudes towards one and the same object. All that has been established is that love and hatred have certain features in common, for instance that both turn attention towards their intentional objects. But of course this is not sufficient to claim that they are intertwined. The *second* interpretation, by way of contrast, says that love and hatred are always present as *complementary* attitudes towards *different*, in fact opposed, objects. I shall now turn to this latter interpretation.

3. SECOND INTERPRETATION: COMPLEMENTARITY

The second interpretation of the claim that love and hatred are intertwined presents these emotions as our attitudes towards our friends and our enemies respectively. The suggestion is that we cannot have friends without having enemies, and the other way round. Whether this leaves us with the uneasy sense that love consummates an unholy union with hatred, or whether we rather welcome the second interpretation as a beautiful and heroic picture of the world, does not matter much; what matters is whether the connection actually holds. The evidence seems to be clear enough. Any group, in order to be strong against an outside enemy, must be harmonious and peaceful inside. Conversely, the cohesive power which binds a group together is, or can be, strengthened by hostile feelings towards other groups.

However, understood in this way the thesis does not seem to be tenable either. To begin with, it is already obvious from our discussion of polar concepts (2.2.) that complementarity must have a pretty weak meaning here. It cannot be equivalent to polarity. While it does not make sense to speak of a south pole if there is no north pole, it does make sense to say of a child that she loves her parents without being able to answer the question "And whom does she hate?", or without presupposing that she hates anyone. And this is not because children are so innocent that they are still incapable of such an emotion. It makes sense to say of Tristan, if he is the lover *par excellence*, that he loves Isolde without presupposing that he hates King Mark, or anyone else.

Of course we cannot love everybody, or, to be more precise, if we did the word would change its meaning. We should rather have a different term for what is sometimes called love of mankind. Love as a passion is necessarily exclusive. But, as such, it is possible against a background of indifference and all gradations of milder sympathy, not necessarily against a background of hatred.

As regards the evidence from conflict, the only thing that seems obvious to me is that nationalism and tribalism flourish whenever a tribe or a nation are at war. To treat these words as synonyms of love, however, would be eccentric usage. During the Falklands War, the British probably felt more British than they ever had since 1945, but I have no reason to believe that there was more *love* around. And while it is true that a group has to be internally disciplined to some degree in order to be successful against an outside enemy, discipline is not exactly the same thing as love either. The groups which are most successful against enemies, which have made this purpose into a profession, are today called armies, and love does not seem to be the principle on which they are built, at least not any more than other institutions with wholly different purposes.

Accordingly, as Kolnai points out, love and hatred are not governed by anything analogous to the law of communicating pipes in hydraulics, which they would have to be if they were strictly complementary. We do not automatically hate our enemies or anyone else more when we fall in love. In fact, it seems to me much more plausible to say that, in the normal case, we forget all about our enemies for a time when we fall in love. Again, it seems implausible to claim that once I stop hating somebody, an equal diminution of my love, say towards my wife, would have to ensue.

At any rate, the burden of proof would be on anyone claiming this, and it would be quite a heavy one.[20]

Perhaps we want to say that someone who is not even *able* to hate must be a pretty shallow character, *too* nice, as it were, and hence hardly capable of passionate love.[21] But that is a very different thesis, not one about people's actual emotions but rather one about what people are capable of. It seems to turn the idea that love and hatred are intertwined into an incontrovertible dogma. For wherever no hatred at all was manifest, the advocate of the thesis could still claim that somehow, invisibly, the *capability* to hate was still there. Since I am not aware how this version of the idea could be turned into a hypothesis testable against reality, I shall drop it.

4. CONCLUSION

I shall begin my conclusion by saying what the argument has *not* demonstrated. It has not demonstrated that we should or could abandon hatred altogether. Perhaps we neither should not nor could not.[22] It is not hard to imagine some situations where hatred is precisely the appropriate human reaction. Yet there are others where it is not; the transformation of this highly focused personal emotion into a political programme, as in Nazism, is a flagrant abuse.

So what follows from the argument developed here along the lines drawn by Kolnai? It follows that the link between love and hatred is less tight than is sometimes assumed. In particular, there is no reason to think that, should we get rid of some, if not all, forms of hatred we would turn into emotional cripples, beings no longer capable of love.

NOTES

1 Kolnai's essay is to be found on pp. 147–87 in no. 2/3 of vol. XLVIII of that yearbook. Page numbers inserted in the text refer to this publication.

2 Kolnai was a Catholic convert, but for the Nazis being Jewish was a matter of race, not of religious denomination.

3 It should be noted, however, that the Nazis, unlike the Bolsheviks, did not take philosophy very seriously; hence, in the early years, a certain amount of carnival licence was granted. Another publication one might not expect is Leo Strauss's *Philosophie und Gesetz: Beiträge zum Verständnis Maimunis und seiner Vorläufer*, Berlin: Schocken, 1935.

4 Heinrich Mann, *Der Hass. Deutsche Zeitgeschichte*, Amsterdam: Querido, 1933. The title essay is on pp. 69–78.

5 "Ein *Nebeneinander von Liebe und Haß* gibt es in zwiefachem Verstande: nämlich in der Bedeutung der komplementären Entsprechung mit gegensätzlichen Gegenständen, und in der Bedeutung einer ambivalenten, 'paradoxen' Haltung zu einem und demselben Objekt" (p. 171).

6 "Im Grunde 'aller' Liebe soll Haß lauern, und 'aller' Haß soll auf irgendwie 'unglückliche', zielabgeschnittene, enttäuschte, verbitterte oder uneingestandene Liebe zurückzuführen sein. Wenn man dies nun in hinreichender Allgemeinheit faßt, läßt es sich in der Tat streng beweisen. Jede Liebe bringt die Möglichkeit des Hasses gegen den betreffenden Gegenstand mit sich, denn in ihr wird eine enge Verknüpfung mit demselben hergestellt, und alles Mißfällige und Gegenstrebige von seiner Seite eignet sich daher, infolge der (relativen) Unaufhebbarkeit der Verbundenheit echten 'Haß' auszulösen. Beispiele: Haß gegen den mißratenen Sohn, den treulosen Geliebten, den 'Angeschwärmten', der sich hochmütig abweisend gebärdet. Andererseits beruht der Haß stets auf Liebe: die geistige 'Würdigung' des Gegenstandes selbst, die für den Haß Bedingung ist, die im Hasse gegenwärtige Hinwendung wären ohne eine beginnende, abortierte Bewegung der 'Liebe' nicht denkbar. Kein Haß kann brennender und schärfer 'persönlich' sein, als der gegen einen Gegenstand, welcher den zunächst 'Liebenden' enttäuscht, ihn gleichsam ob seiner als 'falsch' erkannten Liebe bestraft und ihn zum 'Hassenden' gewandelt hat. Selten durch bloße Abweisung oder Verhöhnung der Liebe, Verweigerung der Gegenliebe: meist spielt in überwiegendem oder geringerm Maße mit, daß der Gegenstand sich im Zuge der Beziehungsentwicklung 'enthüllt', seine Wertwidrigkeiten und noch mehr den bloß scheinbaren Charakter mancher seiner anfänglich bewunderten Werte offenbart" (pp. 171–72).

7 Like others before him, e.g. Vilfredo Pareto, *The Mind and Society: Trattato di Sociologia generale*, trans. Arthur Livingston, London: Jonathan Cape, 1935, vol. II, §1357, p. 841.

8 "Zunächst darf man aufeinanderfolgende Haltungen nicht mit gleichzeitigen verwechseln" (p. 172).

9 Max Black, *Critical Thinking*, Englewood Cliffs, N.J.: Prentice-Hall, 1952, p. 46.

10 Benedictus Spinoza, *Ethica Ordine Geometrico demonstrata*; *Opera*, Carl Gebhardt (ed.), vol. II, Heidelberg: Winter, 1925, III, prop. XVII, p. 153: "Si rem, quæ nos Tristitiæ affectu afficere solet, aliquid habere imaginamur simile alteri, quæ nos æquè magno Lætitiæ affectu solet afficere, eandem odio habebimus, & simul amabimus."

11 *Ibid.*, scholium.

12 *Ibid.*, propositio XXVII, scholium, p. 160.

13 Wilhelm von Humboldt notices this shallowness when he states that the anti-Semite "einen Menschen nicht nach seinen eigenthümlichen Eigenschaften, sondern nach seiner Abstammung und Religion beurtheilt und ihn, gegen allen wahren Begriff von Menschenwürde, nicht wie ein Individuum, sondern wie zu einer Race gehörig und gewisse Eigenschaften gleichsam nothwendig mit ihr theilend ansieht" ('Über den Entwurf zu einer neuen Konstitution für die Juden' [1809], *Gesammelte Schriften*, Königlich Preußische Akademie der Wissenschaften (ed.), vol. X, Bruno Gebhardt (ed.), Berlin: Behr, 1903, pp. 97–115, p. 99).

14 On the connection between hatred and annihilation cf. Kolnai, pp. 151–55. The conclusion is on p. 155: "Jeder Haß ist seinem konkreten Zweck nach unbestimmt und führt, ohne Rücksicht auf das konkrete Wollen, das sich an ihn knüpft, eine Atmosphäre 'absoluter' Vernichtung, einen Blick auf Töten und Auslöschen, bei sich", and repeated on p. 162: "daß jedem Hasse eine Intention der 'Vernichtung' innewohnt". Kolnai (p. 152) refers in this context to Alexander Pfänder, *Zur Psychologie der Gesinnungen*, Halle: Niemeyer, 1913, p. 41. Cf. also Kolnai, "The Standard Modes of Aversion: Fear, Disgust and Hatred", David

Wiggins (ed.), *Mind*, CVII, 1998, pp. 581–95, p. 590: "Prototypically, the 'movement' proper to hatred is directed to the destruction of its object."

15 "Der Sprachgebrauch allerdings, daß wir einen Menschen lieben und einzelnes an ihm 'hassen', oder umgekehrt, ist ein unerlaubt laxer. Liebe und Haß gehen auf real auftretende Wesensganzheiten, nicht auf abstrakte 'Züge'" (p. 173).

16 C. Valerius Catullus, *Carmina*, R. A. B. Mynors (ed.), Oxford: Clarendon Press, 1958, carmen LXXXV, p. 94: "ODI et amo: quare id faciam, fortasse requiris? / nescio, sed fieri sentio et excrucior." In an influential article, "Emotional conflict and its significance in the Lesbia-poems of Catullus", *American Journal of Philology*, LXX, 1949, pp. 22–40, p. 35, Frank Olin Copley argues that the usual interpretation that takes *odisse* to be the opposite of *amare* is misguided. With reference to carmina LXXII and LXXV, Copley claims that *odisse* is the opposite of *bene velle*, and *odium* thus the equivalent of ill-will rather than "hatred" in modern English. Cf. also Kenneth Quinn, *Catullus: An Interpretation*, London: Batsford, 1972, p. 108.

17 *Ibid.*, propositio XXXV, scholium, p. 167.

18 For a closely related point cf. Friedrich Nietzsche, *Die fröhliche Wissenschaft*, §12, *Sämtliche Werke, Kritische Studienausgabe in 15 Bänden*, Giorgio Colli and Mazzino Montinari (eds.), Munich: Deutscher Taschenbuch Verlag; Berlin: de Gruyter, 1980, vol. 3, pp. 383–84.

19 *The Maxims*, French and English, ed. and trans. F. G. Stevens, Oxford: Oxford University Press, 1940, no. 324, p. 104: "Il y a dans la jalousie plus d'amour-propre que d'amour."

20 "Eine starre Polarität, wonach jeder Abnahme des Hasses eine gleiche Abnahme der Liebe nach der Gegenrichtung hin entsprechen müßte, besteht nicht. (...) 'Freund' und 'Feind' sind nicht Beziehungsglieder von der Art mathematischer Reziprokwerte; vielmehr steht es dem Menschen frei, auf der Plusseite ein Uebergewicht seiner Personbeteiligung zu sammeln" (pp. 184–85).

21 Kolnai contemplates this for a moment, without taking a definitive stance: "Vielleicht gibt es keine Liebesfähigkeit ohne Haßfähigkeit" (p. 185).

22 In line with this, Kolnai cautiously speaks of "die Möglichkeit einer gewissen Ueberwindung des Hasses" (p. 184). Cf. pp. 185–87.

Kolnai's Idea of Emotional Presentation

THOMAS NORGAARD

INTRODUCTION

What I would like to gain from the brief study I am about to present is insight into Kolnai's idea of emotional presentation. The expression "emotional presentation" comes from Alexius Meinong, whose work *Über Emotionale Präsentation* was published in 1917. However, I shall bracket possible questions about the relation between Meinong and Kolnai, and concentrate my effort on understanding the latter. My interest in Kolnai is part of a broader interest in cognitivist axiology and ethics, and my particular interest in the idea of an emotional presentation derives from a hope, so far encouraged, that it may be of help in a cognitivist study of compassion. In what follows I do not intend to contribute to the elucidation of any particular mental state, however—neither those in which Kolnai took an interest nor the one that triggered my own interest in emotional presentation. What I present here is meant to be a *preparatory* study. Before embarking on elucidations of the particular emotional presentations that interest us, it is worth while investigating the philosophical advantages of the general idea. So, in the present context, when I make use of examples, Kolnai's or my own, they are offered as mere illustrations and the reader is invited to substitute others more apt or plausible according to personal preference. What matters to me here is a general sense of direction.

THE CENTRAL PASSAGE

As far as I know, there is only one brief passage in the work of Kolnai, less than a page long, in which he offers a general characterisation of the idea of emotional presentation. Here I quote from what I shall refer to as "the central passage". Emotional presentations are:

> Acts or attitudes or conative states of consciousness which, on the one hand, are clearly governed by an intentional object, and, on the other hand, express something like a passion aroused in the self, an impact exercised upon it down to its somatic sounding-board; in other words intention (*Gegenständlichkeit*) as linked essentially, though not in a uniform or unequivocal or causally necessary fashion, to condition (*Zuständ-*

lichkeit). This close linkage is emphasised in both phrasings: "emotive response" and, more profoundly perhaps, "emotional presentation". ...Our range of interest here is marked off, on the one side, against a more or less purely judgement-like and...intellectual apprehension; and, on the other side, against such almost pure condition-types as joy, depression or excitement. ...In still other words, our interest fastens on the intimate and, as it were, indissoluble juncture-point between objects as intentionally present, and the possible correlative motions of the soul as somehow significantly involving states of the body.[1] (SMA 582)

A more detailed understanding of Kolnai's idea must be worked for. It requires some disentangling from his particular analyses, and this is what I shall begin to do. Such disentangling is humble, some would say unexciting, work, but I have found it rewarding and for that reason I go on to present my findings. At certain points in the exegesis I go beyond what there is strict textual evidence for in Kolnai. When this is most obvious, I have made it explicit.

GEGENSTÄNDLICHKEIT

In the central passage Kolnai refers to states of consciousness which are "closely governed by an intentional object". I shall begin with an attempt to unfold the contents hidden in that phrase.

The "intentional object" of an emotional presentation is that object towards which a mind is "directed" in that particular presentation. So, for instance, in fear, my mind is directed towards a *dangerous* or *terrible* object, and in hatred towards a *hateful* or *odious* object (SMA 587). "Intentional object" must be understood in contrast with "real object". Ideally, these are identical, but they need not be. There is room for error here. For instance, if I fear a burglar, then that burglar is the intentional object of my fear. The real object of my fear could be a burglar, but it could also be a shadow that I took to be a burglar, or perhaps just a phantom of my imagination (cf. SMA 585, 592). Henceforward, when I refer to "objects" I mean "intentional objects".[2]

When writing about the proper intentional object of some emotional presentation, Kolnai tends to offer a twofold analysis: firstly, he concerns himself with the basic *kind* of object that essentially figures in the emotional presentation. Here Kolnai distinguishes between objects (or individuals), features of individuals, events and situations (SMA 584). So, for instance, the difference between pleasure and gladness, Kolnai would say, is that pleasure is taken in some object, whereas we are glad about some state of affairs.[3] Another example would be Kolnai's claim that hatred is properly directed at a person, that is, a kind of *individual* (SMA 591), whereas disgust is properly directed at *features* or *qualities* of some entity.

We need a qualification here, however. Sometimes one cannot identify the object of some emotional presentation with a simple reference to any one of the different kinds of object just mentioned. An emotional presentation may have as its *main* object a person, say, but also essentially focus on some quality of that person, or on a situation that the person is in. When trying to identify the object of compassion, for instance, one may begin with a point made well by Wittgenstein: "If someone has a pain in his hand, then…one does not comfort the hand but the sufferer: one looks into his face"—or into his *eyes*, as the German text has it.[4] This suggests that the main object of compassion is a person. However, compassion must also—somehow—be directed at the state or situation the person is in, namely one of *suffering*. Adopting a helpful distinction from Lawrence Blum,[5] we may suggest that the sufferer is the *object* of compassion, and suffering its *focus*. It may be suspected that this example from the debates about compassion is symptomatic; that we *need* distinctions like the one between object and focus when describing objects of emotional presentations.

Secondly, Kolnai goes on to explore what he at one point refers to as the "object area" (*Gegenstandsbereich*)[6] of an emotional presentation (OD 30). The object area consists of something like a list, more or less systematic, of the typical particular objects of that emotional presentation. So, for instance, in the case of disgust, Kolnai systematises his list by distinguishing between the *physically* disgusting and the *morally* disgusting. In the first class we find, for instance, rottenness and secretions, and in the second mendacity and moral "softness" (cf. OD 52–72).

The intentionality of an emotional presentation is not necessarily identical with its object or object area, however. This is easily illustrated with an example: the object of fear is the *dangerous* object. However, in an important sense the frightened man's mind is not directed at the dangerous object, but at his own safety:

> What interests us about the fearsome, terrible or dangerous object as such is only the threat it embodies, and thus not properly speaking its nature or value and disvalue, not the landscape of its features and qualities. (SMA 585)

Kolnai goes on to describe the intentionality of fear as "unfilled", as similar to *instrumental* interest in not *really* being interested in its object.

"No doubt [fear] may stimulate—indeed necessitate or compel—a keen study…of its object: but that remains wholly subordinate to the dominant theme of averting its threat to our own security" (ibid.). Accordingly, Kolnai describes the intentionality of fear as "circumscribed" and "poor" (SMA 585–86). In order for a mental state to be an emotional presentation it has to be directed towards another object to a sufficient degree.

When Kolnai describes the affectivity of an emotional presentation as *governed* by an intentional object, we may understand this first of all in contrast with *caused* affectivity. Feelings of nausea can be mechanically produced, for instance, whereas disgust—and emotional presentation—cannot (cf. OD 34–5). Secondly, governed affectivity is one thing, *instinctual* affectivity another. Whereas the instinctual hunger feelings of a newly born child imply no transcendence, emotional presentation does. In the latter we break through our immanence and conform emotionally to an object, whereas in the former we merely unfold a need or inner structure.

A more precise understanding of the significance of the word "governed" may be achieved by considering the word "presentation" itself.[7] A suggestive contrast to presentation is "disclosure". Kolnai claims, for instance, that whereas sounds merely disclose or "betray" (*verraten*) their objects, sights and smells *present* theirs. Shape, texture and colour belong to an object more intimately than a tone engendered by it. "It is as if the sound only acquires its 'origin', as it were, from the object that engenders it and thereafter constitutes an essence, perhaps even a world, of its own" (OD 49). Whether or not we think Kolnai is right here, we achieve a better understanding of what it is to be a presentation. When writing in German, Kolnai uses the distinction between *Dasein* and *Sosein* to articulate this point. *Dasein* may be translated as "existence" and *Sosein* as "essence" or "character"; or, literally, "being-there" and "being-so". In hearing we only discover that something is there, whereas in seeing we are, at least more than in hearing, presented with an object's character. The word "presentation" is always most apt when the mental state is governed—ideally comprehensively and intimately—by some object's *Sosein*. Generally, visual sensation provides a person with a more "comprehensive" presentation of an object than does olfactory sensation, which to some extent can be "irresponsibly one-sided" in its presentation (OD 51). On the other hand, the olfactory sense "is the organ of an intimate grasping of so-being" (OD 52), and so tends to bring us closer to an object's essence than sight.

Zuständlichkeit

In order for a mental state to be an emotional presentation it must be "enough" of a condition. Take disgust as an example. Kolnai thought of disgust as a paradigmatic example of emotional presentation, and contrasted it with mental states like depreciation, dislike, contempt and detestation, all of which, he claimed, are intellectual apprehensions, or at least too intellectual to be thought of as emotional presentations (SMA 583). "Too intellectual" here means "not enough of a condition". In the central passage, Kolnai describes a condition as "motions of the soul somehow significantly involving states of the body" and also as "something like a passion aroused in the self, an impact exercised upon it down to its somatic sounding-board". As Smith and Korsmeyer put it, when Kolnai speaks of the conditionality of a mental state he has in mind the degree to which it "affects the subject's total condition or state, including bodily condition" (OD 115

n. 4). In order not to misunderstand what Kolnai has in mind here, two disclaimers may be useful.

First, an emotional presentation does not wax and wane with its bodily impact, or even its conditional aspect in general. This is important because of a problem we would otherwise face, namely that a passion can fluctuate in a manner that might force us to say "Now I hate, now I don't. Now I hate again…", and so on. Kolnai seems to have this problem in mind when he suggests that a mental state may be "too episodic and one-sidedly emotional" to be an emotional presentation (SMA 583). The best way to overcome this problem, I think, is to distinguish between emotional *presentation* and emotional *episode*. An emotional presentation is a single, particular state of mind that may last for anything between a moment and a lifetime. Yet it is typically not static but dynamic: it tends to develop over time, and also its conditional aspect may fluctuate. We may think of the periods in which the conditional aspect of an emotional presentation is "high" as emotional episodes. It is difficult to decide just "how much" of a condition a mental state must be in order for it to be thought of as an emotional presentation. But maybe we need not say anything general about this; and perhaps we should not accept a question in terms of "how much", but just express ourselves in terms of "tendency" and suggest that in emotional presentation there is an *essential tendency* for the presentation to affect the subject's total condition, the somatic sounding-board included.

Secondly, it is important to note that conditionality is not the same as body-dependence (*Leibgebundenheit*). Kolnai distinguishes these quite clearly (OD 31–2). For instance, anger is more of a condition than disgust, but disgust more bound to the body than anger.

> Hate and even anger are less bound up with bodily phenomena than is disgust, in spite of the more violent physical phenomena attendant upon anger. This is because the sensuous impressions involved in disgust and the suggestion of a physical reaction of vomiting play here a more essential role in a way that is much more specific and concrete than the raging, kicking and throwing which may arise through anger. (OD 32)

In other words, it is one thing for an emotional presentation to have a tendency to involve strong or "violent" physical phenomena, and another thing for such a tendency to be strong or "essential".

AN INDISSOLUBLE JUNCTURE-POINT

So, a mental state can be more or less intentional *and* more or less of a condition—and in order for a mental state to be an emotional presentation it must be *both* "sufficiently" intentional *and* "enough" of a condition. But, furthermore, these two aspects must be intimately linked in a juncture-point that is "sufficiently" indissoluble in order for the descriptive phrase "emotional presentation" to be apt at all. The important point to appreciate here is that the intimate juncture-points of different emotional presentations are of *varying degrees* of intimacy. This is important since the more intimate a juncture-point is, the more apt it is for us to use the phrase "emotional presentation" about it. When writing about the *most* intimate juncture-points, Kolnai uses the word "harmony" to describe the intimacy. So, for instance, when writing about disgust:

> It is in disgust that intention and condition form the most perfect, interpenetrating and reposeful harmony: we float in nausea intimately adapted to the object we are intentionally—reluctantly but somehow responsively—immersed in. (SMA 590)

At this point we may begin to appreciate the relevance of Kolnai's idea of emotional presentation for cognitivist axiology and ethics. *The central idea, which has the air of a regulative idea, is that of an emotional responding to, even absorption in, an object's* Sosein. *With the idea of emotional presentation Kolnai envisages the possibility of varying degrees of affective participation in, or submission to, meaningful reality.* To see which role this idea plays in Kolnai's particular brand of axiological epistemology, consider the following introduction to what I shall refer to as "the problem of opacity":

> No doubt, in my plain sense perceptions as such I am myself concomitantly "given" as a perceiver; but this aspect, however inseparable from my object-experience, is peripheral and wholly unemphatic; my awareness of the object is what luminously predominates. On the contrary, in my reporting an evaluative experience my own pleasure, delight, satisfaction or admiration, etc.—or inversely, in the case of an unfavourable judgement, my own dislike, unpleasure, horror, etc.—inevitably comes into play and fills an important place. I do not hesitate to say (on many occasions) with complete firmness, "This is good", "This is lovely", "This is beautiful", etc.; but such judgements include a factual reporting of my own emotive response: "I am enjoying the taste of this", "The sight of this attracts me greatly", and so forth. And these factual reportings are invested with a status of objectivity quite on a par with my factual reporting of *what* I am tasting, looking at, conjuring up in my mind, etc.; whereas the corresponding value-judgements proper, *about* objects (that is, specified values and disvalues), not about my emotive responses, are precisely for that reason less objective. Essentially less objective, I mean: as if an additional layer of subjectivity, opaque to some extent, that is, imperfectly transparent, intervened between my sense of evidence and the object it refers to.[8]

Later on in the same passage, Kolnai concludes that "moral evidence... while definitely claiming a cognitive status...lacks the straightforward cognitiveness of sense-perception, logical inference or fact-finding".[9] So, compared to other forms of cognition, evaluation (*because* it is emotional) is *less* straightforward; more *opaque*.

It seems safe to say that part of the *point* of the idea of emotional presentation is to address the problem of opacity. In evaluation a "layer of subjectivity" tends to prevent the object from "filling" my awareness. In fear this is particularly obvious, but, according to Kolnai, this is a general (indeed essential) problem. The idea of emotional presentation, I believe, is partly an envisaging of a certain possibility; namely of the problematic layer of subjectivity being more or less "transparent", and perhaps even in some cases approaching an ideal of "full transparency". This suggestion is confirmed when, in another context, we find Kolnai claiming both that all value-experience must to some extent be self-directed, since it involves either pleasure or displeasure, and that, even so, this self-directedness is "compatible with a most intense emotional penetration of the object".[10] The compatibility claimed here depends on the possibility of transparency. The problem we are faced with is one according to which the very medium through which our evidence is given also tends to distract us from that which the evidence is evidence of. It would not be odd, I think, to describe the problem of opacity as one of "epistemological disharmony". When Kolnai describes disgust as "the most perfect, interpenetrating and reposeful harmony between intention and condition" I think he means to say that, in the case of disgust, the problem of opacity tends to be less disturbing than in most other cases of evaluation. It follows from this that disgust is likely to play a cognitive role more pronounced than many other affective states, and this is what Kolnai claims (OD 39).

MOTIVATION

Kolnai's idea of emotional presentation commits him to a thesis which we, using a technical term from current debates about motivation, may refer to as "internalist".[11] According to an internalist, moral belief or insight may motivate a potential agent without the addition of an independent desire. So, for instance, if I believe that a person in front of me is suffering, then this belief may, on its own, motivate me to help or comfort that person. In contrast, an externalist claims that the belief that there is a suffering person in front of me cannot on its own motivate me. A belief motivates only when combined with an independent, relevant desire; in this case a desire, presumably, to help or comfort sufferers.

In order not to misunderstand internalism, it is worth stressing that the internalist does not have to deny that someone helping a suffering person has a desire to help. The internalist claim is "merely" that no *inde-*

pendent desire is needed. An internalist may imagine (a) that a belief motivates entirely on its own, or (b) that a belief causes a relevant desire in us (so that we "see" and then desire accordingly), or (c) he may hold something like (a) but add that we can always "ascribe" a desire to a motivated person, this being a linguistic point rather than a metaphysical one. In none of these cases does an independent desire play a role in the agent's motivation.[12]

Today, British cognitivist ethics tends to be internalist (in contrast, we may add as an aside, to the most prominent forms of cognitivism in the United States, which tend to be externalist. This claim is somewhat "rough and ready", of course, but possesses truth enough to give a first impression of an important difference within today's cognitivism[13]). However, when Kolnai entered the British scene in 1956 things were different. Not only was mainstream ethics *non*-cognitivist, the best-known forms of cognitivism—W. D. Ross is a good example here—were *externalist*. In other words, internalist cognitivism is a recent achievement in British ethics—and still developing.

Although Kolnai's commitment to internalism is not made explicit in the central passage, this commitment is clear throughout his writings. An emotional presentation is an affective submission to reality from which action tends to flow or follow directly. So, to use Kolnai's own examples, the movements proper to fear, hatred and disgust are flight, destruction and ejection (see, for instance, SMA 584–93). In the next three sections I outline what I take to be some of the main features of Kolnai's internalism. Those familiar with this difficult topic, and with the complexity of the current debates regarding it, will realise that what I provide in the following pages are mere pointers. All I hope to achieve is a first sense of direction for those of us who are interested in the relevance of emotional presentation for the development of internalism.

THE FOCUS OF INTERNALISM

If we compare Kolnai's internalism with the internalism defended by some of the best advocates of the position today—I shall focus on work by David McNaughton and Jonathan Dancy[14]—we find an interesting difference of focus. Both Kolnai and these two British internalists try to make sense of a certain link, and in an important sense they should be understood as allies. *But whereas the link focused on by McNaughton and Dancy is the internal one between belief and desire, Kolnai focuses on the indissoluble juncture-point between intention and condition; and this, I suggest, is a significantly different focus.* What Kolnai tried to make sense of was the idea that certain beliefs are also *conditions*. With the connection between intention and condition in place, the problem of motivation seems to disappear; it does so by making internalism seem obvious. Kolnai can explain the internal connection between moral convictions and motivation as readily as any emotivist. It is symptomatic that Kolnai does not spend time making a *point* about the internal link to motivation; it is, more or less, taken for granted. In contrast, the focus investigated by McNaughton and Dancy is exactly the link to motivation. Kolnai would probably find that what he refers to as "condition" or *Zuständlickeit* is under-described by McNaughton and Dancy. These writers seem to think of "desires" as *strictly* or *narrowly* "conative". A symptom of this is their taking seriously the possibility of merely *ascribing* such a desire to someone motivated. These desires appear to be quite insubstantial compared to Kolnai's "expressions of condition". At times McNaughton moves towards something like the idea of emotional presentation when describing "beliefs",[15] but, as far as I know, this is not something focused on or explored in depth, but rather something gestured towards.

Someone who is convinced that all evaluation is affective, and for this reason subjective in a sense which sense-perception, logical inference and fact-finding are not, may, upon reading McNaughton and Dancy, perhaps wonder whether something like Kolnai's internalism is what these writers have been striving for, but not yet achieved. Further, such a person might speculate whether these writers have been held back by a pair of concepts (belief and desire) which are not the best possible with which to articulate the point they wish to make.

However, perhaps it is *not* obvious that *all* evaluation is affective in this sense. Those of us who are reluctant to think so will not be able to see Kolnai's internalism as a general solution to the problematic link that moral cognitivists are trying to describe and understand. It may even be that there is no general model that would fit all cases: perhaps this link takes a variety of forms which must be treated individually. If this is so, then Kolnai, McNaughton and Dancy are indeed allied thinkers working on a common project.

THE STRENGTH OF INTERNALISM

Internalism takes a bewildering variety of forms, partly because the *strength* of the internal link in focus is phenomenologically complex and difficult to describe. On the one hand, certain kinds of insight are, at least sometimes, so compelling that they tend to silence other motives and move the knowing person to action without further ado. This fact has been stressed at least since Socrates. On the other hand, many internalists feel that this point, though basically true, may also be exaggerated. Without wishing to deny that insight motivates, such internalists tend to moderate their internalism so as to make space for various kinds of complexity. As far as I can see, the idea of emotional presentation lends itself to both stronger and weaker forms of internalism.

Consider first the strong version of internalism defended by Socrates: "Knowledge is a fine thing capable of ruling a person, and if someone were to know what is good and bad, then he would not be forced by anything to act otherwise than knowledge dictates..."[16] One way to make sense of the Socratic doctrine is to operate with an ideal concept of moral knowledge: rather than attributing a moral belief to someone on the basis of his "satisfying some appropriate subset of a cluster of criteria", we may think of moral knowledge as a matter of degree; "the virtuous person" may be understood partly as the embodiment of perfect moral knowledge, whereas "imperfectly virtuous people only approximate, in varying degrees, towards this paradigm".[17] This idea could well be developed further in the light of the idea of emotional presentation. Thus Max Scheler, for instance, who took upon himself to defend a qualified version of the Socratic claim, thought that a value can be "given in various degrees of adequation", and that when it is fully given, then one's will is compelled accordingly.[18] All evil willing rests on a mistake, just as claimed in the *Meno*, although the mistake involved is not "intellectual error" but "deception or aberration" which are *sui generis* emotional mistakes—essentially different from intellectual errors, yet quite on a par with them.

Kolnai's internalism is weaker than Scheler's (perhaps because Kolnai's value pluralism is less touched by hierarchical thinking than Scheler's[19]). An emotional presentation is such that there is a "movement proper" (SMA 590) to it—however, though emotional presentation *motivates*, it does not necessarily *move* the agent.[20] In other words, claiming an internal link between emotional presentation and action does not prevent Kolnai from stressing the *distance* there is between them:

> In some important sense our receptive and responsive way of being definitely precedes and underlies our properly elective and practical acts. *A* pleases us and *B* displeases us, or *A* pleases us more or displeases us less than *B*: "therefore", or at any rate consecutively upon this, other things being equal, we choose *A* and reject *B*. To be sure, "other things" are rarely "equal"; and this provides space for our complex and subtle deliberations, our *liberum arbitrium indifferentiae*, our taking "calculated risks" and sometimes our acting "at random". But in principle we "first" sense, perceive, know, imagine and evaluate, and "then" decide, bring ourselves to act, and make or urge others to act.[21]

Even though action somehow "follows" or "flows" from belief, one may also underestimate the complex relations there is room for between them; and overlooking the distance here may distort the phenomena as much as missing the link.[22]

THE SCOPE OF INTERNALISM

So much about the focus and strength of internalism. Let me end by adding a few remarks about the *scope* of Kolnai's internalism. In two ways we may think of it as a fairly *broad* internalism.

(i) First of all, Kolnai's internalism is not restricted to moral experience. In general, evaluative experience comes with an impulse to act. So, for instance, when writing about aesthetic experience, Kolnai stresses that though "man *qua* aesthetical being *may* be an appraiser only…on the whole he is not only an appraiser but also an *artist*…"[23]

(ii) In my articulation of the internalist thesis, I described the claimed link between condition and action by saying that action somehow flows or follows from condition. Kolnai describes the link further by saying that the action "expresses" the condition. My interpretation at this point brings me beyond what there is strict textual evidence for in Kolnai; in my somewhat speculative reading, Kolnai's use of the word "express" in the central passage suggests that he might have taken a serious interest in a perspective I shall refer to as "expressivist internalism". Some may find this form of internalism too broad, but it tends to throw light, I think, on any narrower form of internalism by placing it in its proper context. It relates our ability to form an intention to a broad range of other phenomena: from semi-involuntary facial expressions like frowning and smiling, to half-conscious behaviour (such as, say, fleeing or flirting may sometimes be), to artistic expression (*dance* may be a particularly good example here). The perspective I ascribe to Kolnai was adopted explicitly by Edith Stein:

> Feeling in its pure essence is not something complete in itself. As it were, it is loaded with an energy which must be unloaded. This unloading is possible in different ways. We know one kind of unloading very well. Feelings release or motivate volitions and actions, so to speak. Feeling is related to the appearance of expression in exactly the same way. The same feeling that motivates a volition can also motivate an appearance of expression. And feeling by its nature prescribes what expression and what volition it can motivate. By nature it must always motivate something, which must always be "expressed". Only different forms of expression are possible.[24]

Adopting this perspective does not imply denying that there is something altogether new and significantly distinct about the human ability to form intentions and to act on these; but expressivist internalism allows us to describe grey areas and to understand certain important forms of tension (by which I mean "potential conflict"). Take fear as an example. It is fairly easy to grasp, I think, the difference between being paralysed with fear (or trembling too much to perform the simple task needed to remove oneself from that causal chain that threatens one's safety) and, on the other hand, taking flight. The point of expressivist internalism is (a) to remind us that sometimes we find an "outlet" for some emotional presentation which is somehow less than "action" (at least in one sense of the word "action"); (b) to make sense of potential conflicts between different "outlets"; and (c) to bring onto the agenda of ethics the question of the *proper* outlet in cases of conflict. It is not obvious that the proper outlet is always action, narrowly understood, rather than "mere" expression. To think so is a kind of prejudice—grief may be a good example here.

The expressionist internalism just sketched is not explicitly present in Kolnai, and he might well have disagreed with various things I have suggested. On the other hand, he does use the word "express" in the central passage, and sometimes he uses "the language of expression" when writing about the motivational aspect of emotional presentations (cf. SMA 586). Even if he would have resisted my interpretation, I think the view I have in mind goes well with the other features of his internalism and his idea of emotional presentation in general.

CONCLUSION

My modest ambition in this paper has been to unfold in outline a general, central idea in Kolnai's moral psychology, which, in his own pages, is largely left to work in the background. Inspired by a single exception to this rule, I have tried to achieve a better grasp of this idea—the idea of emotional presentation—in the hope that it may be of help to those of us interested in affectivity's role in evaluation and motivation. I have worked on the assumption that, to some extent, we may understand this idea, and the philosophical advantages gained with it, in general. However, a serious study of affectivity and its role in evaluation and motivation may well begin with the thought that all of these phenomena are too heterogeneous to allow much general treatment.[25] And if this is so, then the *relevance* of the idea of emotional presentation must be assessed in particular studies; of disgust, and compassion, and other affective mental states.[26]

NOTES

1 Aurel Kolnai, "The Standard Modes of Aversion: Fear, Disgust and Hatred", *Mind*, CVII, 427, 1998, pp. 581–95, with an afterword by David Wiggins. Referred to in the text as SMA with page number.
2 For a more detailed and historically informative introduction to Kolnai's idea of intentionality, *see* pp. 5ff. of Barry Smith and Carolyn Korsmeyer's introduction to

their trans. of Aurel Kolnai, "Der Ekel" (first published in *Jahrbuch für Phänomenologie und Philosophische Forschung*, X, 1929, pp. 515–69), as *On Disgust*, Chicago and La Salle: Open Court, 2004. Referred to in text as OD with page number.

3 "Aesthetic and Moral Experience", in Aurel Kolnai, *Ethics, Value and Reality*, Francis Dunlop and Brian Klug (eds.), London: The Athlone Press, 1977, p. 193, note 3.

4 Ludwig Wittgenstein, *Philosophical Investigations*, trans. G. E. M. Anscombe, Oxford: Blackwell, 1958, §§ 286–87.

5 Lawrence Blum, "Compassion", in Amelie O. Rorty (ed.), *Explaining Emotions*, Berkeley, Cal.: University of California Press, 1980, p. 508.

6 Smith and Korsmeyer translate this as the object's "range".

7 In the central passage Kolnai speaks of representation rather than just presentation. One could pause here and consider which of the two words would be best for Kolnai's purposes. Kolnai himself, however, uses the words interchangeably, and so on this occasion I just hold onto Meinong's original "presentation".

8 From "Moral Consensus", in op. cit., note 3, p. 145.

9 *Ibid.*, p. 146.

10 From "Aesthetic and Moral Experience", in *op. cit.*, note 3, p. 196.

11 To avoid confusion, it may be useful to point out that "internalism", in current ethics, may refer to at least two different kinds of position. The kind of internalism discussed here is not the one associated with the writings of Bernard Williams.

12 Cf. Jonathan Dancy, *Moral Reasons*, Oxford: Blackwell, 1993.

13 *See* Margaret Little, "Recent Work on Moral Realism, I: Naturalism", in *Philosophical Books*, vol. 35, no. 3, 1994, pp. 145–53; and II: Non-Naturalism, in *op. cit.*, vol. 35, no. 4, 1994, pp. 225–33.

14 *See*, for instance, David McNaughton, *Moral Vision*, Oxford: Blackwell, 1988, chs. 3.3 and 7; and Jonathan Dancy, *op. cit.*, chs. 1 and 2. Both of these writers have written further on internalism since their cited works were published, but my comments are strictly limited to these two books.

15 *See*, for instance, *op. cit.*, 7.3.

16 Plato, *Protagoras*, 352c. Cf. also *Meno*, 78a: "No one...wants what is bad."

17 Sabina Lovibond, *Ethical Formation*, Harvard: Harvard University Press, 2002, p. 5.

18 Max Scheler, *Formalism in Ethics*, translation of *Der Formalismus in der Ethik und die Materiale Wertethik*, Halle a.d. S.: Max Niemeyer, 1921, by M. S. Frings & R. L. Funk, Evanston: Northwestern University Press, 1973, pp. 68–69.

19 Cf. "The Concept of Hierarchy", in *op. cit.*, note 3, p. 179.

20 I borrow this distinction from Parfit, 1997, p. 100, but I think it fits Kolnai.

21 "Aesthetic and Moral Experience", in *op. cit.*, note 3, p. 199.

22 See Francis Dunlop's introduction to his translation of the *Early Ethical Writings of Aurel Kolnai*, Aldershot: Ashgate, 2002, pp. xiv–xviii for more contrasts between Scheler and Kolnai.

23 *Op. cit.*, note 21, p. 202.

24 Edith Stein, *On the Problem of Empathy*, Washington, D.C.: ICS Publications, 3rd revised ed., 1989, pp. 51–52.

25 On the heterogeneity of affectivity see Dietrich von Hildebrand, "Die Geistigen Formen der Affektivität", in *Situationsethik und kleinere Schriften* (Gesammelte Werke VIII), Stuttgart: W. Kohlhammer, 1960, pp. 195–208.

26 I am grateful to Francis Dunlop, Michael Lacewing, David McNaughton, Sabina Lovibond, David Wiggins and the audience in Budapest for helpful discussion of earlier drafts of this paper.

Aurel Kolnai's "Disgust": A Source in the Art and Writing of Salvador Dalí

ROBERT RADFORD

In his essay "The Object as Revealed in Surrealist Experiment", published in *This Quarter* (an English-language journal based in Paris) in September 1932,[1] Salvador Dalí compiles a list of propositions for new surrealist actions or "experiments", and includes the following suggestion:

> *Collective Study of Phenomenology* in subjects seeming at all times to have the utmost surrealist opportuneness. The method which can most generally and simply be employed is modelled on the method of analysis in Aurel Kolnai's phenomenology of repugnance. By means of this analysis one may discover the objective laws applicable scientifically in fields hitherto regarded as vague, fluctuating and capricious. It would in my opinion be of special interest to surrealism for such a study to bear on *fancies* and on *caprice*. They could be carried out almost entirely as polemical enquiries needing merely to be completed by analysis and co-ordination.

My aim in this note is to consider the potential benefits of a reading of Kolnai's essay to expand our understanding of Dalí's painting and theoretical position during that most crucial and productive period of his working, between 1929 and 1932, but also to suggest the limitations of such a reading. Prior to David Lomas's imaginative commentary in his essay in the catalogue for the exhibition *Salvador Dalí: A Mythology,* currently at the Tate Gallery Liverpool,[2] I am not aware of this reference having been explored in the Dalí literature, and this must, to some extent, be due to the relative unfamiliarity of Kolnai's text and its limited accessibility.[3]

Aurel Kolnai was born in Budapest in 1900 and, after studying in Vienna, became associated with Husserl and the methodology of phenomenology. He might be described as a conservative liberal in his later political and ethical writing, which includes an attack on Nazism in *The War against the West* of 1938, and then on Communism in *Errores del anti-comunismo* of 1952.[4] "Der Ekel" first appeared in German in 1929,[5] and was also published in the same year in *Revista de Occidente,*[6] the Madrid journal edited by Ortega y Gasset, who introduced the essay "El Asco" as demonstrating the methods of phenomenology which aimed at "scientifically determinable, objective laws" applicable to the description of human feelings. The similarity of Ortega's language here with that used in Dalí's article can only add support to this being the latter's source for his citation of Kolnai, who would have been little known in Paris at that time outside specialist philosophical or Christian Socialist circles.

There is no doubt that Dalí would have found much of interest, both in Kolnai's methodology of objective and detailed categorisation in "Disgust" and in the specific terms of description he employed, which seem to parallel very closely much of Dalí's imagery both in his paintings and in the various forms of his writing at that time, certainly including the script for the film *Un chien andalou*. Kolnai formed detailed arguments isolating the specific features of disgust in order to distinguish it from the related phenomena of fear, anxiety, repulsion, tedium, hatred, contempt and so on. He notes its linkage with physical bodily reactions such as shuddering and nausea, rather than with more mental or specifically ethical reactions. He remarks on the importance of the principle of proximity—disgust arising in terms of an uncomfortable and unsought intimacy with the object of disgust, including obsessive or freely induced fantasies of closeness within the imaginative sphere: this sense of proximity extends so far as to suggest a "harmonious" merging of the surfaces of the subject and object. The disgusting object "looks at us sarcastically, fixedly, and directs its stink against us".[7] This element of the coupling of subject and object goes further, since "No doubt there is an element of invitation in disgust. I might say a lure, an enticement."[8] The physical reaction induced by disgust of an urge to vomit is appropriate because of the impression received that something alien could gain entry into the body.

It is at this stage we should note that Kolnai feels the need to distinguish the project of phenomenology categorically from that of psychoanalysis, ridiculing the latter for the tendency of its adherents to adopt the paradoxical position which contends that all hatred should be understood as repressed love, and love as an overcompensated hatred. In the process of examining the nature of disgust in relation to the various senses, he notes the priority of smell and taste in this and sets up a chain of connection between "disgust—smell—putrescence—decay—secretions—life— food",[9] which might instantly remind us of Dalí's reference in "The Stinking Ass", an essay written in 1930, to "the three great simulacra—excrement, blood and putrefaction".[10] When Kolnai goes on to examine the specific nature of disgust as visually presented, Dalí might well have found an incidental endorsement of his own precisionist painting technique: "The visual sense procures for us the object alone—or at least in its most salient points—the structure and form, with its colours, lines and perspectives",[11] as opposed to blurred impressions. It is perhaps in the next section of "Disgust", where the signal features of the disgusting object are most categorically listed and described, that we are likely to be reminded of the typical ingredients of Dalí's paintings of the *William Tell* period. Bodily excretions, notably faeces, are significant as marking a transition from living matter to dead, and secretions, such as mucus, which are described as "viscous, sticky and indelicately clinging"[12] betray their disgusting nature in constituting an improper surplus of living matter. Kolnai later expands this fundamental principle of "excess of life" as being the essence of the disgusting object. Among animal life it is chiefly insects and invertebrates that are found to be disgusting, again in as much as they demonstrate an excess of life in their swarming and wriggling as a mass. The potential for food to be in some circumstances disgusting is manifest. Food which is left over or which is in excess of comfortable needs, which is viscous or potentially putrid, clearly has this aspect of excess of life too. There are of course problems with cheese or gamy meat, where the discrepant signals between taste and smell obviously present complications; this leads Kolnai to propose an erotics of disgust.

In respect of the disgust which is attributable to the over-intimate presence and the inappropriate sexuality of the body of the other, Kolnai has surprisingly little to say, although he does offer the instance of an unwelcome homosexual advance, as well as the minor disgust of encountering a seat still warm from previous use. What is abundantly obvious, then, is that the whole territory of transgressive erotic experience, so fundamental to the concerns of Dalí and Bataille, deriving from the polemic of de Sade, was quite alien to Kolnai's world-view. The precise theme of masturbation, which so dominated Dalí's work during this period, is also not mentioned by Kolnai, despite its apparent relevance to the themes of secretion and excess of life as aspects of disgust. In a further category of sources of disgust which are "moral" or simply mental in nature (rather than ethical as such), he does however designate "irregular" sexuality (Kolnai's quotation marks) as representing excess of life in being "disorderly, dirty, humid, spumous and unhealthy".[13]

The final section of Kolnai's study does confront the question of the ethical aspects of disgust. It is obvious that Dalí, or indeed any surrealist, would not have followed the moral philosopher revealed within the phenomenologist. Since Kolnai is ready to conclude that disgust has a number of purposes which are certain and effective, that it has a "cognitive indispensability from the biological, metaphysical and ethical point of view",[14] he addresses the question of overcoming and transcending disgust. He quotes from Werfel's poem "Jesus und der Äser-Weg", in which Christ inserts his hand in the putrefying flesh of a human corpse in an act of ultimate compassion, whereupon the carrion flesh responds by miraculously emitting the fragrance of roses. Kolnai draws from this example a conclusion about the redeeming power of love overcoming natural disgust in accordance with conventional Christian theology. It is unimaginable that

the surrealist Dalí would have found any value in this account of the function of disgust, for, as he wrote in 1930 in "The Stinking Ass": "Being con-
noisseurs of simulacra, we have long since learned to recognise the image
of desire behind the simulacra of terror, and even the new dawn of the
'Golden Age' behind the shameful scatological simulacra... The ideal
images of surrealism in the service of the imminent crisis of consciousness, in the service of Revolution."[15]

It is necessary, then, to try to clarify the nature and extent of the
impression that Kolnai's essay might have exerted on Dalí following its publication in Spanish in 1929. The first thing to be noted is that much of the
imagery of those areas of disgust referred to by Kolnai, including decom-
posing animals and birds, swarming flies, soft, deliquescent forms, were
already established in Dalí's paintings from 1927 and 1928, such as *Honey
is sweeter than blood* or *Little ashes (Cenicitas)*. Similar imagery also occurs
in his prose piece "St Sebastian" of 1927, dedicated to Lorca. He makes
use here of the term *putrefacto*, in the sense long-established among his student coterie, of referring to the bourgeois sentimentalist, including "the
blubbering, transcendental artists, far removed from all clarity".[16] This
should remind us of that dominating theme of Dalí's rhetoric of this period,
in praise of objective visualisation and freedom from romantic emotional
involvement of the artist, which directed him towards the qualities of pho-
tographic and cinematic imagery. We should return again to his original
reference to Kolnai where he advocated the *method* of phenomenology as
a potential surrealist mode of research rather than approving the substance of Kolnai's analysis.

Kolnai's "Disgust" is a valuable and lucid document of its time. Dalí
was no doubt struck by its topicality and the parallels displayed by its objects
of analysis to his own interests as a surrealist, but the philosophical and
ethical distance between the two was too broad to allow us to consider
Kolnai as exerting a major influence on Dalí beyond agreeably appearing
to confirm his current preoccupations. There would be much to be said for
the publication of Kolnai's text in English as a contribution to the continuing discourse concerning repulsion and the abject in cultural studies,
since his position and methodology would form a useful counterpoint to
those of Georges Bataille and Julia Kristeva.[17] But Kolnai has a spirited
warning to anyone who might engage in this activity with an excess of
analytic conviction:

> There is something disgusting in the way in which anything and every-
> thing in the world is fastened onto with subtleties, reflections, calcula-
> tions and minutiae. The sterile, exhaustive and hair-splitting consider-
> ations, the stagnation of thought, produces a sensation of insipidness
> which is, ultimately, disgust.[18]

NOTES

1 Salvador Dalí: "The Object as Revealed in Surrealist Experiment", *This Quarter*, VIII, 1, 1932, reprinted in R. L. R. Lippard (ed.): *Surrealists on Art*, New York, 1970, pp. 87–96. No original version in French is cited in the literature, but some of the idioms used are questionable; for example we might prefer "fantasies" to "fancies" in the section quoted. Dalí also makes a passing reference in this short essay to the theories of subject/object relations of Feuerbach, but this is not developed.

2 D. Lomas: "The Metamorphosis of Narcissus: Dalí's Self-Analysis", in D. Ades and F. Bradley (eds.), *Salvador Dalí: A Mythology*, exhibition catalogue, London, 1998, pp. 78–100.

3 The text has not been published in English [Editor's note: but *see* now Aurel Kolnai, *On Disgust*, ed. and tr., with an introduction, by Barry Smith and Carolyn Korsmeyer, Chicago: Open Court, 2004]; for the Spanish translation see note 6 below. A French translation has been published recently as A. Kolnai: *Le dégout*, tr. Olivier Cossé, Paris, 1997.

4 A. Kolnai: *The War against the West*, London and New York, 1938; *Errores del anticomunismo*, tr. Salvador Pons, Madrid, 1952.

5 A. Kolnai, "Der Ekel", *Jahrbuch für Philosophie und phänomenologische Forschung*, X, 1929, pp. 515–69.

6 A. Kolnai "El Asco", *Revista de Occidente*, XXVI, 77 and 78, Madrid, 1929, pp. 161–201, 294–347. Reprinted in *Selección y Recuerdo de la Revista de Occidente*, II, 1950, pp. 243–312. The quotations which follow have been translated by the present author from this text.

7 Kolnai, *loc. cit.* at note 6 above, p. 179.

8 *Ibid.*, p. 181.

9 *Ibid.*, p. 194.

10 Originally published as "L'Âne pourri", in *La Femme visible*, Paris, 1930, reprinted in *Dalí: Retrospective, 1920–1980*, exhibition catalogue, Centre Georges Pompidou, Paris, 1979, pp. 276–78.

11 Kolnai, loc.cit. at note 6 above, p. 196.

12 *Ibid.*, p. 201

13 *Ibid.*, p. 313.

14 *Ibid.*, p. 345.

15 Dalí, *loc. cit.* at note 10 above; translated by the author in preference to the frequently cited translation by J. Bronowski in *This Quarter*, VIII, 1, 1932, pp. 49–54, which sacrifices too much of Dalí's idiomatic style.

16 S. Dalí: "Sant Sebastià", *L'Amie de les Arts*, XVI, Sitges, 1927, reprinted in M. Raeburn (ed.), *Salvador Dalí: The Early Years*, London, 1994, p. 215.

17 [Ed.: *see* note 3.]

18 Kolnai, *loc. cit.* at note 6 above, p. 313.

About the Contributors
to This Volume

LORÁND AMBRUS-LAKATOS is Assistant Professor at the Central European University, Budapest.

ZOLTÁN BALÁZS is Associate Professor at the P. Pázmány Catholic University, Budapest-Piliscsaba, and author of *The Political Community*, Budapest: Osiris, 2003.

JOHN BEACH taught at the Philosophy Department of Marquette University, Milwaukee, USA.

LEE CONGDON is Professor of History at James Madison University, author of *Seeing Red: Hungarian Intellectuals in Exile and the Challenge of Communism*, DeKalb: Northern Illinois University Press, 2001; and editor (with Béla Király) of *The Ideas of the Hungarian Revolution: Suppressed and Victorious, 1956–1999*, Boulder: Social Science Monographs, Atlantic Research and Publications, distributed by Columbia University Press, 2002.

ANDREAS DORSCHEL is Professor of Aesthetics at the University of the Arts, Graz, Austria. Among his recent publications are Nachdenken über Vorurteile, Hamburg: Meiner, 2001, and Gestaltung-Zur Ästhetik des Brauchbaren, 2nd edn., Heidelberg: Universitätsverlag Winter, 2003.

FRANCIS DUNLOP is Honorary Lecturer at the University of East Anglia, Norwich, UK, and author of *The Life and Thought of Aurel Kolnai*, Aldershot: Ashgate, 2002.

JOHN P. HITTINGER is Professor of Philosophy at the Sacred Heart Major Seminary, Detroit, MI: USA, and author of *Liberty, Wisdom and Grace: Thomism and Democratic Political Theory*, Lanham, Md: Lexington Books, 2002.

DANIEL J. MAHONEY is Chairman of the Political Science Department at Assumption College in Worcester, Massachusetts. He is the author of *De Gaulle: Statesmanship, Grandeur, and Modern Democracy* (1996), and *Aleksandr Solzhenitsyn: The Ascent from Ideology*, Lanham, MD: Rowman and Littlefield, 2001.

PIERRE MANENT is Director of the Ecole des Hautes Etudes en Sciences Sociales, Paris, and author of *Modern Liberty and Its Discontents*, Lanham, MD: Rowman & Littlefield Publishers, 1998; *The City of Man,* Princeton, NJ: Princeton University Press, 1998; and *Cours familier de philosophie politique,* Fayard, 2001.

THOMAS NORGAARD is Assistant Professor at the European College of Liberal Arts, Berlin, and author of the entry on Iris Murdoch in the *Routledge Encyclopedia of Philosophy Online.*

ROBERT RADFORD is Visiting Fellow at the University of East Anglia, and the author of "Dalí", in the series *Arts and Ideas,* Phaidon Press.

M. W. F. STONE is Professor at the Hoger Instituut voor Wijsbegeerte, Katholieke Universiteit Leuven, and author of *The Subtle Arts of Casuistry,* vol. 1, *The Casuistical Tradition from Aristotle to Kant;* vol. 2, *Ordinary Morality and Practical Reason,* both forthcoming from Oxford University Press.

DAVID WIGGINS is Emeritus Wyckeham Professor of Logic at the University of Oxford, and author of *Sameness and Substance Renewed,* Cambridge University Press, 2001; and *Needs, Values, Truth,* 3rd amended edn., Oxford University Press, 2002.

INDEXES

Aurel Kolnai

NAME INDEX

Acton, Harry, 4 Acton, Lord, 75
Ambrus-Lakatos, Loránd, 11
Anscombe, G. E. M., 106n, 132,
   141n
Aquinas, 127, 168
Aranguren, J. L. L., 13 5, 141 n
Arendt, Hannah, 211, 218n
Aristotle, 10, 12, 45, 54, 68. 80, 95,
   101–2, 104–5, 106 & n, 127,
   172–74, 188, 213, 224, 233, 239,
   270, 282–83
Aron, Raymond, 163
Augustine, St., 138

Balázs Zoltán, 1, 11
Baroja, Pio, 107n
Bataille, Georges, 329–30
Beach, John, 10
Behrendt, R., 40n
Belloc, Hilaire, 167
Bentham, Jeremy, 111, 161
Bergson, Henri, 17
Bernhardi, F. von, 41 n
Besançon, Alain, 218n, 220
Black, Max, 310n
Blum, Lawrence, 315
Boos, Roman, 44n
Burckhardt, Jacob, 222, 229n
Burke, Edmund, 161–63, 165n, 193,
   264n
Buss, Sarah, 265n

Carritt, E. F., 104
Carey, John, 220–22
Catullus, 305, 311n
Chesterton, G.K, 164, 167
Clark, Norris, 191n, 192n
Cole, G. D. H., 23
Coleridge. S. T., 74
Congdon, Lee, 10
Copley, F. O., 31 ln
Cossé, Olivier, 331n

Dalí, Salvador, 327–30, 331n
Dancy, Jonathan, 320–21, 325n
D'Arcy, Eric, 111
Derrida, Jacques, 220
Dillon, R. S., 258, 263n
Dollfuß, Engelbert, 2

Domenach, Jean, 75
Dorschel, Andreas, 12, 13n
Dostoevsky, Fyodor, 258
Dunlop, Francis, 11, 12n, 13n, 14n, 17,
   143, 165n, 168, 207, 220–21, 279n,
   293n, 325n
Duns Scotus, 127, 135
Dworkin, Ronald, 227, 230n

Ewing, A. C., 139n, 140n

Farrer, Austin, 139, 142n
Feinberg, Joel, 265n
Fejtő, Ferenc, 1
Ferguson, Adam, 207, 218n
Feuerbach, Ludwig, 331n
Findlay, J. N., 89, 93n
Foucault, Michel, 220
Frankena, William, 264n
Frankfurt, Harry, 248n
Franklin, Benjamin, 204
Freud, Sigmund, 220

Gellner, E. A., 92, 93n
Gilson, Étienne, 11, 191
Glasson, P., 106n
Goebbels, Joseph, 300
Gomperz, Heinrich, 167
Gottlieb, Gidon, 249n
Grant, C. K., 107n
Grant, George, 192
Guizot, François, 195

Hampshire, Stuart, 136
Hare, R. M., 10, 14n, 83–5, 92, 93n,
   106n, 294n
Hartmann, Nicolai, 125
Havel, Vaclav, 204
Hayek, F. A., 229n
Heidegger, Martin, 17, 169–70, 209
Heller, Hermann, 42n
Henderson, G. P., 142n
Hermens, Ferdinand A, 44n
Hildebrand, Dietrich von, 2, 13n, 42n,
   279n, 325n
Hill, Thomas, 263n
Hitler, Adolph, 1, 299, 305
Hittinger, John P., 11, 13n, 191n, 194,
   196, 206

SUBJECT INDEX

*For Product Safety Concerns and Information please contact
our EU representative GPSR@taylorandfrancis.com Taylor & Francis
Verlag GmbH, Kaufingerstraße 24, 80331 München, Germany*

T - #0016 - 270426 - C0 - 229/152/20 - PB - 9789637326011 - Matt Lamination